CREATING VALUE

SPREADA

NEW YORK UNIVERSITY PRESS ⧠ NEW YORK & LONDON

HENRY JENKINS, SAM FORD, & JOSHUA GREEN

AND MEANING IN A NETWORKED CULTURE

BLE MEDIA

NEW YORK UNIVERSITY PRESS
New York and London
www.nyupress.org

Library of Congress Cataloging-in-Publication Data
Jenkins, Henry, 1958–
Spreadable media : creating value and meaning in a networked culture /
Henry Jenkins, Sam Ford, and Joshua Green.
p. cm.   (Postmillennial pop)
Includes bibliographical references and index.
ISBN 978–0–8147–4350–8 (cl : alk. paper)   ISBN 978–0–8147–4351–5 (ebook)
ISBN 978–0–8147–4390–4 (ebook)
1. Mass media and culture. 2. Mass media and technology. 3. Mass media—Social
aspects. 4. Social media. I. Ford, Sam. II. Green, Joshua (Joshua Benjamin) III. Title.
P94.6.J46   2012
302.23—dc23   2012028526

New York University Press books are printed on acid-free paper,
and their binding materials are chosen for strength and durability.
We strive to use environmentally responsible suppliers and materials
to the greatest extent possible in publishing our books.

Manufactured in the United States of America

Acknowledgments   vii

How to Read This Book   ix

Introduction: Why Media Spreads   1

1 Where Web 2.0 Went Wrong   47

2 Reappraising the Residual   85

3 The Value of Media Engagement   113

4 What Constitutes Meaningful Participation?   153

5 Designing for Spreadability   195

6 Courting Supporters for Independent Media   229

7 Thinking Transnationally   259

   Conclusion   291

   Notes   307

   References   313

   Index   333

   About the Authors   351

CONTENTS

The ideas we present in this book were inspired by a range of people who we want to recognize here.

We want to thank all the graduate student researchers and staff who took part in the MIT Convergence Culture Consortium. In particular, we want to acknowledge the significant impact Xiaochang Li's work had on our thinking presented in chapter 2 and chapter 3 of this book. We also owe significant credit to Xiaochang and Ana Domb for coauthoring with Henry Jenkins the white paper that inspired this book. And we owe a debt of gratitude to the rest of the C3 team: Ivan Askwith, Alec Austin, Eleanor Baird Stribling, David Edery, Alex Leavitt, Geoffrey Long, Daniel Pereira, Shiela Seles, Parmesh Shahani, and Ilya Vedrashko.

We also want to thank all our Futures of Entertainment Fellows, the community that has surrounded our work over the past several years. Their collaboration, brainstorming, and feedback shaped our thinking and challenged us all along the way. Many of these Fellows contributed to the enhanced book (explained in the "How to Read This Book" section). We want to thank them, along with all those whose work inspired our thinking and with whom we were proud to collaborate on this project.

A special thanks to the institutions that provided support to our work along the way and to our colleagues at those institutions: the Program in Comparative Media Studies at MIT; the Annenberg School for Communication and Journalism and the School of Cinematic Arts at the University of Southern California; Peppercomm Strategic Communications; Undercurrent; and the Carsey-Wolf Center's Media Industries Project at the University of California, Santa Barbara. We

ACKNOWLEDGMENTS

also want to thank our corporate partners that collaborated with us in the Convergence Culture Consortium project: Turner Broadcasting, Petrobras, MTV Networks, The Alchemists, GSD&M, Nagravision, Yahoo!, Fidelity Investments, and Internet Group do Brasil.

A deep debt of gratitude is owed to the staff of NYU Press and specifically to Eric Zinner and Ciara McLaughlin for helping guide this project and brainstorming with us every step of the way. We also thank the reviewers of our proposal and manuscript along the way for their thinking and feedback.

We can't imagine how a project of this magnitude would have been completed if not for the support, advice, and editing expertise of several key people: Zhan Li at the University of Southern California, whose meticulous work as a research assistant on this book challenged us for accuracy down to every minute detail; Amanda Ford, for both her hard work coordinating and editing as an administrative assistant for Henry at USC and as a supportive (and understanding beyond reason) spouse for Sam at home; Cynthia Jenkins, for providing regular feedback, proofreading, and other tasks all along the way; Nina Huntemann for her support (and listening intently to Joshua's long opines on the topic); Sarah Banet-Weiser, for being a critical thinking partner who challenged our arguments and increased the rigor of our analysis; and family and friends who provided the moral support, interest, encouragement, and understanding we often needed to push this project through.

Finally, we want to thank our colleagues who devoted time and energy to providing us feedback on the manuscript along the way, including danah boyd, Scott Ellington, Mizuko Ito, Lynn Liccardo, Kim Moses, Whitney Phillips, Carol Sanford, Suzanne Scott, Sangita Shresthova, Lana Swartz, Jerry Swerling, Dessewffy Tibor, Nikki Usher, Lance Weiler, Pamela Wilson, and Tim Wintle.

We envision three readerships for this book: media scholars, communication professionals, and people actively creating and sharing media content who are interested in how the media industries—and our culture(s)—are changing as a result. *Spreadable Media* has been designed to find common ground for conversation among these audiences and their perspectives. As you read through the book, however, you may find particular passages that speak more directly to one group than another. Bear with us in those cases, and perhaps even take it as an opportunity to consider these phenomena through other eyes. We want all three of our audiences (and others who may find this discussion beneficial) to use our argument as a provocation to ask some fundamental questions about how everyday people are producing meaning and value in a changing communication environment.

Many of this book's core arguments were developed through our work at the Convergence Culture Consortium, a five-and-a-half-year academic research project (2005–2011) aimed at speaking to and facilitating dialogue among these three groups. The Consortium's research was led by a team of faculty, staff, and graduate students at MIT's Program in Comparative Media Studies. This core team worked in conjunction with a community of leading media studies scholars around the world and a diverse range of corporate partners that funded the project: television media companies (Turner Broadcasting, MTV Networks), Internet and digital technology companies (Yahoo!, Internet Group do Brasil, Nagravision), and major brands and marketers (Petrobras, Fidelity Investments, advertising agency GSD&M, and transmedia storytelling agency The Alchemists). The Consortium created a variety of forums—from the Futures of Entertainment and

HOW TO READ THIS BOOK

Transmedia Hollywood conferences to blog posts, newsletters, white papers, and corporate brainstorms—aimed at bringing these three perspectives together, and the project has fostered a community around the annual Futures of Entertainment conference dedicated to continuing such collaboration.

The Convergence Culture Consortium was created for several reasons. A growing number of media studies graduate students were seeking industry rather than academic jobs upon graduation, and the Consortium wanted to take even more seriously the charge to help students turn the thinking they do in the classroom into the "\thought leadership" (to use the corporate term) that might help transform the media and marketing industries. Our team recognized that a great many corporate communicators and media creators providing such thought leadership through their own publications and digital platforms were actively interested in the work being done inside the academy. Indeed, many of our corporate partners not only supported our research but also became collaborators. Our dialogue with these and other industry thinkers informed our work and, in return, helped them apply some of our thinking to their own companies and industries. The Consortium brought together a community of scholars and researchers from a range of disciplines interested in meaningful dialogue between "academy" and "industry." Given how little dialogue often crosses academic boundaries (consider the disconnects between cultural studies and the social sciences or between the humanities and business schools, for instance), we have been particularly energized by this interdisciplinary collaboration enabled by our research initiatives.

Though all three of us once managed the Consortium together, our career paths have diverged, and we now bring our different vantage points to the range of issues discussed in this book. Sam Ford works for a strategic communications firm that consults with a variety of brands and media companies; Joshua Green, after managing an academic research program investigating the media industries, now works at a management consultancy that specializes in digital strategy; and Henry Jenkins serves as a professor of communications, journalism, cinematic arts, and education, calling himself an "aca-fan" to reflect the ways his life has straddled the worlds of academia and fandom.

Throughout, you'll see references to the enhanced version of this book. If you visit http://spreadablemedia.org, you'll find additional material by a range of contributors that shaped our argument and are referenced directly throughout the book—case studies and deep thinking that extends the work discussed here, along with counteropinions to some of the arguments we make. We have drawn liberally on these contributions in this edition, all of which were collected as we worked on this project over the past few years. Many, though not all, of these contributors have been part of the Convergence Culture Consortium, have spoken through our Futures of Entertainment or Transmedia Hollywood conferences, and have thus been part of the larger conversation out of which this book emerged.

We each have strong feelings about the issues we discuss here, but we have made great efforts to keep this book from being a polemic. *Spreadable Media* is fueled by our collective desire to foster conversation among media scholars, communication professionals, and citizens who create and share content, as well as by our frustrations with some of the ways each group engages with the issues we consider throughout.

In part, our work stems from disappointment with the way some companies have reacted to the "convergence culture" our research has examined. Some companies continue to ignore the potentials of this participatory environment, using their legal authority to constrain rather than to enable grassroots participation or cutting themselves off from listening to the very audiences they wish to communicate with. Worse, many marketers and media producers have embraced simplified notions for understanding these phenomena, notions that distort how they perceive their audiences' needs, wants, and activities. Ideas such as "user-generated content" and "branded platforms" ignore the larger history and power of participatory culture in attempting to define collaboration wholly on corporate terms.

This book will best serve those readers from the media industries who strive to listen to their audiences more deeply and to understand the "big picture," rather than those looking for easy ways to "exploit" or "leverage" the people their company purports to serve. *Spreadable Media* offers examples from many noncorporate media producers—nonprofit organizations, activist groups, churches, educators, and independent artists—who have developed strong relationships with their audiences and who often think as actively about people's goals for circulating material as they do their own goals in creating it.

In short, this book argues that the companies that will thrive over the long term in a "spreadable media" landscape are those that listen to, care about, and ultimately aim to speak to the needs and wants of their audiences as crucially as they do their own business goals. The following chapters, among other things, will examine a range of emerging community and business practices which point toward ways companies might build more sustainable models through seeking relationships with audiences that find mutual benefit in a loss of corporate "control."

Ours is a reformist rather than a revolutionary agenda, offering pragmatic advice in hopes of creating a more equitable balance of power within society. We accept as a starting point that the constructs of capitalism will greatly shape the creation and circulation of most media texts for the foreseeable future and that most people do not (and cannot) opt out of commercial culture. Our arguments are thus often directed toward corporations, recognizing that the policies that most directly impact the public's capacity to deploy media power are largely shaped by corporate decision-makers—true in the U.S. in particular and increasingly so in a global context.

While great value comes from media studies academics acting as outside cultural critics of industry power and policy, this mode of discourse has historically made engagements between cultural and media studies and the creative industries contentious.[1] Instead, our intervention takes the form of fostering dialogue between industry and academy. As such, our rhetorical tone differs from many other works in critical and cultural studies. While we are certain our focus on transformative case studies or "best practices" throughout may be dismissed by some readers as "purely celebratory" or "not critical enough," we likewise challenge accounts that are "purely critical" and "not celebratory enough," that downplay where ground has been gained in reconfiguring the media ecology. We believe media scholarship needs to be as clear as possible about what it is fighting *for* as well as what it is fighting *against*. This book is unhesitatingly in support of expanding and diversifying opportunities for meaningful participation in the decisions impacting our culture and society. We feel that making this positive argument and contribution is essential, even as *Spreadable Media* points toward the tensions and unevenness of this new media landscape.

One of this book's goals is to actively critique the neoliberal rhetoric that has emerged as marketing and business models take into account an increasingly participatory culture. *Spreadable Media* examines how current industry discourse masks conflicts between the interests of the media companies/brands and their audiences, drawing on a variety of powerful academic critiques of Web 2.0 logics and practices to focus on issues surrounding audience surveillance, free labor, and the inequalities of access and participation. In the process, though, we point out how industry logic and academic critiques alike focus too often on the value or sovereignty of the individual rather than on the social networks through which audience members play active roles in spreading material.[2]

Spreadable Media is a book about more than just how technology is changing culture. The champions of new technologies write frequently about how the next medium or tool will democratize communication, while media critics often focus on the loss of citizen control, as the platforms for distributing media content are concentrated in the hands of conglomerates. Meanwhile, corporate communicators and professionals in the media industries regularly write about how new platforms are destabilizing their business (and perhaps causing them to "lose control"). Yet new communication platforms do not determine some inevitable "end," whether that be democratization or destabilization. What people collectively and individually decide to do with those technologies as professionals and as audiences, and what kinds of culture people produce and spread in and around these tools, is still being determined. Those media scholars, industry practitioners, and active media participants who care about seeking an inclusive, equitable, and robust media landscape cannot accept the evolution of media platforms and content creation as if it were the unalterable consequence of technological developments. Our hope is to examine the tensions among these various views but also to explore what is missing: the ways the activities of connected individuals are currently, or could potentially, help shape the communication environment around them. If these technologies and logics were not still subject to change, this book would be pointless.

Furthermore, a media system is more than simply the technologies that support it. Culture drives these changes; the realities of the current communication environment are far messier than any one of these perspectives can acknowledge. The growth of networked communication, especially when coupled with the practices of participatory culture, provides a range of new resources and facilitates new interventions for a variety of groups who have long struggled to have their voices heard. New platforms create openings for social, cultural, economic, legal, and political change and opportunities for diversity and democratization for which it is worth fighting. The terms of participation are very much up for grabs, though, and will be shaped by a range of legal and economic struggles unfolding over the next few decades.

This book is not designed as a handbook to teach the creative industries how to make more money by "leveraging" the growing platforms of Web 2.0. Similarly, rather than design a guide for viral media success, we question the cultural logic of "viral media" in ways that point out how such models harm audiences, content creators, and marketers. In each of our explorations, we will look at products and practices that will often be familiar to us, and yet we will question the easy answers and the overly simplistic ways of understanding culture that often come attached. Complex forces shape the flow of media, and we reject simple answers in favor of more sophisticated explanations.

We aim to help all our audiences better understand the shift from a culture shaped by the logics of broadcasting toward one fostering greater grassroots participation. We examine how people are playing a more active role in shaping the flow of media for their own purposes in an increasingly networked culture; the implications of these changes for all involved; and the significant challenges, frustrations, and complications of media production and circulation in a world of spreadable media. We will locate and defend the public's collective right to meaningful participation. *Spreadable Media* proposes an approach to media production, promotion, and circulation which encourages a greater respect for the agency of grassroots participants, calling attention to the clashes occurring as media texts move between commercial and noncommercial spheres.

Spreadable Media is now literally and figuratively in your hands. Make of it what you will. Read it; debate it; critique it; trash it. Above all, expand the conversation we are starting here. Spread the word to others who you think may be interested. Transform these ideas through your conversations. Build on the arguments that resonate with you. Speak out against those that don't. That's how spreadable media works.

This book is about the multiple ways that content circulates today, from top down to bottom up, from grassroots to commercial. As we explore circulation, we see the way value and meaning are created in the multiple economies that constitute the emerging media landscape. Our message is simple and direct: if it doesn't spread, it's dead.

We don't mean the kinds of circulation that have historically concerned publishers—that is, how many readers pick up this morning's edition of the *New York Times* or the *Wall Street Journal*. Any publication can cite its "circulation," especially since the rates paid for advertising are calculated based on those numbers. Like the "impressions" that online publishers tout, such circulation is concerned with making audience members into receptacles for mass-produced and mass-distributed content: as eyeballs in front of a screen (in television terms), butts in seats (in film or sports terms), or whatever other body parts media companies and brands hope to grab next. But those definitions of "circulation" are really talking about distribution, where the movement of media content is largely—or totally—controlled by the commercial interests producing and selling it. These logics of distribution best apply in a broadcast media world, where a small number of producers—Random House or CBS or Warner Brothers—create discrete and finished products for mass audiences.

Instead, *Spreadable Media* examines an emerging hybrid model of circulation, where a mix of top-down and bottom-up forces determine how material is shared across and among cultures in far more participatory (and messier) ways. The decisions that each of us makes about

INTRODUCTION:
WHY MEDIA SPREADS

whether to pass along media texts—about whether to tweet the latest gaffe from a presidential candidate, forward a Nieman Marcus cookie recipe email, or share video of a shoplifting seagull—are reshaping the media landscape itself.

This shift from distribution to circulation signals a movement toward a more participatory model of culture, one which sees the public not as simply consumers of preconstructed messages but as people who are shaping, sharing, reframing, and remixing media content in ways which might not have been previously imagined. And they are doing so not as isolated individuals but within larger communities and networks, which allow them to spread content well beyond their immediate geographic proximity. Henry Jenkins (1992) coined the term "participatory culture" to describe the cultural production and social interactions of fan communities, initially seeking a way to differentiate the activities of fans from other forms of spectatorship. As the concept has evolved, it now refers to a range of different groups deploying media production and distribution to serve their collective interests, as various scholars have linked considerations of fandom into a broader discourse about participation in and through media. Previous work on participatory culture stressed acts of reception and production by media audiences; this book extends that logic to consider the roles that networked communities play in shaping how media circulates. Audiences are making their presence felt by actively shaping media flows, and producers, brand managers, customer service professionals, and corporate communicators are waking up to the commercial need to actively listen and respond to them.

While many content creators are struggling with the growing prominence of such grassroots audience practices, an array of online communication tools have arisen to facilitate informal and instantaneous sharing. These platforms offer new capacities for people to pass along media artifacts—and, in the process, to seek models to generate revenue through the activities of their users. However, while new tools have proliferated the means by which people can circulate material, word-of-mouth recommendations and the sharing of media content are impulses that have long driven how people interact with each other. Perhaps nothing is more human than sharing stories, whether by fire or by "cloud" (so to speak). We must all be careful not to suppose that a more participatory means of circulation can be explained solely (or even primarily) by this rise of technological infrastructure, even as these new technologies play a key role in enabling the shifts this book describes.

Spreadable Media focuses on the social logics and cultural practices that have enabled and popularized these new platforms, logics that explain *why* sharing has become such common practice, not just *how*. Our approach doesn't presume that new platforms liberate people from old constraints but rather suggests that the affordances of digital media provide a catalyst for reconceptualizing other aspects of culture, requiring the rethinking of social relations, the reimagining of cultural and political participation, the revision of economic expectations, and the reconfiguration of legal structures.

Throughout this book, we use terms such as "spread," "spreadable," or "spreadability" to describe these increasingly pervasive forms of media circulation. "Spreadability" refers to the potential—both technical and cultural—for audiences to share content for their own purposes, sometimes with the permission of rights holders, sometimes against their wishes. As we have been working on this book, some critics have challenged the term "spreadable," suggesting it sounds more appropriate for describing cream cheese or peanut butter. (The term originated in relation to "stickiness," as we will soon explain.) However, think of "spreadability" as a placeholder, perhaps like a stub in Wikipedia; it is something we can shape a conversation around. Our goal is not to create a new buzzword. Instead, we want to challenge readers to think through the metaphors we all use when talking about how content moves across the cultural landscape—to resist terminology that might distort how we understand these trends and to continue seeking terms that more accurately describe the complexity of how we all engage with media texts.

Our focus on terminology is more than mere semantics. We believe that language matters deeply and that the metaphors we all use to describe the patterns we see shape how we understand our world. We become blind to some phenomena and biased toward others. By discussing "spreadable media," we aim to facilitate a more nuanced account of how and why things spread and to encourage our readers to adopt and help build a more holistic and sustainable model for understanding how digital culture operates.

Sticky Content, Spreadable Practices

"Spreadability" refers to the technical resources that make it easier to circulate some kinds of content than others, the economic structures that support or restrict circulation, the attributes of a media text that might appeal to a community's motivation for sharing material, and the social networks that link people through the exchange of meaningful bytes.

Our use of "spreadability" is perhaps most effective as a corrective to the ways in which the concept of "stickiness" has developed over time to measure success in online commerce. A term that emerged through marketing discourse and which was popularized by its use in Malcolm Gladwell's *The Tipping Point* (2000) and elsewhere, "stickiness" broadly refers to the need to create content that attracts audience attention and engagement. Gladwell proposes, "There is a simple way to package information that, under the right circumstances, can make it irresistible. All you have to do is find it" (2000, 132). Gladwell uses "stickiness" to describe the aspects of media texts which engender deep audience engagement and might motivate them to share what they learned with others. In short, to Gladwell, sticky content is material that people want to spread.

As online business models have been built, the use of "stickiness" in the business setting refers to centralizing the audience's presence in a particular online location to generate advertising revenue or sales. This notion of stickiness closely resembles the "impressions" model that has shaped the measurement of audiences for broadcast content. In broadcast media, impressions are measured by how many people see a particular piece of media, whereas stickiness refers to the mechanisms motivating people to seek out and spend time at a particular site. Applied to the design of a website, companies hope to achieve stickiness by placing material in an easily measured location and assessing how many people view it, how many times it is viewed, and how long visitors view it.

Under the stickiness model, companies gain economic value by offering merchandise through some kind of e-commerce catalog, charging for access to information (through some kind of subscription or service fee), or selling the eyeballs of site visitors to some outside party, most often advertisers. Such advertising deals are sold by juxtaposing advertising messages on a page alongside content, and advertising rates are based on the number of impressions a page generates or the number of clicks an ad receives. This conception of stickiness focuses on monitoring and generating specific data on the actions of each site visitor.

This mindset has also come to define the way companies understand the popularity of content online. Online publications look at which articles are viewed the most and which hold people's attention the longest. Media companies assess which videos are viewed the most and longest. Nonprofits and corporate websites alike define success online based on web traffic. Audiences themselves often think about the popularity of content in terms of views at a particular destination. In short, even beyond the instances when advertising deals are being brokered, this narrow definition of "stickiness" has provided the logic by which success has come to be understood.

Stickiness capitalizes on the easiest way companies have found to conduct business online—rather than the ways audiences want to and do experience material online. It privileges putting content in one place and making audiences come to it so they can be counted. Such "destination viewing" often conflicts with both the dynamic browsing experience of individual Internet users and, more importantly, with the circulation of content through the social connections of audience members.

What we mean by "spreadability" will become clearer by contrasting it with this stickiness model. We compare the terms here not to indicate that web traffic shouldn't matter or to suggest that spreadability is the "opposite" of stickiness, but rather to demonstrate the limits of models too closely focused on stickiness.

The Migrations of Individuals versus the Flow of Ideas • Like other impressions-based constructs, stickiness models focus on counting isolated audience members. Spreadability recognizes the importance of the social connections among individuals, connections increasingly made visible (and amplified) by social media platforms. This approach may still include quantitative measures of how frequently and broadly content travels, but it makes important actively listening to the way media texts are taken up by audiences and circulate through audience interactions.

Centralized versus Dispersed Material • Because deep quantitative audience measurement is at the center of stickiness, online destinations can become a virtual "roach motel." For instance, at an extreme, some sites disable the Back button, making it difficult for users to escape once they have stumbled on the site, without closing their browser. The key to stickiness is putting material in a centralized location, drawing people to it, and keeping them there indefinitely in ways that best benefit the site's analytics. (The process is not that unlike a corral; audiences are pushed along predefined routes matching a publisher's measurement needs and are then poked and prodded for analytics data.) Spreadability emphasizes producing content in easy-to-share formats, such as the embed codes that YouTube provides, which make it easier to spread videos across the Internet, and encouraging access points to that content in a variety of places.

Unified versus Diversified Experiences • A sticky mentality requires brands to create a centralized experience which can best serve the purposes of multiple audiences simultaneously, offering limited and controlled ways for individuals to "personalize" content within a site's format. A spreadable mentality focuses on creating media texts that various audiences may circulate for different purposes, inviting people to shape the context of the material as they share it within their social circles.

Prestructured Interactivity versus Open-Ended Participation • Sticky sites often incorporate games, quizzes, and polls to attract and hold the interests of individuals. The participatory logic of spreadability leads to audiences using content in unanticipated ways as they retrofit material to the contours of their particular community. Such activities are difficult for creators to control and even more difficult to quantify.

Attracting and Holding Attention versus Motivating and Facilitating Sharing • Since sticky business models are built on demographic data, audiences are often constructed as a collection of passive individuals. Spreadability, by contrast, values the activities of audience members to help generate interest in particular brands or franchises.

Scarce and Finite Channels versus Myriad Temporary (and Localized) Networks • Stickiness retains the broadcast mentality of one-to-many communication, with authorized official channels competing against one another for the audience's attention. The spreadability paradigm assumes that anything worth hearing will circulate through any and all available channels, potentially moving audiences from peripheral awareness to active engagement.

Sales Force Marketing to Individuals versus Grassroots Intermediaries Advocating and Evangelizing • By "grassroots intermediaries," we mean unofficial parties who shape the flow of messages through their community and who may become strong advocates for brands or franchises. Grassroots intermediaries may often serve the needs of content creators, demonstrating how audiences become part of the logic of the marketplace and challenging what "grassroots" means, as such activities often coexist or even coincide with corporate agendas. They are not, however, employed or regulated by content creators and also may act counter to corporate goals.

Separate and Distinct Roles versus Collaboration across Roles • In a stickiness model, it's clear who the "producer," the "marketer," and the "audience" is. Each performs a separate and distinct purpose. In a spreadable model, there is not only an increased collaboration across these roles but, in some cases, a blurring of the distinctions between these roles.

•

While stickiness may provide the prevailing logic for the creation of online business models, any content or destination that has gained relevance with audiences online has done so through processes of spreadability, whether authorized or not. From the word-of-mouth spread of recommendations about a brand to the passing along of media content that might ultimately drive interest (and traffic) back to a particular destination, success in the stickiness model has always ultimately depended on audience activity that happens away from the site—in other words, from spreadability.

However, in our focus on spreadability, we are not arguing against the creation of online destinations; we recognize that creators and audiences alike benefit from a central base for their brand or content, whether to serve a business model or simply to have an easy-to-find location. After all, mass-media channels are still valuable resources for getting information out and sharing content of great common interest because they have such widespread reach.

Instead, the "distribution" reach of sticky destinations and the "circulation" reach of spreadable media should coexist, a relationship aptly illustrated by a 2010 experiment by advertising agency Hill Holliday. The firm created an online microsite called Jerzify Yourself that allowed visitors to remake their image in the style of the stars of popular MTV television show *Jersey Shore*. Hill Holliday created the site as part of a project researching the ways word spread about content. The site generated substantial word of mouth, and was featured in a variety of articles and blog posts. Beyond just researching the audiences of those blogs (their immediate "reach" or "distribution potential"), Hill Holliday also used a URL-tracing mechanism to see what additional traffic came from the ongoing spread of those stories and posts.

The experiment created a unique URL for Jerzify Yourself for every site that linked back to the page. Ilya Vedrashko (2010a) reports that five of the top six sites in terms of driving direct traffic to Jerzify Yourself created almost as much traffic through reshares, as people who first discovered the site through that article/mention passed the link on to their networks. One site's coverage generated twice as many eventual visits through ongoing recirculation of the link as it did via direct click-throughs from the original story. Writes Vedrashko, "Counting only the direct clicks from any site is likely to underestimate the site's total value. [. . .] Content that's designed to be spreadable can nearly double the referred traffic through re-shares." Meanwhile, some sites were more "spreadful" than others. In particular, Vedrashko notes that the site which sent the most direct traffic to Jerzify Yourself actually led to the least amount of resharing.

Despite changes in communication and culture, stickiness still matters. Returning to Gladwell's use of the term, stickiness acts as a measure of how interested an audience member is in a media text. Any creator—whether media company, fan, academic, or activist—produces material in the hope of attracting audience interest. (Perhaps peanut butter isn't such a bad way to represent spreadable media after all: content remains sticky even as it is spread.)

What Susan Boyle Can Teach about Spreadability

What happens when many people make active decisions to put content in motion by passing along an image, song, or video clip to friends and family members or to larger social networks? As this question suggests, much of what is being exchanged at the current moment is entertainment, as fan communities have been among the first to embrace the practices of spreadability. These fan activities will thus be a recurring topic throughout this book. Yet what we say about the spread of entertainment content also increasingly applies to news, branding and advertising, political messages, religious messages, and a range of other materials, and we will draw on a variety of these examples to provide a multidimensional picture of the current media environment.

To start, let's contrast a U.S. "broadcast" phenomenon with a widespread entertainment clip. The finale of the 2009 season of *American Idol* drew 32 million viewers in the U.S., making it one of the year's most viewed two-hour blocks on broadcast television. In comparison, a video of Scottish woman Susan Boyle auditioning for *Britain's Got Talent* was viewed more than 77 million times on YouTube. This latter figure reflects only the viewership of the original upload; YouTube is a space where success often encourages duplication. A cursory survey showed more than 75 different copies of Boyle's audition performance of "I Dreamed a Dream" available on the site when we conducted our research, with versions uploaded from users in Brazil, Japan, the Netherlands, the U.S., and various parts of the U.K. We found edited copies, high-definition copies, and copies with closed captioning and subtitles in various languages. Many of these versions have themselves been viewed millions of times. Even this scan of the Boyle phenomenon considers YouTube alone, ignoring other large online video-sharing platforms such as Chinese site Tudou (where a quick glance showed at least 43 copies of the original performance) or Dailymotion (where there were 20 easily found copies of her first audition video).

Since any of these videos can be watched more than once by the same person, it is difficult, if not impossible, to reduce these views to a raw "eyeball" count equivalent to television ratings. No matter how you look at it, however, the viewership of the widely spread Susan Boyle clip dwarfs that of the highest-rated show on U.S. broadcast television. The Boyle video was broadcast content made popular through grassroots circulation.

The Susan Boyle audition was the result of mainstream commercial media production, to be sure. The original video was professionally produced and edited to maximize its emotional impact. One segment introduced a character and set up ridiculing expectations, while the next swept the rug out from under those expectations with a spectacular performance of a popular West End song, followed by the emotional responses of the overwhelmed judges and audience. Audience enjoyment of the event was shaped by people's general familiarity with the genre conventions of reality television and/or by particular perception of and investment in Simon Cowell's tough judge character, whose schoolboy grin at the segment's end represents the ultimate payoff for her spectacular performance. And, once the video had been widely spread, the visibility of Boyle was amplified through mainstream media coverage; she was, for instance, interviewed on *Good Morning America* and spoofed on the *Tonight Show*.

Nevertheless, Boyle's international success was not driven by broadcast distribution. Fans found Susan Boyle before media outlets did. The most popular Susan Boyle YouTube video reached 2.5 million views in the first 72 hours and drew 103 million views on 20 different websites within the first nine days of its release. Meanwhile, Boyle's Wikipedia page attracted nearly half a million views within a week of its creation.[1]

While the performance was part of a mainstream television program in the U.K, it was not commercially available at all to viewers in the U.S. and many other countries. Instead, the video was circulated and discussed through a variety of networks online. Her entry into the U.S. market and her spread around the Internet was shaped by the conscious decisions of millions of everyday people functioning as grassroots intermediaries, each choosing to pass her video along to friends, family members, colleagues, and fellow fans. The Susan Boyle phenomenon would not have played out in the same way if not for the relationships and communities facilitated by social network sites, media sharing tools, and microblogging platforms.

Part of what allowed the Susan Boyle video to travel as far and as fast as it did was the fact it *could* travel so far so fast. People had the right tools and knew what to do with them. Sites such as YouTube make it simple to embed material on blogs or share it through social network sites. Services such as bitly allow people to share links quickly and efficiently. Platforms such as Twitter and Facebook facilitate instantaneous sharing to one's social connections. All of these technical innovations made it that much easier for the Susan Boyle video to spread.

However, the mere existence of individual technologies to facilitate the sharing of the clip does little to explain how the Susan Boyle performance was spread. We must consider the integrated system of participatory channels and practices at work that support an environment where content could be circulated so widely. For instance, uses of particular services should not be viewed in isolation but rather in connection, as people embrace a range of technologies based on if and when a particular platform best supports the cultural practices in which they want to engage.

But, more fundamentally, we have to understand the cultural practices that have both fueled the rise of these sharing technologies and evolved as people discover how these platforms might be used. For instance, the Susan Boyle video was widely shared because the participating public is more collectively and individually literate about social networking online; because people are more frequently and more broadly in contact with their networks of friends, family, and acquaintances; and because people increasingly interact through sharing meaningful bits of media content.

Taken together, this set of social and cultural practices, and the related technological innovations which grew up around them, constitute what we call a "networked culture." These cultural practices were certainly not created by new technologies. We've long known that news stories generate conversations; many of us have a cousin or grandmother who (still!) clips newspaper articles to put on the refrigerator, in an album, or in the mail to us. Social historian Ellen Gruber Garvey (2013), for example, has offered a glimpse into how circulation and value were connected in the scrapbook culture of nineteenth-century U.S. readers. Their primary activity was sifting through newspapers, magazines, and other periodicals, gathering material to archive. In an era when news publications themselves actively engaged in "recirculation"—local papers reprinted stories originally published elsewhere if they seemed of interest to local readers—scrapbook collectors stored the most appealing of these ephemeral accounts for future generations. In turn, newspapers sometimes capitalized on this early form of "user-generated content," publishing retrospectives featuring reader-curated material. These archival practices accelerated with the twentieth-century rise of photocopiers, which facilitated easier reproduction and sharing of found material.

However, what happened in a predigital world now occurs with exponentially greater speed and scope, thanks to the affordances of online social tools. According to a CNN research project ("Shared News" 2010), the average global Internet user receives 26 news stories per week via social media or email and shares 13 news stories online. According to a report from the Pew Research Center (Purcell et al. 2010), 75 percent of respondents received news forwarded through email or posted on social network sites, and 52 percent shared links to news with others via those means.

This news gathering is shaped by a strong desire to contribute to ongoing conversations with friends, family, and co-workers. Of the respondents to the Pew study, 72 percent said they follow the news because they enjoy talking with others about what is happening in the world, and 50 percent said they rely to some degree on people around them to tell them the news they need to know. All of this suggests a world where citizens count on each other to pass along compelling bits of news, information, and entertainment, often many times over the course of a given day.

In this networked culture, we cannot identify a single cause for why people spread material. People make a series of socially embedded decisions when they choose to spread any media text: Is the content worth engaging with? Is it worth sharing with others? Might it be of interest to specific people? Does it communicate something about me or my relationship with those people? What is the best platform to spread it through? Should it be circulated with a particular message attached? Even if no additional commentary is appended, however, just receiving a story or video from someone else imbues a range of new potential meanings in a text. As people listen, read, or view shared content, they think not only—often, not even primarily—about what the producers might have meant but about what the person who shared it was trying to communicate.

Indeed, outside the U.K., most people probably encountered the Susan Boyle video because someone sent a link or embedded it in a Facebook update or blog: many people shared the video to boast their accomplishment of discovery. They could anticipate sharing the video with people who hadn't seen it, precisely because the material was not widely available on television. Some may have heard conversations about it and searched on YouTube; for many more, the message came in the midst of other social exchanges, much as an advertisement comes as part of the commercial television flow. Yet, while an advertisement might feel like an intrusion or interruption, people often welcome spreadable media content from friends (at least discerning ones) because it reflects shared interests.

It is apparent that some people were passing Boyle's performance along as a gesture of friendship to build interpersonal relationships, while others used the material to contribute to a community organized around a key interest. This difference is a key distinction: between friendship-based and interest-based networks (Ito et al. 2009). An avowed Christian, Boyle became the focus of online prayer circles. Science blogs discussed how someone with her body could produce such a sound. Karaoke singers debated her technique, reporting an incident when she was thrown out of a karaoke bar because she was now viewed as a professional performer. Reality-television blogs debated whether her success would have been possible on U.S. television given that *American Idol* excludes people her age from competing. Fashion blogs critiqued and dissected the makeover she was given for subsequent television appearances. Boyle's video spread, then, as a result of the many conversations it enabled people to have with each other, whether among friends or within communities of common interest. (And, of course, many may have done some of both.)

From a commercial perspective, *American Idol* had a full season to build public interest in its finale yet failed to attract the scale of attention the seven-minute clip of Boyle sparked. Contrary to speculation that the Boyle phenomenon would be short-lived, her debut album released by Columbia Records months later enjoyed groundbreaking advance sales, surpassing The Beatles and Whitney Houston on Amazon's charts (Lapowsky 2009). The album sold more than 700,000 copies in its first week, the largest opening-week sales of any album released that year. As Columbia Records chair Steve Barnett explained, "People wanted to get it and own it, to feel like they're a part of it" (Sisario 2009). Of course, those who helped circulate the video already felt they were "a part of it."

While such success makes for an impressive business story, the initial international popularity of the Susan Boyle moment wasn't driven by a plan for counting impressions and raking in the cash. Most of the many millions of people who streamed the Boyle clip were part of a "surplus audience" for whom producers had not built a business model. Boyle's performance was part of a British program with no commercial distribution in most other countries, so the majority of people sharing the video couldn't turn on a television network—cable or broadcast—and watch the next installment of *Britain's Got Talent*. They couldn't stream the show legally online. They couldn't buy episodes from iTunes. Despite relationships with multiple television networks, FremantleMedia couldn't get the show into commercial distribution quickly enough for transnational viewers to catch up with the Brits. Given the global circulation of information about Susan Boyle online, anyone who wanted to know what happened on *Britain's Got Talent* heard about it within seconds of its airing. In short, market demand dramatically outpaced supply.

The spread of Susan Boyle demonstrates how content not designed to circulate beyond a contained market or timed for rapid global distribution can gain much greater visibility than ever before, thanks to the active circulation of various grassroots agents, while television networks and production companies struggle to keep up with such unexpected, rapidly escalating demand.

The case also allows us to challenge the commonplace assertion that, in the era of Web 2.0, user-generated content has somehow displaced mass media in the cultural lives of everyday people. Lucas Hilderbrand notes, "For mass audiences, broadcast, cable and satellite television still dominate, [. . .] and network content will continue to feed these streams. And I suspect that for many audiences, network content—new or old—still drives users to YouTube, and amateur content is discovered along the way, through the suggested links, alternative search results, or forwarded emails" (2007, 50). What Hilderbrand's account misses, though, is that much of the mass-media content encountered on YouTube and other such platforms is unauthorized—not so much user-generated content as user-circulated content. While audiences' sharing and spreading of Susan Boyle's video may still fit within the broad logic of capitalism, the capacity of audiences to alter the circulation of content is nevertheless causing consternation for companies and artists trying to figure out how to reshape broadcast business and marketing models or to design new businesses altogether. In cases where bottom-up activities have not been ordained by content creators, various corporate entities have labeled many of these activities "piracy" or "infringement"—even when unauthorized forms of sharing create value for both the people circulating the material and those who created it, as was clearly the case with the Boyle video.

Piracy is a concept that will surface repeatedly throughout the book, and every reader will probably draw the line between "appropriate" and "inappropriate" practices at different points. In fact, one of the problems of the current use of "piracy" is that it shortcuts important conversations we should all be having about the economic and cultural impact of different types of media sharing. Such discussions might draw on legal notions that consider the nature of the use (commercial or noncommercial, education or entertainment), the degree to which the use is transformative, the portion of the work being taken, and so forth in determining what constitutes piracy.

As a rule, though, we are reserving the term "pirate" in this book for people who profit economically from the unauthorized sale of content produced by others. This is not a legal distinction but a moral one that matters for many of those whose activities we will discuss. Yet, as the Boyle example suggests, piracy is as much a consequence of the market failures of media companies to make content available in a timely and desirable manner as it is a consequence of the moral failure of audience members seeking meaningful content by hook or by crook if it is not legally available. We will thus make the case that the appropriation and recirculation of even entire works may sometimes work in the best interests of not only the culture at large but also of the rights holders.

One can only speculate whether Boyle's album and career could have been even more successful or whether *Britain's Got Talent* could have been a transnational hit had the show's producers been prepared to react quickly to this clip's spread. The failure to reconceptualize the way *Britain's Got Talent* circulates reduced what could have been a season-long event into one discrete moment: a single video. For instance, one imagines that few viewers of Boyle's audition video know that multiethnic dance troupe Diversity won the season rather than Boyle. This case not only demonstrates the cultural and technological system at the core of a networked culture but also the inability of the media industries—whose structure and models are still largely configured to a "broadcast" and "sticky" mentality—to actively listen and respond to unanticipated interest in their material.

We've Found a Cure for Viral Media!

As we question how and why content circulates today, it is all too easy to accept an inadequate answer, a theory of media distribution that makes a media text sound more like a smallpox-infected blanket. Many observers described the Susan Boyle phenomenon as an example of "viral media," a term whose popularity has been fueled by the rapid rise of social network sites alongside declining advertising rates and an extremely fragmented audience for broadcast media.

Viral metaphors do capture the speed with which new ideas circulate through the Internet. The top-down hierarchies of the broadcast era now coexist with the integrated system of participatory channels described earlier in the chapter which have increased access to tools for communication and publishing. As marketers and media companies struggle to make sense of this transformed media landscape, one of the most common explanations is that media content now disseminates like a pandemic—spreading through audiences by infecting person after person who comes into contact with it. Even if the media industries must accept the shift from an environment where people congregate around media texts to a context where audiences do the circulating, they hope to preserve creator control. The promise is simple, if deceptive: create a media virus, and success will be yours. Thus, marketers and media distributors that are unsure of how to reach audiences through traditional "broadcast" or "sticky" methods now pray material will "go viral."

The term "viral" first appeared in science fiction stories, describing (generally bad) ideas that spread like germs. Something of the negative consequences of this simplified understanding of the viral are suggested by this passage from Neal Stephenson's science fiction novel *Snow Crash*: "We are all susceptible to the pull of viral ideas. Like mass hysteria. Or a tune that gets into your head that you keep on humming all day until you spread it to someone else. Jokes. Urban Legends. Crackpot religions. Marxism. No matter how smart we get, there is always this deep irrational part that makes us potential hosts for self-replicating information" (1992, 399). Here, the viral is linked to the "irrational," the public is described as "susceptible" to its "pull," and participants become unknowing "hosts" of the information they carry across their social networks.[2]

Echoing this theme, Douglas Rushkoff's 1994 book *Media Virus* argues that media material can act as a Trojan horse, spreading without the user's conscious consent; people are duped into passing a hidden agenda while circulating compelling content. Rushkoff writes that certain "media events are not *like* viruses. They *are* viruses," and such a virus seeks "to spread its own code as far and wide as possible—from cell to cell and from organism to organism" (1994, 9; emphasis in original). There is an implicit and often explicit proposition that the spread of ideas and messages can occur without users' consent and perhaps actively against their conscious resistance; people are duped into passing a hidden agenda while circulating compelling content.

This notion of the media *as* virus taps a larger discussion that compares systems of cultural distribution to biological systems. Rushkoff describes the culture through which modern U.S. residents navigate as a "datasphere" or "mediaspace"—"a new territory for human interaction, economic expansion, and especially social and political machination"—that has arisen because of the rapid expansion of communication and media technologies (1994, 4). He writes,

> Media viruses spread through the datasphere the same way biological ones spread through the body or a community. But, instead of traveling along an organic circulatory system, a media virus travels through the networks of the mediaspace. The "protein shell" of a media virus might be an event, invention, technology, system of thought, musical riff, visual image, scientific theory, sex scandal, clothing style or even a pop hero—as long as it can catch our attention. Any one of these media virus shells will search out the receptive nooks and crannies in popular culture and stick on anywhere it is noticed. Once attached, the virus injects its more hidden agendas into the datastream in the form of ideological code—not genes, but a conceptual equivalent we now call "memes." (9–10)

This theme of comparing the spread of cultural material to biological processes extends beyond the "virus" metaphor. In the 1976 book *The Selfish Gene*, famed British evolutionary biologist Richard Dawkins introduced the "meme," which was to become both an incredibly important and incredibly overused idea, just like its viral companion. The meme is a cultural equivalent to the gene—the smallest evolutionary unit. "Cultural transmission is analogous to genetic transmission," Dawkins argues (1976, 189), writing,

Just as genes propagate themselves in the gene pool by leaping from body to body via sperms or eggs, so memes propagate themselves in the meme pool by leaping from brain to brain via a process which, in the broad sense, can be called imitation. If a scientist hears, or reads about, a good idea, he passes it on to his colleagues and students. He mentions it in his articles and his lectures. If the idea catches on, it can be said to propagate itself, spreading from brain to brain. (192)

Dawkins notes in later editions (1989, 2006) that the notion of the meme has itself spread in memelike fashion—it provides a compelling way to understand the dispersion of cultural movements, especially when seemingly innocuous or trivial trends spread and die in rapid fashion. In a moment when the meme pool—the cultural soup which Dawkins describes as the site where memes grow—is overflowing with ideas, being able to create or harness a meme seems to promise anyone the chance to ride the waves of participatory culture.

However, while the idea of the meme is a compelling one, it may not adequately account for how content circulates through participatory culture. While Dawkins stresses that memes (like genes) aren't wholly independent agents, many accounts of memes and viral media describe media texts as "self-replicating." This concept of "self-replicating" culture is oxymoronic, though, as culture is a human product and replicates through human agency.

Simplified versions of these discussions of "memes" and "media viruses" have given the media industries a false sense of security at a time when the old attention economy has been in flux. Such terms promise a pseudoscientific model of audience behavior. The way these terms are now used mystify the way material spreads, leading professional communicators on quixotic quests to create "viral content."

The term "viral marketing" was first popularized in relation to Hotmail in 1995, after the creators of the service used the phrase to describe why their service gained millions of users within months (Jurvetson and Draper 1997). At the bottom of every email sent, a marketing message appeared which offered, "Get your free Web-based email at Hotmail." The term described the process well. People communicated and—in the process—sent along a marketing message, often without realizing it had happened.

Yet the viral metaphor does little to describe situations in which people actively assess a media text, deciding who to share it with and how to pass it along. People make many active decisions when spreading media, whether simply passing content to their social network, making a word-of-mouth recommendation, or posting a mash-up video to YouTube. Meanwhile, active audiences have shown a remarkable ability to circulate advertising slogans and jingles against their originating companies or to hijack popular stories to express profoundly different interpretations from those of their authors.

"Viral marketing," stretched well beyond its original meanings, has been expected to describe all these phenomena in the language of passive and involuntary transmission. Its precise meaning no longer clear, "viral media" gets invoked in discussions about buzz marketing and building brand recognition while also popping up in discussions about guerrilla marketing, exploiting social network sites, and mobilizing audiences and distributors.

Ironically, this rhetoric of passive audiences becoming infected by a media virus gained widespread traction at the same time as a shift toward greater acknowledgment that audience members are active participants in making meaning within networked media. Shenja van der Graaf maintains that viral marketing is "inherently social": "the main feature of viral marketing is that it heavily depends on interconnected peers" (2005, 8); van der Graaf uses "viral" to describe content that circulates in ways linked to network behavior, citing participation within a socially networked system as a central requirement of "viral" behavior. This focus on how audiences pass material along, however, is distorted by the metaphor of infection that "viral" invokes.

Confusion about viral media will not be easily resolved. The term is at once too encompassing and too limiting, creating false assumptions about how culture operates and distorted understandings of the power relations between producers and audiences. As we have been making this argument over the past few years while working on this project, we have found a growing number of marketers and media professionals also challenging the term. (See, for instance, Yakob 2008;

Arauz 2008; Caddell 2009b; Askwith 2010; Hasson 2010; Chapman 2010.) The term even received the most nominations for elimination in Lake Superior State University's annual "List of Banished Words from the Queen's English for Mis-use, Over-use, and General Uselessness" (2010). Bluntly put, an antidote for the viral needs to be discovered; we hope this book contributes to that growing charge.

In contrast, the concept of "spreadability" preserves what was useful about earlier communication models—the idea that the effectiveness and impact of messages is increased and expanded by their movement from person to person and community to community. Spreadability recognizes the ways later theorists such as van der Graaf have revised the earliest, relatively static and passive conceptions of "viral" to reflect the realities of the new social web, while suggesting that this emerging paradigm is so substantively different from the initial examples that it requires adopting new terminology. Our use of "spreadable media" avoids the metaphors of "infection" and "contamination," which over-estimate the power of media companies and underestimate the agency of audiences. In this emerging model, audiences play an active role in "spreading" content rather than serving as passive carriers of viral media: their choices, investments, agendas, and actions determine what gets valued.

However, while this book combats the use of "viral" to describe many processes in which people are actively involved in circulating and shaping the meaning of content, we want to acknowledge that there still remain examples of "viral marketing." Ilya Vedrashko (2010b) argues that, as marketers (hopefully) shift away from "viral market-ing" as a catch-all term, they cannot forget that there are still literal examples of viral marketing which do not seek to engage audiences but rather deploy automated ways to induce audience members to unwittingly pass along their marketing messages.

As Iain Short (2010) points out, for instance, many applications for Twitter and Facebook send automated marketing updates to a person's followers without a user actively passing this material along. Thus, downloading an app might cause a Facebook user's friends to get pinged with a message encouraging them to join, or buying an animal on Farmville might send an update to all of a user's Facebook friends (whether or not they play the game). In the instance of Facebook's Open Graph feature, users receive notice that a friend is reading a particular story or watching a certain video in his or her Facebook news feed. In order to see the content, users have to download an application for that publisher, which then starts sharing what they read to their friends' feeds. In all these cases, messages are sent "from the user," without the user crafting the messages or often even being aware the message has been generated.

The use of "viral marketing" should be reserved only for those marketing concepts that really do not rely on the agency of audience members to circulate media texts for their own purposes and through their own relationships. Vedrashko writes,

> The entire debate over the terminology might look to a marketing practitioner like an Ivory Tower nitpicking but it is an important one because metaphor-based terms rely on our understanding of the underlying concepts to guide our actions. An attempt to create a "viral" video will be informed by what one knows about viruses, which among marketing professionals isn't a lot, anyway. On the other hand, a creator of a "spreadable" video will be drawing upon an entirely different body of knowledge, perhaps a theory about *why people gossip*, or the related *theory of social capital*. (2010b)

As Vedrashko suggests, the choice of metaphors sets expectations. If viral success means elements of a campaign have to be spread rapidly among audiences in pandemic proportions, then many companies are likely to be disappointed by the distribution they achieve. For instance, a 2007 JupiterResearch report found that only 15 percent of marketers launching viral campaigns were successful in "prompting their consumers to promote their messages for them." By using the term "spreadable media," we refer to (and draw on cases that describe) not just those texts which circulate broadly but also those that achieve particularly deep engagement within a niche community. In many cases, such content does not obtain the type of scale that would qualify for many people's definition of "viral success," yet the text became highly spread among the particular audiences the producer hoped to reach.

Further, if companies set out thinking they will make media texts that do something to audiences (infect them) rather than for audiences to do something with (spread it), they may delude themselves into thinking they control people. Conversely, understanding spreadability will allow audiences and activists to form new connections and communities through their active role in shaping the circulation of media content. The concept of spreadability also gives these groups new means to mobilize and respond to decisions made by companies and governments in ways that challenge decisions that adversely effect them and to exploit gaps in the system which may allow them to serve their own needs.

"Comcast Must Die"

Companies are not just worried about making their content "go viral," though. Marketers have also been using the metaphor to make sense of how their customers' communication about a company now has the potential to circulate widely.

Fifteen years ago, the degree to which audiences had direct access to brands, and vice versa, was limited. Direct mail may have targeted messages at particular customers. Brands with retail outlets had a direct customer touchpoint, but the brand ambassadors in this case—retail employees—were (and remain) among the least respected, trained, and compensated members of the organization. Some companies had sales forces that aggressively contacted potential customers but often only through a one-way message, as during the "telemarketing craze." The most robust site of contact between customer and company was customer service, a division in most companies that has been marginalized and is often measured by efficiency—how quickly employees can get customers off the phone—rather than any prioritization of customer engagement (Yellin 2009). Thus, most correspondence between brand and company was one-way, providing little room for the customer to shape the experience.

These conditions persist. However, when corporate websites emerged by the mid-1990s, no one fully realized how substantially they would shift a company's relationship with its audiences. Few of the companies creating brochure-like websites at the time completely considered that brands had the opportunity to tell their stories directly to the audience outside the constraints of advertising spots on television and radio and without going through the third-party voice of journalists. There would be a fundamental shift in how everyone "consumes," as interested people could seek content from companies when they wanted it—to juxtapose and assess corporate messages directly from the source and to publish what they find online for family, friends, colleagues, and strangers to see.

Brands and entertainment properties cannot return to the one-directional communication flows of the broadcast era, when they had the perception of control, so companies must listen to and learn from their audiences if they want to enjoy long-term success.

This "lack of control" is particularly noticeable when it comes to customer complaints. In a world of spreadable media, what were once considered solely "customer service" issues are increasingly "public relations" issues as well (which is ironic, considering "customer service" was, in the early twentieth century, once called "public relations" [Yellin 2009, 22]), as customers spread their own stories about companies.

Comcast, the largest cable operator in the U.S., has learned this lesson with particular pain. Cable operators have long struggled with customer complaints and dissatisfaction, displeasure well illustrated by a 2006 video of a Comcast technician falling asleep on customer Brian Finkelstein's couch while on hold with the company's own help line. Finkelstein's video spread rapidly and widely and received coverage in a variety of traditional media outlets as well. The drowsy technician was fired, and Comcast received a steady stream of negative publicity online as frustrated customers added their own commentary to the video.

The sleepy Comcast technician was only one of their spreading troubles. For instance, there was the much-recounted tale of LaChania Govan, the Illinois Comcast customer whose repeated attempts to resolve a customer service issue in 2005 led to employees changing her account name—and bill—to "Bitch Dog." Similar attention was heaped on 75-year-old Virginia Comcast customer Mona Shaw, who became so angered at her customer service treatment in 2007 that she smashed up the office with a hammer (Yellin 2009, 2–8). Journalist Bob Garfield (2007) shared his own "Hell on Earth" story about Comcast customer service, beginning his *Advertising Age* column with the declaration "Comcast must die." Garfield started a campaign against the cable operator on the site ComcastMustDie.com. And amid these videos, stories, and campaigns were the myriad individual complaints that Comcast customers increasingly voiced across blogs, microblogging platforms, and discussion forums.

Companies now face building pressure to use their online presence not just to communicate their own messages but to respond to the demands of disgruntled customers as well. Comcast listened to some degree, one could argue out of necessity, over time creating a specific department to respond to issues raised online. In February 2008, Comcast Executive Support Manager Frank Eliason (who had been with the company six months) was named the company's "Director of Digital Care." The department Eliason created now reaches out to bloggers, Twitterers, and other online discussants, attempting to proactively resolve their problems. In the process, the "Comcast Cares" initiative has addressed thousands of customers and simultaneously generated significant publicity. *BusinessWeek*, for instance, named Eliason (who has since gone on to work for financial services company Citi as its head of social media) "the most famous customer service manager in the U.S." (Reisner 2009). Although in 2009 Bob Garfield still called Comcast "a vast, greedy, blundering, tone-deaf corporate colossus," he noted that the company "has heard our angry voices and taken concrete steps in the process of putting customers first." Meanwhile, many people in customer service and communications look to Comcast's online customer service response as an exemplar that companies should follow to create online communication platforms which respond to customer questions and reach out to those who complain.

Despite the praise, Comcast's customer service remains far from ideal. Its pioneering work using social media platforms to listen and respond to negative customer experiences still serves as a quick fix to the larger issues that plague service providers. In 2010, for example, Gizmodo published a letter received by a customer who was told his service would be disconnected if he didn't pay the $0.00 he owed (Golijan 2010), while another customer who praised Comcast's Twitter communication shared his ongoing frustrations once he was connected to others within the company (Paul 2010). These are only two of a regular stream of customers expressing frustrations with the company's traditional communication modes.

Further, the "Comcast Cares" initiative, and the general perspective that customer service issues become a higher priority when customers have their own online presence, means that some customers get better treatment than others. See, for instance, this account from *Slate*:

> People with more clout seem to get better service. One Twitterer with fewer than 20 followers told me that though he's tweeted about Comcast frequently, the company has responded only to tell him its customer-service phone number. Another—with about 300 followers—told a better story: When she complained about a service problem, Comcast made special arrangements for a refund. And Glenn Fleishman, a tech journalist with more than 1,600 followers, got the best deal of all. [He] quickly got a call from an executive in the escalation department, who offered to waive [a $1,300 early-cancellation] fee. (Manjoo 2009)

As long as companies treat customer service issues online with some degree of concern about whether the customer is "an influencer," customers will receive different levels of response based on their perceived "public relations threat" (not to mention the lack of recourse for those who lack easy access to these communication platforms). And, in devoting significant energy to responding to those customers who complain loudest, without fixing underlying customer service issues companies might, if anything, encourage people to "spread their complaint" as their first course of action, influenced by the horror stories of phone trees and endless hold times awaiting them at a customer call center.

Even though Comcast and all large companies still have miles to go in fairly and fully prioritizing customer service, the spreadable media environment has made listening to audiences a greater priority for many marketers and media companies. Public relations and corporate communication departments are increasingly using their online presence to address the messages customers are circulating, a sign of the power which visible and socially connected audience members have to shape the agendas of companies through the messages they spread (an issue we will return to in greater detail in chapter 4). In other words, companies are feeling more pressure to think not just about how audiences might spread messages about a brand (and content from the brand) but also about how their own corporate presence might "spread" to connect with the messages audiences are circulating about them.

Participatory Culture Reconsidered

Spreadability assumes a world where mass content is continually repositioned as it enters different niche communities. When material is produced according to a one-size-fits-all model, it imperfectly fits the needs of any given audience. Instead, audience members have to retrofit it to better serve their interests. As material spreads, it gets remade: either literally, through various forms of sampling and remixing, or figuratively, via its insertion into ongoing conversations and across various platforms. This continuous process of repurposing and recirculating is eroding the perceived divides between production and consumption.

Whitney Phillips's doctoral work at the University of Oregon focuses on the cultural practices, productions, and performances associated with 4Chan, an online community that actively encourages behavior which is often described as "antisocial" or "troll-like." Phillips argues that even disrespectful remixing is generative. In our enhanced book, she argues that 4Chan members have adopted a distinctive model for thinking about the "contributions" they make to culture, actively seizing on memes as tools for creativity and production:

> As understood by trolls, memes are not passive and do not follow the model of biological infection. Instead, trolls see (though perhaps "experience" is more accurate) memes as microcosmic nests of evolving content. [. . .] Memes spread—that is, they are actively engaged and/

or remixed into existence—because something about a given image or phrase or video or whatever lines up with an already-established set of linguistic and cultural norms. In recognizing this connection, a troll is able to assert his or her cultural literacy and to bolster the scaffolding on which trolling as a whole is based, framing every act of reception as an act of cultural production.

For 4Chan members, the concept of the meme as a self-perpetuating phenomenon beyond human control might contribute to the spontaneity and disruption the group hopes to achieve. Phillips (2009) has argued elsewhere that 4Chan may have been the birthplace for widely spread images that represented U.S. President Barack Obama as Batman character The Joker, which some supporters of the U.S. conservative Tea Party movement adopted for protest signs during their public opposition to President Obama's national health care plan.

While the *Los Angeles Times* (Grad 2009) identified the artist of one of the most widely spread versions as college student Firas Alkhateeb, the image emerged from a larger series of remixes by the 4Chan community as they toyed with marketing material produced for the 2008 Batman film *The Dark Knight*. Other remixes included transforming John McCain into The Joker, along with Sarah Palin, Hillary Clinton, various pop stars, and, of course, pictures of cute cats. While most of these remixes didn't circulate broadly outside 4Chan, some members of the Tea Party found particular resonance in the image of Obama as the antisocial Joker. Within 4Chan, memes serve as themes for ongoing conversations and fodder for creative activity, with each variation demonstrating and requiring particular cultural knowledge. Much as 4Chan hijacked images from Christopher Nolan's movie, the Tea Party poached these images from 4Chan, changing their political valances yet again. All of this suggests the ways that the appropriation, remixing, and recirculation of content via the mechanisms of participatory culture are increasingly impacting conversations far removed from what once might have been seen as niche communities. As this happens, we are seeing the erosion of traditional boundaries—between fans and activists, creativity and disruption, niche and mainstream in the 4Chan example, or between commercial and grassroots, fan and producer in some of the examples we will consider later in this section.

This book will suggest a range of groups who are strongly motivated to produce and circulate media materials as parts of their ongoing social interactions, among them activists who seek to change public perceptions of an issue of concern to the group; religious groups who seek to spread "the Word"; supporters of the arts—especially of independent media—who seek to build a base to bolster alternative forms of cultural expression; enthusiasts for particular brands that have become signposts for people's identities and lifestyles; bloggers who seek to engage others about the needs of local communities; collectors and retro audiences seeking greater access to residual materials; members of subcultures seeking to construct alternative identities; and so forth.

In particular, we will frequently use entertainment fandom as a reference point because fans groups have often been innovators in using participatory platforms to organize and respond to media texts. As early as the mid-nineteenth century, amateur publishers began to print newsletters about shared interests and to circulate them across the country, ultimately leading to the formation of the Amateur Press Association (Petrik 1992). The rise of science fiction fandom in the 1920s and 1930s (Ross 1991) built on this foundation, representing one of the most prominent and enduring examples of organized fan communities. Television fandom, in turn, has provided a supportive context through which many women, excluded from the male-only club that science fiction fandom had largely become, could develop their skills and hone their talents. By the 1970s, many women were remixing television footage to create their own fanvids, writing and editing their own zines, creating elaborate costumes, singing original folk songs, and painting images, all inspired by their favorite television series (Bacon-Smith 1992; Jenkins 1992; Coppa 2008). With the rise of networked computing, these fan communities did important work, providing their female participants with access to new skills and technologies as their members took their first steps into cyberspace, reversing early conceptions about the gendering of digital culture as a space only for masculine mastery. In particular, female fans were early adopters of social network technologies such as LiveJournal and Dreamwith, using the resources offered by new media technologies (podcasting, mp3s, video-sharing sites) to create their own distinctive forms of participatory culture.

These types of communities have embraced new technologies as they emerged, particularly when such tools offered them new means of social and cultural interactions. Rather than looking at platforms such as YouTube and Twitter as "new," we consider these sites where multiple existing forms of participatory culture—each with its own historical trajectory, some over a century old—come together, which is part of what makes such platforms so complex to study. The popularity of Twitter, for instance, was driven by how efficiently the site facilities the types of resource sharing, conversation, and coordination that communities have long engaged in. The site's early success owes little to official brand presence; big-name entertainment properties, companies, and celebrities began flocking to the microblogging platform only after its success was considered buzzworthy (a few exceptional early adopters notwithstanding, of course). Launched at the 2007 South by Southwest Interactive festival, a favorite event for people in media-related industries, Twitter quickly enabled individual marketers to build their personal brands, to connect with one another, to demonstrate their social networking abilities, and to share their "thought leadership." Marketers, advertisers, and public relations professionals constituted a good portion of the early professionals using the site at a time when the rules of marketing were rapidly changing and a new crop of professionals were cementing their status and demonstrating their prowess in the "digital era."

The same year Twitter launched, so too did *Mad Men*, AMC's multi-Emmy-award-winning series about 1960s advertising agency Sterling Cooper. *Mad Men* celebrates what many people consider a "golden era" of U.S. mass marketing. The series serves as both a retrospective on the broadcast era and an exploration of another time in marketing when the rules were in flux and new advertising practices were developing around an increasingly important new media form (in this case, television).

It almost seems inevitable now that Twitter would prove a natural extension for the drama of *Mad Men*. Since season one, ad man Don Draper and fellow Sterling Cooper employees Pete Campbell, Joan Holloway, and Roger Sterling (or, rather, someone performing their identities) had been providing advice to readers through a Tumblr blog. However, on August 12, 2008, in the midst of the series's second season, Draper showed up on Twitter, gaining several thousand followers in a few days. Soon, Pete, Joan, Roger, and almost the full cast of *Mad Men* characters arrived. During and between episodes, their followers could watch the characters interact and even join conversations with them. Some wholly new creations began to appear in the Twitter/*Mad Men* narrative as well, including Sterling Cooper mailroom employee Bud Melman and the office's Xerox copy machine.

The *Mad Men* characters on Twitter were often playful and self-referential. Despite the obvious questions about how characters from the 1960s were using a modern communication platform, why they would share personal thoughts publicly, or how a Xerox machine could tweet, the interaction largely fit within the parameters of the show's storyline, deepening engagement with existing stories rather than challenging the narrative or taking it in new directions. Some tweets referenced facts the audience knew but most characters didn't, such as the closeted homosexuality of art director Sal. Others alluded to contemporary political events in relation to developments on the show, such as the rise to prominence of Joe "the plumber" Wurzelbacher as the quintessential middle-class citizen during the 2008 U.S. presidential election (King 2009).

A growing number of high-profile bloggers, especially in the fan and brand spheres, praised AMC's marketing prowess. This praise was somewhat misdirected, however: as it turned out, the tweeting *Mad Men* (like their Tumblr forebears) were not affiliated with AMC or the show. Instead, fans of the show had inhabited the identities of favorite characters. As the popularity of these virtual versions of *Mad Men*'s characters escalated, AMC contacted Twitter to ascertain who was behind the accounts. Twitter interpreted this inquiry as a copyright challenge from AMC and suspended several user accounts, under the guise of the Digital Millennium Copyright Act, on August 26, 2008, about two weeks after Draper's first tweet.

Twitter's suspension of the accounts fit a narrative that media fans and marketers alike knew well. Cease-and-desist orders have become an all-too-familiar means of correspondence between brands and their audiences in an era when prohibitionist corporate attitudes have collided with the collaborative nature of online social networks. There was immediate outcry against AMC for disrespecting its fans, pointing out that this activity had become an engine for generating interest and deepening engagement in a niche cable show with high critical praise but underwhelming ratings.

Part of AMC's ambivalence about *Mad Men*'s Twitter popularity was likely driven by marketers' uncertainty about ceding control, in some ways paralleling *Mad Men* creator Matthew Weiner's own reputation as a self-professed "control freak" who "approves every actor, costume, hairstyle and prop" (Witchel 2008). Weiner's reputation for tight control has extended beyond careful monitoring of the production; he has spoken out vehemently against ways of viewing or experiencing the show of which he disapproves. Says Weiner, "I met this guy who was creating software where you could watch *Mad Men* and you could chat with your friend while you're watching it, and things would pop up, and facts would pop up, and I said, 'You're a human battery. Turn the fucking thing off! You're not allowed to watch the show anymore. You're missing the idea of sitting in a dark place and having an experience'" (quoted in Jung 2009). Weiner's response is emotional rather than legal, but both his complaint and AMC's actions in response to tweeting fans reflect a desire on the part of the media industries to maintain a tight grip on the reception and circulation of content. While the attention to detail that Weiner and his staff consistently display is part of what drives the show's reputation and its audience's enjoyment, expanding that tight control over how *Mad Men* is viewed, discussed, and spread restricts the show's circulation and dampens audience enthusiasm.

In many cases, however, the people writing as *Mad Men* characters had professional as well as personal interest in the show. Several were marketers themselves (Draper, for instance, was performed by strategist Paul Isakson with digital agency space150), and these fans drew on their professional identities to lobby for account reinstatement. Strategist Bud Caddell (who created the original character Bud Melman on Twitter) launched WeAreSterlingCooper.org to act as "command central" for the community of fans participating in the Twitter fan fiction and to articulate their rights to continue posting. The site issued "a rallying cry to brands and fans alike to come together and create together":

> Fan fiction. Brand hijacking. Copyright misuse. Sheer devotion. Call it what you will, but we call it the blurred line between content creators and content consumers, and it's not going away. We're your biggest fans, your die-hard proponents, and when your show gets cancelled we'll be among the first to pass around the petition. Talk to us. Befriend us. Engage us. But please, don't treat us like criminals. (Caddell 2008)

In the midst of the controversy, marketer Carri Bugbee, who had tweeted as @peggyolson, opened up new Twitter account @Peggy_Olson to continue writing. She started with, "I worked hard. I did my job. But the boys at Twitter are just as churlish as the boys at Sterling Cooper. Such a pity that they're so petty" (quoted in Siegler 2008). As fan tweeting and public discussion about the controversy increased, AMC did a swift about-face. Reportedly, AMC was following advice from its digital marketing agency Deep Focus, which itself had suffered criticism from marketers for preaching the value of social media while working with a client blatantly stomping on fans' passion and expressions (Learmonth 2008). More visible after the suspension controversy, the Sterling Cooper Twitterers returned to their posts.

Perhaps the *Mad Men* snafu resulted from the continued prevalence of "stickiness" as the chief way to measure success. If AMC evaluated the success of promoting *Mad Men* only by the easily measurable traffic through its official channels, then discouraging anything that might distract people from these destinations makes sense. From that mindset, fan-created material off official *Mad Men* channels is in competition with the show, and any traffic those outlets receive dilutes the reach of the show's official presence. This approach assigns no value to how fan-created-and-circulated content might drive awareness and engagement in a show indirectly, because it cannot be easily quantified.

Beyond the lingering desire to cling to a stickiness model, companies are often just uncertain about audiences spreading material for their own purposes. Though marketers idealize a dream audience that will passively pass along official (viral) messages, they know that the reality is much messier: fans who create new material or pass along existing media content ultimately want to communicate something about themselves. Fans may seek to demonstrate their own technical prowess, to gain greater standing within a niche community, to speculate about future developments, or to make new arguments using texts already familiar to their own audiences. As the *Mad Men* Twitter example proves, content often gains traction when people are given the latitude to use "official" media texts to communicate something about themselves.

The clash of professional concerns and fan enthusiasm within the *Mad Men* Twitter community caused particular consternation. Since the *Mad Men* Twitterers were marketers, professional motivations also drove their fan creation. Because of this, Deep Focus initially indicated that the Twitterers shouldn't be considered fans (Caddell 2008), suggesting their professions removed them from the logics of fandom, locating them instead squarely within the economics of "corporate America."

Further, Caddell describes infighting among the Twitterers as their popularity grew, with multiple contenders vying to portray popular characters and some more secretive members concerned that, if their true identities were "outed," their professional standing could be compromised. Meanwhile, some of these fans used their role in this controversy to demonstrate their own knowledge about Twitter and their understanding of fan enthusiasm, building recognition within the marketing community. After the controversy subsided, Caddell published the report "Becoming a Mad Man"; Bugbee built a new agency, Big Deal PR—drawing, in part, on the controversy and the Shorty Award she won for her Twitter portrayal of Peggy Olson; and several others have drawn on their participation in this fan activity through professional publications or conference presentations. In the process, tension over who claimed ownership of the fan activity and which Twitterers took credit for this moment of success became public. For instance, when Bugbee created a South by Southwest Interactive panel about the *Mad Men*/Twitter phenomenon, Caddell (2009a) publicly discussed the politics of panelist selection, blogging about the omission of himself and other prominent "fans" who were pivotal in the movement.

The circulation of media content within participatory culture can serve a range of interests, some cultural (such as promoting a particular genre or performer), some personal (such as strengthening social bonds between friends), some political (such as critiquing the construction of gender and sexuality within mass media), some economic (such as those which serve the immediate needs of everyday individuals, as well as those which serve the needs of media companies). We are not arguing that fans are somehow resisting consumer capitalism and its intellectual property regimes through these various processes and practices, as many of even these unauthorized activities might indirectly profit media companies and brands. Whatever audiences' motivations, they may discover new markets, generate new meanings, renew once-faded franchises, support independent producers, locate global content which was never commercially introduced in a local market, or disrupt and reshape the operations of contemporary culture in the process. In some cases, these outcomes are the direct goal of participatory culture; in others, they are a byproduct. Companies that tell audiences to keep their hands off a brand's intellectual property cut themselves off from these processes, many of which might create and prolong the value of media texts.

The media industries understand that culture is becoming more participatory, that the rules are being rewritten and relationships between producers and their audiences are in flux. Few companies, however, are willing to take what may be seen as substantial risks with potentially valuable intellectual property. Fans' desires and corporate interests sometimes operate in parallel, yet they never fully coincide, in part because even companies that embrace the ideals of audience engagement are uncertain about how much control to abdicate. Watching AMC and Deep Focus sometimes reject and sometimes embrace the efforts of their fans to promote *Mad Men*, regardless of these fans' alternative motivations, provides a glimpse into the limits of current industry understanding of what we call spreadable media. The fans in the *Mad Men* case are themselves part of the branded entertainment industry, using their recreational time to consider how this new cultural economy might operate. Some have publicly acknowledged that their actions crossed the lines which normally separate producers from their audiences, while others were wary to speak out, unsure what was at risk as they ventured into this uncertain terrain. However, these marketers/fans and their fictional characters articulated audience desires to participate more actively in producing and circulating media and professional desires to make marketing and media texts more participatory.

Corporate interests will never fully align with those of participatory culture, and frictions will frequently emerge. For instance, people are deeply ambivalent about how media companies and corporate communicators participate in such an environment. With audiences' greater autonomy, they seek more explicit acknowledgment from companies but are concerned with how the active participation of corporations might distort communities or that corporations will only embrace audience practices in the ways they can most easily profit from them. Participatory culture is not synonymous with the business practices that have been labeled Web 2.0, a distinction we will explore more fully in chapter 1. We are all struggling over the shape our culture(s) will take in the coming decades, a struggle being tackled on uneven terms and with unequal resources. We see participatory culture as a relative term—culture is more participatory now than it was under older regimes of media power in many places. Yet we are a long way away from anything approaching full participation.

All of this suggests ways we are revising the concept of participatory culture to reflect the realities of a dramatically altered and still-evolving mediascape. We are moving from an initial focus on fandom as a particular subculture to a larger model that accounts for many groups that are gaining greater communicative capacity within a networked culture and toward a context where niche cultural production is increasingly influencing the shape and direction of mainstream media. We are moving from focusing on the oppositional relationship between fans and producers as a form of cultural resistance to understanding those roles as increasingly and complexly intertwined. We are moving from a celebration of the growth of participatory opportunities toward a view tempered by concern for the obstacles blocking many people from meaningful participation. We will return throughout the book to debates about the terms of our participation, about how our participation is valued or blocked through various corporate policies and practices, and about which participants are welcomed, marginalized, and excluded.

Papyrus and Marble

The innovations, and struggles, of participatory culture that take place within the broad interplay between top-down institutional and bottom-up social forces have shaped the spread of media within and across cultures. There is a long history of such cultural exchanges, conducted through various channels and practices. The rise of networked computing and the ways its components have been absorbed into participatory culture and deployed through social network sites represents a new configuration of long-existing practices. (MIT media historian William Uricchio traces some key chapters of that history in our enhanced book, showing how media from coins to printed books have flowed within and across cultures.) Even if grassroots channels of communication may have disruptive effects on existing monopolies of knowledge, spreadable media needs to be understood in evolutionary rather than revolutionary terms.

How media circulates has been a central concern of media studies at least since the 1951 publication of Harold Innis's *The Bias of Communication*. In Innis's formulation, the dominant means of communication in a given society influences the production and control of information. Calling for an approach to media studies centered on "the dissemination of knowledge over space and over time," Innis noted that some media (stone or marble, for example) are "heavy and durable," preserving information for long periods but also leading to top-down control over what information is preserved. Other media (papyrus, for example) are "light and easily transported," allowing for their quick and easy spread across a geographically dispersed area (1951, 33). Often, those media that enable mobility are also low cost, allowing for their deployment by and among more people and resulting in more decentralized communication.

Innis argues that ongoing tension between durability and mobility—between marble and papyrus—has determined what kinds of information gained visibility in its own time and what has been preserved for subsequent generations. In his account, shifts in the technological infrastructure have the potential to construct or undermine "monopolies of knowledge" closely associated with other sources of institutional power. Innis's focus on how different configurations of technologies may enable or constrain the circulation of information has been taken up by more recent writers seeking to explain the rise of phenomena such as digital rights management systems (DRM) as attempts to shape audience behavior. Tarleton Gillespie describes the system of constraints determining how users can engage with and share digital media texts:

> Constructing technology to regulate human activity, such that it limits all users in a fair and effective way, is never simply a technical matter. It is a heterogeneous effort in which the material artifacts, the institutions that support them, the laws that give them teeth, and the political and cultural mechanisms that give them legitimacy, must all be carefully aligned into a loosely regimented but highly cohesive, hybrid network. (2006, 652)

Different technological choices, then, can shape the uses the public makes of media content, facilitating some while constraining others, but technologies can never be designed to absolutely control how material gets deployed within a given social and cultural context. Indeed, both popular and niche uses of technology always emerge far outside anything foreseen by the designer.

Yet the more companies and governments roadblock the spread of media texts, the more grassroots circulation requires advanced technical skills to work around those obstacles. In the process, many people are shut out of being able to meaningfully shape the circulation process. Gillespie describes user agency as a mixture of technical capacities (being able to "act with a tool and on that tool") and social capacities ("the user's perception of their ability and right to do so") (2006, 661). Using transportation as an example, Gillespie discusses the range of cultural resources, economic incentives, and technological innovations which have encouraged some users to fix their own cars, even as he describes ways current car design has made this less likely than in the past and has limited which groups of people feel able to do so without causing more damage than they are fixing. Spreadability is coming to a head right now because a complex set of changes has made it easier for grassroots communities to circulate content than ever before, yet the requirements of skills and literacies, not to mention access to technologies, are not evenly distributed across the population, an issue which we will examine throughout this book.

However, we again do not wish to ascribe too much power to any particular technology or platform. While Innis's formulation presumes there will always be a dominant communication medium "biasing" society in one direction or another, this present moment of media convergence is one when there are multiple (sometimes competing and sometimes complementary) media systems whose intersections provide the infrastructure for contemporary communication (as the Susan Boyle and *Mad Men* examples suggest about the interplay between broadcast and digital networks). Some of these structures (such as the digital rights management systems Gillespie describes) seek the weight and authority prescribed to previous durable media. Often, such structures seek to lock down content, limiting or controlling its circulation. Other current platforms (such as YouTube, which makes it easy to embed its content elsewhere) have the freedom and mobility once ascribed to papyrus, enabling their rapid circulation across a range of social networks. Some media texts are made to last, while others (such as Twitter) are intended to be timely and disposable.

If various platforms offer divergent opportunities for participation, preservation, and mobility—and each system of communication sustains different relations between producers and citizens—then the established geopolitical system also creates hierarchies which make it harder for some groups (and some nations) to participate than others.

Anthropologist Arjun Appadurai, a leading theorist of globalization, is another who has followed in Innis's footsteps. Appadurai observes that "cultural objects, including images, languages, and hairstyles, now move ever more swiftly across regional and national boundaries. This acceleration is a consequence of the speed and spread of the Internet and the simultaneous, comparative growth in travel, cross-cultural media and global advertising" (2010, 4). Appadurai sees this accelerated flow of information and culture being facilitated not simply by the efforts of multinational capitalism but also through the expansion of illegal and unauthorized markets. These markets often cobble together systems of exchange that support the spread of media content and cultural values (but also guns and drugs) outside official and commercial channels. Often, he suggests, these underground, grassroots circuits—which serve the needs of less-affluent or marginalized peoples—"ride on" older systems of exchange which emerged from even more longstanding processes of globalization.

Appadurai's model concedes fundamental inequalities in terms of which countries have access to these different forms of circulation, which face roadblocks that make it difficult to meaningfully participate in such exchanges, and how these inequalities of participation shape which ideas get put into circulation. There are, as Appadurai's work demonstrates, many different kinds of networks which reach many different layers of societies and which travel between many different nodes in the system. While our book details the potentials of spreadability as a means of ensuring that more people have access to the means of cultural circulation, we believe it's crucial to always be cognizant that not everyone has equal access to the technologies and to the skills needed to deploy them.

Despite (or perhaps because of) these inequalities, though, we are seeing some spectacular shifts in the flow of information across national borders and, as a consequence, in the relations between the peoples of different countries. As Appadurai notes, "This volatile and exploding traffic in commodities, styles, and information has been matched by the growth of both flows of cultural politics, visible most powerfully in the discourse of human rights, but also in the new languages of radical Christianity and Islam, and the discourse of civil society activists, who wish to promote their own versions of global equity, entitlement, and citizenship" (2010, 5).

Journalists, bloggers, and other cyber-enthusiasts have celebrated the use of sites such as Twitter, Facebook, and YouTube by protesters across the Muslim world and their supporters from the West as a decisive sign that grassroots communicators might be able to route around government censors and that citizen journalists might be able to force international concerns onto the agenda of the professional news media. Consider, for example, the role such technologies played in the aftermath of Iran's hotly contested summer 2009 elections. Between June 7 and June 26, the Web Ecology Project (2009) at Harvard University recorded 2,024,166 tweets about the Iranian election, involving 480,000 people. Meanwhile, CNN's iReport received more than 1,600 citizen-produced reports from Iran (Carafano 2009), mostly photographs but including videos of the actions in the street, recorded and transmitted via mobile phones. (Our enhanced book features a more involved discussion by Henry Jenkins on how "spreadability" applies to these events in Iran and the 2011 Arab Spring movements as well as the Occupy Wall Street movement in the United States.)

Sean Aday et al.'s 2010 report *Blogs and Bullets: New Media in Contentious Politics* argues that Twitter participation inside Iran was too low to have made much difference on the ground (estimating that as few as 100 people may have produced most of the Twitter traffic out of the country) and that the regime in power likewise used social network tools to monitor the behavior of protesters and often to circulate counterrevolutionary materials. However, the report concludes, "Where Twitter and other new media clearly did matter is how they conveyed information about the protests to the outside world. Traditional media were at a disadvantage in covering events inside Iran because of restrictions placed on journalists, and thus ended up relying on new media for content. Hence, the outside world's perceptions of the protests were crucially shaped by Twitter (as conveyed through blogs and other means), amateur videos uploaded to YouTube and Facebook, and other sources" (22). In Innis's terms, what happened challenged two "monopolies of knowledge" which potentially regulated the flow of information from Tehran to the United States: the

Iranian government's desire to contain news of the protest and the mainstream news media's ability to determine the priority it gave to covering specific events. For Appadurai, the same data might have illustrated continued inequalities in the speed and spread of communication, such that people struggling for power within Iran were forced to rely on influence and attention from the Western world to shape events within their own country.

Clay Shirky has argued that Twitter's impact in this instance was more affective than informational: "As a medium gets faster, it gets more emotional. We feel faster than we think. [. . .] Twitter makes us empathize. It makes us part of it. Even if it's just retweeting, you're aiding the goal that dissidents have always sought: the awareness that the outside world is paying attention is really valuable" (2009). These strong emotions reflected the cumulative effect of an ongoing but always fragile flow of messages from the streets of Tehran. Much as daily digital communication about mundane matters led to people using social network sites feeling stronger personal ties to their friends, the flow of political messages through Twitter helped make them feel more directly implicated by the protest. Global citizens (including a strong diasporic community in North America and western Europe) helped the Iranian protesters evade potential censorship and technical roadblocks, translated their thoughts into English and other Western languages, flagged reliable information from rumors, passed what they had learned onto others, and rallied news outlets to pay closer attention.

Newsrooms are still struggling to figure out what their new roles may be in an environment where the demand for information can be driven by affect and shaped by what happens within online communities, where citizens may make demands on what journalists cover and may cobble together information from a range of resources if traditional news outlets fail to provide desired information. While smooth relations between grassroots and commercial media can be rare, the two can coexist within a more layered media environment, each holding the other accountable for its abuses, each scanning the other for potentially valuable content that might otherwise fall through the cracks.

However, one could argue that these acts of circulation (and discussions of circulation) substituted for actual political action. Jodi Dean contends in an essay on what she calls "communicative capitalism" that the expansion of the public's capacity to circulate messages has too often been fetishized as an end in itself, often at the expense of real debate or action on the ground that might seek to directly change the struggles taking place:

> Today, the circulation of content in the dense, intensive networks of global communications relieves top-level actors (corporate, institutional and governmental) from the obligation to respond. Rather than responding to messages sent by activists and critics, they counter with their own contributions to the circulating flow of communications, hoping that sufficient volume (whether in terms of number of contributions or the spectacular nature of a contribution) will give their contributions dominance or stickiness. [. . .] Under conditions of the intensive and extensive proliferation of media, messages are more likely to get lost as mere contributions to the circulation of content. (2005, 54)

Dean raises an important caveat about how means can become ends in themselves, especially amid the techno-euphoria that has surrounded the expansion of communication capacities. Twitter (as a new company seeking to increase its visibility in the marketplace) benefited from what happened in this case as much or more than the Tehran protestors did. Yet we feel that Dean goes too far in dismissing the meaningfulness of popular acts of circulation. She writes, "Messages are contributions to circulating content—not actions to elicit responses. [. . .] So, a message is no longer primarily a message from a sender to a receiver. Uncoupled from contexts of action and application—as on the Web or in print and broadcast media—the message is simply part of a circulating data stream. Its particular content is irrelevant" (59). For Dean, meaningful participation is a fantasy used to sell products and services rather than a description of contemporary political and economic realities. We disagree. Web 2.0 companies may often seek to sell longstanding cultural practices back to the communities where they originated, but Dean's argument is every bit as disempowering as corporate versions of "viral media" and ultimately fatalistic in its conclusions. Rather than seeing circulation as the empty exchange of information stripped of context and meaning, we see these acts of circulation as constituting bids for meaning and value.

We feel that it very much matters who sends the message, who receives it, and, most importantly, what messages get sent. Acts of circulation shape both the cultural and political landscape in significant ways, as we will demonstrate throughout this book. What happened with Iran was not revolutionary, in the sense that it led to a regime change, but it was profound, in the sense that it made people around the world more aware of the political dynamics on the ground in Tehran and left many of us feeling closer to a group of people who, for most of our lives, we had been told to hate and fear.

What's Next

Innis's distinction between marble and papyrus, storage and mobility, is helpful for considering the ways a more spreadable media culture breaks with the assumptions of both the broadcast paradigm and the "stickiness" model. Both broadcast and stickiness represent different kinds of "monopoly" structures, locking down access and limiting participation. Under the conditions we've been describing here, media content that remains fixed in location and static in form fails to generate sufficient public interest and thus drops out of these ongoing conversations. Throughout this chapter, we've detailed many examples of spreadability at work, including those from the realm of entertainment (Susan Boyle, *Mad Men*), news and politics (Iran), and marketing/customer service (Comcast). Insofar as spreadability becomes an attribute of the contemporary media landscape, it has the potential to dramatically reshape how central cultural and political institutions operate.

If we all accept that the media industries and marketing worlds are moving toward a model of circulation based on the logic of spreadability, and if we also accept that concepts such as the meme and the virus often distort the human agency involved in spreading media content, how might we better understand the ways in which material travels within a networked culture? This core question will structure the rest of this book.

First, we consider the economic and social logics shaping this spreadable media landscape. Chapter 1 critiques the rhetoric and mindset of Web 2.0, examining what gets lost in contemporary business practices which seek to harness participatory culture for businesses' own economic gain and exploring some of the gaps emerging between the social logic that often shapes noncommercial production and the commodity logic that informs much of commercial culture. Chapter 2 digs further into the processes used to evaluate and appraise media content from yesteryear, examining the residual meanings and potential new value for content and brands as they move between commercial and noncommercial exchange.

Second, we consider ways the media industries have begun to reconceptualize their audiences as active participants whose labor helps determine the value of branded entertainment. Chapter 3 focuses on how the television industry is rethinking audience measurement as it seeks new business models built on audience engagement. In particular, we explore how transmedia entertainment has emerged as an alternative strategy for courting and mobilizing audiences behind media franchises. Chapter 4 directs attention toward the nature of participation, suggesting a need to move from the broadcast era's focus on individual audience members to an emphasis on socially active and networked audiences. Along the way, we consider which forms of participation are and are not valued within current business models. We make the case for a greater focus on processes of deliberation rather than aggregation and on the value of "listening" to what audience members say rather than simply "hearing" that a brand or media property has been mentioned. And we examine the gaps in access and participation that persist in our culture.

Third, in chapter 5, we explore why some types of media content spread more widely and more quickly than others. In focusing specifically on marketing (in the first part of the chapter) and on activist and civic media (in the second), we seek to link the spread of material with the social needs of online communities. We draw on John Fiske's (1989b) notion of "producerly" media texts to explore how networked communities transform mass-produced media into "resources" which fuel their ongoing conversations with each other.

Finally, our book explores how spreadable practices may support a more diverse array of media options than the old broadcast paradigm—focusing on independent and Christian media in chapter 6 and transnational media flows in chapter 7. In chapter 6, we examine how independent media makers from film, publishing, music, comics, and games are building new kinds of relations with their audiences. While these practices may not match the economic advantages enjoyed by mass-media producers, they have allowed independent artists to expand access to and increase the visibility of their productions. Chapter 7 argues that a combination of pirates, immigrants, and pop cosmopolitans have helped circulate more media content beyond geographic borders than ever before. Much like the creations of independent media makers, these cultural goods often still operate from a position of marginality, unable to compete directly with dominant media industries. Yet there are signs that their cultural and economic impact is increasing, thanks to their ability to travel through grassroots media channels.

In December 2009, Capitol Records filed a suit against online video-sharing site Vimeo, claiming the site "induces and encourages its users" to engage in copyright infringement (Lawler 2009). Capitol argued that Vimeo failed to take sufficient action to monitor infringing material that was uploaded to its servers. They also claimed that Vimeo staff actively participated in the production and promotion of videos infringing Capitol's copyrights. In particular, the complaint targeted the site's regular promotion of the "lip dub"—a form of high-concept music video featuring intricate lip-syncing and choreography. Lip dubs are regularly highlighted on the site's front page, and Vimeo staff has produced its own (some of which have drawn substantial attention online).

As word of the suit spread, people responded with a mixture of cynicism about Capitol's motives, defenses of the recording industry's need to protect its business models, and a litany of frustrated barbs about the lack of innovation from major industry players. At TechDirt—a site covering online technology, policy, and legal issues—readers suggested that Capitol's actions occurred at a time when parent company EMI was suffering from massive losses. (See comments at Masnick 2009.) *Rolling Stone*'s Daniel Kreps (2009) noted that the action against Vimeo came soon after EMI had signed licensing deals with start-up Vevo—a site developed by YouTube and supported by a number of major U.S. labels as a central, officially sanctioned depository for music videos online. At both collaborative news site Digg and online journal *Ars Technica*, some commenters

WHERE
WEB 2.0 WENT WRONG

pondered why Capitol's suit was necessary, given that there was no proof lip dubs result in any harm. Many people contended that such videos constituted free advertising and publicity for recording artists (see comments at LeechesofKarma 2009 and N. Anderson 2009), an argument regularly mobilized by those who disagree with "antipiracy" lawsuits.[1]

Conflicts between media rights holders and the platforms, such as Vimeo, which host that material have become increasingly common, particularly as the ideas behind Web 2.0 have led to a proliferation of start-ups looking to monetize and commodify user-generated content. These dramatic technological and economic shifts have disrupted normative practices but not yet produced a model satisfying any party. Throughout this chapter, we will map the varying conceptions about fair economic and social relations held by media companies and their audiences. As we do so, we will examine how value, worth, and trust are negotiated and legitimized in this shifting social-economic-technological context through a few crucial concepts—the idea of a "moral economy" derived from the work of historian E. P. Thompson and the relations between commodity and gift economies as envisioned most notably by philosopher Lewis Hyde. Both of these models suggest ways that economic relations are shaped, at least in part, by social and moral understandings between the participating parties, aspects which often get dropped out of popular representations of debates about who "owns" media content and who should be "paid" for creative "labor."

What Is Web 2.0?

The idea of Web 2.0 was introduced at a 2004 conference of the O'Reilly Media Group. In Tim O'Reilly's formulation, Web 2.0 companies rely on the Internet as the platform for promoting, distributing, and refining their products: treating software as a service designed to run across multiple devices, relying on data as the "killer app," and harnessing the "collective intelligence" of a network of users (O'Reilly 2005). Since Web 2.0's introduction, it has become *the* cultural logic for e-business—a set of corporate practices that seek to capture and exploit participatory culture.

More than "pasting a new user interface onto an old application" (Musser et al. 2006, 3), Web 2.0 represents a reorganization of the relations between producers and their audiences in a maturing Internet market, as well as a set of approaches adopted by companies seeking to harness mass creativity, collectivism, and peer production (Van Dijck and Nieborg 2009). The emerging business superstars in this category have promised users greater influence over the production and distribution of culture, and "users," "consumers," and "audiences" have been reimagined as "co-creators" (Banks and Humphreys 2008) of content and services. These co-creators are engaged as collaborators as they upload, tag, organize, and categorize content on YouTube, Flickr, and myriad other sites. Meanwhile, marketers have increasingly emphasized transmedia campaigns, interactive experiences, and participatory platforms encouraging such co-creation. The tenets of Web 2.0 entice audience members to join in the building and customizing of services and messages rather than to expect companies to present complete and fully formed experiences.

In theory, Web 2.0 companies relinquish a certain degree of control to users. What has been described as "putting the We in the Web" (Levy and Stone 2006), however, has brought with it contradictions, conflicts, and schisms, particularly around the imperfectly aligned interests of media producers and audiences.

As José Van Dijck and David Nieborg note in their critique of Web 2.0 management and business manifestos, many corporate practices effectively erode the line between "collective (non-market, public) and commercial (market, private) modes of production." Such efforts "cleverly combine capital-intensive, profit-oriented industrial production with labor-intensive, non-profit-oriented peer production" (2009, 856). There is a considerable gap between the Web 2.0 rhetoric of happy collaboration and users' actual experiences working with companies. On the one hand, the mechanisms of Web 2.0 provide the preconditions for spreadable media; many of the key tools and platforms through which material is spread operate according to Web 2.0 principles. On the other hand, conflicting expectations of what constitutes fair participation means that the actual spreading of media content remains a contested practice.

Taking the "You" Out of YouTube

Video-sharing platform YouTube has struggled since its inception to balance the activities of its users with the interests of large copyright holders. Founded in February 2005 and acquired by Google in October 2006, YouTube's principal business strategy relies on advertising revenue from the attention drawn by the site's wide range of videos (predominantly created and uploaded by users themselves). From its earliest days, YouTube has also signed revenue-sharing deals with corporate producers to distribute their videos—everything from the latest movie trailers to music videos—alongside user-created content and to provide licenses for some of the varied uses of these texts (Knowledge@Wharton 2006). YouTube has also sought to acquire, develop, implement, and refine digital fingerprinting technologies to identify texts belonging to major copyright holders and to automatically issue "takedown" notices to users presumed to have violated intellectual property law through the unauthorized uploading of videos.

Critics (Aufderheide and Jaszi 2008) have noted that automatic takedown notices fail to protect legitimate "fair use" claims, creating a "chilling effect" on a site where creative remixes of existing cultural materials have long been among the most visible and cherished contributions. However, the enforcement mechanisms and related revenue-sharing deals were developed to shield YouTube from accusations that their business rests primarily on directly or indirectly encouraging copyright infringement, a claim that Viacom leveled at the company in its 2007 legal action (Helft and Fabrikant 2007). Indeed, large media companies have sought compensation from YouTube since the site launched. (See Burgess and Green 2009; Driscoll 2007; Knowledge@Wharton 2006.) Holding users and rights holders in balance is especially difficult for YouTube given the scale of the site (as YouTube reports, more than 24 hours of video is uploaded to the site every minute; see YouTube n.d.) and the diverse range of users—professional and amateur, market and nonmarket driven—who share content through it (Burgess and Green 2009).

On January 14, 2009, some YouTube uploaders found that the soundtracks to their videos had suddenly vanished. After a breakdown in licensing negotiations with Warner Music Group (WMG), YouTube had used an automatic tool to remove audio from videos featuring music from WMG artists. In a controversial post no longer available on the site's blog, YouTube explained that removing audio shielded users whose videos would have otherwise faced an infringement claim: "Instead of automatically removing the video from YouTube, we give users the option to modify the video by removing the music subject to the copyright claim and post the new version, and many of them are taking that option" (quoted in M. Campbell 2009).

Unaware of the decision, many uploaders wondered whether they were encountering technical difficulties (Arrington 2009), while some were enraged over market forces intruding on their user-created content. One user wrote, "How does a song playing in the background of a slideshow about a colonial reenacting unit harm anyone—least of all Warner Music Group?" (quoted in M. Campbell 2009). Meanwhile, others mused that their use of the audio tracks added value for the music industry: "If we can use it then that would probably get more people to listen to the audio. It's pretty much like us helping the artist, right?" (quoted in M. Campbell 2009).

While upsetting users, this strategy made business sense for You-Tube. It provided the company a way to woo back Warner Music Group while minimizing the likelihood of further legal troubles. Indeed, as Michael Driscoll discusses, YouTube's strategies for copyright management are generally focused on forging relationships with large copyright holders (2007, 566–567). Even though the site has expanded its "Partner Program" to "ordinary" users, promising them a cut of advertising revenues for videos that might suddenly "go viral" (Kincaid 2009), the company remains primarily focused on policing the copyrights held by large media companies for which the fingerprinting software is made available (Driscoll 2007, 566). Smaller professional and amateur producers who feel that their intellectual property has been infringed—those less likely to constitute a legal threat, to purchase significant ad inventory, or to provide licensed material—must still apply through formal channels to generate a takedown notice under the U.S. Digital Millennium Copyright Act. These various struggles to negotiate between YouTube as a platform for sharing and YouTube as a business model—which have taken place since the platform's genesis—encapsulate the tensions that run throughout the Web 2.0 model. The rest of this chapter will explore those tensions in detail.

Toward a New Moral Economy

Having embraced rhetoric about enabling and empowering participants, YouTube should scarcely be surprised when users push back against shifts in the site's policy and practice. Such shifts represent a unilateral reworking of the social contract between the company and its contributors and damage the "moral economy" on which the exchange of user-generated content rests.

The idea of a moral economy comes from E. P. Thompson (1971), who used the term to describe the social norms and mutual understandings that make it possible for two parties to conduct business. Thompson introduced the concept in his work on eighteenth-century food riots, arguing that when the indentured classes challenged landowners, their protests were typically shaped by some "legitimizing notion": "The men and women in the crowd were informed by the belief that they were defending traditional rights and customs; and in general, that they were supported by the wider consensus of the community" (1971, 78). The relations between landowners and peasants—or, for that matter, between contemporary media producers and audiences—reflect the perceived moral and social value of those transactions. All participants need to feel that the parties involved are behaving in a morally appropriate fashion. In many cases, the moral economy holds in check the aggressive pursuit of short-term self-interest in favor of decisions that preserve long-term social relations among participants. In a small-scale economy, for example, a local dealer is unlikely to "cheat" a customer because the dealer counts on continued trade with the customer (and, the dealer hopes, the customer's friends) over an extended period and thus must maintain his or her reputation within the community.

Economic systems ideally align the perceived interests of all parties involved in a transaction in ways that are consistent, coherent, and fair. A dramatic shift in economic or technological infrastructure can create a crisis in the moral economy, diminishing the level of trust among participating parties and perhaps tarnishing the legitimacy of economic exchanges. This moral economy might empower corporations that feel their customers, employees, or partners have stepped outside the bounds of arrangements. Or it can motivate and empower individuals or communities when they feel a company has acted inappropriately. In these contexts, both producers and audiences make bids for legitimization, proposing alternative understandings of what constitute fair and meaningful interactions. "File sharing" and "piracy," for instance, constitute two competing moral systems for characterizing the unauthorized circulation of media content: one put forth by audience members eager to legitimize the free exchange of material and the other by media companies eager to mark certain practices as damaging to their economic interests and morally suspect.

This sense that the moral economy was being violated motivated peasants in early modern Europe to push back against the feudal economy which had shackled them for hundreds of years, and it surely has and is motivating audience resistance in an era with much more pronounced rhetoric about audience sovereignty. Given how much the practices of participatory culture were marginalized throughout the broadcast era, many communities (particularly fan and activist groups) developed a strong sense of social solidarity and a deep understanding of their common interests and shared values, and they have carried these over into their interactions with Web 2.0 companies.[2] A persistent discourse of "Do-It-Yourself" media (Lankshear and Knobel 2010), for example, has fueled not only alternative modes of production but also explicit and implicit critiques of commercial practices. Meanwhile, the rhetoric of "digital revolution" and empowerment surrounding the launch of Web 2.0 has, if anything, heightened expectations about shifts in the control of cultural production and distribution that companies have found hard to accommodate. (Game designer Alec Austin considers the emotional dimensions of a "moral contract" between producers and audiences in our enhanced book.)

Communities are in theory more fragmented, divided, and certainly more dispersed than the corporate entities with which they interface, making it much harder for them to fully assert and defend their own interests. Fan communities are often enormously heterogeneous, with values and assumptions that fragment along axes of class, age, gender, race, sexuality, and nationality, to name just a few. Yet the moral certainty shaping the reactions of such groups to debates about business models, terms of service, or the commercialization of content reflect how audiences may be more empowered than we expect to challenge corporate policies, especially as they gain greater and easier access to communication platforms which facilitate their working through differences and developing shared norms. It is important, however, to remember that the values associated with fan communities, for instance, may differ dramatically from those of other kinds of cultural participants—activists, members of religious groups, collectors, and so on. As we emphasize throughout this book, these different types of participatory culture do not command equal levels of respect and attention from the media industries.

Stolen Content or Exploited Labor?

New technologies enable audiences to exert much greater impact on circulation than ever before, but they also enable companies to police once-private behavior that is taking on greater public dimensions. Some people describe these shifts as a crisis in copyright and others a crisis in fair use. Fans defend perceived rights and practices that have been taken for granted for many years, such as the long-standing practice of creating "mix tapes" or other compilations of quoted material. Corporations, on the other hand, want to constrain behaviors they see as damaging and having a much larger impact in the digital era. Both sides accuse the other of exploiting the instability created by shifts in technology and media infrastructure. The excessive rhetoric surrounding such digital circulation suggests just how far out of balance the moral understandings of producers and audiences have become.

Consider these two quotes:

> This next block of silence is for all you folks who download music for free, eliminating my incentive to create. (Baldwin n.d.)

<dsully> please describe web 2.0 to me in 2 sentences or less.
<jwb> you make all the content. they keep all the revenue. (Quote
Database n.d.)

The first, from a cartoon depicting an artist preparing to sit in silence onstage during a concert in protest of his audience, demonstrates a sense that media audiences are destroying the moral economy through their expectations of "free" material. The second sees the creative industries as damaging the moral economy through expectations of "free" creative labor from media audiences or platform users. Both constructs represent a perceived breakdown of trust.

Sunny Web 2.0 rhetoric about constructing "an architecture of participation" papers over these conflicts, masking the choices and compromises required if a new moral economy is going to emerge. Instead, we feel it's crucial to understand both sides of this debate. Both ends of this spectrum interpret the process of creating and circulating media through a solely economic lens, when we feel it's crucial not to diminish the many noncommercial logics governing the engaged participation of audiences online. Further, both positions ignore the ongoing negotiation over the terms of the social contract between producers and their audiences, or between platforms and their users, while we believe that neither artist/company nor audience/user can be construed as stripped of all agency.

Writers such as Andrew Keen (2007) suggest that the unauthorized circulation of intellectual property through peer-to-peer networks and the free labor of fans and bloggers constitute a serious threat to the long-term viability of the creative industries. Here, the concern is with audience activity that exceeds the moral economy. Keen's *The Cult of the Amateur* outlines a nightmarish scenario in which professional editorial standards are giving way to mob rule, while the work of professional writers, performers, and media makers is reduced to raw materials for the masses, who show growing contempt for traditional expertise and disrespect for intellectual property rights. Similarly, Jaron Lanier has labeled peer-to-peer production and circulation of media content "digital Maoism," devaluing the creative work performed under a free-enterprise system: "Authors, journalists, musicians and artists are encouraged to treat the fruits of their intellects and imaginations as fragments to be given without pay to the hive mind" (2010, 83).

Here, we can see that the concept of the moral economy is crucial to understanding the business environment facilitating—or restraining—what we are calling spreadable media. As arguments such as Keen's and Lanier's demonstrate, the mechanisms of Web 2.0 may provide the preconditions for the sharing of media texts, but the moral position that many content owners take demonstrates how spreading material remains a contested practice. Corporate rights holders are often so threatened by the potential disruption caused by "unauthorized" circulation of their content that they seek to lock it down, containing it on their own sites—decisions justified through appeal to the "stickiness" model. Others take legal action to foreclose the circulation of their intellectual property through grassroots media, using threats to contain what they cannot technologically restrain. However, such knee-jerk responses to unauthorized audience circulation have rarely been more than temporarily effective and have left media companies that take this approach continuously frustrated. (In our enhanced book, Queensland University of Technology researcher John Banks examines how creative professionals can be frustrated by the growing need to involve audiences in the process of making and circulating media content and argues that such questions are organizational challenges professionals must engage with rather than bemoan.)

On the other hand, critics of commercial models built from profiting off audience activity with no compensation deploy labor theory to talk about the exploitation of audiences within this new digital economy, a topic we will return to several times in this book. For instance, Tiziana Terranova has offered a cogent critique of these economic relationships in her work on "free labor": "Free labor is the moment where this knowledgeable consumption of culture is translated into productive activities that are pleasurably embraced and at the same time often shamelessly exploited. [. . .] The fruit of collective cultural labor has been not simply appropriated, but voluntarily channeled and controversially structured within capitalist business practices" (2003).

Consider also Lawrence Lessig's critique (2007) of an arrangement in which Lucasfilm would "allow" fans to remix *Star Wars* content in return for granting the company control over anything fans generated. Writing in the *Washington Post*, Lessig described such arrangements as modern-day "sharecropping." Terranova and others have argued the corporate capitalization of free labor, coupled with the precarious employment conditions surrounding the creative and service industries in the early twenty-first century, have reconstituted the labor market in ways which further undercut the possibilities of collective bargaining around benefits, pay scales, or other terms of employment. (In our enhanced book, University of California–Berkeley media studies professor Abigail De Kosnik examines the labor that fans often provide for media producers and questions whether fans may have settled for too little in their implicit bargain with rights holders.)

However, as Mark Deuze and John Banks have warned, we must be careful that critiques of "free labor" do not paint audiences as somehow always unaware of the economic value being generated by their actions (2009, 424). Indeed, taking part in free labor may be meaningful and rewarding (as compared to previous corporate structures), even when a company may be perceived as providing too little value or recognition for that work. Instead, it seems audiences are increasingly savvy about the value created through their attention and engagement: some are seeking ways to extract something from commercial media producers and distributors in return for their participation. These fans see their attention—and the data mined when they visit sites—as a growing source of value for commercial interests, and some are demanding greater compensation, such as more control over and access to content, in recognition of the value they are generating. Individually, they may choose among a range of competing sets of arrangements and transactions which shape their access to material. Collectively, they can work through their responses together, organizing large-scale protests (such as those directed against Facebook when it sought to change its terms of service concerning users' privacy) which can have a real impact on the public perception and economic fortunes of the companies involved. Of course, the potential for collective action and discursive struggle are limited when audience members are forced to use a corporation's own platforms to pose their critiques of that company's practices. All too often, Web 2.0 companies have not really opened up their governance to the communities they claim to enable and serve (Herman, Coombe, and Kaye, 2006).

The frictions, conflicts, and contestations in the negotiation of the moral economy surrounding such labor are ample evidence that audiences are often not blindly accepting the terms of Web 2.0; rather, they are increasingly asserting their own interests as they actively renegotiate the moral economy shaping future transactions. For instance, Hector Postigo (2008) has documented growing tensions between video game companies and modders (developers who build new games or other projects through appropriating and modifying parts of an original platform). While many game companies have made their code available for grassroots creative experiments, others have sought to shut down modding projects that tread uncomfortably close to their own production plans or head in directions of which rights holders do not approve. In return, because modders are aware of the many economic advantages game companies often receive from these "co-creation" activities, they may reject the moral and legal arguments posited for restraining their practice. We feel it is crucial to acknowledge the concerns of corporate exploitation of fan labor while still believing that the emerging system places greater power in the hands of the audience when compared to the older broadcast paradigm.

Engaged, Not Exploited?

When it comes to the matter of profits, it is clearly the media companies that win out in current economic arrangements. If, however, we are to truly explore who benefits from these arrangements, we need to recognize the varied, complex, and multiple kinds of value generated. Critiques of "free labor" sometimes reduce audience labor to simply alienated labor.

Richard Sennett (2008) complicates classical economic models that view labor as motivated almost entirely by financial returns. Rather, he notes, the craftsmen of old were also rewarded in intangible ways such as recognition or reputation, status, satisfaction, and, above all, their pride in a "job well done." These craftsmen set higher standards on their own performance than necessitated by a purely commercial transaction. It was not enough to produce commodities to be exchanged for money; these were also artifacts that displayed professional accomplishments. Craftsmen performed labor that benefited others yet also created structures of self-governance on the level of the guild that helped shape the conditions of their production. (Of course, historically, guilds also sought to construct monopolies, making it harder for newcomers to enter trades, thus protecting the economic interests of their members. Though tempting, we must not overly romanticize such arrangements.) It is precisely the shift from this system in which individual craftsmen felt pride in their own labor to one in which they became anonymous and interchangeable contributors to an assembly line that resulted in the concept of "alienated labor."

Sennett's work is crucial to think through as we examine why participants engage in activities which may not yield them immediate financial returns or which may even cost money to sustain but which get appraised through alternative systems of value. Sennett himself cites the open software movement as an example of a modern social structure which in many ways replicates the self-motivation and shared governance of craftsman guilds (2008, 24), contrasting this system of voluntary labor with the kinds of compensating-yet-regulated performance associated with work in industrial or bureaucratic systems.

Like Sennett's craftsmen, the millions of individuals producing videos for YouTube take pride in their accomplishments, quite apart from their production of value for a company. They create media texts because they have something they want to share with a larger audience. Certainly, as writers such as Sarah Banet-Weiser (2012) suggest, this process—whether the work of celebrities such as Tila Tequila or of an average teen posting videos of herself dancing with her friends—always involves some degree of "self-branding," which can make the participants complicit in the systems of values through which commercial companies appraise their material. Users generating online content are often interested in expanding their own audience and reputation. They may measure their success by how many followers they attract on Twitter, just as television executives value the number of eyeballs their programs attract.

Yet, even if we agree that some degree of self-promotion plays a role in all communication, we must likewise recognize a desire for dialogue and discourse, for solidifying social connections, and for building larger communities through the circulation of media messages. The material emerging from DIY or fan communities provides a vehicle through which people share their particular perspectives with the world, perspectives often not represented in mass media. When audience members spread this content from one community to another, they do so because they have a stake in the circulation of these messages. They are embracing material meaningful to them because it has currency within their social networks and because it facilitates conversations they want to have with their friends and families.

We should thus describe such audience labor as "engaged" rather than "exploited." Talk of "engagement" fits within industry discourse which has sought new ways to model, measure, and monetize what audiences do with content within networked culture (as we will examine in chapter 3). However, "engaged" also recognizes that these communities are pursuing their own interests, connected to and informed by those decisions made by others within their social networks. Perhaps this is what Terranova means when she describes the activities associated with "free labor" as "pleasurably embraced" by participants, even as they are also being commodified and "exploited" by corporate interests.

If Sennett offers us a way to frame labor that does not rest exclusively on economic relations, others have suggested ways of thinking about notions of ownership which respect the emotional and moral investments fans make in media properties and not simply the economic stakes of media corporations. Flourish Klink, Chief Participation Officer at transmedia branding and entertainment company The Alchemists, developed a statement of best practices to govern corporate relationships with a fan base. Reflecting her own involvement as a fan in debates around "free labor," Klink contends in this "fan manifesto,"

A person who works in an office probably doesn't own their own desk—it probably belongs to their company. But they feel like they own the desk; it's *their desk*. In the same way, when you love a story, you feel like it's *your story*. That's a good thing. If you didn't feel that way, you obviously wouldn't care very much about the story. As storytellers, we want to encourage people to own their favorite stories. We want them to incorporate their favorite stories into their lives, to think about them deeply, to discuss them passionately, to feel like they know the characters and they've really been to the locations. (2011)

Klink goes on to argue that storytellers can increase their audience's emotional investment in properties through respecting and recognizing the contributions fans make to the value of stories, thus strengthening the moral economy surrounding a brand or text. As she stresses, fans may be motivated to make creative contributions to content for many reasons—only some of which involve financial motives. Companies, she argues, are obligated to learn from and respond to fan expectations, not the other way around, since fans do not owe companies anything but rather freely give their labors of love.

The motives shaping cultural production within a commercial economy are multiple and varied; they cannot be reduced to purely economic rewards, as Richard Sennett shows us. In addition to remuneration, artists (both professional and amateur) seek to gain recognition, to influence culture, and to express personal meanings. Only a complex set of negotiations within the creative industries allow artists to serve all these various goals. The social motives for sharing media are also varied and cannot be reduced to the idea of "stealing content," a phrase which still values the transaction almost entirely in economic terms. Within many peer-to-peer exchanges, "status," "prestige," "esteem," and "relationship building" take the place of cash remuneration as the primary drivers of cultural production and social transaction. Across this book, we will explore a range of informal relationships which generate meaning through the exchange of media: economies based on reputation or status, competition and "bragging rights," mentorship and learning, and the exchange of curatorial expertise and fan mastery. All these practices and motives are examples of an informal economy which coexists and complexly interacts with the commercial economy.

Giving Gifts, Creating Obligations

The social obligations audience members feel toward each other within audience groups may be as important for understanding how and why media spread as the economic relations between producers and audiences are (thus our emphasis later in this chapter on the concept of a gift economy). Indeed, many behaviors that have primarily been discussed through the lens of producer-audience relations look quite different when examined in terms of the relations among audience members. As Ian Condry explains, "Unlike underwear or swim suits, music falls into the category of things you are normally obligated to share with your dorm mates, family, and friends. Yet to date, people who share music files are primarily represented in media and business settings as selfish, improperly socialized people who simply want to get something—the fruits of other people's labor—for free" (2004, 348). Industry discourse depicting file sharers as "selfish" ignores the investment of time and money people make toward facilitating the sharing of valued content, whether individually among friends or collectively with any and all who want to download. Enthusiasts bear these costs because they feel an obligation to "give back" to their "community" and/or in the hope that their actions will direct greater attention and interest to the media they love.

When a firm moral economy exists, audiences will often police their own actions, calling out those who they feel damage the integrity of a platform or who undercut informal agreements with commercial producers and distributors. Consider, as another example, anime fans actively circulating underground copies of their favorite series with fan-translated subtitles, an activity called "fansubbing." While their videos often attract takedown notices, fans (and some producers) view fansubbed material as mutually beneficial, demonstrating demand for properties not yet legally and commercially available. So long as the fans do not turn a profit, some content owners have chosen to overlook the use of their material in exchange for the work fans perform in testing markets and educating potential customers. According to this fandom's moral economy, fansubs circulate when a show is unavailable commercially in their market, but fans often withdraw unauthorized copies voluntarily when titles secure commercial distribution (Leonard 2005). Mizuko Ito (2012) notes further that fans who actively participate in fansubbing refer to those who do not contribute to the community as "leechers," an expression that signals the perceived obligations fans have toward each other to provide value within this informal cultural economy.

It's crucial to realize that audiences and producers often follow different logics and operate within different economies (if, by "economies," we mean different systems of appraising and allocating value). Painting in broad strokes, we might describe these two worlds as "commodity culture" and "the gift economy." One (commodity culture) places greater emphasis on economic motives, the other (the gift economy) on social motives.

Certainly, most of us who have grown up in capitalist economies understand the set of expectations surrounding the buying and selling of goods. Yet we all also operate in another social order that involves the giving and accepting of gifts and favors. Within commodity culture, sharing content may be viewed as economically damaging; in the informal gift economy, by contrast, the failure to share material is socially damaging. We do not mean to imply that these cultures are totally autonomous; rather, at the current moment, they are complexly interwoven in ways both mundane and profound. All of us, from the poorest individual to the hugely profitable conglomerate, operate within an economic context of capitalism. And, at the same time, Web 2.0 companies—and neoliberal economics more generally—seek to integrate the social and economic in ways that make it hard to distinguish between them.

A "barn raising" might be considered a classic example of the social exchange of labor. In this nineteenth-century social ritual, established members of a community gathered to welcome newcomers and help them establish a homestead. The labor involved in a barn raising is productive, contributing real value to the new community member. However, it is also expressive, signaling the community's embrace. Since barn raisings are recurring rituals, the value created through this labor gets passed forward to future arrivals, and thus, participation is a kind of social obligation, a repayment of contributions that earlier community members had made toward one's own well-being.

Social bonding takes place as the newcomer works side-by-side with other community members for common ends. Participants accept the unequal exchange of value through labor involved in the barn raising because the process knits the newcomer into the system of reciprocity on which the community depends for its survival. The message of the barn raising is that the community benefits when each member's economic needs are protected.

Insert commercial logic into any aspect of a barn raising, and we alter the meaning of these transactions, creating discomfort for participants. Suppose the newcomers refused to join in on the work, seeing their neighbors' labor as an entitlement for purchasing land in the area. Suppose the newcomers turned the productive labor into a public spectacle, charging admission for outsiders to watch the construction. Suppose the newcomers sought to sell parts of the barn to various community members, charging rents for the areas their neighbors were developing. Suppose they sold outside economic interests the rights to sell snacks and drinks to those who were laboring or sold information about their neighbors which would give these outside interests advantages in future economic exchanges. Or suppose they were to seek to use their neighbors' labor to complete other tasks around their property or else to use the barn, once completed, for radically different purposes than the community perceived (for the sake of argument, let's say to house a brothel). Each of these alterations would violate the spirit of the barn-raising ritual, making it less about the community's efforts to promote its mutual well-being and more about exploiting the economic opportunities that arise as a consequence of the neighbors' labor. Any newcomer who adopted such practices would not be welcome in the community for long, and the practice of raising barns would grind to a halt.

As absurd as such exploitative arrangements seem in the context of a barn raising, they are taken for granted in the Web 2.0 model, as companies generate revenue through monetizing the attention created by user-generated content. Web 2.0 business practices inevitably involve the exchange of labor. However, this labor may or may not be freely given. It may or may not be motivated by the desire to serve the collective interests of the participating community. It may or may not be viewed as a gift that creates obligations and encourages reciprocity. And participants may or may not benefit in intangible ways (such as enhancing their reputation or advancing their "brand") from their participation. Over time, tapping free labor for economic profit *can* turn playful participation into alienated work. Insofar as the terms of this transaction are not transparent or are not subject to negotiation with all participants, they corrode the moral economy.

The concept of the gift economy has its origins in classic anthropology, dating back to Marcel Mauss's 1922 book *The Gift* ([1922] 1990). There are substantial differences between the communities Mauss describes as organized entirely around gift exchanges and the digital cultures we are examining here, imbricated as they are into capitalist logics. As such, we can't simply map one onto the other. The concept of the gift economy, however, has been adopted by digital theorists as a helpful way to explain contemporary practices, in which "the gift economy" functions as an analogy for the informal and socially based exchanges which characterize some aspects of the digital ethos.

Howard Rheingold's 1993 book *The Virtual Community*, for instance, mentions the gift economy as central to relationships across the online world. Describing information as the web's most valuable "currency," Rheingold argues that the generalized spread of knowledge is one way of giving back to the larger community, suggesting, "When that spirit exists, everybody gets a little extra something, a little sparkle, from their more practical transactions" (59). Richard Barbrook (1998), another early cybertheorist, argues that "network communities are [. . .] formed through mutual obligations created by gifts of time and ideas," practices that actually superseded commodity culture in the priorities of those who were the first to form online communities.

The early web was dominated by the ethos of the science community and a mindset in which researchers were obliged to address each other's questions when they had relevant information to share. Rheingold describes this ethos less as a tit-for-tat exchange of value than as part of a larger reputation system in which one's contributions are ultimately recognized and respected, even if there is no direct and explicit negotiation of worth at the time someone contributes. Companies were relative latecomers to the web, even though they now enjoy a dominant presence online. As commercial values have spread into the web, though, they have had to negotiate with the older web ethos.

That said, as anthropologist Igor Kopytoff (1986) reminds us, there remains a great deal of permeability in the relations between commodity and gift economies—especially within complex societies. The distinction between gifts and commodities does not describe their essence. Kopytoff explains, "The same thing may be treated as a commodity at one time and not another. [...] The same thing may, at the same time, be seen as a commodity by one person and as something else by another. Such shifts and differences in whether and when a thing is a commodity reveal a moral economy that stands behind the objective economy of visible transactions" (1986, 64). Kopytoff understands commodification to be a "cultural and cognitive process" which shapes our understanding of the objects we exchange with each other (64). Though we idealize "gifts of the heart" and "labors of love," most gifts these days are manufactured and store bought. There is often a magic moment when we remove the price tag from what we purchased and transform it from a commodity to a gift. People do not necessarily fear that gifts' origins as commodities diminish the sentiments expressed through their exchange, though such exchanges may never fully escape the tendency to appraise gifts at least in part on the basis of what was spent on them. Conversely, as companies talk about their desire to build "relationships" with their audiences, their transactions will be judged—at least in part—on the basis of the norms and values of the gift economy. Objects in movement—media that spreads—thus may travel across different systems of exchange, often multiple times in the course of their life cycle.

In *Remix*, Lawrence Lessig (2008) describes contemporary culture as shaped by the complex interactions between a "sharing" economy (which he illustrates through reference to Wikipedia) and a "commercial" economy (which he discusses through the examples of Amazon, Netflix, and Google). Not everyone agrees these two economies can coexist. Jaron Lanier (2010) argues that an ethos which assumes information and media content "wants to be free" can destroy the market for anyone who wants to sell material for a profit—whether a big company or a small-scale entrepreneur. At the same time, since the logic of Web 2.0 tends to commodify all works—assuming they will make a profit for someone—it thus undercuts the desires of people who wish to share their material with each other as "gifts."

For Lessig, as for us, the way forward is to explore various points of intersection between the two systems. Lessig writes about "a third economy," a hybrid of the other two, which he thinks will dominate the future of the web (177–178). Evoking something similar to what we are calling a "moral economy," Lessig stresses that any viable hybrid economy needs to respect the rights and interests of participants within these two rather different systems for producing and appraising the value of transactions.

Value, Worth, and Meaning

In the 1983 book *The Gift*, Lewis Hyde sees commodity culture and the gift economy as alternative systems for measuring the merits of a transaction. Gifts depend on altruistic motivations; they circulate through acts of generosity and reciprocity, and their exchange is governed by social norms rather than contractual relations. The circulation of gifts is socially rather than economically motivated and is not simply symbolic of the social relations between participants; it helps to constitute them. The commodity, Hyde suggests, moves toward wherever there is a profit to be made, while a gift moves toward resolving conflicts or expanding the social network (29). By contrast, he writes, "To convert an idea into a commodity means, broadly speaking, to establish a boundary of some sort so that the idea cannot move from person to person without a toll or fee. Its benefit or usefulness must then be reckoned and paid for before it is allowed to cross the boundary" (105).

For Hyde, a commodity has "value," while a gift has "worth." By "value," Hyde primarily means "exchange value," a rate at which goods and services can be exchanged for money. Such exchanges are "measurable" and "quantifiable" because these transactions can be "reckoned" through agreed-on measurements of value. By "worth," he means those qualities associated with things on which "you can't put a price." Sometimes, people refer to what he is calling "worth" as sentimental (when personalized) or symbolic (when shared with a larger community) value. Worth is variable, even among those who participate within the same community—even among those in the same family.

In that sense, worth is closely aligned with meaning as it has been discussed in cultural studies; the meaning of a cultural transaction cannot be reduced to the exchange of value between producers and their audiences but also has to do with what the cultural good allows audiences to say about themselves and what it allows them to say to the world. Talk about audience members making "emotional investments" in the television programs they watch or claims of a sense of "ownership" over a media property (such as those offered by Klink earlier) capture this sense of worth.[3]

The past couple of years have brought myriad examples of new Web 2.0 companies and longstanding brands alike misunderstanding what motivates audience participation. On the one hand, audiences are increasingly aware of the ways companies transform their "labors of love" (in the case of fan culture) or expressions of personal identity (in the case of profiles on social network sites) into commodities to be bought and sold. There is a growing recognition that profiting from freely given creative labor poses ethical challenges which are, in the long run, socially damaging to both the companies and the communities involved.

California-based online video start-up Crunchyroll.com found this out right after securing more than $4 billion in venture capital to support the development of its video-sharing platform for East Asian video. The company's business plan was built around aggregating fansubbed material. However, the anime community was concerned that Crunchyroll.com was profiting without returning any value to dedicated anime fans and without bearing any of the potential legal liability that might emerge from effectively "commercializing" fansubbed material. As researcher Xiaochang Li notes, Crunchyroll.com hoped to profit on the back of fan labor while placing any costs of legal problems onto the fans, potentially damaging the implicit relationship between anime producers and fans in the process (2009, 24). Similarly, start-up company FanLib's business model to commercialize fan fiction drew vocal objection in 2007. Fans who protested the company's practices saw their work as gifts circulating freely within their community, rather than as commodities, and believed the companies that held intellectual property rights to appropriated characters were more likely to take legal action if a business model was built around these activities/creations (Jenkins 2007b). While some fans chose to accept the terms the company was offering (Li 2007), others formed the Organization for Transformative Works to create community-managed platforms where they could resist efforts to commodify their culture.

On the other hand, many participants are frustrated when companies offer them financial compensation at odds with the informal reciprocity that operates within some forms of peer-to-peer culture. Imagine how your lover would respond if you left money on his or her bedside table after a particularly passionate encounter, for instance. Far from accepting this reward for "services rendered," it might well damage the intimacy of the relationship and send altogether the wrong message.

Contrasting such situations with the questions of audience labor earlier in the chapter highlights the complexity inherent in the contemporary media environment. How might we alleviate these misunderstandings if we infuse the idea of worth, in addition to our traditional reliance on value, into these discussions? How might we negotiate the range of possible exchanges—value-to-value, worth-to-worth, value-to-worth, worth-to-value—that such a vocabulary implies?

These complex negotiations of value and worth are examined in a 2008 episode of the CBS sitcom *The Big Bang Theory* entitled "The Bath Item Gift Hypothesis." Sheldon, the series's comically maladjusted protagonist, experiences an emotional crisis when he discovers that his perky next-door neighbor, Penny, plans to give him a "silly neighbor gift" for Christmas. Sheldon's initial reaction is one of shock and outrage: "Wait! You bought me a present? Why would you do such a thing?" Sheldon has clearly read Lewis Hyde and has a firm grasp of the meaning of gift giving in capitalist society: "I know you think you are being generous, but the foundation of gift giving is reciprocity. You haven't given me a gift; you've given me an obligation."

Sheldon's friends, having suffered through this cycle of anxiety and recrimination many times before, delight at seeing the drama played out with a new gift giver, until their friendship "obligates" them to take their needy and nerdy friend to the local mall in search of a gift of "comparable value." There, Sheldon confronts his distaste for the goods on offer at a Bed, Bath & Beyond–type store, finding little he thinks a woman would value. He chases a shop clerk, trying to get her to describe the social relationship implied by gifts of different economic value: "If I were to give you this gift basket, based on that action alone and no other data, infer and describe the hypothetical relationship that exists between us. [. . .] Are we friends, colleagues, lovers? Are you my grandmother?" If the gift is a representation of a relationship, he ponders, can one read the relationship from the gift given?

In the end, Sheldon buys several gift baskets with a range of values in the hope that he can appropriately match the price range of the gift Penny bought him. He plans to open her gift first, sneak out of the room, look up the cost online, and return with something that approximates absolute parity. However, Sheldon is taken off guard when Penny gives him a gift of no fixed economic value—a soiled napkin—but great sentimental worth: it is autographed by Leonard Nimoy and personalized to Sheldon. What he first took to be worthless turns out to be priceless instead. When he learns that Nimoy has wiped his mouth on the napkin, Sheldon excitedly proclaims that he now possesses Nimoy's DNA, enough that he can grow his own Spock if only he were provided access to an ovum.

Penny, obviously uncomfortable, makes it clear that she did not have such an intimate relationship in mind. It is Penny's turn to feel uncomfortable about the "obligations" implied—or at least read from—this exchange of gifts. Sheldon retreats, only to return with every gift basket he purchased. Deciding that, even collectively, their value does not approximate the worth of the autographed napkin, he finally, awkwardly, gives Penny a hug, a gesture which is touching in its unexpectedness and which seems, at last, to bring the negotiations to their proper close. The episode offers us a comic dissertation on the differences between value (as negotiated around the exact alignment of the prices of the various gift baskets) and worth (as understood in terms of the personal meaningfulness of the gifts being exchanged).

Throughout this discussion, we have deployed a range of analogies to earlier historical practices—to the moral economy that shaped peasant uprisings in early modern Europe, to the barn raising as a nineteenth-century community ritual, to medieval craftsmen and their guilds as an alternative to alienated labor, and to the gift economy as a system of exchange in traditional societies. Our point here is not to romanticize these earlier moments in the historical relations between production and "consumption," nor is it to depict what contemporary audiences do as somehow "authentic" and free of economic constraints. However, we also want to argue against totalizing accounts which subsume people's social and cultural lives fully into the economic sphere: whether those associated with Web 2.0 discourse which often erase the conflicting interests of producers and audiences or those worried that the mechanisms of capitalism overwhelm any potential for us to pursue alternative agendas. In many ways, these older values of craftsmanship—reciprocity, collectivity, and fairness—continue to exert a residual influence on contemporary commercial culture, much as new forms of participatory culture can be understood as involving the application of traditional folk culture practices onto the materials of mass culture.

Part of what has given the discourse of Web 2.0 its power has been its erasure of this larger history of participatory practices, with companies acting as if they were "bestowing" agency onto audiences, making their creative output meaningful by valuing it within the logics of commodity culture. To maintain a balanced perspective, it is vital to be able to imagine alternative forms of value and meaning. Social and cultural practices operate in an economic context, but economic practices also operate in a social and cultural context. There is a relative autonomy between these spheres of activity, even as many of the practices we describe in this book are working to blur the boundaries between them. Holding onto a notion of the relative autonomy of cultural life gives us a way to critique the logic of Web 2.0, insisting on respect for prior cultural identities and practices, which often are deeply important to the communities involved.

For media properties to move from the commodity culture in which they are produced to informal social contexts through which they circulate and are appraised, they must pass through a point where "value" gets transformed into "worth," where what has a price becomes priceless, where economic investment gives way to sentimental investment. Similarly, when a fan culture's "gifts" are transformed into "user-generated content," there are special sensitivities involved as the material gets absorbed back into commercial culture. When people pass along media texts, they are not doing so as paid employees motivated by economic gain; rather, they are members of social communities involved in activities which are meaningful to them on an individual and/or social level. Such movement—and the transformations that media texts undergo as they are circulated—can generate both value and worth. However, content producers and online platforms alike have to be keenly aware of the logics of worth being employed by their audiences or risk alienating those who are emotionally invested in the material.

Nothing Is Ever Free

In 2008 and 2009, the Internet buzzed about the idea of "free" things. Media giants such as Rupert Murdoch's News Corporation worried about services such as Google News "taking their content for free" and profiting from it (Smillie 2009). Rumors circulated about television-network-owned online video site Hulu introducing subscription models for its material, effectively cutting off the "free" stream (J. Herrman 2009). (In June 2010, Hulu indeed introduced the subscription service "Hulu Plus" [Stelter 2010].) *Wired* editor Chris Anderson wrote about "the economics of giving it away" (2009), and terms such as "freeconomy" popped up (The Freeconomy Community n.d.).

In an especially prominent example illustrating this "freeconomy," rock music group Nine Inch Nails released digital copies of its 2008 album *The Slip* under a Creative Commons license. When physical versions were released a few months later for a fee, *The Slip* remained available on the band's site as a free download. While press buzz focused on the cost of the album—its economic value—and talked about the band "giving away" its content, Nine Inch Nails front man Trent Reznor discussed the decision differently. On the official NIN site, Reznor called the free download "a thank you" to the band's fans for their "continued support" (Nine Inch Nails 2008), adding elsewhere, "This one's on me" (Visakowitz 2008). Rather than "giving the album away," Reznor was giving *back* to the fans for what they had already given him—their previous support and purchases—with an unspoken request that they continue to support him. What at first glance seemed to be "free" was actually a reciprocal exchange of social worth within an ongoing relationship between producer and fans.

Reznor's efforts may be somewhat unconventional, yet the notion that no-cost exchanges aren't truly free can be seen in types of "give-aways" with which we've been familiar for generations. Prior to the widespread introduction of air-conditioning, churchgoers in the U.S. once cooled themselves on hot summer days with paper fans branded by local funeral homes. Jewelry stores in shopping malls often offer services as marketing: providing "free" ring cleaning to passersby with the unspoken hope of gaining the loyalty of potential future customers. And brands—from local banks to presidential candidates—put their logos on pens, stationery, and T-shirts for "giveaways." Those giving such gifts hope the receiver will incorporate the objects into their everyday lives, the brand regularly reminding them of the company, while the utility of the gift generates some sense of goodwill. Such branded goods also often turn users into brand promoters. In that sense, these branded goods are not "free"—there is some labor performed in exchange for these gifts. And, as people share their pens or other swag, these items become "spreadable media" themselves.

The exchange of "gifts" brings social expectations, as both Hyde (1983) and the writers of *The Big Bang Theory* note; as a result, not all gifts can be accepted. In that sense, there are goods and services which literally cannot be given away because we are all wary of hidden obligations, unstated motives, or covert interests smuggled inside the gift. This focus on the expectations which shape the exchange of gifts is especially important if we hope to explore how media spreads online, because many systems of peer-to-peer sharing, cooperation, and collaboration generate value through creating mutual ties, reciprocal expectations, and social "payments."

Indeed, when we describe such goods and services as "free," we mean that people have not purchased them with money, not that they have not paid for them via some other means. In each case, the producers and laborers working for "free" expect some form of (social) payment, and each person provides his or her time and labor under an expectation that others will contribute similarly, to the benefit of all. Understanding the popularity of many Web 2.0 platforms, then, means considering what motivates people to contribute their time and energy without expectation of immediate financial compensation—whether these motives are attention, recognition, and identity building; the development of community and social ties; the creation of a useful tool; or myriad other considerations.

Technology has made the flow of content across systems of exchange easy, allowing people to take media texts from one context and transplant them into the other without much difficulty. But, as we have already discussed with regard to disputes over terms of service or control over intellectual property rights, these transitions aren't always smooth. This is why the clarification regarding "free" is so crucial. The use of "free" attempts to describe transactions based in reciprocity while clinging to the language of the market, obscuring the underlying social mechanisms in a way that invites conflicts and violations on both sides.

Often, commercial motives for offering a platform or text for "free" include commodifying audience labor, creating opportunities for gathering data, adding people to a contact list to be sold to marketers, or bringing together an audience to sell to advertisers (concepts we explore throughout the rest of this book). In other cases, these "free" offers generate benefits by attempting to enlist those who accept them as grassroots intermediaries or else encouraging those users to create content themselves and thus to attract greater audiences to expand the reach of a platform or brand. YouTube might offer its web platform to users at no cost, but the efforts of users to create social value through the site generates page views and data which are the basis for YouTube's advertising and licensing relationships. As a result, these exchanges create implicit social contracts not just within the user community but between the community and the platform—contracts that, when violated, can generate a sense of being cheated, much as workers would object to having their wages changed on payday.

Toward Transparent Marketing

As companies come to terms with an online environment that records, amplifies, and proliferates the audience's collective interpretation and appropriation of their marketing materials, and as companies try to make sense of how their material spreads in environments governed by peer-to-peer logics, those companies are spending more energy trying to engage their audiences directly. Consider, for instance, the public relations field. As noted in the introduction, "public relations" was once a term used for customer service; however, for most of the twentieth century, PR primarily stood for "press relations," as companies sought to influence "the masses" through the intermediaries of professional journalists. Today, however, people tasked with promoting a brand are increasingly trying to bring the "public" back to public relations.

This doesn't mean that traditional media is no longer a significant focus, since they remain a crucial and prominent amplifier in a spreadable media environment. However, suddenly, the importance of recommendations from "the average person" have become a renewed priority, and word of mouth, the original form of marketing, is treated as a new phenomenon due to one major distinction: online communication creates a textual trail of the conversations audiences have about a brand or media property which may be archived indefinitely for all to see.

If brands and media properties admit that the word-of-mouth recommendations of fellow audience members hold the greatest opportunity for influencing others, many questions remain. What implicit contracts exist between brands and those recommenders? What moral codes and guidelines should brands respect when encouraging, soliciting, or reacting to comments from those audiences they wish to reach? What types of compensation, if any, do audience members deserve for their promotional labor when they provide a testimonial for their favorite television show or company? Do some forms of compensation compromise the integrity of all involved? After all, as Hyde notes, a thin line separates gifts from bribes, but the distinction carries enormous moral implications (1983, 237).

North Carolina State University marketing professor Stacy Wood has conducted extensive research on the value people place on recommendations from everyday people and their potential impact on brands. In a world where audiences are bombarded by thousands of messages daily and where they have become incredibly suspicious of the authenticity and credibility of marketing messages in response, word-of-mouth recommendations are an incredibly important source of credible information. Brand managers and marketers have begun to capitalize on this, encouraging customers to write testimonials or to produce content recommending products. This encouragement needs to be carefully applied, however: Wood's research suggests that, when customers are provided rewards for writing about their experiences, they often exaggerate, resulting in less genuine testimonials that no one (even the recommenders themselves) trusts. As Wood elaborates further in our enhanced book,

> Firms must be careful to create a testimonial-giving space that is clearly not linked to prizes or other financial benefits, a space that highlights the voluntary nature of testimonial contributions. In this way, the facilitation of consumer engagement and testimonials must occur in the social economy (moral/gift) rather than in a traditional commodity-based economy. This acts as a signal of credibility, not only to the testimonial writer but also to other consumers who read the resulting testimonies.

As marketing disciplines tackle how best to encourage participation while still sounding bona fide, two buzzwords have consistently appeared in popular literature surrounding Web 2.0: "transparency" and "authenticity." Both of these words have deep histories in various disciplines. In current Web 2.0 business rhetoric, "transparency" refers to the degree to which brands and audience members alike are forthcoming about their ties to one another, ensuring that potential customers have access to all the information needed to assess the credibility of a recommendation. Meanwhile, in the recent parlance of marketing, "authenticity" represents the overall assessment of the credibility of a brand or audience member. Here, the test of authenticity asks, Is the messenger being fully transparent? Is this piece of content or recommendation consistent with what is known about and expected from the messenger? And does the messenger genuinely have the knowledge, experience, and credentials necessary to back up the message?

Both these concepts are crucial to the moral economy presented in this chapter. Taken together, they help to establish "trust" among participants in an economic transaction, and they remain crucial as producers/advertisers and their audiences renegotiate relations managed by the logics of the gift economy. As companies seek to sustain and encourage supportive word of mouth, however, their transparency and authenticity is often brought into question.

In the past few years, corporate communicators have repeatedly been caught speaking as if they were unpaid customers or fan reviewers. Such practices are labeled "astroturf"—that is, fake grassroots. Few examples of astroturfing angered people more than a 2006 campaign from Zipatoni for Sony centered on "All I Want for Xmas Is a PSP," a site portrayed as the creation of two teenage fans to convince their parents to buy them a Sony PlayStation Portable gaming system for Christmas. When gamers discovered that the videos from the blog were hosted on Zipatoni's servers, the site was outed as astroturf. This discovery made the site "viral" (at least in the sense that it made those who came into contact with it sick), as myriad gamers saw the situation as an example of Sony's disrespect for the gaming community. Marketers profiled the site as a "worst practice" example; watchdog groups highlighted the campaign as an example of the need for greater regulation of corporate marketing; and journalists and bloggers used the story (as we do here) to highlight missteps made by major companies (Snow 2006).

However, many examples of astroturfing are not so blatant. Take another now-canonical "lesson learned" from the public relations world: public relations firm Edelman's collaboration with Walmart in supporting the website "Wal-Marting Across America." A couple bought an RV and planned to blog about a trip around the country to visit their respective children. In the process, they realized that Walmart parking lots allowed for the free parking of RVs and decided their experiences could provide a unique look at the country. Since the blog series would fundamentally be about their experiences at Walmarts, however, the couple decided to contact Working Families for Walmart, an organization started by Edelman on the company's behalf, to ensure they had the right to move forward with the project (Gogoi 2006a). Edelman and Walmart not only gave permission; they offered to support the couple, providing another RV and funding a much wider journey than originally planned.

While the impetus behind the resulting blog was truly "user" driven, Walmart and Edelman did not disclose their intervention, save a Working Families banner on the couple's site. Thus, when bloggers and watchdog groups discovered Walmart's and Edelman's involvement, both the retailer and its public relations firm were the target of significant scorn. Many marketing bloggers were particularly upset that Edelman, which had been an industry leader in defining appropriate Web 2.0 strategies, would make this misstep (Gogoi 2006b). While the blog and the couple's interest had not been fabricated, the situation was a reminder that astroturfing includes not only blatant lies but also initiatives that fail to be completely transparent.

The ethical questions that corporate communicators and audience members both face are crucial and demonstrate the challenges of a hybrid world where goods and media texts move fluidly between the logics of commodity and gift economies. What types of tie-ins or relationships must be made public? Clearly, corporate communicators pretending to be audience members or brands paying fans who speak favorably without disclosing that relationship violate the implicit contract of spreadable media. But what of bloggers who are reviewing a product provided to them by a company or fans being rewarded for their commentaries or promotional work with access to creators? In reverse, were professional marketers participating in the fan activities around *Mad Men* examined in the introduction inauthentic as fans because of their dual identity as marketers, as Deep Focus intimated?

Did they have an obligation to be up-front from the outset about their professional identities?

Numerous questions such as these have led to consistent appeals for governmental regulators to intervene. In the U.S., the Federal Trade Commission updated its guidelines to require disclosure of paid relationships in 2009, sparking discussion among marketers and bloggers alike. While most agreed on the general need for policing unscrupulous behaviors, some bloggers questioned how to handle many of the less clear issues that could lead to their violating guidelines unknowingly. Online journalists questioned whether overly restrictive rules could target too wide a swath of online commentary in the interest of prohibiting unscrupulous behaviors. And some industry leaders felt that government-mandated rules rather than industry guidelines and self-policing could lead to overly onerous restrictions that would create a chilling factor among marketers. Do the guidelines encourage companies to persist in a broadcast-era mentality for fear that collaborating with audiences could lead to legal vulnerability?

What's certain is that media producers and brands are becoming increasingly cognizant of the potential for profit and promotion in embracing "spreadable media." However, there exists a strong need for a more nuanced discussion of the economic implications behind Web 2.0. Already, prominent communities are finding themselves increasingly barraged by marketers looking to create a "viral phenomenon" or to generate word of mouth. The "mommy blogger" community, prominent Twitterers, and active fan discussion forums are now on the target lists of marketers and public relations professionals tasked with "reaching out to influencers." While paid journalists are monetarily compensated for their time liaising with corporate communicators, many of these audience members maintain their blogs out of social rather than economic interests: because their contributions are valued within their communities. As more brands want to foster community and "join the discussion," brand managers, internal marketers, and the agencies and industry associations need to become better informed about the implicit and sometimes explicit assumptions audiences make about corporate participation in these conversations. Likewise, fans, bloggers, gamers, Twitterers, and other online community participants need to develop a more nuanced understanding of the implications of their new entanglements with advertisers and producers.

We Don't Need Influencers

While public relations professionals have accepted that they can no longer just think about journalists when hawking their wares, some now contend instead that there exist a few elite members of any given community who—if convinced of a brand's message—can convince everyone else to follow suit. We argue throughout this book that content creators need to pay attention to the audience's agency in circulating content; however, we are not claiming that so-called influencers are more apt to be effective at circulating content than the rest of us are. In fact, the influencer is one of the major myths of the Web 2.0 world. In *The Tipping Point* (2000), Malcolm Gladwell based his theory of the influencer on the now well-known "Small World Problem" study (Milgram 1967; Travers and Milgram 1969), in which, through multiple experiments, Nebraska and Kansas residents were asked to get a letter to someone in Boston by passing it through social contacts they thought would be closer to the eventual target. Famously, among those instances when the letter successfully transferred, it took an average of five exchanges to get it to its intended target, or "six degrees of separation," as it has now popularly been labeled. In his use of these studies, Gladwell emphasized that the letter eventually reached its intended target through the same few friends in most cases and argued that these "influencers" were ultimately the ones who needed to be engaged to reach the target audience.

Since Gladwell made this argument, the "influencer" has been emphasized in countless marketing case studies discussing why the attention and endorsement of key audience members is crucial for success. The argument is that the best way to reach anyone in a community is to find the few prominent people who influence most of the members. In particular, the language of the "influencer" has been used often by public relations professionals to justify the importance of reaching beyond traditional journalists to bloggers.

However, Peter Dodds, Roby Muhamad, and Duncan Watts (2003) tested such thinking by asking more than 60,000 people to reach 18 "target persons" in 13 countries by forwarding an email along to an acquaintance who might know them. Their study found a median of five to seven steps for the message to reach one of its intended targets (reinforcing the "six degrees" concept), but they did not find any evidence of "influencers." As summarized by Clive Thompson, "[Watts] found that 'hubs'—highly connected people—weren't crucial. Sure, they existed. But only 5% of the email messages passed through one of these superconnectors. The rest of the messages moved through society in much more democratic paths, zipping from one weakly connected individual to another, until they arrived at the target" (2008). This research shifts the question from how to reach "influencers" to what social structures best support the spread of media texts. Certainly, people exercise varying degrees of influence. We all take the recommendations of trusted sources over strangers, experts over neophytes. However, that influence typically is contextual and temporal, depending on the subject, the speaker's credibility, and a variety of other factors. Sure, there are influencers, but who those influencers are may shift substantially from one situation to another.

It's easy to see how this concept of the "influencer" became popular alongside notions of viral marketing: both assume there is some shortcut to building interest around one's message. In the case of viral marketing, the myth is that something inserted into the content's "DNA" will infect people and give them no choice but to spread its messages. In the case of "influencers," the myth is that, if a marketer reaches a very small set of taste makers, those few will bring "the sheep" along. In short, brand developers and media producers are still trying to figure out any angle of "public relations" that doesn't require much in the way of relating to the public.

In marketer Scott Gould's (2010) writing on spreadability, he examines the tension between "scattering" and "gathering." Using a farming metaphor, he argues that marketers have to scatter seeds through many potential relationships and then identify which relationships develop and are worth deepening:

> We don't know which relationships will end up returning the greatest to us, which tweets return the deals, which bits of marketing make

the biggest difference—and trying to carefully plant our seeds rather than scatter them neglects all the potential relationships that we could have, that we'd never normally pick. [. . .] The conundrum is this: how do we go from a volume approach to a value approach? How do we filter all that we scatter, and know what relationships or opportunities to begin investing in with greater value?

Here, Gould rejects the influencer theory; a marketer doesn't know at the outset which audience members might embrace a brand. Gould insists that the marketer build relationships through listening and interacting, deepening relationships with audience members when it's contextually relevant and when both parties have common ground.

If the search for "influencers" is a vestige of a distribution mindset in an environment built on circulation, Gould's suggestion of "scattering" content broadly and then "gathering" potential supporters follows the logic of online social connectivity: open communication that often leads to temporary and contextualized connections, a few of which might become long-term relationships. The media industries and marketing professionals must abandon the illusion that "targeting" the same nine "mommy bloggers" or a handful of celebrities on Twitter is all it takes to get one's message circulated broadly. Such a model limits the meaningful relationships a producer or brand might build, devalues people not initially considered "influencers," and ultimately reinforces a "one-to-many" mindset, seeking out a handful of affiliates to share a message rather than seeing it develop and build through many everyday interactions.

Moving Beyond Web 2.0 (But Not Just to "Web 3.0")

For the media industries, for marketers, and for audiences, then, where has Web 2.0 ultimately gone wrong? Much as "viral media" pushed us toward embracing a false model of audience behavior, one which simplifies the motives and processes through which grassroots circulation of media content occurs, the language of Web 2.0 oversimplifies the "moral economy" shaping commercial and noncommercial exchanges. In the process, these terms mask some fundamental differences in how producers and audiences value what gets generated through their interactions with each other.

Web 2.0 discourse assumes that fan participation is highly generative—yielding new insights, creating new value, reaching new audiences—but the business model often isolates the resulting texts from the social contexts within which they were produced and circulated, thus devaluing notions of reciprocity. Many Web 2.0 companies have sought to assert total ownership over content generated by their fans, even after having sought to strengthen participants' sense of personal stakes in the space. In other cases, platforms too quickly sell out user interests in order to placate the contested assertion of intellectual property claims posed by other commercial interests. All of this has contributed to a sense of instability and insecurity about the promises of Web 2.0.

Further, as companies embrace and desire to harness the credibility of customer testimonials and the recommendations of grassroots intermediaries, marketers and audiences alike must take a new set of ethical considerations into account. Brands must strike the balance—appropriately valuing and collaborating with enthusiasts while respecting both the autonomy and voice of its audiences. They must avoid crossing the nuanced ethical boundaries of "authenticity" and "transparency," lest shortsighted marketing tactics put a company's reputation in crisis. And they must abandon the illusion that they can effectively relate to a whole community or audience through reaching a few key "influencers" who everyone else mindlessly follows. Instead, corporate communicators must accept the complications and nuance necessary to truly engage with the public.

The flaws in Web 2.0, at their core, can be reduced to a simple formulation: the concept transforms the social "goods" generated through interpersonal exchanges into "user-generated content" which can be monetized and commodified. In actuality, though, audiences often use the commodified and monetized content of commercial producers as raw material for their social interactions with each other. This misrecognition is perhaps most profoundly expressed when companies seek not simply to "capture," to "capitalize on," or to "harvest" the creative contributions of their audiences but also to lock down media texts so they can no longer spread beyond their walled boundaries. In chapter 2, we will further explore the sometimes parallel, sometimes conflicting, and sometimes unrelated motives that drive the production, circulation, and appraisal of media content at the juncture between commodity culture and the gift economy.

Chapter 1 suggested that each party involved in exchanging material may have a different conception of its value and/or worth. We use the term "appraisal" to describe the process by which people determine which forms of value and worth get ascribed to an object as it moves through different transactions. Appraisal is often used to talk about the monetary value of a commodity in a commercial transaction. However, the same term is also used in processes of curation, which create value not through buying and selling commodities but through critiquing, organizing, and displaying/exhibiting artifacts. An appraisal performed in an archive or museum may be just as concerned with an artifact's historical, cultural, or symbolic value—with whether the material is worth preserving for future generations—as it is with the item's monetary value. Further, museums and archives may be reluctant to take gifts if the costs of preserving an artifact exceed its symbolic worth or cultural significance. As the rise of digital networks has accelerated the flow of texts and objects, such processes of curation have become part of the everyday lives of many people. Such competing forms of appraisal are especially visible in the case of "residual" materials—antiques, hand-me-downs, collectors' items, and so on. Such "old stuff" may have lost much of its economic value and cultural centrality but still carries enormous sentimental value for some enthusiasts. As the chapter progresses, we will develop a more nuanced understanding of the "residual" as a specific site of cultural transactions, exploring how and why negotiations of older media content are gaining new

REAPPRAISING THE RESIDUAL

centrality within a culture where sites such as eBay and YouTube support grassroots exchange of items which otherwise no longer command the attention of commercial interests.

Assessing economic value and determining cultural or sentimental worth are two increasingly connected notions when talking about grassroots forms of appraisal. As artifacts (whether a physical object or a piece of content) travel through different exchanges, the various groups involved might apply different systems of appraisal that reflect divergent goals and interests. We might broadly distinguish between market and nonmarket exchanges, between purchases and gifts; however, even within a market exchange, there may be more than one kind of value at play.

While many of the examples we raise in this book consider how media texts circulate through peer-to-peer exchange, not all spreadable media begins that way, and not all spreadable media ends that way. Rather, material is shared by virtue of its adaptability to different conditions and its ability to be adjusted to fulfill a wide range of needs and motivations. Clips from U.S. television shows, for instance, are created within the logic of market-driven commodity culture but get repurposed by fans to establish social relations as they are passed along. Conversely, many forms of user-generated content created within primarily social exchanges get leveraged commercially when hosted on revenue-generating websites. Mentos, for instance, claims to have received more than $10 million worth of publicity from videos posted online of people dropping Mentos into Diet Coke, a coup for a brand which, at the time, spent less than $20 million a year annually for U.S. advertising (Vranica and Terhune 2006).

In other cases, content generated and spread through the digital gift economy is also eventually used directly by companies as promotional material, as in the case of a Chicken McNuggets commercial that appropriated user-generated video of two friends rapping about the meal. The original video clip was posted to YouTube a year before McDonald's acquired it. McDonald's used the clip mostly intact, interspersing some title cards and adding a tagline at the end. As both these cases show, spreadable media can travel through both market and social exchanges and in both directions.

If we could decide that some things bear a market value and others don't, there would be less tension or confusion over what something is worth. But goods or services don't inherently possess market or nonmarket characteristics. Rather, these values and conditions are assigned to goods and services via the context of the exchanges in which they are involved. Purchasing a bottle of wine to bring to a dinner party begins as a market exchange—the store purchase—where its value is communicated through price. When you give the wine to your hosts to thank them for their hospitality (and perhaps in the process show them you were thinking of them by knowing their favorite variety), however, it is considered a social faux pas if you leave the price sticker on the bottle. Removing the sticker is a ritualized gesture of the transformation between market and nonmarket exchanges. Even though no one would think you've made the wine yourself, the dinner party represents a gift exchange where the value is not determined primarily by the price of the wine.

Systems of Appraisal

There is a tendency to describe appraisal, at least as performed within a commercial context, as a highly rationalized process designed to determine an object's absolute value. Yet appraisal is also a negotiation between different systems of evaluation, determining not only the object's value but also how that value can be measured. When one evaluates a gold coin, for example, it matters whether the appraisal is based on the value of the gold, the value of the coin as a historical object, collector interest in the coin, or the circumstances of the coin as a token passed from one family member to another.

Consider two sites where appraisal is performed in contemporary media culture—the television series *Antiques Roadshow* and the Internet auction site eBay. These two sites apply different processes of appraisal—one relying on experts who estimate market value, the other allowing buyers and sellers to directly negotiate prices. If *Antiques Roadshow* transforms the act of appraisal into a public spectacle, eBay transforms appraisal into a participatory practice. Both make the negotiations between competing forms of value visible and explicit, while the relations between these different systems of appraisal are often taken for granted when purchasing an item at a store.

One of the all-time most successful PBS programs (Clouse 2008; Bishop 2001), *Antiques Roadshow* feeds people's growing fascination with the process of appraisal, transforming the negotiation between different systems of value into the basis for public spectacle. On an average episode, U.S. viewers can watch ten to twenty transactions during which a team of professional appraisers and experts render their judgment about the exchange value of various artifacts—often, family heirlooms—which the public has brought to the taping location. An assessment session usually begins with a personal or sentimental narrative, typically involving the passing of the object across generations. The object's meaning and value rests on its place within these personal narratives and is bound with intimate family relations. As one owner explained, "We've never really thought about the value at all. It's such a personal thing to me." Of course, bringing these items to the studio already signals the owner's willingness to reintroduce them to the logics of commercial transactions, where their primary value is economic and not sentimental. Not surprisingly, there is often something startling for these owners about seeing objects which have long been part of their everyday lives get reread through the language of exchange value. Thus, the appraisal process often involves a swapping of stories. The owner shares the history of the individual item as it has gone through its unique trajectory through various exchanges, while the expert shares a more generalizable historical narrative about who made the object under what circumstances and how the object's value may have shifted over time.

Within this system, the appraiser is presented as neutral (admiring the object's beauty but indifferent to its sentimental value) and expert (discerning its true character and measuring its potential exchange value in the market). Once the appraisal is completed, owners can determine which of a competing set of values will guide their future treatment of the object. They may be tempted to part with goods when the exchange value becomes too high ("My wife is going to want to sell this"), may become concerned about how everyday use or family rituals may risk damage ("My fear is that you were going to tell me it was so pricey that I wouldn't be able to keep it hanging on my wall"), or may reassert the priority of sentimental value over exchange value ("I feel really glad handing this down to my children").

Antiques Roadshow focuses on only two participants in the transaction—the object's owner and the expert evaluator—while two other potential parties remain off-stage: the collector, often cited as the final arbiter of value, and the auction house, whose role in the economic transaction remains unremarked. Also implicit, but hovering in the background, are viewers, who take pleasure in developing more discernment about the value of everyday objects and who are invited to entertain the fantasy that items in their own attic may be worth much more than previously imagined.

By contrast, the online auction site eBay strips aside both the expert appraiser and the professional auctioneer to create what founder Pierre Omidyar hoped would become a "frictionless" exchange between sellers and buyers: "The playing field would be level. Buyers would all have the same information about products and prices, and sellers would all have the same opportunity to market their wares. The auction format would, as classic economic theory taught, yield the perfect price, because items would sell at the exact price point where supply met demand" (quoted in Epley 2006, 151). Each day, sellers on eBay list approximately 4.8 million items across more than 40,000 categories, creating a space where many more people than ever before are involved in the process of appraisal (Hillis, Petit, and Epley 2006, 1). The rise of networked exchanges makes it possible for each item to get assigned its price and to find a new owner without undergoing any formal appraisal. There is no guarantee of authenticity; sellers often misidentify content, material, and origins, and buyers have to trust their own judgment in assessing what's on offer. The categories through which objects circulate are not fixed but constantly fluctuating, with the same good potentially appealing to multiple interests and the success of the sale often resting on the ability of the seller to correctly identify and flag the attention of diverse groups of potential buyers. In many cases, the terms of the exchange are not grounded in the material value of the objects, which may be disposable or cheaply made, but rather in the sentimental or symbolic value ascribed to them: their desirability. Desirability may be mutually recognized within a particular collector community or may be idiosyncratic as people seek to reacquire objects from their childhood that got lost along the way. Mary Desjardins describes such goods as "throwaways not thrown away" (2006, 32), and Zoe Trodd discusses them as "dynamic debris" (2006, 86). Both concepts capture the contingency of their survival and the variability of their value. Goods once seen as cheap, mundane, and everyday become special, distinctive, and collectible.

As Desjardins notes, these exchanges take place within communities which are themselves usually ephemeral, since they are "often based on individuals temporarily competing with one another as bidders" (2006, 33) and among people who have very limited if any social ties with each other outside the process of bidding on a particular item. These transactions may leave social traces, since both buyer and seller participate in a reputational economy that influences future transactions. And, in some niche areas, the communities that emerge around particular classes of objects may interact many times across multiple sites of transaction, with buyers and sellers getting to know each other as members of a collector subculture. Over time, these particular collector communities develop norms that shape the negotiation of value, norms based on criteria that participants might not be able to fully articulate but have nevertheless internalized and that many more casual sellers have little comprehension of or access to.

The Hybrid Audiences of YouTube

The online transactions around nonmaterial goods—such as segments of media—further blur the line between differing regimes of value. Whereas a particular physical good (or physical media products such as a DVD or a book) may only be used for one purpose at a time, digital goods are shared resources that can be used by a variety of audiences simultaneously. When guests give their host a bottle of wine, they no longer have possession of it (and, once the host decides to "consume" the gift, it's gone). However, digital goods can be shared under a variety of contexts simultaneously, and access to the item can be sold or offered as a gift without the content ever leaving one's possession. Paul Booth has coined the term "digi-gratis" to describe the way peer-to-peer exchanges operate within digital economies. Booth writes, "The new gift, the digital gift, is a gift without an obligation to reciprocate. Instead of reciprocity, what the gift in the digital age requires for 'membership' into the fan community, is merely an obligation to reply" (2010, 134). Such transactions depend on sociality but not necessarily reciprocity. As Booth explains, "When one 'gives' a blog fan fiction entry, it is public and universal, and one does not lose it. To reciprocate is therefore unnecessary—one acknowledges the presence of the blog gift (usually with positive reinforcement or constructive criticism) through a response, but does not have to fill the void the gift left" (quoted in Jenkins 2010a). Booth's "digi-gratis" term takes us back yet again to Lawrence Lessig's (2008) notion that to move forward we must be more explicit about recognizing the hybrid status of online exchanges. Of course, it is precisely the hybrid nature of these exchanges, the fluidity with which digital content moves between different kinds of transactions, sometimes functioning as a gift and sometimes as an advertisement (for commercial gain or social advancement), which makes it so hard to determine the value, worth, and meaning of such materials.

The idea that digital media may be escalating or even facilitating new hybrid models of exchange can be appreciated more fully by observing how such hybrid systems operate in more longstanding types of transactions. Gretchen Herrman (1997), for example, has explored the rummage sale as such a site. As she notes, the rummage sale (whether taking place in the seller's yard or garage) is a market transaction insofar as it involves the "payment of money and the display and merchandising of goods," yet this focus on the commercial nature of these exchanges masks the "range of exchange styles, from the saliently commercial and individualistic to a concern with the needs of others": "Contrary to the market model, the garage sale encompasses acts of outright giving, partial giving, and the connection of people through the spirit of the gift in which something of the original owner is passed along. Garage sale goods are used as gifts, and the proceeds from sales are often donated to worthy causes" (925–926). Similar ambiguities about the motive and nature of transactions surface in the thrift shop, a special kind of commercial establishment dealing with individualized rather than bulk transactions and run to raise money for a charity. These are often sites where goods are donated as gifts rather than sold to the store as inventory and where prices are subject to negotiation rather than fixed (Tinkcom, Fuqua, and Villarejo 2002). (As filmmaker and MIT media historian Hanna Rose Shell examines in our enhanced book, clothing has passed between different kinds of exchanges for centuries, acquiring different meanings and values in the process.)

A model based purely on producers and audiences can't adequately account for the diverse points of intersection between a variety of stakeholders in such hybrid value systems. Yochai Benkler argues in his book *The Wealth of Networks* (2006) that the emergence of Web 2.0 platforms results in a media ecology where commercial, amateur, nonprofit, governmental, and educational media producers interact in ever more complex ways, often deploying the same media channels (and particular texts) toward very different ends. For instance, with relatively low barriers to entry, YouTube supports many types of users, ranging from casual participants to independent producers, cultural institutions, political parties, professional producers, and a myriad of categories in between. Indeed, the success of the site is due in part to a certain flexibility which makes it accessible and valuable to such a diverse user base. With few real limits on what can be uploaded to the site (aside from restrictions around pornographic material, copyright infringement, and a few categories that violate "community standards"), YouTube is a platform offering potentially great reach to almost all comers. The site encourages users to think of attention as itself a kind of currency, with participants gaining social prestige through the number of hits they attract.

Viacom's claims that YouTube's early successes were due to the value of its copyrights—that its most popular videos were produced by large media companies—cast the site as a place where mass attention makes content valuable. Nevertheless, many homegrown

YouTube stars have built viable businesses through leveraging interaction with their niche audiences, not merely through distributing material for mass consumption. Further, there is a breed of "entrepreneurial vloggers" (Burgess and Green 2009) who have built businesses through concerted and active engagement in the space rather than merely distributing videos across it. These vloggers are superusers, building audiences and successful careers by actively responding to commenters and viewers, explicitly inviting responses and subscriptions. As Bill Wasik writes, "Aware they're always being watched, [bloggers and vloggers] act accordingly, tailoring their posts to draw traffic, stirring up controversy, and watching their stats to see what works and what doesn't. They develop a meta-understanding of the conversation they're in and how that conversation works, and they try to figure out where it's going so they can get there first" (2009, 11). These users are entrepreneurial in the sense that they don't just produce video blogs, but they use the trappings and practices of vlogging to court YouTube viewers, rather than just serve viewers content.

However, not all those who upload content to the site use YouTube as a means to aggregate attention or to explicitly build notoriety. For instance, some share material primarily on a communal level, because they have access to something that they think others may find valuable and that might fuel personal or community exchange. Some upload videos to YouTube because it is a space for information gathering, either through the conversation and social connections it can support or through the opportunities it provides for users to track down news, archival footage, oddities, or DIY content. Further, recent work on the significance of YouTube for educational or archival purposes demonstrates that the site serves as a valuable resource for specialized users in ways that often escape mass attention (Snelson and Perkins 2009; Gehl 2009).

As a result, many competing ideas about what is valuable on YouTube coexist. These competing ideas extend even to individual users. YouTube Inc. defended itself against Viacom's claims that it harbored and profited from copyright infringement, producing emails showing that companies and brands owned by Viacom itself uploaded content to the site in order take advantage of YouTube's distribution channels. Some of these videos were later flagged as copyright infringing and removed, many in response to infringement notices sent by Viacom itself. The example is telling not because it marks Viacom as hypocritical but because it points to the many ways the site can be understood, even by individual parts of a single company. There are, in fact, many "YouTubes," depending on the logic applied to understanding and appraising content on the site.

YouTube has a particular impact on the classroom, where ephemeral material from the past or content from niche archives may be accessed for educational purposes. In an era of greater corporate sponsorship of education, classrooms are often becoming branded spaces, shaped by commercial imperatives. However, instructors continue to pursue the historically noncommercial values that shape the classroom itself, with increased access to digital content and tools driving new forms of collaborative learning. In our enhanced book, Western Kentucky University film studies director Ted Hovet examines the way archival content is appraised for value by students and instructors alike and how the activity of assessing archival material itself becomes part of the learning process. Hovet writes that the role of students changes when they are encouraged to actively bring new texts into the media studies classroom from the vast archives of content available online and that "the role of the instructor, then, comes in helping students find appropriate criteria by which to appraise these alternative materials."

On the whole, the kinds of appraisal taking place on YouTube are much closer to those performed by curators at museums, archives, and libraries than those performed by dealers in antiques or secondhand books. On one level, the videos shared on YouTube are "free," in the sense that there is no direct financial transaction involved between uploader and viewer. At the individual level, viewers appraise this content, often trying to figure out who is circulating it and what the circulator's goals are as the viewers decide which videos to watch and which to spread through their social networks. These decisions, on the level of the individual, are often made in terms of sentimental value and personal interest.

As people move to circulate media texts more broadly, they are also making assessments of the value of these texts as a resource for social exchange. Yet, as the Susan Boyle YouTube video examined in the introduction illustrates, these individual decisions—when aggregated—may help determine the economic value of a particular video, assisting media companies in mapping large-scale patterns of taste and interest that may cut across multiple social networks. Given the sheer volume of content uploaded to YouTube every hour, most videos remain static, appealing to small clusters of users (or perhaps just the uploader). When material starts to spread on a larger scale, however, it allows companies and researchers alike to track shifts in attention and interest with greater sociocultural depth than would have been possible in an era of traditional broadcasting, when they might have counted the number of eyeballs but not understood how specific acts of reading, viewing, or listening fit into larger patterns of social interaction.

This range of uses for YouTube means that some videos circulate within a clearly defined and relatively confined niche, while others (the Boyle video, for example) may spread across different interest groups, reflecting a much more generalized cultural interest. Some videos represent what Grant McCracken (2009) calls "fast culture," moving at such a rapid rate that their spread becomes highly visible and trackable, while others represent "slow culture," often evergreen material which has a longer shelf life but may never percolate to the point that it becomes visible to industry cool-hunters who are looking for "the next big thing." Just as audience members are appraising the value of content as they decide whether to pass it along, the media and marketing industries are often appraising the value, scale, scope, and timeliness of different contributions as they decide which trends to prioritize next.

Residual Culture

The British cultural critic and theorist Raymond Williams (1977) suggests that cultural change occurs at variable rates. As a result, we can be influenced by things—experiences, practices, values, artifacts, institutions—long after they have lost cultural centrality.

Ultimately, Williams asserts that how culture operates can only be fully understood by looking at the ebb and flow of cultural influences rather than taking a static snapshot of specific content or groups.

Williams's account distinguishes four types of cultural practices: emergent, dominant, residual, and archaic. Emergent cultural practices might be represented by "lead users," the term Eric Von Hippel (2005) uses for early adopters whose decisions help manufacturers anticipate future uses or identify potential bugs for a newly issued product, or by the "fast culture" described in McCracken's work. In this chapter, we've been looking at the other end of this continuum: "slow culture," in McCracken's terms. *Antiques Roadshow*, eBay, garage sales, thrift shops, and YouTube clips of archived media content each in its own way illustrates the "afterlife" of ephemeral goods and commodities, demonstrating what happens when these items slide into the residual and the archaic.

Historically, people have imagined that, once an initial purchase has been made, a product loses its value or that, once a program's ratings decline, the content no longer has any cultural currency. There are myriad horrifying accounts of television networks or production companies tossing canisters of film into dumpsters, convinced they would have no lasting interest. Yet, at the present moment, we are all seeing the emergence of a range of alternative channels where value gets produced through the reappraisal and recirculation of what Williams would call the residual. People interested in media texts from the past comb through the landfill of history and identify artifacts which still have currency and desirability. For example, Paul Booth (2010, 27–28) recounts the story of how the BBC had to rely on amateur collectors who had recorded episodes of *Doctor Who* on audiocassette to help restore missing soundtracks for episodes that the television network had trashed decades before, pooling resources to reconstruct lost episodes which later commanded tremendous audience interest.

Whereas the archaic refers to historical forms that no longer serve any recognized cultural functions, Williams sees the residual as representing "areas of human experience, aspiration, and achievement which the dominant culture neglects, undervalues, opposes, represses, or even cannot recognize" (1977, 123–124). The residual can linger in popular memory, become the object of nostalgic longing, be used as a resource for making sense of one's present life and identity, serve as the basis of a critique of current institutions and practices, and spark conversations. In short, residual content may become a prime candidate for spreadability.

Will Straw argues that the introduction of digital media has altered people's relationships with the residual through the collecting and recycling of the "stuff" of past eras:

> A significant effect of the Internet, I would argue, is precisely this reinvigoration of early forms of material culture. It is not simply that the Internet, as a new medium, refashions the past within the languages of the present, so that vestiges of the past may be kept alive. [. . .] In fact, the Internet has strengthened the cultural weight of the past, increasing its intelligibility and accessibility. On the Internet, the past is produced as a field of ever greater coherence, through the gathering together of disparate artifacts into sets or collections and through the commentary and annotation that cluster around such agglomerations, made possible in part by high-capacity storage mechanisms. (2007, 4)

Straw's essay starts with a discussion of a site called Longlostperfume.com. Promising "perfume beyond the touch of time," Longlostperfume.com remakes and resells scents that have long ago gone out of production. As Straw writes, "The internet has become a repository for wide varieties of knowledge that have predated it: the rhetorics of old fandoms, folksy family genealogies, film buff checklists, and so on. Around something as minor as old perfumes, the Internet has gathered together the resources (old photographs, personal reminiscences, and the logos of now forgotten companies) that pull old objects into the limelight of cultural recognition and understandings" (4).

Straw, who says this exchange of residual media fosters new forms of historical consciousness and collective memory, is far more optimistic than music critic Simon Reynolds, whose book *Retromania: Pop Culture's Addiction to Its Own Past* (2011) argues that this kind of "total recall" is deeply destructive to the generative capacities of a culture. Reynolds is concerned that, in a world where vintage music can be increasingly recovered instantaneously through YouTube or file-sharing services such as BitTorrent, less incentive exists for audiences to seek out distinctive new sounds or for musicians to explore new directions. Instead, musicians imitate their predecessors and engage in retro stylings. In what Reynolds acknowledges is potentially an "unnecessarily apocalyptic" framing, he asks in the book's opening, "Could it be that the greatest danger to the future of our music culture is . . . *its past?*" (ix; emphasis in original). Yet even the curmudgeonly Reynolds is forced to admit that audiences are drawn not so much "backwards" as "sideways" (85), taking advantage of these new delivery technologies to reappraise and revalue B-list titles which never were fully experienced by previous generations and even to seek out unreleased or narrowly released music which never found any audience in its own time. Such reappraisals become increasingly central as Reynolds's book continues, suggesting, contrary to the author's own argument, the ways that collectors may nevertheless generate new value for a culture rather than sink into the "hyperstasis" he fears (427).

As Philipp Blom notes in his book *To Have and to Hold: An Intimate History of Collectors and Collecting*, many collections consist of "collected objects, taken out of circulation and pinned up like butterflies, regarded now as specimens, as 'examples of,' as links to another realm of history, of authenticity, of beauty" (2002, 165). The value of the object shifts as it is removed from its natural life cycle and inserted into a collection to be preserved and protected. Blom writes, "Collected objects lose their utilitarian value (there are exceptions, of course) and gain another one, are imbued with meaning and qualities of representation beyond their original station. [. . .] The collected objects have a value for the individual collector that only other collectors can understand" (165). At the same time, Blom finds that collectors find value in "cast-offs," "disposable, outmoded, disregarded, unfashionable" objects, mapping their own fantasies and desires onto things others have left behind (165). The concept of collector's items involves an anticipation of a moment when goods will no longer be produced or circulated. Comic collectors bag and store comics, almost afraid to read them; toy collectors never remove the toy from the box, transforming them from objects of play to objects of display. And many cabinets are full of trading cards, soda cans, magazines, and a variety of other merchandise which is implicitly or explicitly labeled a "collector's item." The objects may be valued as potential investments, with the possibility of their subsequent resale, and isolated objects may be gathered into a set to increase their desirability. Both forms of collecting point toward the "hyperstasis" that Reynolds fears.

Focusing on the phenomenon of retrogaming, Swarthmore College film and media studies professor Bob Rehak examines in our enhanced book how grassroots interest in residual media and culture may coalesce online, sparking new kinds of cultural practices and production (at both the grassroots and commercial level). As Rehak notes, the continued engagement generated by games as residual media challenges/complicates our typical understanding of technology, as quick to shed anything obsolete amid our search for the "next new thing." According to Rehak, retrogames are valued as embodying a "golden age" marked by innovation and experimentation. Such games, however, are not experienced as "hopelessly antiquated museum pieces lacking the good sense to stay buried in gaming history." Rather, the culture around retrogames involves the creative generation of new texts based on older aesthetics and on emulators that allow older games to be played on new platforms. Retrogames (whether older games reprogrammed for emulators or new games based on older aesthetics) remain objects of nostalgia for older players who recall them fondly from their own childhood (which coincidentally was also the childhood of a still-evolving medium), while other players embrace them as objects of camp and pastiche. Both sets of aesthetic considerations shape the ways materials associated with retrogames circulate online.

From the Residual to the Retro

Media collectors have historically behaved more or less the same way as other kinds of collectors. They acquired old prints of movies or tracked down old recordings and locked them away, watching them rarely so as not to damage them, taking pride (and perhaps gaining some recognition from their niche community) in their exclusive access to these rare texts. But the emergence of digital media seems to be shifting the nature of these curation processes, allowing collectors of media artifacts to "have" and to "share" with fans of content from previous generations simultaneously. Collectors are digitizing rare media materials and posting them on YouTube as part of renewed interest in "retro" material, gaining prestige by what they are able to put back into circulation. In the process, old archival media materials are gaining greater visibility online, educating a new public that comes to recognize previously unsuspected value in the past, whether in an educational setting or among game collectors.

If traditional collectors erase use value almost entirely in favor of sentimental value, these retro media fans restore use value by discovering new uses for forgotten materials. Thus, the ready availability of old media texts may inspire new acts of creation and performance—leading not simply to the making of new meanings but also to the creation of new texts and the emergence of new subcultural communities. Here, the residual becomes the emergent, to return to Williams's terms, as collector culture coexists with and even fuels the retro culture which may value these objects in a mode of camp or ironic appreciation.

Sam Carroll (2007) explores the complex set of co-relationships between collectors and retro fans in her account of the uses of YouTube by the neo-swing movement. Twenty-plus years ago, the dance community made conscious efforts to recover the Lindy Hop and other swing dances from historical neglect. They quickly discovered that these steps were most vividly preserved in old musical shorts and obscure films, many of which rested in the hands of archivists and collectors. By the 1990s, neo-swing music began to appear in clubs, Hollywood films, advertisements, and other places throughout U.S. culture.

In some cases, these groups were recovering old songs from forgotten albums left moldering in someone's basement. In other cases, they were writing and performing new songs, further revitalizing the genre. The people who had been learning swing dancing were natural audiences for this new swing music, and the new swing music brought new audiences into the swing-dance community. Labels reissued old albums they hadn't sold for decades. Old songs that had fallen into public domain were assembled and released on albums. And, as YouTube became a prominent site for sharing video content, clips—from both old and contemporary musical numbers alike—spread online. While traditional collector cultures have been governed by preservationist impulses, these new retro subcultures are often more generative, more imaginative, and more playful in the ways they recontextualize and reimagine the residual.

Consider the case of steampunk, a subgenre of science fiction focused on the active reimagining of the technologies and cultural practices of the Victorian era (Bebergal 2007). From the earliest steampunk works, the subgenre has explicitly pitted the virtues of old mechanical devices (sometimes steam driven, but not always) against the perceived defects of digital technologies (the domain of cyberpunk). The themes of steampunk have emerged explicitly through science fiction novels such as *The Difference Engine*, *Infernal Devices*, and *The Diamond Age*; graphic novels such as *The Five Fists of Science* and *The League of Extraordinary Gentlemen*; and films such as *The Wild Wild West*. Steampunk quickly became a global phenomenon, as illustrated by European works such as *City of Lost Children* and Japanese anime such as *Steamboy* and *Howl's Moving Castle*.

Yet to see steampunk simply as a new media genre is to miss the degree to which its fans have built an entire lifestyle around their interests (Guizzo 2008). Some of these fans are using eBay to acquire old devices and mechanisms—from stereoscopes and magic lanterns to old laboratory equipment—which may be enjoyed as is or scavenged for parts for their own modification and fabrication projects. Steampunk craftspeople are producing handmade objects, and small-scale companies are beginning to mass-produce objects in the steampunk mode, much as they used to create objects for circulation in the closely related yet distinctly different goth culture (itself framed around an imaginative rethinking of the Victorian era, albeit more focused on romance and horror literature). In one of the few ethnographic accounts of this steampunk subculture, Rebecca Onion explains,

> Steampunks seek less to recreate specific technologies of this time than to re-access what they see as the affective value of the material world of the nineteenth century. The steampunk ideology prizes brass, copper, wood, leather, and papier-mâché—the construction materials of this bygone time. Steampunks fetishise cogs, springs, sprockets, wheels and hydraulic motion. They love the sight of the clouds of steam that arise during the operation of steam-powered technology. [. . .] How did these technologies, once so reviled, enter back into the cultural lexicon as icons of a new utopian landscape? (2008, 138–139)

Her final question is one which will be asked increasingly as today's networked society churns through once-private collections, seeking fodder for the construction of new identities and the creation of new cultural experiences from this retro content.

York University marketing professor Robert V. Kozinets has long traced the revitalization of old and often forgotten brands that are embraced by collector communities and fan groups online. He was among the first to conceptualize the link between brand narratives and stories, myths and legends, fan communities and brand communities, and the "retroscaping" of the past as a means of generating new meaning and value around brands. In our enhanced book, Kozinets discusses the strategies through which companies engage in "retro-branding," reviving or relaunching brands from the past in ways that capitalize on existing fandoms and provide launching points for the creation of new markets:

> Retrobranding research [. . .] builds on the idea that brand allegories are stories, narratives, or extended metaphors in symbolic form. Successful

branding is successful world-building, and the world it builds can be a window into the brand's own (often rosy-colored or stereotyped) past. Successful brand narratives will possess an almost utopian evocation of past worlds and past or present communities.

Kozinets writes about how the enduring appeal of certain brands has helped "spur a type of residual and actual 'brand fandom,'" leading to their eventual revival. For instance, the ongoing cultural relevance of the Volkswagen Beetle led to a relaunch of the vehicle in 1998, while the ongoing interest in *Star Wars* led to three new prequel installments. Kozinets's discussion of retrobranding shows the economic stakes behind the retro movement: patterns of retro interest in brands do not simply generate new meanings, recharging the cultural significance of once-static icons. They do not simply inspire new cultural production and subcultural activity. They also generate new value, creating new markets for cultural goods and media texts which had come to carry little to no exchange value. These patterns both generate new products inspired by the old and extend or renew the shelf life of products otherwise believed to be past their prime. As such, they are sources of profit for those companies that own those brands and the rights to those stories.

The processes that generate these values and renew these interests are complex, involving many possible feedback loops among producers, marketers, and audiences, each monitoring and seeking to influence the others. If lead users are early adopters, then retro users might be late adopters. However, both function as scavengers and innovators whose activity, if mapped, may fuel the next phases of cultural and economic development. Audiences may benefit if this process allows for a better fit between the goods available and their particular needs and desires, if the culture provides resources that better sustain their fantasies and interests. Simultaneously, companies profit through the expansion of this market activity and through the discovery of potential new sources of revenue.

Of course, where brands are concerned, one has a different relationship to the fantasies they enhance, depending on whether one can afford to buy the commodities to which one has assigned these values. Brands are certainly sustained by aspiration—the mystique of the Rolls Royce is supported by those who dream of buying such a car—but the company depends on the actual purchases of people with the money to buy the vehicles to sustain their business. Thus, while companies may invite all interested parties to make meanings with their content, these stories will ultimately focus on the fantasies of a subset who can afford to become customers.

Residual Economics

Raymond Williams's choice of the term "residual" to describe the value of this content that has fallen out of the cultural mainstream is an interesting one, since "residual" carries economic as well as cultural meanings. In accounting, "residual value" is another term for salvage value. It is the value that remains in an object—say, an automobile—once its "useful life has ended" and once the costs of disposing of the artifact have been subtracted. Meanwhile, in the entertainment industry, a residual is a form of profit sharing through which talent continues to receive compensation when their work gets recirculated or reperformed in supplemental markets. Labor contracts in Hollywood often center as much on residual payments as they do on payments for the initial production, and there is an ongoing recalibration and renegotiation of these terms because digital distribution was not anticipated in many pre-1990s contracts and has to be reappraised after the fact.

In both those uses, "residual" refers to the economic value generated through the afterlife of material objects and media performances. These multiple uses of "residual" suggest that materials' ongoing sentimental and symbolic interest may still generate profit long after their initial exchange and use value has vanished from memory. Media producers have historically acted as if they needed to protect their franchise from the rough handling of their fans, seeing fans as potentially depreciating the value of their intellectual property by changing its meaning in popular perception. Yet our exploration of the residual here suggests the opposite—that retro fans appreciate media properties, in the sense that they like them and thus make them a site of emotional investments. Fans might then "appreciate" this material in an economic sense as well, increasing these artifacts' potential value by expanding their shelf life and opening them up to new potential markets.

As an example of how media content can stay relevant for decades, through a combination of corporate promotional practice and fan activity, Kevin Sandler (forthcoming) has mapped the trajectory of the Hanna-Barbara cartoon character Scooby-Doo as he moves in and out of cultural currency with various audiences. As Sandler notes, Scooby-Doo spans more than four decades of television programming from 1969 to the present, appearing in thirteen different original series on various broadcast and cable television networks. While some of the Great Dane detective's success is tied to his capacity to reinvent himself to reflect contemporary children's taste, his continued relevance also involves maintaining relations with older fans who grew up with this goofy character, and the character then becomes the object of both camp and nostalgia.

Here, a media franchise operates very much like a retro brand, with new value generated by inserting Scooby into new contexts or putting him in front of new audiences. Sandler describes the tensions which emerge around the competing bids on this character, with the hip and ironic strategies the Cartoon Network deployed to hold the attention of adult viewers sometimes clashing with the more earnest targeting of next-generation fans. Creators of new content are constantly trying to juxtapose the perspectives of multiple audiences. For instance, Sandler points out that, despite the fact that adult players are the largest group of gaming customers, Scooby-Doo video games have repeatedly reflected more juvenile interests in the character because of the risk that more adult readings might be perplexing or inappropriate for children. In a similar vein, the way in which adult fans appropriate cartoon characters from their childhood can create tensions as well, as was the case with a 2010 unauthorized fan film which manipulated the digital versions of Scooby's Hanna-Barbera cartoon brethren Yogi Bear and Boo Boo (who were set to appear in a feature film aimed at family audiences) to restage a sequence from *The Assassination of Jesse James by the Coward Robert Ford*, in which a watery-eyed Boo Boo shoots his longtime buddy in the back in return for reward money.

The dark tone of this video generated much controversy because of the prospect that it might traumatize young fans of the picnic-basket-stealing bears.

Sandler's account suggests ways that marketing and programming decisions often privilege certain audience members and their interests at the expense of others. While several groups may equally value Scooby-Doo, those groups are not equally valued by television-network or advertising executives. Here, we might note yet another potential meaning of residual as "what gets left behind" through the perpetual processes of sedimentation and crystallization. Media companies typically identify (sometimes unconsciously and sometimes strategically) certain groups that are a desired audience and then other groups that are considered excess or irrelevant. The process is a major source of friction. As we'll see again in chapter 3, these surplus fan communities, along with nonmarket fan uses of a text, are often ignored or even suppressed by media producers and brands; however, companies could learn much by listening to what these audiences are saying and doing.

WWE Classics on Demand

World Wrestling Entertainment is one company than has observed and responded to transactions from its retro fans. In the process, WWE discovered new sources of revenue for what once were considered "fringe fan behaviors." For decades, prior to the rise of cable television, U.S. pro wrestling was regionalized, with promoters "owning" an area comprising a few key cities. Local fans only saw their area's troupe, and a weekly television program promoted live events. Regional promoters saw the television show as a vehicle to drive the only business metric that mattered: ticket sales. Thus, these videos were seen as ephemeral promotional material with no residual value. They either aired live from the studio or, if taped, were often recorded over because of the significant expense of videotape.

Yet some dedicated fans were curious where new performers in their territory had come from and where departing performers were headed. While wrestling magazines were often outdated or incomplete because they relied on information from promoters (and were skewed by the relationships those publications had with those who ran particular regions), some ardent fans from different territories alternatively began creating and trading their own media. These loose relationships were manifested in fan newsletters such as the *Wrestling Information Bulletin* from California fan Burt Ray in the 1960s or the *Illustrated Wrestling Digest* from Illinois fan Ronald Dobratz in the 1970s. Newsletters carried reader-contributed match results and news accounts from each territory, allowing subscribers to trade ephemera and live audio recordings of themselves doing commentary from the stands at local wrestling events (and even the occasional eight-millimeter film).

There may have been nominal fees for postage or to help support someone putting the newsletter together, but these networks were developed with a gift-economy logic. Fans received information from other territories in exchange for providing information from theirs. While these publications' subscription bases were small, they helped to create a network of "expert" fans who could then act as go-to resources for the more casual fans in their local arena. Subsequently, the information shared in these underground publications had an influence far greater than their circulation number. Wrestling promoters were annoyed at these developing audience networks, feeling that sharing results from various cities "exposed" the business—demonstrating, for instance, that local promoters basically put on the same show from town to town.

With the rise of home video recording, this preexisting fan infrastructure became the basis of an active tape-trading community, in which fans would swap video of their local televised wrestling for episodes from another territory. Some of those fans amassed personal archives, collecting matches from as many territories as possible. They saw great value in media texts that were not otherwise considered commercially viable by wrestling promoters, and these media texts gained increasing traction and interest while circulating through nonmarket exchanges.

Fan collectors saw value in replicating and sharing material rather than having it remain scarce, particularly because there were no official commercial means to access these shows after their first airing. As a result, local shows or particular matches were dubbed in multiple generations of recordings (with the quality often wearing thin after a few iterations), and these collectors and distributors gained special "expert" status within their own community as wrestling curators, with their reputations tied to the size of their collection.

The impact of tape trading was felt in many ways. Fans now had the ability to watch wrestling from other territories as if they were locals, learning how stories built over time rather than just reading match results. Fans also had new benchmarks through which to measure and discuss the quality of wrestlers' performances. Prior to the VCR, fans treated pro wrestling show results quite like legitimate sports. With tapes, fans could start evaluating wrestling as performance art, comparing the ability (or "workrate") of performers rather than their character's win-loss records. This mindset allowed fans to debate, for instance, performances on a "five-star" scale. While tape trading remained a wholly nonmarket exchange system, it was governed by both a gift-economy system of reciprocation and a developing mode of quality appraisal, providing a new lens for determining what matches were "must-see."

Some promoters enjoyed the novelty of having viewers from far away, but such bragging rights had no commercial impact: these fans couldn't buy seats at the local arena. Cheaper archiving technologies eventually led to more shows being saved, but promoters still didn't have a business reason for saving shows, in some cases only keeping some episodes to access clips for future episodes rather than seeing any commercial value in the content. In short, these wrestling videos held great value as gifts within the fan community but not as a commodity in the commercial industry.

Yet, as demand grew, this material began to accrue market value as well. For instance, tape traders with the largest archives eventually began selling compilations of matches, storylines, and interviews. While some exchanges became impersonal, with content being sold through listed catalogs, many built on personal relationships and thus included a variety of nonmarket considerations. Likewise, newsletters took on greater prominence in the tape-trading era. For example, Dave Meltzer's *Wrestling Observer Newsletter* gained popularity through his news and reviews based on tapes he received from around the country (and the world). Meltzer, a professional journalist, turned his personal passion into a business model and eventually quit his job as a sportswriter to work full-time as the editor of his self-published newsletter, supported by annual subscription fees from fellow fans.

The Internet only amplified both business models. Those fans looking to profit from their dedication to archiving were able to more actively promote their tape compilations through websites. Meanwhile, the thousands of readers of newsletters became millions in the Internet era, as myriad subscribers distributed news through their own fan forums and sites, a practice which also increased newsletter readership, even as the content of Meltzer and others was often shared broadly with nonsubscribers. And the nonmarket exchange of wrestling content proliferated as well, with online discussion forums providing greater opportunities for fans to share contact details and to trade video.

Meanwhile, the wrestling industry had undergone massive change as well. The rise of cable television killed the territory system, as Vince McMahon's World Wrestling Entertainment (then known as the World Wrestling Federation) began to tour its act nationally in the 1980s, driven by weekly programs on the USA Network and a variety of shows syndicated in local markets. WWE Home Video capitalized on the VCR, making limited use of its own archive to translate "super events" into tapes for purchase or rental. However, limited shelf space in video stores forced the WWE (and other national wrestling brands) to choose only special events or compilations for distribution, whereas online fans were able to actively trade weekly shows, not to mention content from wrestling's past and from more underground local promotions.

In 2001, the WWE bought out its major national competitor, World Championship Wrestling, acquiring WCW's full archive. Combining this material with its own holdings, WWE suddenly became interested in actively exploring the value of archived wrestling content. Because these "ephemeral" texts had circulated in both nonmarket and market exchanges among fans for decades, the company realized they might hold deeper economic value than "the industry" had realized. The centerpiece of its efforts was the development of a cable video-on-demand subscription service, now called WWE Classics on Demand, which makes 20–30 hours of archived wrestling video footage available to fans each month. While some of these are special events, many are weekly wrestling shows from WWE or the territories of yesteryear.

What was once disposable content has now been labeled "classic." The WWE has worked for the past several years to tag its massive archive, allowing it to be accessed for an increasing number of DVD releases of "retro" material. These DVDs are amassed around themes: stipulation matches (e.g., *Bloodbath: The Most Incredible Steel Cage Matches*), wrestling history (e.g., *The Spectacular Legacy of the AWA*), and performer compilations (e.g., *20 Years Too Soon: Superstar Billy Graham*). The WWE has also built more commercial offerings around its Hall of Fame, including DVD releases of Hall of Famers' matches and regular video-on-demand Hall of Fame features. Further, WWE.com, a prominent part of WWE's modern business model, increasingly features classic content to draw visitors and its own monthly subscription channel, WWE Greatest Matches. And the WWE maintains plans as this book goes to press to launch its own full cable channel, primarily featuring content from its pro wrestling video archive.

Even as pro wrestling's general popularity waned from a peak at the beginning of the twenty-first century, the WWE has kept profits relatively consistent in part by offering new types of material to dedicated fans, such as these various uses of archived material. Thus, the company's reappraisal of the wrestling archive has played a substantial role in its business model.

Alongside these new business practices, wrestling content circulates through nonmarket logics now more than ever. Fans continue seeking a copy when they have missed the last week's show, uploading content from "indie promotions" across the country (often from fans of a particular local personality looking to make it to WWE or from the talent himself), and sharing matches from archives WWE doesn't own. Meanwhile, one can find a proliferating collection of matches and clips from WWE's history uploaded by fans on YouTube, for instance, where WWE very actively polices for what it considers misuses of its intellectual property (such as clips from pay-per-view events or WWE DVDs) but still lets a large portion of content stand. Perhaps, since WWE has way too much material in its archive to make commercially available at any one time, the company realizes that such circulation has no economic downside but potential promotional upside for the company.

The history of any media property, brand, or text likely includes the flow of material through both market and nonmarket exchanges. Here, wrestling television shows developed initially for marketing purposes were seen as having no long-term value. These archives only gained traction through noncommercial circulation, but this peer-to-peer circulation of wrestling content generated new commercial uses of the material for big brands and individual fans alike. And these market uses now thrive alongside the ongoing nonmarket spread of archived videos. A constant process of reappraisal among fans and the wrestling industry alike governs the movement of these texts, allowing content to serve multiple functions as it circulates over time.

We are not suggesting here that every fan activity lends itself well to "monetization." As we have seen, the common industry parlance—"capitalizing," "leveraging," or "taking advantage of"—sounds quite exploitative and indeed can feel that way. Several of our examples demonstrate that audience uses of cultural material can backfire when companies violate their implicit contract with their audience (to borrow language from chapter 1). Instead, we are suggesting that companies need to get much better at truly listening to their audience and at understanding their various audience's motivations for spreading their content. The WWE realized over time that there was interest in archival wrestling material by paying attention to fans' grassroots archiving and sharing practices. As a result, the company built new business models to better serve these fans and subsequently put historical wrestling video, which had only circulated through fan communities for years or even decades, back into widespread availability.

At times when the audience's motivation and the company's desire to make a profit align, new business opportunities might result. Often, they will not. The media and marketing industries still have not, as a whole, developed an attuned ear to their audiences and how their intellectual property is circulating between these two logics. In chapter 3, we will discuss more fully some of the ways the television industry in particular is appraising different forms of attention and engagement, reading some audiences as desirable and others as "excess," and the dangers of dismissing or marginalizing these "surplus audiences."

In January 2010, the SyFy Channel site Blastr posted an article with the provocative headline "*Heroes* Is a Hit—as the Most Pirated TV Show, That Is" (Huddleston 2010). As the article reported, TorrentFreak.com tracked how often the average episode of particular series had been downloaded illegally in 2009. Many cult shows—*Heroes* and *Dexter* among them—attracted as many or more illegal downloads as television viewers, at least as counted by Nielsen. If all these viewers were counted equally, some canceled or soon-to-be-canceled series would become television-network hits. *Heroes*, for example, had 6,580,000 illegal downloads for a single episode, as compared to 5,900,000 legal viewers (the Nielsen number the show was hovering around at that time). Meanwhile, a hit such as *Lost* had 6,310,000 illegal views per episode, in addition to its 11,050,000 legal viewers.

Torrents represent only one of several possible mechanisms by which someone might illegally access television content, so even these expanded numbers underestimate the full range of viewers. Strikingly, almost all these torrent "hits" were "cult shows" that rely on dedicated niche audiences and serial structures to attract "engaged" audiences. Most were serial programs that depended on regular viewership in order to be comprehensible. These shows are also among the most heavily viewed on alternative legal platforms (such as video on demand and commercially available online platforms) and are top sellers on DVD.

Many illegal viewers come from countries where a series is shown on a delayed schedule. These fans want to sync their viewing schedule with international online discussions about shows, but they can't easily

THE VALUE OF
MEDIA ENGAGEMENT

join the conversation if they have to wait until programs become locally available. Meanwhile, some come from countries where a series is not available on any schedule, delayed or otherwise; illegal downloads are their only chance of accessing the content. Many other viewers want to skip advertisements, view shows on their own schedules, watch video on their preferred platform, and/or avoid policies of legal streaming television sites they find frustrating. These "pirates" are not taking content because they refuse to pay for it (especially since they could watch it free when it is originally aired); they are seeking to change the conditions under which they view it (De Kosnik 2010).

Such viewers don't count within the current logics of audience measurement. They are watching the series but not in ways television channels can value. The industry seeks audience members who fit into particular markets, defined by age and gender demographics desirable to advertisers, which are most easily constructed around a common, "sticky" advertising time slot.

Heroes executive producer Tim Kring responded to Blastr's revelation by saying, "The general attitude of the networks towards this massive audience that's out there has been to stand on the sideline and heckle these people when, in fact, these are people who actively sought these shows out. They went some place and actively pirated the show. These are fans that should be embraced, and, somehow, figured out how to monetize" (quoted in Jenkins 2010b). *The Middleman*'s Javier Grillo-Marxuach saw these illegal viewers as part of the mechanism for generating awareness of, and interest in, his cult property:

> The more people talk about the show, the more other people will end up buying the DVD. Eventually, anybody who looks at a pirated copy will tell somebody to buy the T-shirt or the DVD or the keychain, and the money will come back to us. [. . .] I'd rather have the show I work on be seen, and, frankly, given the way that the studios have dealt with the royalty compensation for writers on alternative platforms . . . I'm so sorry about your pirating problem, really! (Quoted in Jenkins 2010b)

Heroes was then in ratings peril and was eventually canceled, while *The Middleman* was already canceled and recovering its production costs through DVD sales. However, the perspectives of both Kring and Grillo-Marxuach reflect the potential value that rights owners might ultimately find in these alternative views. These fringe audiences are often highly engaged at a time when the media industries are concerned about disengaged audiences and declining viewer loyalty. Yet these illegal downloads are most often routed to the legal team rather than to the research or marketing divisions. Instead of seeking ways to engage these torrenting viewers in legal practices, to recognize the potential value of their engagement, or to understand what might motivate them to step outside the law to access content, the preferences and interests of unauthorized viewers of *Heroes* and other shows are more often delegitimized.

Grillo-Marxuach's comments echo the logic of Jason Mittell (2005), who writes that his using file sharing to watch the first season of *Veronica Mars* "actually offered more value to the industry" than had he watched on the network itself. Mittell suggests, as a TiVo user, he wouldn't have watched commercials, and as a non-Nielsen family, his "viewing habits do not factor into the elaborate exchange of audiences between networks and advertisers via the currency of ratings."

However, as an "illegal" viewer, Mittell's viewing through torrenting could actually have been tracked as an indicator of *Veronica Mars*'s popularity. Further, he encouraged others to watch and even rewatched the series to "hook" his wife. He also converted to a legal viewer on network television once he had caught up and even used the show in his classes, requesting that his university library buy *Veronica Mars* on DVD.

Grillo-Marxuach and Mittell both challenge the assumption that unauthorized viewing holds no commercial value, pointing to alternative revenue streams which might count within U.S. television's evolving business models. They suggest how audience members generate value through their direct purchases (of downloaded legal episodes, of DVDs, of program-related merchandise) and through their role as grassroots intermediaries drawing in new audience members. In doing so, both Grillo-Marxuach and Mittell evoke a logic of engagement, one of several that will help us decode the kinds of viewing most valuable to media industries.

Are You Engaged?

One might describe what is happening in contemporary U.S. television as a shift from an appointment-based model of television viewing toward an engagement-based paradigm. Under the appointment model, committed viewers arrange their lives to be home at a certain time to watch their favorite programs. Content is created and distributed primarily to attract this attention at a certain time—viewership which can be predicted and subsequently metered and sold to advertisers for profit. Traditional television ratings represent the audience as the primary commodity exchanged through the practices of broadcast media.

By contrast, engagement-based models see the audience as a collective of active agents whose labor may generate alternative forms of market value. This approach places a premium on audiences willing to pursue content across multiple channels as viewers access television shows on their own schedules, thanks to videocassette recorders and later digital video recorders (DVRs), digital downloads, mobile video devices, and DVD boxed sets. Such models value the spread of media texts as these engaged audiences are more likely to recommend, discuss, research, pass along, and even generate new material in response.

The increased fragmentation of the audience and the multiplication of delivery platforms has led to uncertainty about how much value to place on different kinds of audiences. Those who measure and value more active audience practices often conflict with others who want to lock down content in order to preserve the value coming from traditional models. Even among those who understand that developing business models around such engagement is key, there has been little consensus on how, or even which, measures of engagement are valuable or how to agree on a model for business transactions around such measures.

The Nielsen ratings system, the gold standard within the industry, has experimented with alternative formulas that at least expand beyond the strict appointment model. Nielsen's new standard, the "C3s," measures same-day viewing plus those who watch within the three following days via time-shifting technologies (such as DVRs). This approach remains focused on the appointment-based model;

Nielsen now counts not just those who made the appointment on time but also everyone who was "fashionably late."

Comments from CourtTV's Deborah Reichig demonstrate the difficulties of coming to a consensus on how to measure engagement:

> We're talking to one agency who thinks that loyalty is an important factor, and they measure that by the number of people who have watched three out of four episodes. Another thinks it's persistence, and that's measured by numbers of minutes watched per show. And there's others who want to look at "persuasiveness." We actually did a literature review, and there are 85 different words and phrases that people have used to get at this concept. (Quoted in Sass 2006)

Audiences confront an ever-shifting configuration of platforms and financial arrangements as they seek the content they want from an industry not yet able to sell it to them in the forms or contexts they desire.

A focus on engagement is central to the reconfiguration of audience power that we are discussing throughout this book. If chapter 2 dealt with how audiences "appraise" media texts, chapter 3 explores the way media industries assign value to audiences as a case study for how to better understand this overarching issue of engagement on any platform. Our focus here is on the television industry, site of some of the greatest tensions about how to measure audience value, but similar questions are surfacing across the entertainment industry. Current debates around authorized and unauthorized access to television content illustrate emerging tensions as fans share material outside traditional broadcast structures and flows. Unauthorized circulation of content often emerges from the frustrations which audiences have as they deal with the transitional state of alternative delivery channels, with the frustrations of trying to navigate through a system that seems to promise them the media they want when they want it but frequently disappoints. This situation is what we mean to describe when we suggest that "piracy" is more often a product of market failures on the part of media industry than of moral failures on the part of media audiences. This chapter looks at the tensions between how audiences engage and how the media industries measure and reward engagement. Such tensions are what all parties will need to work through if we are to construct an alternative "moral economy" around the production and circulation of media. In the second part of the chapter, we will explore a range of different transmedia strategies that have emerged as producers and marketers have sought to court and sustain the interests of active fans in the hope that they may also help motivate engagement from more casual viewers.

The Challenges of Measurement

The television industry requires knowledge about the people who watch, but that audience is, to a great extent, unknowable. As Ien Ang suggests, the actual people watching television are, to a great extent, "invisible" to media companies, a mass "hidden behind the millions of dispersed closed doors of private homes, virtually unmanageable and inaccessible to the outsider" (1991, 30). Even as new formats such as the DVD, video on demand, and electronic rentals are providing the television industry with direct-to-the-audience markets for programming (Kompare 2006, 337), and even as online delivery services and communities have increased the visibility of audiences (niche, fan, or otherwise), the television industry is still defined by a condition of "centralized transmission and privatized reception" (to draw, as Ang does, on Raymond Williams [1974, 30]).

The technologies of ratings systems attempt to render the audience visible to the television industry. Using survey technologies to achieve scale, the industry constructs a statistical representation of who might be watching and how they might be watching. This model uses demographics to segment the television audience into easily definable groups, differentiated by factors such as age, income, gender, and ethnicity, but "the audience" is otherwise held to be relatively coherent.

This approximated television audience provides the industry with a manageable object it can measure, design programming for, and sell to advertisers. Audience members are read as "consumers," and ratings assume that reception (the fact that a given television set was on) equates with communication (that the message was received). This model reduces the range of factors that need to be accounted for when discussing "watching television," an act that occurs in a diverse array of everyday contexts and circumstances (Ang 1991, 62) and with an enormous variety of audience engagement. These ratings, though a great simplification, have become the standard currency for business transactions.

Additional measurement strategies (such as Q Scores that provide a more qualitative account of audience familiarity with and preference for certain performers, characters, and brands) provide more nuanced accounts of audience experience. Nevertheless, the model Ang describes still predominates because of the structural relationships that organize the television industry. Eileen Meehan (2005) argues that advertisers' demand for access to particular "consumers" (certain high-value demographics) shapes the industry's programming practices. Thus, media conglomerates use multiple platforms and synergistic practices to attract these highly sought audiences. This situation rewards the development of franchises, reducing competition across the media industry and narrowing the range of interests (potentially) represented.

Television networks *and* advertisers purchase the ratings from a single accredited supplier (Nielsen) with a longstanding interest in pleasing both. The resulting ratings system has an inertia that makes it difficult for new competitors and blocks significant shifts in the methods of measurement. The ratings system is configured to provide a consistent currency for business deals to be conducted, not primarily to provide an accurate account of all who watch. Changes can be made to the system to improve the breadth and depth of how the audience is understood but only in ways that do not disrupt the reason this data is being gathered in the first place. Even if the data is far from perfect, business can continue as usual as long as everyone is using the same numbers.

Despite steps toward developing delivery alternatives to the broadcast model (from television networks' own websites to online distribution initiatives such as Hulu and Fancast), studio and television-network structures still privilege advertising revenue from first-run content. In a post titled "Why Watching TV Online (Mostly) Doesn't Help Ratings (for Now)," SyFy Digital Senior Vice-President Craig Engler explains that, at least for the time being, the industry is structured to separate audiences for broadcast and audiences for streaming:

> TV ratings specifically measure the audience watching shows on TV, while a different kind of ratings system (actually several kinds of systems) measures audiences who watch online. Even though they share a lot of the same content and are integrally linked, online streaming and TV are fundamentally separate businesses that are usually distributed, funded and monetized in different ways. (2010)

Perhaps unsurprisingly, then, given that ratings are commodities that networks sell to buyers, Engler puts the onus on advertisers. He indicates that advertisers are (quite understandably) only interested in viewers for the platform they have purchased:[1] "If an advertiser buys an ad in the [show] on TV, they don't care how many people watched the show on iPhones because they didn't pay to have their ad run on iPhones. Sometimes advertisers will buy on air, online and mobile simultaneously, but it's not the standard (yet)" (2010). Even for the teams that create a work, tracing the profit that material generates can be quite complicated. The deals struck for revenues generated from advertising sold for television, online, and on-demand viewing may all have different configurations of how the profit is split, not to mention DVD sales, rental arrangements, syndication rights, and so on. Portions of the profit stream not only to the company that distributed the content, the company that owns the content, the team that created the content, and so on but often to multiple divisions within each of those entities, depending on the particular platform. While those cumulative revenues may be able to mark the program a success (or failure), these numbers are dispersed and thus harder to track and interpret. Further, as new business models are still developing for alternative forms of video distribution, the value of a viewer shifts from platform to platform. Engler says, "We'd rather have a million TV viewers than a million streaming viewers because we make more money from the TV viewers, which means they contribute more to the health and success of a show" (2010).

Given the television industry's internal challenges, media companies send confusing messages to their audiences. The life and death of CBS drama *Jericho* illustrates these conflicting signals. Premiering as part of the fall 2006 season, *Jericho* (a series about a rural Kansas community coping with the aftermath of a nuclear holocaust) drew a small (for a U.S. television network) but passionate audience. When the program was canceled at the end of the first season, fans showed their support by launching a large and well-organized online campaign. CBS spokesperson Chris Ender proclaimed the campaign the biggest outpouring of support via digital means they'd ever seen for a program. (See Collins 2007.) In addition to bombarding CBS with emails, fans sent somewhere between 20 and 25 tons of peanuts to CBS's offices in New York and Los Angeles, a reference to a line from the last episode of the first season (Serpe 2007).

The outpouring was enough to have the program renewed. Seven new episodes were commissioned with a stern warning to *Jericho* fans: that they needed to watch the live broadcast or there was no future for the show. In an interview with *Ad Age* (Steinberg 2007), Leslie Moonves, CBS Corporation's chief executive, announced that the broadcaster had been surprised by fan support for the program. CBS hadn't noticed that this relatively poor ratings performer had a significant audience that watched on its official streaming platform and on their home DVRs. To be appropriately counted, viewers needed to "show up" in measured ratings by watching television live. It wasn't just Moonves; star Brad Beyer (quoted in Tarnoff 2007) and president of CBS Entertainment Nina Tassler both separately warned viewers that they needed to watch live broadcasts. As Tassler told the *New York Times*, "We want them to watch on Wednesday at 8 o'clock, and we need them to recruit viewers who are going to watch the broadcast" (quoted in Wyatt 2007). These warnings conflicted with the message Moonves projected just three days later in a Q&A session at Syracuse University:

This is a major time of transition, where our goal basically is to get our product—our content—everywhere it can be, anywhere it can be. So, at the end of the day, as long as I'm getting paid for it, I don't care whether you are watching *CSI* on CBS at 9 o'clock on Thursday night, on your DVR, if you are getting it on Amazon.com, or CBS.com. [...] You are still watching *CSI*. It doesn't matter how you get it. (2007)

In response to a question at the end of the interview, Moonves conceded that the discrepancy between this "everywhere, anywhere" mentality and the statements about *Jericho* was due to a lack of comprehensive measurement for online viewing. However, presuming CBS could count views on CBS.com and elsewhere, the larger issue was actually the difference advertisers would pay from one medium to the next. (And, of course, only those viewers who happened to have a Nielsen box would have been counted in the "comprehensive measurement" for traditional television viewing, even if all the fans did what CBS was advising.)

Jericho was canceled before the end of its second season. Ultimately, CBS had done nothing to change its model. The depth of engagement from *Jericho* fans surprised them into bringing the program back for a limited run, but they still measured success through an appointment model.

While *Jericho* fans again lodged their protests to CBS, fans of another network-television show—NBC's *Chuck*—followed Engler's logic by instead appealing to the other side of the business transaction: the advertiser. As Sheila Seles, marketing manager at Bluefin Labs, details in our enhanced book, these fans chose to demonstrate the potential economic value of audience engagement in a tangible way. When fans of the NBC spy comedy heard of the program's potential cancellation at the end of the 2008–2009 television season, they targeted an individual sponsor, restaurant chain Subway, to demonstrate the value of their attention. Less than a month later, NBC renewed *Chuck* through an advertising partnership with Subway.

As Seles discusses, the *Chuck* fans recognized that watching the show did not do enough to demonstrate their size as a viewing community or their investment in the program. By targeting an individual sponsor, these fans focused their energies on making an impression NBC could recognize:

Chuck fans bought sandwiches to demonstrate that they were the people Subway was trying to reach—people who would buy foot-long sandwiches. If the ratings system could effectively measure the real value of the television audience, Nielsen would have been able to tell NBC that these sandwich-buying people were watching *Chuck* in numbers that justified Subway's ad dollars. But they couldn't or didn't. And so fans bought sandwiches and saved a show.

Highlighting the television industry's difficulty navigating between the dominant appointment model and the emergent engagement model, Seles contrasts the rescue of *Chuck* with NBC's efforts to create programming that would succeed in spite of poor ratings. In fall 2009, NBC replaced an hour of scripted programming every weeknight with a talk show hosted by veteran host Jay Leno. Cheaper to produce than scripted programming and filled with product placement and sponsored segments, "Leno's show was so inexpensive to produce that it could recoup costs and turn a modest profit even without high ratings." While swiftly canceled after disastrous ratings and a negative impact on the news programs that followed, the Leno experiment serves as a counterpoint to the success of the *Chuck* fans. Writes Seles, "Both *Chuck* fans and NBC wanted to outsmart the ratings system: *Chuck* fans did it by appealing directly to sponsors, and NBC did it by making a show that didn't need ratings to make money."

Such changes require a rethinking of popular models of consumerism; a useful model, for advertisers and producers alike, is the past several decades of work in cultural studies, which has explored media "consumption" as acts of meaning production. In viewers' everyday activities, they contribute to the cultural value (sentimental, symbolic) of media products by passing along content and making material valuable within their social networks. Each new viewer that these practices draw to the program could, in theory, translate into greater economic value (exchange) for media companies and advertisers.

Anthropologist Grant McCracken has proposed shifting the descriptor away from "consumer" altogether, as the term locates people at the end of a chain of value creation—perhaps even a dead end, since the life of the product closes with its consumption. In our enhanced book,

McCracken notes that "consumer" has been useful in evoking "the distinction between producer and consumer, reminding the corporation that capitalism is not about the art of the possible but the art of the desirable." However, he writes that many people object to the term "consumer," not just because it indicates a destructive force incapable of generating value but also because it is insufficient for describing the purchase of a wide variety of goods (such as digital content) which "are not diminished by the act of 'consumption.'" Somewhat provocatively, McCracken proposes "multiplier" as an alternative, arguing that his new term acknowledges the ways audience members generate value through their activities:

> A "multiplier" is someone who will treat the good, service, or experience as a starting point. Multipliers will build in some of their own intelligence and imagination. They will take possession of a cultural artifact and make it more detailed, more contextually responsive, more culturally nuanced, and, lest we forget the point of the exercise, more valuable. Using a term like "multiplier" will help the meaning maker keep new realities front and center. If there is nothing in the product, service, or experience that can be built on, well, then it's back to the drawing board.

"Multipliers" may or may not be the right descriptor for this new relationship, but McCracken asks the right questions about how companies describe the economic and cultural value generated by audience activities, such as the media sharing that is central to the spreadable media paradigm.

Right now, only a few producers fully grasp what is at stake in shifting from an appointment-based to an engagement-based model, and only a few fans are experimenting with alternative ways of claiming the value their activities generate. Television networks have tried and failed (through the Leno experiment) to lower the costs of appointment-based viewing; perhaps they would be better served by developing new ways of appraising engaged viewership.

In our enhanced book, Eleanor Baird Stribling—director of client services and research at online video distribution, promotion, and analytics company TubeMogul—offers a rigorous quantitative model for valuing engagement. Stribling categorizes the "broad spectrum of fan behaviors that contribute economic value" into four categories of activity, two which provide direct economic value—"watching, listening, or attending" and "purchasing primary or secondary products"—and two which provide indirect economic value—"endorsing" and "sharing and recommending." These latter two activities are more difficult to quantify and measure than the first two but "are immensely valuable because of the social elements that help to both retain and recruit audiences," sustaining and proselytizing a media property.

Stribling argues there are two keys to developing a model to effectively transform these varied expressions into measures companies can use. The first is balancing breadth of expression with depth of expression, a balance which Stribling acknowledges may shift for a media property over time as it is sustained by dedicated fans but sees its more casual popularity wax and wane. The second is accounting for the way time affects the value of the expressions: "Too often, we see a statistic such as the number of Facebook fans or Twitter followers of a media property and an assertion that this number represents value. However, these data do not indicate what those fans do once they've friended or followed in order to participate in, promote, or support the media property." To do so, Stribling proposes looking at "the amount of time spent with a media property compared to others," "how frequently fans interact with or around a media property," and "changes in how fans interact with or around a media property over time."

Stribling's model raises questions about how fans' investment can be recognized, quantified, and rewarded in ways fans, producers, and advertisers can *all* recognize. Both McCracken and Stribling propose new terms for discussing these relationships, a language which might have increased the effectiveness of fans of series such as *Jericho* and *Chuck* who wanted their perspectives to be heard within the broadcast industry. In identifying signs of deeper engagement and then proposing ways to engage fans as grassroots intermediaries, Stribling's proposal moves beyond impressions-based counting, even as she recognizes the significance of tracking the number of times a fan touches base with a property.

Certainly, there will still be cases in which companies might see audiences as "dividing" rather than "multiplying" the value of their intellectual property. The interests of fans and producers will not always align. And, perhaps more importantly, the dysfunction of the present system is becoming more and more obvious in our increasingly complex media environment. The ratings industry's focus on passive measures of audience response—and our acceptance of their logic—means that companies undervalue efforts by committed viewers to actively demonstrate the value of their engagement.

Audiences as Commodity and Labor

The title of Dallas Smythe's classic 1981 work "On the Audience Commodity and Its Work" points toward a core contradiction: the audience's attention may be a "commodity" approximated, packaged, and sold in commercial transactions between broadcasters and advertisers, but audiences also "work." Both as a commodity and as labor, audiences produce economic value. Smythe says,

> [Work is] regarded generally as doing something which you would prefer not to do, something unpleasant, alienating, and frustrating. It also is thought of as something linked with a job, a factory, an office, or a store. It is not always this way. At its base, work is something creative, something distinctly human—for the capacity to work is one of the things that distinguishes human beings from other animals. (256)

Smythe is interested in how watching television becomes commodified labor which the ratings company packages as data and which becomes a currency of exchange between advertisers and television networks.

Mark Andrejevic (2009) writes that the traditional broadcasting flow creates a context for advertising in which the desired content is consistent with, and often actively reasserts, a "consumerist" logic; companies are not going to act counter to their ultimate customer, the advertiser. Andrejevic suggests that media producers and advertisers have found new ways to generate value from audience labor—in part by the often covert practices of data mining mentioned in chapter 1. Says Andrejevic,

Users are offered a modicum of control over the product of their creative activity in exchange for the work they do in building up online community and sociality upon privately controlled network infrastructure. As a condition of their "free" acquiescence to engage in this productive exchange, they both construct popular websites and submit to the forms of monitoring and experimentation that are becoming an integral component of the interactive economy. (419)

Such an account suggests that audiences, wittingly or not, create economic value for commercial interests through generating the content around which attention gets collected and commodified and through the valuable information they shed, which can be sold to the highest bidder.

While a consistent business model has not yet been built for online video-sharing platforms, these practices provide media measurement companies a greater chance to directly capture and value audiences as commodity. (Indeed, one of the most compelling arguments that Internet platforms make, in attempting to capture more of the advertising dollars spent by brands, is that they provide actual and detailed rather than approximate audience data.) Andrejevic is right to stress the different ways that Google and other media companies profit from the activities of their users, whether in generating content or shedding data, but his account makes little distinction between audience labor under the logics of Web 2.0 and the far more expansive possibilities that exist in what we are calling participatory culture.

Within an engagement model, this relatively simple construction of the industry's "exploitation" of passive audience labor is no longer adequate for describing the many ways fans and other audiences generate value—not just through the "commodity" value of their own attention but also through their "work" as McCracken's "multipliers," shaping and framing the circulation of material. Smythe's model assumes that watching television is essentially unskilled labor. Yet engaging with television texts in a social context—especially in its more complex and dispersed forms—constitutes skilled labor. Fans and other active audiences develop an expertise in the content and a mastery of distribution technologies which increase their stakes in these media properties. When they interact with media through social networks, they begin to act more as Sennett's crafts guilds (2008), actively pursuing mutual interests. They are deploying both media texts and brand messages as carriers of cultural meaning and as resources for everyday life. Indeed, companies are often profiting from this audience labor, but it's crucial not to paint this wholly as exploitation, denying the many ways audience members benefit from their willing participation in such arrangements.

While accounts such as Smythe's focus on audience labor performed in the private sphere and Andrejevic's account focuses on how the media companies are data mining the individualized activities of a user, networked audience practices increasingly involve many dynamics beyond that which can be easily turned into data. Robert V. Kozinets describes the emergence of "communities of consumption," groups of people with similar interests who "actively seek and exchange information about prices, quality, manufacturers, retailers, company ethics, company history, product history, and other consumer-related characteristics" (1999, 10). Such trends have made interventions such as those of the *Chuck* fans possible. Kozinets argues that commercial transactions are increasingly being appraised and policed by such communities: "Loyal customers are creating their tastes together as a community. This is a revolutionary change. Online, consumers evaluate quality together. They negotiate consumption standards. Moderating product meanings, they brand and rebrand together. [. . .] Organizations of consumers can make successful demands on marketers that individual consumers cannot" (12). The decision about what kind of computer or car to buy may now be shaped by the evolving consensus of a community of potential customers. And, similarly, the decision about what television content to watch and where to watch it is shaped by the emerging norms of social associations as organized around fan communities, religious groups, racial and ethnic communities, political groups, and other interest-driven networks.

For instance, Joshua Green (2008) traces early Hulu users' passionate discussions about the site's terms of service as they sought to barter the value of their attention for greater and more timely access. While the company had conducted varied surveys to measure audience responsiveness to its pricing and delivery schemes, its users hoped to assert their voice to gain greater power and control over what the site offered. Hulu's marketing defined the site in relation to appointment-based broadcast platforms, but many of these users read the platform in comparison with the free but illegal downloads by torrenting. Hulu framed its site as offering expanded service, while these active users saw it as a place to barter their attention to advertisements for ease of use and guaranteed high-quality videos. These highly vocal audience members resemble Kozinets's "communities of consumption," displaying a sophisticated understanding of their status as both commodity and labor.

The Value of Surplus Audiences

In the appointment-based model, it isn't possible to have a surplus of the show's target audience. As long as a show is "producing" the "right" audience, there is an infinite demand for those audience members. Advertisers wouldn't complain, for instance, if every teenage female in the U.S. watched a television show or flocked to a website, if that were the demographic they desired. The cost of advertising during the television lineup would be driven to astronomical amounts, of course, and the incremental advertising budgets often used for online video would be blown through very quickly; yet neither advertiser nor content provider would argue that the content drew "too many" of the desired audience.

However, audience members outside the target demographic are often treated as "surplus." In some cases, these audience members might provide supplementary income through purchasing merchandise related to an entertainment property, but they are often considered irrelevant in an appointment-based model. When these "undesired" segments overwhelm the core demographic, they can even be seen as a nuisance, confusing advertisers about the media property's value for delivering targeted audience groups.

The U.S. daytime serial drama genre has been shaped in recent years by decisions among broadcast networks to focus on target demographics and to write off surplus audiences. "Soap operas" age (with the youngest, CBS's *The Bold and the Beautiful*, having launched in 1987), and so do their audiences. Yet, at present, the industry predominantly brokers advertising deals focused on women 18–49 and especially women 18–34. Meanwhile, television-network decision-makers and analysts increasingly talk about soaps' lackluster numbers for the target demographic, and the continued viewership of women over 49 (and men) is sometimes negatively referred to as another sign that these shows no longer primarily appeal to young adult women.

The transgenerational nature of these soap operas' stories, casts, and fan communities could be considered a drawback when looking at the audience solely in terms of impressions to sell. However, understood as part of a larger social network, these surplus audiences look different. Active viewers over the age of 49 are often veteran fans who perform important work in the offline and online fan communities around these shows. Fans who have watched a particular soap opera for decades are elders in the dual sense of the meaning, not just older viewers but also authorities in the fan community. As C. Lee Harrington and Denise Bielby describe, the process of becoming an involved viewer of soap opera texts takes time and a lot of patience (1995, 87–88). Veteran fans often help neophytes understand the relationships among all the characters; the entirety of the narrative's history cannot ever be completely learned and understood by any one person.

Many actors, writers, and executives in the soap opera industry have long realized and appreciated the key role these veteran fans play, yet economic pressures have pushed the emphasis away from satisfying these crucial fans. The need to appeal to a younger demographic has justified downplaying program history or dumping more expensive veteran actors to put greater emphasis on newer and younger stars.

With low production values compared to prime-time shows, complicated relationships among large ensembles of characters, and a dialogue-heavy format with a multi-hour weekly viewing commitment, these shows are a major gamble for new viewers if they have no history with the characters and no social structure in place which encourages continued viewing. Charlotte Brunsdon writes, "To millions of fans production values are clearly not the point—or at least not the main point. [. . .] It is partly a ritual pleasure, which offers reassurance in its familiarity and regularity" (1984, 86). To achieve this ritual pleasure, though, the soap opera has to become a familiar part of fans' lives. That is one reason why fan communities, both online and offline, are so important—these communities form social spaces for maintaining fans' engagement even when particular storylines fail to generate immediate audience interest. Often, fans active in online message boards state that they are disillusioned with the show but continue watching as a prerequisite for participation in discussions about the show's mistakes or debates about character continuity and/or motivation. While many people in the soap opera industry bemoan fans' constant complaining, the fan parodies and rants that result may encourage viewers to hold onto the community they have built around the ritual of watching the program.

Soap opera magazine editor and columnist Mary Ann Cooper said of CBS soap opera *As the World Turns* (canceled in 2010), "People remember growing up with *As the World Turns*, watching the show while Grandma was baking cookies or Mom was folding the laundry. Today, when they tune in, they're reminded of those times at home with their loved ones" (quoted in Waldman 2006). Many of the show's most faithful viewers within the target demographic started watching because their mother, grandmother, or older sibling watched the show when they were growing up, and those ongoing conversations with their close friends or family members often remain an important part of their viewing experience.

But soaps have consistently diminished their transgenerational appeal through solely courting their target demographic. Fewer mothers and grandmothers watching means fewer sons and daughters joining the audience. The only way to foster a new generation of soap opera fans might thus be to regain the trust of veteran viewers and to work with them to help construct a sustained social infrastructure around the soap opera, but this requires looking at viewers as part of a larger network rather than as individual impressions, as an engaged audience and not just as eyeballs.

While U.S. soap operas are increasingly leaving the airwaves (with four long-running soaps being canceled by networks from 2008 to 2011 and others continually rumored to be on the chopping block) to be replaced by game shows, talk shows, and "lifestyle programming,"

ABC has sold rights for ongoing original production for two of these "daytime" series: *All My Children* and *One Life to Live*. Prospect Park Productions had plans for launching both series as ongoing online serials, a model built on the belief that dedicated soap opera fans can sustain a show outside of the logics of broadcast television. However, the venture publicly struggled to gain necessary financial backing and announced in November 2011 that it was suspending its plans to launch the two soaps online. The difficulty bringing the soap operas to online distribution demonstrates how uncertain the entertainment industry is with these new models, as well as how existing models, guild arrangements, and the like make it hard to scale projects such as these in ways that are profitable. Nevertheless, Prospect Park's interest in both shows after their ABC cancellation raises questions as to whether traditional television networks are well equipped to be sites where programming focusing on audience engagement rather than audience demographics flourishes or whether such new forms of measurement might better suit cable networks or online ventures.

Transmedia Engagement

Soap operas have staying power because they provide a storytelling universe substantially larger than the show itself, offering almost infinite material for fan discussions and debates—and thus ensuring "spreadable" content across fan networks. Such "immersive story worlds" (Ford, De Kosnik, and Harrington 2011) are defined by large back-stories that cannot be neatly summarized; an ensemble of characters within the current narrative and across its larger history; substantial reliance on program history; a wide variety of creative forces over time; a serialized structure of storytelling; and a sense of permanence and continuity within the fictional universe.

The U.S. networks' logic that soap operas are solely a vehicle for selling young adult females to soap companies has remained relatively static for the past eight decades and remains in place even as these properties are leaving daytime television. Meanwhile, comic book franchises, sports leagues, and other media properties built on immersive story worlds have built business models that identify multiple ways of engaging with a narrative and thus open up multiple revenue streams.

For instance, professional wrestling builds its weekly soap-opera-like serialized television shows around a business model which includes live events, pay-per-view shows, merchandise, DVD sales, original website content, video games, and various other types of storytelling, many of which generate direct revenue from audiences. If someone buys a ticket to a show, it's worth the same to the WWE, whether that person is male or female, 8 or 80. And, in chapter 2, we looked at how the sustained interest of wrestling fans led to a reappraisal of archived video. Such examples are driving the media industries to think more deeply about their material as an ongoing and renewable generator of value (whether it be exchange, symbolic, or sentimental), rather than as merely a one-time commodity. Rather than striving to move audience interest onto the next new release in a system of planned obsolescence, this model seeks to prolong audience engagement with media texts in order to expand touchpoints with the brand. In the process, it also provides the economic base that supports the creation of new kinds of texts which allow audiences to more fully explore favorite fictions and to dig deeper into stories that matter to them.

As Derek Johnson, a media and cultural studies professor at the University of Wisconsin–Madison, suggests in our enhanced book, the idea of extending a fictional franchise across platforms is not new. Yet these practices are taking on new visibility in a networked culture. Transmedia strategies are often discussed as emerging practices. Instead, as Johnson suggests, transmedia represents a reconfiguration of older industry logics (such as licensing and franchising), frequently adopting new platforms and new ideas about audience engagement toward familiar goals. The licensing and coproduction arrangements sustaining transmedia practices have evolved over several decades, and so has audience appreciation of "world building." The challenge is to recognize the new energies motivating transmedia strategies as the media industries move from an appointment model toward an engagement model more suited for a spreadable media landscape without dismissing the lessons that can be learned and the models which may remain useful from decades past.

In addition to this history of franchising and licensing, transmedia storytelling draws on a longstanding push toward heightened serialization. Jennifer Hayward (1997) traces this type of storytelling back to serial fiction published by Charles Dickens and others in the nineteenth century. From the start, serialized entertainment was assumed to demand a committed and engaged reader, one who would track down each new installment and make links between chunks of information dispersed across the unfolding narrative. Hayward cites the response of contemporary critics to Dickens's serialized storytelling, including cautions against spoiling the narrative for other readers, anxieties that Dickens might be making up the stories as he went along, and concerns that the tension and anticipation about forthcoming elements were too prolonged and distracting.

Such longstanding genre traditions of serial fiction seem ideally suited to the current era of engagement television. Writers such as Jason Mittell (2006) and Steven Johnson (2005) have noted the increased complexity of contemporary television storytelling, suggesting that such stories tap into the expanded cognitive capacities of networked audiences. This is especially the case in an era when people can pool knowledge and compare notes online, as occurred around the development of Lostpedia, a large-scale Wikipedia-like online reference site which was built by the audience of *Lost* (Mittell 2009). And, as Ivan Askwith (2009) notes, *Lost*'s producers often found themselves balancing the interests of people watching their series week-by-week and those watching many episodes back-to-back on DVD, suggesting their increased consciousness of alternative modes of viewing. The concerns of Dickens's nineteenth-century critics sound like the concerns of twenty-first-century critics writing about *Lost*.

These complex serialized narratives are now extending beyond the medium of television into webisodes, printed and digital comics, computer games, and alternate-reality experiences, each becoming new sources of revenue and each further fueling audience fascination (at least, that is, when these extensions are of comparable quality and up until that still-unpredictable moment when the market becomes saturated and interest satiated). The industry calls such practices "transmedia entertainment," a term solidified in 2010 with the decision by the Producers Guild of America to recognize "Transmedia Producer" as a standard job title within its labor negotiations (Powell 2010).

Writing about so-called viral media (such as the Susan Boyle video discussed in the introduction) often assumes that what gets passed along in communities amounts to little more than video "snacks"—superficial, short bursts of content which deliver a straight-forward emotional payoff. (See, for instance, Miller 2007.) Such "snacks" can constitute common currency among office workers seeking fresh content to share with their colleagues.[2] In our enhanced book, Ethan Tussey—an assistant professor of communications at Georgia State University—explores how some producers factor in the specifics of those who are accessing media texts while at work as they design content, adopting certain formal characteristics that help fit the material into the work flows and surveillance practices of the modern office. Tussey argues that the workday now constitutes simply another "day part," much like prime time or "drive time," through which brands and producers can target specific demographics.

In contrast to these quick media experiences which involve little investment of the audience's time and energy, transmedia strategies for complex story worlds often draw their popularity among engaged audiences through what Middlebury College media studies professor Jason Mittell has labeled "forensic fandom." In Mittell's essay in our enhanced book, he explains that these shows foster "long-term commitments to be savored and dissected in both online and offline fora." Mittell argues,

> Perhaps we need a different metaphor to describe viewer engagement with narrative complexity. We might think of such programs as *drillable* rather than spreadable. They encourage a mode of forensic fandom that spurs viewers to dig deeper, probing beneath the surface to understand the complexity of a story and its telling. [. . .] Such programs create magnets for engagement, drawing viewers into story worlds and urging them to drill down to discover more.

While Mittell's phrasing indicates an either/or dichotomy between "spreadable" and "drillable" texts, we would suggest that such texts do indeed foster engagement through spreading—in this case, spreading particularly within these communities of "forensic fandom." In other words, while promotional material for the show or fan-created texts about the show might spread in wider circles among casual fans, conversation about, extensions of, and artifacts from "deep within" these drillable texts might circulate within the engaged fan base, as fans compare notes and trade interpretations. Rather than "snacks," transmedia content surrounding these shows could be thought of as "clues" which shed light on core enigmas, as "puzzle pieces" which forensic fans can assemble to reveal a more complex pattern, or as "probes" which spark debate among these dedicated fans.

Each of these uses represents the kind of "cultural activators" that Jenkins described in *Convergence Culture* (2006b), elements which give audiences something to do. The engagement model suggests that having something to do also gives fans something to talk about and encourages them to spread the word to other potential audience members. Mittell's focus on Lostpedia, for example, suggests that a dense text encourages its fans to become foragers for information (Rose 2011), which they then bring back together as they construct online reference sites to guide others' experiences of the much-loved series. These narrative and promotional strategies tap into social dynamics among fans, moving beyond the solitary viewer imagined under older forms of audience measurement. They provide fans with the resources they need to talk about the program, much as daily soap opera episodes fuel constant conversation among viewers.

Yet there are substantial differences between the ways immersive story worlds build engagement from their fans and the ways fans engage with such "drillable" texts. A show such as *Lost* gains much of its complexity because of the layers of meaning packed into a single episode. Forensic fans can watch these shows repeatedly, unpacking new meanings with each viewing and revisiting old episodes once new truths are revealed in order to gain new understandings. The narrative spreads over multiple seasons (*Lost*, for instance, had 121 installments), but these shows' runs are generally small enough that fans can—collectively if not individually—piece together every minute detail.

On the other hand, the complexity of comic book universes, soap opera towns, and the pro wrestling world (and one could add the active following of political news or following of a sports league) comes through a heightened form of accretion, through story worlds based on a much larger universe of characters than a typical "drillable" story, with installments that come more frequently and have much longer durations. For instance, a U.S. soap opera has more episodes in half a year than *Lost* had for its full run, and soap operas often have lasted for decades. Longtime comic book characters have had their stories built over hundreds or even thousands of issues. And World Wrestling Entertainment generates several hours of new programming each week, with no off-season. Many of these texts aren't so often deeply "drillable"; there may not be as many layers of meaning to unpack in a single episode. However, these shows generate complexity through their volume and duration.

As Mittell demonstrates, drillable texts become spreadable through fans' collective intelligence-gathering and meaning-making processes (e.g., Lostpedia). For texts such as soap operas, which are complex through their accretion, fans might engage through interpreting, contextualizing, continuity-testing, and communally piecing together the relevant backstory for a recent episode, in light of the massive amount of text that has come before. In short, both types of stories provide viable models for engaging particularly dedicated audiences, for creating potentially spreadable material, and for taking a transmedia approach to storytelling—even if they build that engagement in quite different ways.

"The Total Engagement Experience"

As the preceding section demonstrates, there are multiple precedents, reasons, and rationales for this push toward a more transmedia approach, not the least of which is the now well-established configurations of concentrated media ownership, which create strong incentives to develop content across platforms. Creative teams in the media industries are transforming this economic imperative into an artistic possibility—asking not only how companies might profit from the flow of material but also how transmedia approaches yield more meaningful entertainment experiences. These first two motives, however, are closely aligned with a third: the desire to increase engagement by recognizing and rewarding the most heavily committed viewers.

From the start, early experiments in transmedia storytelling (from *The Blair Witch Project* and *The Matrix* on film to *Dawson's Creek* on television) were funded through promotional budgets and thus were evaluated based on their success in attracting and motivating audience attention. Transmedia stories use additional segments to develop their fictional worlds, to construct backstory, or to explore alternative points of view, all in the service of enhancing the core narrative—the "mothership"—and ultimately intensifying audience engagement.

In some cases, transmedia content is assumed to be its own profit center, expected to reach a mass audience—or at least a large enough niche audience to recover its production costs. Such producers want to make material more accessible to a larger audience, anticipating that devices such as the iPad will guide audiences across multimedia texts. Others see fans, in effect, as early adopters who will publicize the property across their social circles. Here, the exclusivity and targeted nature of the content is precisely what drives buzz. Others—such as *Ghost Whisperer* co-creator Kim Moses (2009)—describe transmedia works as "gifts" to their dedicated fans, rewarding their investment with highly desired content.

When CBS agreed to air *Ghost Whisperer* (a supernatural-themed series which ran from 2005 until 2010), wife-and-husband team Kim Moses and Ian Sander recognized that they faced an uphill battle in finding the "right" demographic. While the program's star, Jennifer Love Hewitt, had a primarily youthful following, CBS had a reputation for its maturing demographics. Further, the show's Friday-night time slot has proven to be the kiss of death for most series, especially those targeting young people unlikely to spend Friday evenings at home. Very few of the new series introduced in that time slot over the past decade made it into a second season. Moses and Sander's seemingly impossible goal was to get *Ghost Whisperer* to at least 100 episodes so that it could move successfully into syndication.

Moses notes, "In this day and age, it is not enough for a producer to just deliver a television show. I believe you are also responsible for delivering the audience" (2009). To achieve this, she sought to transform *Ghost Whisperer* into "a total engagement experience." She formulated the beginnings of such an approach when she was working on the NBC show *Profiler* from 1996 to 2000, for which she developed a highly trafficked website depicting key series events from the perspective of Jack of All Trades, the serial killer that the series's protagonist tracks over much of its run. Here's how Moses describes this philosophy: "The total engagement experience gives you a bridge experience in between each broadcast; it drives people to the show week after week through these experiences; and it also gets people to sample the show who have never seen the show before. It also generates press buzz and creates new revenue sources" (2009).

Moses and her *Ghost Whisperer* team closely monitored online fan responses, trying to identify program elements that particularly engaged active viewers. For example, a throwaway detail about "the Laughing Man" on one first-season episode became central to their online storytelling strategy, and the character was ultimately reintroduced on the television program for the season's final episode. And, building on audience fascination with the ghost world, they developed a web serial called "The Other Side." The series, while including no cast members or sets from the television show, explored the same issues from a ghost's perspective.

In *Ghost Whisperer: Spirit Guide*, Moses and Sander describe the total package:

> First and foremost, we are storytellers, so everything we do, from "The Other Side" webisodes to the interactive journey in "Payne's Brain," tells a story relative to *Ghost Whisperer*. [. . .] We test assets we've created online, and as they get traction, we team with department heads at the studios and networks and roll them out into various platforms that service our fan base. The aim is to make *Ghost Whisperer* a multidimensional experience which the viewer can interact with in their own way on their own schedule. Go beyond what Melinda Gordon is experiencing in the spirit world on an episode by interacting online with all sorts of viral initiatives we've created. (2008, 146–147)

Some of the extensions they developed had a long shelf life, while other elements were topical, responding to particular episodes. Some expanded the fiction, while others offered behind-the-scenes looks at the production process. Some sought to organize social gatherings of fans, such as screenings on college campuses or online parties, while others sought to tap their audience's creative abilities, such as a contest to get fans to collectively write "The Scariest Story Ever Told." Much of what they did was accomplished on very low budgets, so they would find themselves collaborating with amateur artists, offering them greater visibility for their work.

Moses discusses this process as one of collaboration between the production team and the active fan base to keep the series on the air. This approach, Moses argues, recognizes that the series's most ardent fans want to become an active part of the world depicted on television:

> We had to collect them, bring them in. We had to court them and date them. It was like the Mickey Mouse Club for people who liked ghosts. As we did this, our relationships in the online world started to grow. And the audience started to feel enfranchised, and they started to do things virally for us. [. . .] We really think that this total engagement experience is the silver bullet for diminishing audiences in the 21st Century. (2009)

Moses's "courtship" metaphor is especially helpful here, if we think of "engagement" as the emotional connections between viewers and desired content. Courtship metaphors stress the importance of relationship building rather than "surveilling," "mining," "taking advantage of," or "leveraging" fan engagement—although they can be misleading insofar as they can mask the ways such efforts are also about expanding revenue streams and profiting from those relationships. However, as Moses's philosophy indicates, an engagement model thrives only when entertainment properties help active audiences connect with one another in and around these properties. By the time the series was canceled at the end of its 2010 season, *Ghost Whisperer* episodes had been successfully syndicated on SyFy, WE, and ION.

As transmedia storytellers design their narratives in ways meant to drive cross-platform interest or to feed forensic fandom, other concerns about how engagement is ultimately discussed and defined have arisen as well. In particular, some cultural critics have grown worried that an era of transmedia extensions might mean the decline of any type of storytelling that doesn't lend itself well to a webisode series, co-creation with the audience, or "user-generated content." Writing about the critically acclaimed television series *Friday Night Lights*, Virginia Heffernan muses,

> The fault of *Friday Night Lights* is extrinsic: the program has steadfastly refused to become a franchise. It is not and will never be *Heroes*, *Project Runway*, *The Hills* or *Harry Potter*. It generates no tabloid features, cartoons, trading cards, board games, action figures or vibrating brooms. [. . .] The exquisite episodes are all you get. The show [. . .] ferociously guards its borders, refines its aesthetic, defines a particular reality and insists on authenticity. It shuts fans out. (2008)

Heffernan highlights a danger that many creatives feel as companies seek to engage viewers online: that good storytelling might fall by the wayside amid a promotional blitz of "extensions." Yet, while Heffernan points out how *Friday Night Lights* will never become a franchise, the spreadability of the show's reputation through active fan discussion and gushing word of mouth argues against too narrow a definition of engagement. A show with ratings considered relatively poor throughout its run nevertheless aired for five seasons on NBC—a traditional "broadcast" network—despite never substantially improving its ratings. Its final three seasons were saved by striking a deal for first run on DirecTV, in exchange for the satellite provider bearing some of the costs of the show's production. *Friday Night Lights* might never have created a "total engagement experience," but the spread of fan support of the show across platforms (including online campaigns for rallying NBC) led to a substantial series that can maintain a long shelf life, rather than the truncated run for a poor-performing teen drama that fans initially feared (a fate, for instance, suffered by the acclaimed *Life Unexpected* on the CW Network in 2011).

Valuing "Cult" Audiences

As media producers develop a more nuanced model of transmedia entertainment, they need to become equally nuanced in identifying the various kinds of audience activity that their properties inspire. Accretion texts and shows that generate passionate fan discussion but little in the way of "transmedia extensions" demonstrate that models of engaged viewing must also take into account the many ways audiences actively participate across media platforms without creating user-generated content or following supplementary stories. For instance, recent Nielsen data (Nielsen 2010) suggests that 10 percent or more of all viewers tap into social network sites or otherwise search the web for relevant material during major television events, such as the series finale for *Lost*, broadcasts of the Oscars or the Super Bowl, or the season finales of certain reality series (*Survivor*, *American Idol*). Program-related topics "trend" on Twitter during broadcasts, and a range of shows now encourage real-time tweeting, based on a burgeoning industry logic that these conversations are creating a stronger incentive for audiences to watch the shows "in real time" (even if only to avoid "spoilers"). Similarly, two researchers from HP Labs—Sitaram Asur and Bernardo Huberman (2010)—have monitored conversations about movie openings on Twitter. Twitter attracts many "media fans" most likely to go to movies on opening days. Their conversations reflect their awareness of and interest in a movie release; their Twitter posts in turn amplify that interest as they spread what they know to friends, family, and followers.

Friday Night Lights fans may seek to engage in critical discussion about character motivations, wrestling fans in reinterpreting the long-standing history of two characters feuding with each other leading into the next pay-per-view event, *Lost* fans in deeply penetrating the mysteries of a complex narrative, and *Ghost Whisperer* fans in following and even helping extend the narrative across multiple media platforms. But all these strategies share one crucial factor: behaviors that were once considered "cult" or marginal are becoming how more people engage with television texts.

In a world where audiences now regularly use Twitter, Facebook, blogs, and video-sharing sites to react to mass-media offerings, media producers and marketers increasingly recognize and respect the influence of these grassroots intermediaries. The notion of "cult" historically connoted potentially dangerous enthusiasms and abnormally tight-knit (and unhealthy) social ties. As early as the 1930s, "cult" referred to religious beliefs and practices that broke from mainstream Christianity. By the 1960s, the term had been applied to niche tastes in media and culture. Matt Hills argues that fans of "cult" media position themselves and their preferred properties "against the mainstream" because the property has a limited appeal to a discriminating audience or because it transgresses mainstream tastes and values (2002, 27). However, increasingly, the definition of "cult media" describes certain modes of fan participation. As the Internet has helped to normalize some of those practices, a series such as *Lost* can be read as "cult" in its mode of engagement and "mainstream" in the size of its audience.

The evolution of the World Wrestling Entertainment "on-demand" model (see Chapter 2) embodies a company's decision to listen to cult fans and ultimately to take their behaviors mainstream. The WWE's overall popularity has diminished from its high in the late 1990s and early 2000s, but the franchise survives by taking modes of engagement once considered "cult"—interest in the company's backstage politics, for instance, or access to news and information between television shows—and incorporating them into promotional and production strategies. The most ardent wrestling fans act as intermediaries in promoting wrestling to a more mainstream audience, even as they define themselves against the more casual viewers through their insider discourse.

Transmedia strategies assume that the gradual dispersal of material can sustain these various types of audience conversations, rewarding and building particularly strong ties with a property's most ardent fans while inspiring others to be even more active in seeking and sharing new information. In this environment, events such as the San Diego Comic-Con have become a key starting point for word-of-mouth campaigns around media properties. San Diego's Comic-Con attracts more than 130,000 active fans each year, many of whom have blogs, Twitter accounts, and influential followings on social network sites focusing on popular culture. Thus, makers of television series such as *Heroes* and films such as *Paranormal Activity* (2007), *District 9* (2009), *Kick-Ass* (2010), and *Scott Pilgrim vs. the World* (2010) have described their presentations at Comic-Con as a cornerstone of their promotional efforts—with varying degrees of success.

Comic-Con was at the center of the campaign for HBO's 2008 launch of *True Blood* developed by Campfire, a marketing agency formed, in part, by members of the team that pioneered "dispersed storytelling" with *The Blair Witch Project*. As Michael Monello, executive creative director for the *True Blood* campaign, explained, "The strategy for season one was to begin small, excite core fans, and then build to wider audiences as we got closer to the premiere" (2010). During what the agency described as its "discovery" phase, fan opinion-leaders received personal mailings, including messages in dead languages or vials of fake synthetic blood intended to spark online discussions. Those who cracked the code were able to access hidden websites or secret telephone messages providing new leads. Their interests were fed by videos distributed via YouTube, "documenting" how human society responded to the discovery of vampires in their midst.

Having snagged these early adopters, Campfire extended the approach to advertisements in magazines and newspapers or billboards in major cities, shifting focus toward more casual fans. As it did so, Campfire and the *True Blood* team counted on those who were already engaged with the property to proselytize to their friends and families. The program's characters (and the property's connection to a popular book series) became a focus of the promotion only after Campfire had educated its interested audience about the basic parameters of the fictional world. This phase began with the first public presentation by the series cast and crew—as a standing-room-only panel at San Diego Comic-Con—out of which came another immense wave of online buzz around the soon-to-start series.

From there, Campfire engaged wider audiences through traditional publicity for the show and by packaging some of this content in more easy-to-access packages that ran on HBO's website, video-on-demand platform, and elsewhere. Throughout the process, the fan buzz inspired news coverage, further increasing mainstream awareness. Ultimately, the online videos alone attracted more than 5.9 million viewers, according to Campfire's internal statistics, and 6.5 million people watched the first episode of the new series, high results for a program on a subscription cable channel. As Monello explained,

Without social networks enabling fans to spread the word widely and quickly, our "start small" strategy wouldn't be nearly as viable. Those initial mailings worked because the people who received them had connections with other fans and could tell the stories to each other, and these stories could be discovered by other fans. [. . .] Freed from the need to make everything big and accessible, we can create elements within our stories for different types of fans, sparking passion and driving people to spread the story. [. . .] Hardcore fans act on their passion much faster, so the key is to create experiences that give them a piece of your story to tell. [. . .] Giving these dedicated fans early access to story elements and empowering them to help circulate the story became key to this highly successful launch strategy. (2010)

However, as Comic-Con takes on an important role in launching cult media content, some once-core Comic-Con supporters have seen that event as perhaps going too broad or mainstream. On the other hand, the media industries have had to learn that the interests of Comic-Con attendees, often described as "tastemakers" or "influencers," may not always reflect the interests of a broader public. For example, the high level of enthusiasm at Comic-Con for *Scott Pilgrim vs. The World* led industry analysts to overestimate its box office, resulting in a short-term backlash against cult audiences when the movie failed to draw anticipated ticket sales. The following year, some major studios declined to participate in Comic-Con, guessing that this core audience would turn out opening weekend for superhero blockbusters regardless, whereas the event remained central to the strategies of television producers seeking to break through the clutter of the fall preview television season and to low-budget and independent genre film producers who might not otherwise gain media coverage and fan attention.

Even a few years ago, the industry saw Comic-Con as a means of rewarding its dedicated fans by providing exclusive early access to footage from forthcoming releases while warning them not to share what they saw with others. In more recent years, a push for exclusivity has given rise to a push for publicity, with panelists sharing their Twitter handles, publicists setting up their own hashtags to sustain the discussion, and videos released to blogs—such as Gawker's io9—which target niche audiences more or less simultaneously with the real-time happenings in San Diego. These strategies suggest a growing recognition both that these fans, as grassroots intermediaries, can become effective publicists for their effort and that the act of helping to spread media may increase the participating fans' engagement with the property, allowing them to feel stronger stakes in its potential success.

Thus, for producers or marketers looking to make such active and engaged audiences a central part of their strategy for unveiling a new story, it's important for them to listen to and thoroughly understand the desires and priorities of these most passionate cult audiences, to ensure both that they are seen as respecting those fans' niche interests (not going too broad or mainstream) and that they are not mistaking the desires of this particularly involved segment for those of their overall potential audience.[3]

These struggles to draw on cult media practices and to engage passionate fans while also appealing to mainstream audiences has been especially challenging for U.S. broadcast networks—as the soap opera and *Friday Night Lights* examples demonstrate. In particular, the end of the 2010 television season signaled a shift in the transmedia strategies informing U.S. broadcast television. Series such as *Heroes*, *Lost*, *Ghost Whisperer*, and *24*, which constituted the first wave of such approaches, ended their runs. Attempts to recapture *Lost*'s audience engagement (such as *Flash Forward*, *V*, *The Prisoner*, and *The Event*, among many others) failed to inspire the "forensic fandom" that Mittell describes. Most of these series did not last an entire season, frustrating those fans who were gathering the clues to decipher their mythologies and halting the rollout of transmedia content before it really began. Yet, as these cult media practices faltered, another successful new series, *Glee*, represented an alternative transmedia approach, one more focused on extending performance rather than storytelling across platforms and supporting different forms of audience participation.

Responding to the commercial success of Disney's *High School Musical* franchise (which spun out through live performances, records, and made-for-television movies), *Glee* combines the narrative conventions of the backstage musical with covers of recent hits and popular older songs. The show creates a space where, much like *American Idol* or soap operas, multiple generations of viewers can coalesce. *Glee* can be understood alongside games such as *Guitar Hero* and *Rock Band* as part of the music industry's own experiments in using alternative media venues to promote new artists and to revive interests in classic songs. Both the original and *Glee* versions of songs are made available through iTunes, allowing them to be integrated immediately into the lives of the series's fans, the Gleeks, often in the same week an episode aired. In all, the *Glee* cast now has more *Billboard* "Hot 100 hits" than any other musical group or performer in history (Trust 2011), surpassing Elvis Presley, James Brown, and The Beatles. By focusing on performance rather than narrative, *Glee* disperses "evergreen" elements that can be engaged with at any time and in any order. Further, the *Glee* cast's performance numbers are watched by many viewers who may not have seen the series and thus work to attract fans to the program.[4]

Existing alongside the commercial and authorized releases, however, the Gleeks have also deployed the practices of participatory culture and the affordances of video-sharing platforms to produce and share their own performances. As Alex Leavitt writes in the enhanced version of this book,

> Passionate Gleeks celebrate *Glee* by consuming media, but more so by creating it. Hundreds of YouTube videos feature individuals or groups dancing and lip-syncing to cast recordings or reenacting scenes, subjectively and uniquely interpreting the show. This isn't fan fiction, in which fans put new spins on preestablished narratives; instead, these videos illustrate a type of "redoing," participatory but respectful of the original creation.

Glee's producers have openly embraced such grassroots productions as reflecting the fans' enthusiasm for the series, in part because the series itself focuses on the joy of amateur performance and new takes on familiar cultural material. The contrast between *True Blood*'s and *Glee*'s grassroots campaigns is striking: one involved the careful rolling out of content to reach different tiers of participants; the other relies on the uncoordinated efforts of the audience itself to create and share content with more casual fans.

But Which Fans?

As the preceding sections indicate, there are many competing models for thinking about how audiences relate to the expanded content becoming ever more normal in our transmedia world. Some envision that transmedia storytelling means a story or narrative world that unfolds in installments across media platforms. In these cases, producers are never certain how deeply fans will be able to engage in each touchpoint, so they either have to make this dispersed material of secondary interest or else must eventually catch up those who follow only certain prioritized installments on what they might have missed in ancillary texts. Meanwhile, some producers envision the transmedia space as offering different appeals to different niche audiences: the people playing the games may not be the same people reading the webcomics.

What is clear, though, is that the sheer number of these models indicates that the industry is changing its perceptions of the audience as new models for content creation arise. Certainly, broadcast mentalities persist. The Nielsen ratings remain central to the television industry, even as they are unequipped to value engaged audiences or to understand viewers who fall outside the target demographic. Yet the many innovations highlighted in this chapter show how longstanding models of audience measurement are coming into question and how the television industry is realizing it is losing potential revenue with a lack of accounting for fan engagement.

As social media has facilitated audience behaviors that were once considered niche or fringe to become commonplace and mainstream, innovative producers (such as Kim Moses) and marketers (such as Campfire) have established new relationships with their audiences using practices that were once only considered for the fans of cult media. Transmedia practices, for example, are designed to give viewers something to do and something to talk about in relation to media content. In some cases, their responses are scaffolded so that the activity of the most actively engaged fans (such as the blog posts around *True Blood*, entries on Lostpedia, or the Gleeks' fan-made music videos) increases awareness among more casual viewers. These "grassroots intermediaries" are thus generating value—especially as measured in terms of viewer engagement—through their attempts to spread media content beyond its initial point of distribution.

Yet, as the industry seeks to engage with its audiences in this new way (and seeks to develop new processes for measuring the value of this engagement), new questions arise about the relative value of different media segments. We've suggested already, for instance, that the old logic based solely (or primarily) on targeting a particular age/gender demographic needs to be rethought to reflect the more complex social network that surrounds a popular media property, in a way that better acknowledges the value that engaged audiences bring to a media property.

Unfortunately, this mentality of narrow age/gender targeting has too often found its way into transmedia storytelling as well. Often, the television industry has viewed transmedia narrowly as a means of attracting certain segments of the audience—for example, young geek males who have the disposable time and income to track a complex, unfolding serial and thus might even expect such engagement. This focus on young male audiences reflects a desire to recapture a valuable audience segment that television has lost in recent years to other media but flies in the face of a longer history of serialized fiction, which has tended to associate a narrative structure that crosses installments or that encourages communal response with female and more mature viewers (Fiske 1987). *Ghost Whisperer* and *Glee* are particularly successful cases of media properties attracting a heavily female following through transmedia extensions, and soap operas and dramas such as *Friday Night Lights* draw substantial female audiences through other strategies which encourage online discussion.

The female-centered community which has sustained fan fiction and fan vidding through the years has been among the most vocal critics of a narrowly defined transmedia approach. We've already seen in chapter 1 that these fans have been deeply ambivalent about their relations to industry, frustrated by their marginalization but also not eager to see their longstanding commitment to "gift economy" values co-opted by commercial ventures. Suzanne Scott (2009) argues that transmedia content may appropriate ideas from grassroots cultural production and reroute them to serve other markets, a process she describes as a form of "regifting." The commercial industry now polices fan material, absorbing what is compatible to mainstream tastes, marginalizing the rest. Transmedia extension, Scott argues, often promotes "a narrowly defined and contained version of fandom to a general audience."

While these practices may expand the reach of particular fan cultural practices (such as fan fiction's focus on secondary characters) and reward some fan interests (such as a fascination with backstory), industry choices reflect producers' sense of what kinds of audience members are desired and what kinds of meanings enhance rather than detract from mainstream interest. Scott describes the result as a "digital enclosure," a sanitized, market-friendly version of the much messier space of grassroots fan criticism and cultural production: "Whether or not ancillary content models are being actively deployed as a device to rein in and control fandom, they are serving as a potential gateway to fandom for mainstream audiences, and they are pointedly offering a warped version of fandom's gift economy that equates consumption and canonical mastery with community" (2009). Some of these fan critics draw distinctions between affirmational fandom, which seeks to construct its fantasies within the terms created by the original text, and transformational fandom, which seeks to rewrite the texts to better serve fan interests. Writes obsession_inc,

> In "affirmational" fandom, the source material is re-stated, the author's purpose divined to the community's satisfaction, rules established on how the characters are and how the universe works. [. . .] It's all about nailing down the details. This is the very most awesome type of fandom for the source creator to hang out with, because the creator holds the magic trump card of Because I'm The Only One Who Really Knows, That's Why. [. . .] They're in charge, they're always the last word on their own works, and the terrifying idea of fanworks taking their works away from them and futzing with them is not one that comes up a lot. These are the sanctioned fans. [. . .]

"Transformational" fandom, on the other hand, is all about laying hands upon the source and twisting it to the fans' own purposes, whether that is to fix a disappointing issue (a distinct lack of sex-having between two characters, of course, is a favorite issue to fix) in the source material, or using the source material to illustrate a point, or just to have a whale of a good time. [. . .] There's a central disagreement there about Who Is In Charge that's very difficult to ignore. These are, most definitely, the *non-sanctioned* fans. (2009)

In many cases, as Scott and obsession_inc note, transmedia extensions are courting affirmational fans—perceived within fan circles as most often predominantly young and male. In so doing, the extensions reward historically "masculine" interests (including those of mastering the complexity of program content) while marginalizing historically "feminine" interests (especially those related to exploring the emotional and erotic relations between characters). Julie Levin Russo (2009), for example, has critiqued the *Battlestar Galactica* Video Maker Toolkit, which provided forty short-action and establishing scenes from which fans might construct their own "tributes" to the science fiction series. As Russo notes, the starter kit includes none of the character scenes central to many female fans' experience of the series, and the rule set actively discourages people from grabbing and adding their own shots. The project's goal was to create a legally sanctioned space for fans to play with media texts, although the choices of what to make available showed a consistent bias toward male fans. Similar attempts to encourage male parody films and discourage female vidding had surfaced around the fan filmmaking competition that Atom Films hosted for the *Star Wars* franchise, practices which Henry Jenkins critiqued in *Convergence Culture* (2006b). In both cases, female fans can either step outside the rules or refuse to participate, either way being marginalized.

We all should be vigilant over what gets sacrificed, compromised, or co-opted by media companies as part of this process of mainstreaming the activities and interests of cult audiences. In this context, it matters how media companies understand the value that fans create around their property. It matters whether audiences are seen as commodities or labor, whether companies assume that valuable content can only originate from the commercial sector, and whether all authority rests with sanctioned contributors or whether legal practices of the networks and studios protect space for more transformative uses. And, crucially, it matters what forms of audience creation and creativity ultimately are labeled as "transmedia."

The television industry's gradual evolution from an appointment-based model to an engagement-based one reflects shifts occurring across the media industries, as networked communication makes visible the once invisible work of active audiences in creating value and expanding engagement around media properties. The logic behind purchasing an imagined mass and passive audience is breaking down, and demographic segmentation by age and gender is being questioned. In this environment, marketers will have to find new ways to account for audiences and to value the purchase of advertising space. Any new system must respect the importance of surplus audiences and the role active audience members play as grassroots intermediaries shaping the experience of other audience members.

This chapter has used the television industry in particular as perhaps the media sector where these tensions have played out most dramatically. However, many of the lessons learned thus far in television have implications across the media industries, where the role of increasingly engaged and social audiences and the active and conscious labor those audiences are dedicating to media content for their own purposes is driving change in how media companies and brands engage with their publics.[5] In the process, as concepts such as audience engagement and transmedia storytelling take greater hold, companies must be careful not to define too narrowly who can participate (leaving out potentially crucial surplus audiences) or how to participate (valuing some types of audience engagement while ignoring, disrespecting, or even attempting to litigate the valuable contributions of others). And creators have to consider how these transmedia touchpoints can offer sites for listening rather than promoting. These concepts of audience participation will be the primary focus of our next chapter.

While chapter 3 explored how the concept of "engagement" is helping redefine audience measurement, chapter 4 is focused on how the shifting relations between media producers and their audiences are transforming the concept of meaningful participation. Consider two quotes that represent a larger discourse proclaiming the end of media "consumption" as it's historically been described:

> Every time a new consumer joins this media landscape, a new producer joins as well because the same equipment—phones, computers—lets you consume and produce. It is as if when you bought a book, they threw in the printing press for free. (Shirky 2005)

> The people formerly known as the audience wish to inform media people of our existence, and of a shift in power that goes with the platform shift you've all heard about. Think of passengers on your ship who got a boat of their own. The writing readers. The viewers who picked up a camera. [. . .] Many media people want to cry out in the name of reason herself: *If all would speak who shall be left to listen? Can you at least tell us that?* (Rosen 2006)

The "consumers," the argument goes, are becoming producers.

Not so fast, warn José Van Dijck and David Nieborg (2009). Their essay "Wikinomics and Its Discontents" dissects and critiques recent Web 2.0 manifestos (including, full disclosure, *Convergence Culture: Where Old and New Media Collide* [Jenkins 2006b]) that describe

WHAT CONSTITUTES MEANINGFUL PARTICIPATION?

fundamental shifts in the economic and cultural logics shaping the media landscape. Citing a 2007 Forrester survey of U.S. adults online which found that 52 percent of people online were "inactives" and only 13 percent were "actual creators" of so-called user-generated content, Van Dijck and Nieborg conclude, "The active participation and creation of digital content seems to be much less relevant than the crowds they attract. [...] Mass creativity, by and large, is consumptive behavior by a different name" (861). What, they ask, has changed—if anything—in a world where "the majority of users are in fact those who watch or download content contributed by others" and where this segment of "spectators and inactives" represents the most "appealing demographic to site owners and advertisers" (861)? They find the shift away from "audiences" or "consumers" toward "users" profoundly misleading, since the latter term merges passive ("merely clicking") and active ("blogging and uploading videos") modes of engagement, making it unclear exactly what "use" is.

However, as we detailed in chapter 3, we think audiences do important work beyond what is being narrowly defined as "production" here—that some of these processes marked as "less active" involve substantial labor that potentially provides value according to both commercial and noncommercial logic. Even though we are excited about lowering the barriers of entry to cultural production, we should not assume that audience activities involving greater media production skills are necessarily more valuable and meaningful to other audience members or to cultural producers than are acts of debate or collective interpretation—or that media properties which drive more technical forms of audience creation and participation are somehow more engaging than content that generates discussion and sharing is. As people push DIY media making as the be-all and end-all of participatory culture, they risk reducing other kinds of participation—the evaluation, appraisal, critique, and recirculation of material—to "consumptive behavior by a different name."

Unlike Rosen, we believe that there are still people who are primarily *just* "listening to" and "watching" media produced by others. However, like Yochai Benkler (2006), we argue that even those who are "just" reading, listening, or watching do so differently in a world where they recognize their potential to contribute to broader conversations about that content than in a world where they are locked out of meaningful participation. (More on this later.)

Van Dijck and Nieborg may also underestimate some changes in cultural production by focusing on data that only include adults. A 2007 survey by the Pew Center for the Internet & American Life (Lenhart et al.) found that 64 percent of U.S. teens online had produced media, with 39 percent circulating that content beyond friends and family. Over the past five years, Pew has seen dramatic increases in youth media production (more than 10 percent), suggesting a trend toward increasingly active participation.[1]

Van Dijck and Nieborg are correct, though, that this is not yet—and may never be—a world where every reader is already a writer and every audience already "the people formerly known as." An individual who "productively" responds to one media property, brand, or cause may be a "passive" listener to many others; activity and passivity are not permanent descriptions of any individual. And we respect Matt Hills's warning that, at times, the concept of "cultural producer" has been "pushed to do too much work" in the hopes of "removing the taint of consumption and consumerism" (2002, 30). Throughout this book, then, we want neither to overstate the prevalence of many active audience behaviors nor to discount forms of engagement too often labeled as "passive."

This clash between a view which sees networked communication as fundamentally altering the nature of audienceship ("the people formerly known as the audience") and as changing nothing significant about existing structures ("consumptive behavior by a different name") is one of a series of competing frames (lurking versus legitimate peripheral participation; resistance versus participation; audiences versus publics; participation versus collaboration, hearing versus listening; consumers versus co-creators) which are shaping our understanding of online participation during this transitional moment. These various binaries come from many different disciplines and perspectives, including marketing research, cultural studies, political science, education, anthropology, and digital studies, suggesting a persistent difficulty for defining what constitutes meaningful participation across many different fields. Throughout this chapter, we will struggle between conflicting and perhaps contradictory pulls—between a corporate conception of participation (which includes within it a promise of making companies more responsive to the needs and desires of their "consumers") and a political conception of participation (which focuses on the desire for us all to exercise greater power over the decisions which impact the quality of our everyday lives as citizens). We will not be able to resolve these tensions here—the uneasy relationship between capitalism and expanded communication capacity remains a vexing one which theorists of all stripes are confronting through their work. We are trying to resist any easy mapping of one onto the other, yet they have been deeply intertwined in our everyday ways of talking about the "digital revolution." Both concepts of participation are at stake in the restructuring of the media ecology that has taken place over the past two decades. And both are worth keeping in focus as we examine what changes and what remains the same in a culture in which grassroots practices of circulation are exerting greater impact on the kinds of media content we encounter and the relationships which exist within and between networked publics.

Lurking versus Peripheral Participation

As illustrated by Van Dijck and Nieborg's critiques of Web 2.0, it has become commonplace for skeptics to assert that the most active contributors represent a very small percentage of the user base for any Web 2.0 platform. Most often, within the industry, this insight is represented via a pyramid of participation, which shows how the population of users narrows as you reach activities that demand more time, money, resources, skills, and passion. As an example, consider the way Bradley Horowitz described how Yahoo! modeled audience participation in its Yahoo! Groups service:

> 1% of the user population might start a group (or a thread within a group). 10% of the user population might participate actively, and actually author content whether starting a thread or responding to a thread-in-progress. 100% of the user population benefits from the activities of the above groups (lurkers). [. . .] We don't need to convert 100%

of the audience into "active" participants to have a thriving product that benefits tens of millions of users. In fact, there are many reasons why you wouldn't want to do this. The hurdles that users cross as they transition from lurkers to synthesizers to creators are also filters that can eliminate noise from signal. (2006)

Such models frequently depict media production as the highest form of audience participation, dismissing many people as "inactive" and seeing audience members as having fairly fixed positions so that changes between those positions are seen as significant. One widely spread representation of Horowitz's pyramid went so far as to label the 90 percent who were not actively producing content as "lurkers," suggesting they drew on the community without contributing back. There are multiple alternative models offering more nuanced ways to think about participation (see, for instance, Hayes 2007; Bartle 2003), with the more sophisticated models mapping the ecology of interactions between different participants, rather than constructing the hierarchies implicit in the pyramid structure.

While these models help us visualize a complex process, we already know that users don't adhere permanently to any one of these roles and often behave in different ways within various communities. Game designer Raph Koster notes, with reference to gaming, that "everyone is a creator": "The question is 'of what.' Everyone has a sphere where they feel comfortable exerting agency—maybe it's their work, maybe it's raising their children, maybe it's collecting stamps. Outside of that sphere, most people are creators only within carefully limited circumstances; most people cannot draw, but anyone can color inside lines, or trace" (2006; emphasis in original). Moreover, seeing participation as a model with increasing levels of more intense engagement masks the degree to which all participants work together in an economy operating under some combination of market and nonmarket logic, with various audiences performing tasks that support one another. From this perspective, a "lurker" provides value to people sharing commentary or producing multimedia content by expanding the audience and potentially motivating their work, while critics and curators generate value for those who are creating material and perhaps for one another. Critics provide ideas about which content to value, and curators provide critics with easy access to the texts being examined.

Educators have long studied how members of communities of practice learn from and sustain each other's participation. Their research suggests that people initially learn through "lurking" or observing from the margins, that certain basic activities may represent stepping-stones toward greater engagement, and that key individuals help to motivate others' advancement. Jean Lave and Etienne Wenger describe this process as "legitimate peripheral participation," noting that new-comers will integrate much more quickly if they are able to observe and learn from more skilled participants (1991, 29). In an oft-cited example, they describe how apprentices are often asked to sweep the shop, giving them access to the establishment's ongoing operations and a chance to see others apply their advanced skills across a range of different transactions. Lave and Wenger note, "As a place in which one moves toward more-intensive participation, peripherality is an empowering position. As a place in which one is kept from participating more fully—often legitimately, from the broader perspective of society at large—it is a disempowering position" (36).

This reframing forces us to pay more attention to the "scaffolding" that different communities provide for participation but also asks us to recognize that "lurkers" may choose to "lurk" for many different reasons. As Susan Bryant, Andrea Forte, and Amy Bruckman write in an account of how one learns to be a Wikipedian, "Through peripheral activities, novices become acquainted with the tasks, vocabulary, and organizing principles of the community. Gradually, as newcomers become oldtimers, their participation takes forms that are more and more central to the functioning of the community" (2005, 2). The Wikipedia community has a strong interest in expanding its ranks and recruiting new members, and they proceed at their work in ways that make it easier for people to become more engaged.[2]

We contrast this strong scaffolding with the conditions of production that surround mass media, where an elite few have the skills, knowledge, and motivations required to make meaningful contributions and where most of us remain observers. The processes of more skilled participants are hidden from public view in order to protect the "magic" and "mystique" of professional media making. Yochai Benkler says digital tools "enable anyone, anywhere, to go through his or her practical life, observing the social environment through new eyes—the eyes of someone who could actually interject a thought, a criticism, or a concern into the public debate. Individuals become less passive and thus more engaged observers of social spaces that could potentially become subjects for political conversation" (2006, 11). We believe "lurkers" experience the content of these conversations differently, even if they never actually contribute, because of their awareness of their potential capacity to participate and their recognition of lower barriers to contribution (though we recognize, as we discuss later in this chapter, that participation is not an option equally available to all). And, if that's the case, it points toward fundamental shifts in the audience's position. Many cultures are becoming more participatory (in relative terms) than previous configurations of media power.

A Brief History of Participatory Culture

Current debates about participatory culture emerge from a much longer history of attempts to generate alternative platforms for grassroots communication. Consider the development of the Amateur Press Association in the middle of the nineteenth century, which saw young people hand set, type, and print their own publications about culture, politics, and daily life and mail them through elaborate circuits which resemble what are now labeled "social networks" (Petrik 1992). Consider how this same community was among the first adopters of amateur radio in the early part of the twentieth century (Douglas 1989). Consider the efforts of alternative political communities, such as the African American community's creation of its own press in reaction to mainstream news coverage on issues it cared about or its own movies in response to the 1915 release of *The Birth of a Nation*. Consider the emergence of amateur camera clubs in the nineteenth century or the growth of home movie production in the twentieth century (Zimmerman 1995). And consider how various minority groups have used the concept of "consumer activism" and tactics such as boycotts and buycotts to struggle for greater social and legal equality (Cohen 2003). Participatory culture, in other words, has a history—indeed, multiple histories—much larger than the life span of specific technologies or commercial platforms.

As early as 1932, Bertolt Brecht imagined the transformation of radio from a technology supporting passive mass audiences to a medium of collective participation:

> Radio is one sided when it should be two. It is purely an apparatus for distribution, for mere sharing out. So here is a positive suggestion: change this apparatus over from distribution to communication. The radio would be the finest possible communication apparatus in public life [. . .] if it knew how to receive as well as transmit, how to let the listener speak as well as hear, how to bring him into a relationship instead of isolating him. ([1932] 1986, 53)

In the U.S. radio context, Brecht's vision came its closest to fruition in the first two decades of the twentieth century, when transmitters were as apt to be in the hands of scout troops, church groups, and schools as they were the hands of department stores and other commercial interests (Douglas 1989). "We the People" eventually lost the battle for radio, with ham operators and "pirate" stations on the periphery of most people's experiences with the medium. The public retained some aspects of Brecht's model in the space carved out for community radio among local AM stations and in some public radio endeavors. However, in an era of personalized mp3 players and "curated" satellite radio, the prominence of these public alternatives to mainstream commercial radio continues to diminish. Ham radio operators are viewed today as nostalgic for an outdated technology. Indeed, the only notable remnant of Brecht's call for two-way communication is the longstanding U.S. CB culture, built on the radio communication devices most commonly associated with truck drivers who communicate on the road with one another using pseudonyms or "handles," the avatars of the open road.[3]

Brecht's agenda was revisited by Hans Magnus Enzensberger, who, in 1970, similarly predicted the emergence of a much more participatory media culture, one in which the means of cultural production and circulation will be "in the hands of the masses themselves" ([1970] 2000,

69). From this starting point, Enzensberger seeks to understand why the public has persistently failed to embrace the participatory potentials of communication technologies. Change, he argues, would come about not by altering the technological infrastructure, since the public was not taking advantage of already existing opportunities, but rather through shifting the social and cultural practices around media and overcoming economic and political obstacles to fuller participation. For Enzensberger, the solution was not simply putting production in the hands of isolated individuals but rather promoting new kinds of publics which might adopt "aggressive forms of publicity" which allowed for the meaningful sharing of media content and enabled "mobilization."

As Aaron Delwiche (2012, 16) notes, Enzensberger's essay needs to be understood as part of a much larger conversation about the potentials of participatory culture, new media technologies, and their relationships to democratic citizenship, a theme which runs through many of the key documents of 1970s counterculture. For example, the Port Huron Statement—issued by Students for a Democratic Society several years prior, in 1962—coupled the demand that a citizen should have a say in those "social decisions determining the quality and directions of his life" with the call to "provide media" for citizens' "common participation" in key deliberations (12). Delwiche points out that this counterculture discourse sought to distinguish between the potentials of technologies and the way their previous uses had been shaped by the "technocratic" structures of dominant institutions (12). The hope was that, if the public could expand its access to new channels and processes of communication, they might use them as a tool through which to fight for a more democratic culture. Fred Turner (2008) has shown how these ideas, in turn, exerted a powerful influence over cybercultural developments in the past few decades, highlighting the importance of mapping these earlier ruminations on cultural and political participation to the types of developments this book documents.

Today's era of online communication demonstrates some decisive steps in the directions Brecht and Enzensberger advocated, expanding access to the means of cultural production (through ease-of-access-and-use tools) and to cultural circulation within and across diverse communities. Brecht's conception of a world where listeners become "suppliers" of material for other listeners has been more fully realized in the digital era than radio ever achieved. Podcasting, for example, has returned the radio format—if not the technology—to a more participatory medium, allowing many different groups to produce and circulate radiolike content.[4]

We should acknowledge that, for many of these writers just discussed, changing the structure of media ownership was central to their analysis of what needed to take place before we could achieve a more participatory culture. But these authors also assumed that greater public access to tools for cultural production/circulation and to core information about how society works would simultaneously result from and create shifts in ownership structures. From that perspective, the current moment, when media concentration remains alongside an expansion in the communicative capacities of everyday people, is paradoxical. To understand it, we may need to separate out different kinds of control over channels of communication. We might, for example, distinguish between the kinds of information control exerted by television networks (which tightly program all the content they distribute) and telecommunications companies (which determine who has access to bandwidth and how much priority is given to different uses of the system but holds little editorial oversight, or liability, for the content shared through their technologies). The shift of the dominant means of communication from broadcast to digital may in the process loosen the grip of corporate control over many types of content, resulting in the active circulation of a greater diversity of perspectives. And yet, as these gains are made, struggles will only intensify over questions of access—particularly for net neutrality—making debates about corporate constraints on access to networks, and the uses of them, ever more crucial.

Resistance versus Participation

As suggested by the quotes from Shirky and Rosen at the beginning of this chapter, the gains made in expanding access to media platforms in a digital world are often painted as resistance to mainstream media industries. For instance, industry voices, activists, and bloggers alike have frequently described the rising power of "the blogosphere" as a challenge to journalists and commercial media, speaking of the diminishing authority of "big media" or the threat these free media sources pose to "legacy" institutions and practices. However, just as pundits have made the mistake of prioritizing audience activities on the basis of the level of technological skill involved, many likewise incorrectly read grassroots media creation solely as a force of opposition or revolution against commercial media. Instead, something more complex is occurring.

This focus on "resistance" is consistent with language deployed by writers in the critical and cultural studies traditions since the 1980s. Today, academics are much more likely to talk about politics based on "participation," reflecting a world where more media power rests in the hands of citizens and audience members, even if the mass media holds a privileged voice in the flow of information. Syntax tells us all something key about these two models. We are resistant *to* something: that is, we are organized in opposition *to* a dominant power. We participate *in* something, that is, participation is organized *in and through* social collectivities and connectivities. Corporate thinkers have also embraced a focus on participation, though they often want to see what we are participating in as some kind of "market" (potential or actual) for their goods and services. At the same time, others have used the concept of "participation" to describe the civic behaviors of publics (concepts we'll be covering in greater detail shortly). Both accounts start from the assumption that participants feel a greater investment in the institutions and practices of networked culture: they are less likely to try to overturn something which has given them greater stakes in the outcome.

Within advertising circles, the kinds of participation desired by companies are often discussed in terms of "brand communities." Companies have been interested in the idea that the audiences they court form strong social bonds through common affinity for a brand, because, hopefully, these affective relations mean increased customer loyalty at a time when brand attachments are viewed as less stable than they have been in previous generations. Many marketers frame this concept as indicating corporate ownership over specific groups of people, reading the "community" as largely reactive to the machinations of the brand.

On the other hand, critics worry that such brand communities can become simple vehicles for promoting particular corporate messages, a vehicle solely for granting the company access to and credibility with members' friends and families.

In many cases, though, companies do not "create" brand communities. Rather, they "court" existing communities whose broad interests predispose them toward the kinds of conversations the company seeks to facilitate. In a few cases, perhaps this idea of communities built around a company fits, broadly speaking—enthusiasts for Harley-Davidson, John Deere, and Apple have developed strong ties to these respective companies and their products. However, what usually happens within these "brand communities" is more complicated than that.

First, to read these communities only as reactive enthusiasts for a company obscures potential conflicts these groups may have with the brand. Just as soap opera fans regularly declare ownership of "their show" and are vocal about the direction they think the producers should take, members of "brand communities" are often vocal about customer service issues and critical about business decisions the company makes, feeling that their passionate support of a company's products makes them an active stakeholder in the brand. Brand communities can thus play a policing role. They might enthusiastically support a brand when it serves them, but they are also just as likely to call for changes in corporate behavior or products when they think a company is acting in ways contrary to its customers' interests.

Second, brands may find themselves at the center of a social group if and when they become a symbol for longstanding cultural affiliations. Motorcycle culture predated Harley's "brand community." Apple didn't invent technology enthusiasts, and John Deere didn't create an agrarian society. Rather, these brands generated deep affinity with socially connected audiences inasmuch as they understood a culture that already existed and demonstrated that understanding through the marketing, design, and focus of their products.

Given efforts by companies to forge such active and affective ties with their audiences, critics legitimately fear a blanket celebration of participation, especially if divorced from discussions of what people are participating in and who benefits from their participation. Mark

Andrejevic, for example, argues that "the simple equation of participation with empowerment serves to reinforce the marketing strategies of corporate culture" (2008, 43), while political theorist Jodi Dean talks about "publicity without publics" (2002, 173), suggesting that the expanded communication capacity enjoyed by new media participants does not necessarily result in the kinds of thinking, debating communities envisioned by traditional understandings of the public sphere. While the notion of the "active reader" was associated with the "resistance" model—responding to earlier theories of media manipulation which assumed the passive absorption of ideological messages—the notion of audience "activity" and "sovereignty" has been absorbed into Web 2.0 business models, requiring us to develop a more refined vocabulary for thinking about the reality of power relations between companies and their audiences. (For a consideration of the strategies by which television producers actively solicit audience participation, see Columbia College Chicago television professor Sharon Marie Ross's essay in our enhanced book.)

We agree that companies have sometimes cynically exploited the public's desire to "participate" in ways which serve commercial ends while ceding very little control to those who participate; companies rarely embrace more participatory practices out of purely altruistic motives. Rather, participation functions as a means of increasing audience engagement, along the lines discussed in chapter 3. But audiences are not simply pawns for commercial interests or political elites; their shared identities and collective communication capacity allow them to speak out about their perceived interests.

Many of the communities we are discussing here have histories prior to the current digital communication and have asserted values, politics, identities, and practices that exist outside the digital platforms through which their activities are currently being conducted. Their collective interests involve shaping representations, asserting meanings and values, altering terms of service and conditions of labor, and deploying the platforms toward larger movements for social change. They often are making calculations about the acceptable trade-offs between the value that companies extract from them and the benefits they gain through their use of corporate tools and platforms. Most of these groups would argue that they have gained communication capacity through online networks, even though they are frustrated by some of the more exploitative aspects of their engagement with these companies. Often, they are publics and not simply audiences.

Audiences versus Publics

In Daniel Dayan's usage, *audiences* are produced through acts of measurement and surveillance, usually unaware of how the traces they leave can be calibrated by the media industries. Meanwhile, *publics* often actively direct attention onto messages they value: "A public not only offers attention, it calls for attention" (Dayan 2005, 52). Publics, Sonia Livingstone tells us, are "held to be collectivities, more than the sum of their parts, while audiences by contrast are merely aggregates of individuals" (2005, 25). Dayan arrives at a very similar conclusion: "A public is not simply a spectator in plural, a sum of spectators, an addition. It is a coherent entity whose nature is collective; an ensemble characterized by shared sociability, shared identity and some sense of that identity" (2005, 46).

Deploying these terms, we might usefully distinguish—as others have—between "fans," understood as individuals who have a passionate relationship to a particular media franchise, and "fandoms," whose members consciously identify as part of a larger community to which they feel some degree of commitment and loyalty. Individual fans can be thought of as parts of audiences, while fandoms start to demonstrate some traits of publics, bound together through their "shared sociality" and "shared identity." Fandoms seek to direct the attention of the media industries and, in the process, shape their decisions—a goal they pursue with varying degrees of success.

Fandoms are one type of collectivity (in that they are acting as communities rather than as individuals) and connectivity (in that their power is amplified through their access to networked communications) whose presence is being felt in contemporary culture. Members of minority or subcultural communities, various kinds of activist and DIY groups, and different affinity groups are also linked through shared "sociality" and "identity" and are also seeking to "direct attention" through their actions online. Much of the rest of this chapter will be spent exploring different models that account for these developing forms of social experience and the kinds of collective power they exert over their communication environment.

Thinking about audiences as publics may give us a new lens through which to understand media fandom. Take, as an example, soap opera fans. While some viewers watch in isolation, the daily broadcast of soaps, with no off-season, facilitates rituals of sharing and debate among family and friends during or after episodes. Such "gossip" (Brown 1990) has become a vibrant source of audience participation in a genre whose plots often focus on town "gossip." Soap fans have long used new technologies to expand the scope of these processes—they have pushed from personal conversations to organized letter-writing campaigns, from the organization of fan clubs to the development of a fan press, from online discussion boards to increasing use of blogs and podcasts (Ford 2008a). The rise of digital platforms has only amplified and widened the scope of the activities of this already socially networked and participatory audience. Further, online forums and digital production practices (such as uploading and remixing program content) have become popular among soap fans chiefly when they facilitate the primary "work" of soap audiences: debating, critiquing, and so on (Webb 2011). Thus, one could argue, fan "production" remains a supplementary activity to what soap opera audiences have been doing since the 1930s. (For more on the historical relations between soap fans, producers, and texts, see Miami University sociology professor C. Lee Harrington's essay in our enhanced book.)

In this environment, the soap text acts as a resource for audiences to build relationships, often engaging in critical debates that move beyond situations on the show to people's personal lives or else larger moral, political, religious, or civic issues—especially as soap operas have tackled "social issues." In summer 2006, for instance, *As the World Turns* featured a storyline about the coming out of teenager Luke Snyder, focusing for the next several years on the reactions of Luke's family and his attempts to manage life in the midwestern U.S. as a gay young adult. In the process, the story generated a variety of active debates among fans. Some gay male soap opera fans began discussing the coming-out storyline in gay chat forums, introducing a new community of viewers to *As the World Turns* (a "surplus audience"). Many used the show to mediate issues of the contemporary gay male identity in the U.S. and media representation of gay characters. Eventually, as Roger Newcomb (2011) discusses, many gay fans protested the story's trajectory, particularly upset at a lack of physical intimacy shown on-screen between Luke and his boyfriend because of what they perceived as network/producer concerns about potential reactions from socially conservative audiences. The fan pressure led to an increase in the couple's on-screen kissing, but the degree to which Luke was allowed to show affection and intimacy remained a focus until the show's 2010 cancellation.

Meanwhile, as longtime *As the World Turns* fans discussed the story in online soap opera forums, conversations delved into viewers' own perspectives and questions about homosexuality. On Michael Gill's Media Domain, for instance, discussion shifted from Luke's coming out to questions about whether sexual preference was genetically or environmentally determined. The question led to detailed and passionate personal responses. Posters shared stories of gay friends who had been molested as children and who had themselves wondered if the event helped shape their sexual identity; gay siblings who said they knew they were gay from an early age or who were raised in otherwise heterosexual families; and an aunt who had experimented with homosexuality but ultimately settled into a long-term heterosexual relationship. An openly gay fan shared her personal stories and views. Another board regular gathered and shared research from a variety of medical sources. While the discussion linked back to the text as the thread moved along, the storyline acted as a catalyst for a fan community with diverse social and political views to discuss issues of great social importance in (largely) civil ways, in part because these fans had developed longstanding social relationships. Such discussions illustrate how fan communities often take on several key aspects of publics, complicating any model that would paint these fans as passive audiences. Instead, a media text becomes material that drives active community discussion and debate at the intersection between popular culture and civic discourse—conversations that might lead to community activism or social change.

Some activist groups seek to transform audiences into networked publics with which they might work in promoting their causes. One such group is Brave New Films, a media production company established by progressive documentary producer Robert Greenwall (*Outfoxed: Rupert Murdoch's War on Journalism*; *Iraq for Sale*; *Wal-Mart: The High Cost of Low Price*). Greenwall was an early adopter of Netflix as an alternative distributor of his content, thus using the commercial service as a low-cost way for his supporters to host house parties "in churches, schools, bowling allies, pizza parties, wherever there was a screen" (Greenwall 2010). Greenwall asked fans not simply to show his films but also to discuss them—inserting the videos into ongoing conversations within communities and tapping social network sites/tools (especially Meetup. com) to rally audiences. In some cases, he linked multiple house parties together with live webcasts where the producer answered questions.

A longtime television producer now running a nonprofit organization, Greenwall was more invested in getting the word out than in capturing revenue, though he uses the web to attract donations to help support future productions. Speaking about *Outfoxed*, his critique of Fox News, Greenwall told the *Boston Globe*, "You have my permission to give it away. This film is meant to be a tool, so you will take it and do with it what you will" (Gorman 2003). Greenwall found audiences who share his cause, many of whom have an active distrust and disdain for commercial interests. Brave New Films constructs itself as a grassroots alternative to concentrated media.

Increasingly, Greenwall's team shares its videos through social network sites such as Facebook, encouraging "friends" to remix and circulate the content. During one of Brave New Films' campaigns, the staff pushed their members to see if they could grow their Facebook community, looking to ensure the Facebook page for *Rethink Afghanistan* had more "fans" than the Department of Defense's own community site. In the process, the company encouraged participants to think of themselves as part of a networked public that could spread the word to its dispersed members. The group has also developed Cuéntame, a Facebook page focused on Latin issues. Here, the Brave New Films team courts interest both through campaigns focused on explicitly political concerns (such as the Tea Party movement's clashes with the NAACP or the protests surrounding Arizona's immigration law) and more cultural interests (linking their progressive platform to discussions about pop stars or the World Cup).

As Chuck Tyron (2009) notes, Brave New Films has long used the flexibility that digital distribution offers to continuously update its documentaries. Frustrated when a film focusing on Tom Delay's ethics was rendered moot after the congressional leader was forced to resign, the team now rolls out feature-length documentaries in ten-minute chunks via the web, capitalizing on their immediacy and topicality before incorporating them into longer works.

Greenwall's approach is consistent with what Jessica Clark (2009) has described as "public media 2.0." Rejecting a paternalistic notion of "public service media" in favor of one where "public media" refers to media that mobilizes and facilitates publics, Clark argues that giving publics greater control over the circulation of media may deepen their investment:

> Rather than passively waiting for content to be delivered as in the broadcast days, users are actively seeking out and comparing media on important issues, through search engines, recommendations, video on demand, interactive program guides, news feeds, and niche sites. This is placing pressure on many makers to convert their content so that it's not only accessible across an array of platforms and devices, but properly formatted and tagged so that it is more likely to be discovered.

In similar fashion to our spreadability model, Clark describes how such works offer resources to sustain public conversations, how audience members intensify their involvement through acts of curation and circulation, and how spreading the word may help prepare them to take action around the issues being discussed. Since the public can only engage with content if they can find it among the plethora of available options, it's becoming increasingly important to use such texts as calls to action to gather such publics or else to develop material which can sustain or engage existing communities.

While Greenwall's group has welcomed people making video responses to, and remixes of, his films, "participation" is not just limited to media creation. The acts of curation, conversation, and circulation that help spread his progressive messages are understood as part of the political process. Undeniably a public, Greenwall's supporters also demonstrate many behaviors and attitudes often associated with fan communities, including the desire to connect with the producer to gain early access to eagerly anticipated material.

The complexities of these relationships might be suggested by the experience of fan activist group Racebending (Lopez 2011). The group consisted initially of the most passionate fans of the Nickelodeon animated series *Avatar: The Last Airbender*, a program noted for its multinational and multiracial cast of characters. Though they come from imaginary ethnicities, the iconography of the program associates the fictional civilizations represented on the program with various East Asian and Inuit cultures. This imagined multiculturalism was central to fans' engagement. When fans heard that a proposed live-action feature film version would cast all white actors in the core roles—a rumor later confirmed by casting calls seen as explicitly preferring Caucasian performers—they rallied against what they saw as a betrayal of the values they associated with the original property. They drew on a variety of the approaches fan communities have taken to put pressure on the film's writer, director, and producer, M. Night Shamalyan—himself Indian American. Fans joined forces with other activist groups dedicated to tackling Hollywood's discrimination and challenging screen representations of people of color, such as the theater group East West Players and the media advocacy group Media Action Network for Asian Americans. Lori Kido Lopez notes, "Some of the organization's strongest and most effective tactics rely on the skills developed as members of the fan community: honing their arguments through community discussions, producing and editing multimedia creations, educating themselves about every facet of their issue, and relying on their trusted networks to provide a database of information" (2011, 432).

This story looks different if interpreted in terms of audience resistance to the feature film or fans' loyalty to the original animated series. Here, the franchise's most ardent supporters are also its harshest critics. While the producers of the original animated series did not publicly challenge Paramount's decisions, the fans felt strongly that their grassroots activities were protecting the integrity of the original vision, even as they called for a boycott. Racebending members spoke as fans and endorsed some commercially produced content; they generated their own videos, often through remixing commercial texts; they sought to reverse unwelcome producer decisions; and they organized a boycott. Each of these behaviors implies a somewhat different relationship between this active audience and (some of) the producers, as both aggressively pursued their own converging and diverging interests.

While the film producers have sought to dismiss the impact of the protest on their casting decisions, the fans were successful in reshaping the discursive context of the film's release, forcing the producers to repeatedly respond to questions and challenges about their racial politics and ensuring that the erasure of ethnic difference was anything but invisible. When the same group of fans raised awareness of a similar whitewashing of an Asian American character in a proposed film adaptation of the *Runaways* comics series, Disney and Marvel moved quickly to reverse their casting call and reassure the group that the casting would be race appropriate. The group's investments as fans have given them a powerful position from which to challenge corporate interests.

Participation versus Collaboration

Drawing on popular representations of characters seeking to negotiate a space for themselves between occupying regimes and resistance movements, Derek Johnson has suggested a move away from metaphors of "warfare" or "resistance" and toward "collaboration," a more morally complex relationship in which collaborators may "have taken up subject positions within an oppressive power structure, seeing it as the best means of serving their individual interests" and ultimately of creating new opportunities and tools "for others to challenge the rules of an occupied social order" (2010).

Johnson's notion of "collaboration" may be less comfortable to corporate and public interests alike, because it calls attention to the messy, uncertain, and contradictory relationships between the two. Participating within a fan or brand community may or may not be a way of influencing the culture and may or may not be a way of intensifying audience engagement with the property or brand. Collaborators are complicit with the dominant regimes of power, yet they often also use their incorporation into that system to redirect its energies or reroute its resources. At the same time, companies often have to tolerate behaviors that may have once been seen as resistant or transgressive if they want to court the participation of these networked communities.

Mary L. Gray, in her work on queer youth living in the rural U.S., proposes the concept of "boundary publics"—"iterative, ephemeral experiences of belonging that circulate across the outskirts and through the center(s) of a more recognized and validated public sphere" (2009, 92–93). Gray explains that such groups may form anywhere people temporarily occupy a space owned and operated by others to engage in serious conversations for their own purposes. Gray discusses, for example, queer youths in a small Kentucky town who gathered in the aisles of Walmart in the wee hours of the morning—cross-dressing, flirting, and engaging in other social behaviors prohibited in other public spaces within that community. As she describes it, the store became a site of struggle when the youth confronted gay bashers, and participants were forced to decide whether to defend or abandon their turf.

The use of commercial spaces for political gathering is not historically unique. Classically, the Habermasian (1962) conception of the public sphere emphasized the independence of such spaces from both government and corporate interests. As Nancy Fraser reminds us, Jürgen Habermas argued that the public sphere "is not an arena of market relations but rather one of discursive relations, a theater for debating and deliberating rather than for buying and selling" (1990, 57). Yet, as Tom Standage documents, the coffeehouses that Habermas used to illustrate his conception of the public sphere were, after all, commercial establishments, often organized around themes or topics which allowed them to bring together desired publics who might wish to use them as their base of operations (2006, 151–165). The proprietors supplied meeting spaces and resources (pamphlets, magazines, newspapers) to sustain conversations and customers. But, ultimately, the coffeehouses were in the business of selling coffee. The coffeehouses might be considered branded spaces that worked in ways surprisingly similar to the spaces being constructed and sold by Web 2.0 companies.

We certainly want to be attentive, as John Edward Campbell (2009) has advocated, to the way such establishments negotiate between competing (and sometimes conflicting) understandings of participants as customers and as citizens. Campbell points to ways "affinity portals" associated with minority groups, such as PlanetOut or Black-Planet, often have to downplay controversial issues that might make them less hospitable to brands. In many cases, though, these establishments—despite their commercial aims—also function as spaces where participants can step outside of their fixed roles and engage in meaningful conversations, identifying shared interests, mutual desires, and collective identities.

In order to accept this more morally complex account of collaboration, it's crucial to move beyond seeing the relations between producers and their audiences as a zero-sum game. Andrejevic moves us in this direction with his critiques of Henry Jenkins's metaphor of "poaching" (1992) in relation to participants on the fan discussion site Television Without Pity (TWoP). Referring to a passage from Michel de Certeau describing readers as moving across "lands belonging to someone else, [. . .] fields they did not write" (1984, 174), Andrejevic argues,

> The metaphor breaks down in the transition from fields to texts: the consumption of crops is exclusive (or, as economists put it, "rival"), the productive consumption of texts is not. Far from "despoiling" the television texts through their practices, TWoPers enrich them, not just for themselves but for those who economically benefit from the "added value" produced by the labor of viewers. (2008, 42)

As we've suggested throughout this book, the owners of those fields do not always welcome and value such contributions and may see them as a threat to their own creative and economic control over those fields. Nevertheless, Andrejevic is right to argue against a binary opposition between "complicit passivity and subversive participation" (43). He points out that the "workplace" where fans labor may at the same time "be a site of community and personal satisfaction and one of economic exploitation" (43). Indeed, fan labor may be exploited for the profit of the "owners," even as fans also benefit from what they create. Such is the nature of collaboration in the belly of the media beast.

We all should approach these emerging structures and practices with healthy skepticism, weighing carefully different bids for our participation. The rapid expansion of participatory culture is an ongoing challenge: communities grow faster than their capacity to socialize their norms and expectations, and this accelerated scale makes it hard to maintain the intimacy and coherence of earlier forms of participatory culture. Members are tempted on all sides to embrace practices which don't necessarily align with their own interests; and, yes, participation often involves some degree of imbrication into commercial logics. But, likewise, networked participation also forces media companies and brands to be more responsive to their audiences. Networked communities can "call out" companies they collectively perceive as acting counter to the community's interests, and their access to tools of mobilization and publicity means they can inflict some real damage.

Hearing versus Listening

Much of the rhetoric around Web 2.0 seeks to conflate the active practices of collaboration and public deliberation with the more passive role of traditional audiences. Tim O'Reilly demonstrates this tendency in his 2005 essay "What Is Web 2.0?" and his 2009 essay, with John Battelle, "Web Squared: Web 2.0 Five Years On." Both pieces discuss the need for an "architecture of participation," which O'Reilly (2005) initially characterizes as "a built-in ethic of cooperation" in which the company acts as "an intelligent broker, connecting the edges to each other and harnessing the power of the users themselves." O'Reilly obscures some important differences between aggregation and deliberation, evading the core issue of whether Web 2.0 companies value participation because of the content consciously submitted or because of the data unknowingly shed.

While still using the concepts interchangeably, O'Reilly and Battelle's 2009 report shows far less interest in collective deliberation than in the aggregation of user data: the "managing, understanding, and responding to massive amounts of user-generated data in real time.

[. . .] Our phones and cameras are being turned into eyes and ears for applications; motion and location sensors tell where we are, what we're looking at, and how fast we're moving. Data is being collected, presented, and acted upon in real time. The scale of participation has increased by orders of magnitude." If there is intelligence that emerges from this system, it is machine intelligence and not the social intelligence of participants. Much as the media industries have long sought ways to "passively" measure audience engagement, fearing the "subjectivity" which occurs when audiences become co-creators of audience data, the Web 2.0 paradigm—for all of its empowering rhetoric—increasingly rests on the passive collection of user preferences.

O'Reilly and Battelle are celebrating what Mark Andrejevic (2007) has critiqued as a new culture of surveillance which transforms users into data sets rather than engaging with them as complex cultural beings. Valuing participants solely as data returns audiences to a state of imagined "passivity" rather than acknowledging them as publics, with the capacity to reshape the companies with which they interact. At the heart of our spreadable media model is the idea that audience members are more than data, that their collective discussions and deliberations—and their active involvement in appraising and circulating content—are generative.

While O'Reilly and Battelle minimize the social and qualitative nature of deliberative models, corporate communicators and advertisers are similarly plagued by a focus on "return on investment" that relies on broadcast-era models of measurement. The types of astroturfing described in chapter 1 prioritize easily quantifiable measures (e.g., numbers of views, numbers of followers, numbers of fans) over more qualitative measures of audience engagement and participation. Further, as brands seek to "track" what their audiences say about them, these monitoring programs often lean disproportionately toward aggregation, perpetuating Andrejevic's culture of surveillance that too often views audience members as little more than data points.

This reliance on quantitative measures leads to marketing strategies that define success by what's easiest to count (echoing the limitations of the stickiness model discussed in the introduction and the challenges of measurement facing the television industry detailed in chapter 3).

Measurement is especially important not just for determining *whether* an initiative was successful but in defining *what* constitutes success. Ilya Vedrashko—head of research and development for advertising agency Hill Holliday—examines in his essay in the enhanced book why the advertising industry has had difficulty incorporating a spreadable media approach into their marketing initiatives. He finds that companies and agencies often venture into participatory spaces to ask their traditional questions of "Who is there?" and "How many of them are there?" rather than soliciting new insights and forming new relationships.

Such approaches not only assign little value to audience engagement; they also can lead companies to design so-called strategies that actually have little strategy at all, to enter online communities or platforms without understanding the context of that community or putting thought into how, or why, audiences might want to interact with the company and its content. Sam Ford writes that such media practices lead to "one social media fad after another" (2010e). Describing the "shiny new object" mentality that companies took toward virtual world Second Life, he writes that the "vast majority had satisfied their goals just by being there and were shocked by the lukewarm response. Unfortunately, the takeaway from Second Life wasn't to question the strategy that took companies there in the first place." Instead, companies have taken the same "gee whiz" approach to Facebook fan pages, mobile applications, and location-based services.

To avoid such fallacies, companies must move from a culture of just "hearing" what audiences are saying to one that prioritizes "listening" to what audiences have to say. On an interpersonal level, we all understand the core difference between "hearing" and "listening." Hearing is the physical act of receiving a message; listening is an active process of waiting for, concentrating on, and responding to a message. Yet, as companies talk about "listening," the term has fallen into the same trap as many otherwise useful words, given the buzzword-driven nature of marketing rhetoric. The marketing/public relations version of listening often refers to little more than quantitative monitoring—the "who is there?" and "how many of them are there?" sorts of questions that Vedrashko refers to. Such quantitative monitoring has likely become the focus because, as is often the case when measuring people (see Ang 1991), it is easiest to do when the people are removed from the process. Quantifying comments and online discussion and semantically filtering them to determine sentiment promises a more consistent measure because the accuracy of gathering data is easier to ascertain and test, the failures of such tools are problems that can conceivably be fixed technologically, and companies can easily hire a platform (a "hearing aid," if you will) to aggregate that data (Ford 2010a).

While companies have spent considerable time perfecting data gathering, on the one hand, and getting corporate messaging out through their "social media touchpoints," on the other, many have not put as much emphasis on connecting what they say with what they hear. In *Chief Culture Officer* (2009), Grant McCracken calls on corporations to become "living" and "breathing" entities. While companies have become adept at exhaling their messaging, they are not so good at inhaling what their audiences are saying about them or the issues they are communicating about. Given how many companies are gasping aggregated audience data, we might imagine them on life support, relying on mechanical devices to inhale outside perspectives, their intakes narrowed to only those messages the company already knows how to suck in (Ford 2010a). From the corporate perspective, the more "listening" can resemble survey results, the better. (Or, if companies want qualitative insights, they turn to focus groups—closed, artificial environments with agendas under company control.) We do not mean to imply that such research has no place. However, we believe that turning the active conversations of communities into aggregated data (and thus turning publics into passive audiences) strips these groups of their agency and rejects their capacity for participation.

Ultimately, listening demands an active response: not just gathering data but doing something about it. Such action might include reaching out in response to what audiences are talking about: thanking them for their enthusiasm, offering support or additional resources, addressing concerns, and correcting misconceptions. In other cases, it might lead, rather, to internal changes: addressing the needs of unexpected surplus audiences, the pleas of lead and retro users, the cultural patterns among the communities the company most wants to reach, or points of contention or misunderstanding that can be addressed through altering communication or business practice.

One of the most daunting reasons companies have concentrated primarily on hearing is that they are not really organized to listen effectively. Media and marketing scholars have long battled to keep audiences from being painted as one passive whole. In that same spirit, we must be careful not to describe organizations as a single, unified entity. Often, the marketing functions of a company have little, if any, connection to IT, legal, or customer service. Each of these divisions reports to a different part of corporate leadership and resides on a different campus; their leaders may only be vague acquaintances.

To the customer, all these touchpoints constitute "one brand." Yet, internally, this fractured communication represents contradictory logics and competing measures of success with little internal alignment or collaboration. For instance, while marketing departments are charged and measured by how many ways they can "engage" the customer—or, at the very least, collect their "impressions" across various platforms—customer service departments are often measured by how quickly they can disengage with the customer, by metrics of efficiency (how many calls can be answered in an hour, for example).

At one time, these internal "silos" (the popular term to describe this problem in the corporate world) could exist separately because customers had fewer opportunities to speak outside the carefully orchestrated mechanisms of feedback a company provided. Today, however, when a brand asks audiences to collaborate in a contest to create "user-generated content" or facilitates the customization and spreading of "official" material, are these activities still within the purview of an advertising division or owned by public relations?

Such questions are more than just semantics. Corporate infrastructure has created rigid disciplinary divides among these various departments, not only in scope of work but—perhaps most importantly—in budget. Who "owns" the customer relationship within a company is ultimately a question of who remains relevant and who keeps their job. And, as corporate communicators throughout an organization adjust to a digital age, the tensions and fault lines between departments shape how brands react to the ethos and practices of what we're calling spreadable media.

Certainly, various divisions of an organization might best be served to provide somewhat different functions in this media environment—advertisers, for instance, might listen to build, sustain, and make more relevant their marketing campaign; public relations professionals to build relationships and make the company responsive to conversations happening beyond the company's marketing; customer service to proactively respond to issues people are having with a company's products or services (Ford 2010b). However, listening to the audience is a goal and activity all these departments might share, one which might provide a central point on which to forge new means of internal communication and collaboration.

Most frustrating of all is that many companies don't truly listen because their leadership doesn't want to. Just as media makers often want to stay within the illusion of a broadcast world, where audiences could more easily be relegated to being passive individuals rather than understood as networked publics, corporate leaders live in a less complicated world when they can simplify how their customers are understood (hence the preference for hearing over listening).

Nevertheless, debates are taking place in every corporate boardroom between prohibitionists who wish to tightly control their intellectual properties and collaborationists who wish to build new relations with their audiences (Jenkins 2006b). As Erica Rand suggests in *Barbie's Queer Accessories* (1995), there are collaborators inside many companies working to liberalize policies, to enable alternative meanings, or otherwise to shift their relationship with their audiences. They may do so not because they want to "liberate" their audiences but rather because they see these concessions to the public as good business logic, or else their personal and professional ethics demand this shift.

For these collaborators, shifting from hearing to listening is important because of the potential benefits that can be achieved through listening and responding to audiences. As an illustration, take this example from the sports gaming community. Fans found that the *Tiger Woods PGA Tour 08* game from EA Sports had a glitch in it wherein a player (playing as the eponymous Tiger Woods) could walk out onto a water hazard and take a shot. Levinator25 was one of those fans, among several, who not only discovered the mistake but uploaded a YouTube video of their performing the shot in the game. When it was time to promote *Tiger Woods PGA Tour 09*, agency Wieden+Kennedy uploaded a 30-second video which begins with handheld footage of a computer showing Levinator25's video, followed by titles that read:

> Levinator25,
> You seem to think your Jesus Shot
> video was a glitch in the game.

The spot then features the "real" Tiger Woods hitting his ball into a water hazard. Woods surveys the ball (which is sitting on a lily pad), removes his shoes and socks, and walks out on top of the water to take his shot. The ad ends with two sentences—"It's not a glitch. He's just that good."—appearing over footage of Woods walking back across the water to the shore.

The ad was posted not as a standalone video but as a "response" on YouTube to Levinator25's upload. Such an approach meant that W+K, EA Sports, and Woods made their commercial part of the community conversation that was already happening, demonstrating that they were paying attention and listening to the community of fans interested in their games. Such processes can lead to opportunities for companies to respond to their audiences in ways the audiences want and need and in ways that fit the conversations audiences are already having, where they are having them, in appropriate ways—if the company really listens to and understands the community to which it is reaching out.

However, listening practices are also crucial because the illusion of the broadcast world has been shattered. Not proactively listening to what customers or other groups are saying about a company's brand means not answering a customer service problem before it becomes a public relations issue or not addressing a concern people have raised with a company's messaging or business practice until it has already damaged the brand's reputation. In other words, listening efforts are important for the company's bottom line not just because they provide a foundation for building positive relationships with audiences but also because they help avoid the types of crises which are becoming increasingly likely when companies ignore what people are saying about them or their products.[5]

For example, beginning in late 2009, Domino's Pizza dumped its traditional marketing in favor of listening to and addressing what people actually said about their pizza: that it wasn't very good. Rather than continue to ignore this reality, Domino's addressed it head-on, announcing publicly that it was committing itself to providing better pizza and asking its customers to help in this endeavor. The company reacted to online conversations about its new pizzas, solicited feedback, and committed to continue addressing issues people still had with Domino's. It asked audiences to document and send in any bad experience they had with the brand and ran a national advertising campaign highlighting what it had done wrong, apologizing, and pledging to fix the problem.

A more participatory media environment focuses not only on better understanding and prioritizing the ways media audiences participate but likewise the activities that media industries and brands must participate in if they want to continue to thrive. In other words, top-down corporate concepts of "alignment" should be replaced by companies who constantly listen to their audiences and who recalibrate their infrastructure to make the company more attuned to address what those audiences want and need.

Everyday Patterns of Co-Creation

If some companies are still learning how to "listen" and respond, networked culture is giving rise to more elaborate (and in some cases, radical) forms of co-creation and "produsage" which further revise our understanding of the relations between companies and audiences. We might consider these practices as collaboration in a different sense—that is, working together to achieve something that the participants could not achieve on their own. In our enhanced book, Ana Domb, director of the Interaction Design Program at Universidad Veritas in Costa Rica, describes the complex forms of participation which have grown up around the Brazilian popular music form Tecnobrega.

Her suggestive case study examines the roles various parties play in sustaining the production and circulation of recorded sound in a context where many dominant ideas about intellectual property have been suspended. As Domb suggests, these various participants—some amateur, some commercial, some occupying the borderlines between the two—form a value network; their activities are mutually sustaining, each contributing to the value of the overall experience.

Within this model, audiences are valued not only as customers within a commercial transaction—as purchasers of recorded music, event tickets, or branded merchandise—but also as active multipliers who contribute symbolic value to the Tecnobrega community. Tecnobrega is a musical subculture organized around thousands of large parties a month, where DJs pilot sophisticated and spectacular sound systems with hydraulic platforms and pyrotechnic effects. Equally crucial to this subculture, however, are the audiences, who organize themselves into "*equipes*, teams of friends that attend the parties and concerts together." As Domb describes it, the *equipes* create value through their promotional activities: circulating music, promoting shows and their favorite acts, creating content (commissioning and composing songs, inventing dances, etc.), and elevating the DJ's status in the community through public displays of fandom. These roles are significant for the success of the Tecnobrega scene at large. While many of these behaviors have been increasingly normalized as the activities of engaged fans, the Tecnobrega context is illuminating because this audience role is embraced as a means of sustaining music production in ways which may not be accounted for in conventional understandings of "audiences" or even "fandoms."

Through examining social network sites, collective ventures such as free and open-source software, and collaborative online spaces such as Wikipedia and Slashdot, Axel Bruns (2008) offers a framework for understanding the different roles audience members play in a networked society. Importantly for our discussion, Bruns argues for a more fluid category of participation that he labels "produsage"—a merging of "production" and "usage," undertaken by "produsers" through collaborative processes of creation and re-creation. Built on technical affordances that encourage iterative approaches to tasks, fluid roles and a lack of hierarchy, shared rather than owned material, and granular approaches to problem solving, network society encourages collaboration on projects by a "hive" community (18–19). This community creates through an "ongoing, perpetually unfinished, iterative, and evolutionary process of gradual development of the informational resources shared by the community" (20).

The blurring of roles that Bruns discusses aptly describes the participation of Tecnobrega's superfans, who act "not simply as passive consumers, but active users, with some of them participating more strongly with a focus only on their own personal use, some of them participating more strongly in ways which are inherently constructive, and productive of social networks and communal content" (2008, 23). Read through Bruns's framework, the activities of Tecnobrega audiences in generating crowd interest, promoting shows, distributing recordings through social network sites, and even begging DJs for recognition at parties, means those fans can be seen as significant creators of the experience they, and other more casual audiences, are enjoying as "the audience." Domb recognizes that the returns Tecnobrega audiences enjoy come as much from members of other *equipes* as from the musicians and the event promoters.

And, given that the actions of effective *equipe* members are rewarded by social status (that is, the more popular your *equipe* is, the higher you are regarded within the community and the greater your celebrity profile), it could be argued Tecnobrega rewards through communal evaluation, as Bruns identifies. These parallels are not altogether unexpected—Bruns notes that practices similar to produsage can be identified in older DIY and enthusiast communities (2008, 390). Tecnobrega is a process, not a product—an ongoing scene, not a singular event. Like other kinds of produsage, the fans' activity is never finished (27–28). One concert ends, and they begin planning for the next.

Practices of liking, recommending, and passing along texts are especially apparent in places that leverage attention, such as You-Tube, where, Bruns argues, "produsage values" have triumphed over "production values" (2008, 255). There, Bruns notes, produsers play curatorial and promotional roles, selecting and promoting content and creating metadata, improving the prospects of the material being found by future users. In doing so, he argues that these "produserly" audiences are more likely to select for salience and resonance, under-mining traditional media producers who have long relied on high production values to distinguish themselves from grassroots and independent media producers. Increasingly, everyone is making media as part of the normal response to reading/listening/viewing rather than out of a desire to be media producers in training.

Such active audience practices are particularly noticeable, for exam-ple, in the popularization of dance crazes. In our enhanced book, Kevin Driscoll—doctoral student at the University of Southern California's Annenberg School for Communication & Journalism—looks at what might be learned from the online video phenomenon of staging dance routines based on Soulja Boy's 2007 "Crank Dat (Soulja Boy)" video. DeAndre Way, a high school student from rural Mississippi recording music as Soulja Boy Tell 'Em, became something of an overnight sen-sation in summer 2007 with his track "Crank Dat (Soulja Boy)." Way's track was one of a number of "snap" tracks posted to music-sharing site Soundclick. As Driscoll explains, snap is a southern hip-hop genre that deviates "the most from the conventional hip-hop template. Snap's minimal drum programming and repetitive lyrics destabilized unques-tioned hip-hop norms such as the value of complex wordplay and the use of funk and soul samples." Way was one of a small number of snap artists posting to Soundclick, each of them reworking a few common elements to create his own version of Crank Dat. Important to snap and the Crank Dat variation is dancing, a feature that distinguishes it from some other genres of hip-hop. Soulja Boy used his blog and social networking profiles to actively encourage fans to perform and build on his performance, to produce and share videos which remixed his song. This approach drove thousands of song downloads and millions of views for his MySpace blog, contributing to his signing a contract with a major record label within three months.

It is tempting to read Soulja Boy's success as the tale of a talented producer crafting a catchy song and designing an easily imitable dance which was then pushed out to the widest possible audience through YouTube. But, as Driscoll notes, the success of Soulja Boy had more to do with the way DeAndre Way engaged audiences to remix and reper-form his content, providing "multiple points of entry," as Driscoll puts it:

For a particular cultural artifact to spread, its expressive potential must be accessible across seemingly disparate audiences. The Cash Camp clique demonstrated, through their idiosyncratic clothes, slang, dancing, and southern accents, multiple points of entry into the "Crank Dat" phenomenon. And Soulja Boy, by debuting his song as the soundtrack to another group's homemade dance video, implicitly invited viewers to create further variations. The audiences that took up this invitation kept only the elements they found relevant. They felt free to create new dance steps, to rework the audio, to alter the video, and to introduce their own symbols of local significance.

Way encouraged audience transformation of his piece, asking people to speak back and say something unique through "Crank Dat." Through this process, Soulja Boy acted as "curator, cheerleader, and embodied symbol for the collective 'Crank Dat' phenomenon," according to Driscoll, encouraging rather than seeking legal action against fans who wanted to build on his own creations. As he explains in the song lyrics, "Y'all can't do it like me / so don't do it like me." At each stage, the performer prompted and rewarded audience participation within a genre which has, as Driscoll points out, strong traditions of appropriation, transformation, performativity, and (local) identity expression.

The versions, interpretations, adaptations, and mash-ups fans created around "Crank Dat" are examples of audience practices that were already widespread on YouTube. Regardless of YouTube's much publicized tagline inviting users to "Broadcast Themselves," communication and dialogue rather than broadcasting and self-branding account for a significant amount of the site's activity. Its architecture allows users to link an uploaded video to an existing one as a "response" and, in the process, to become a direct part of the original video's circulation. Even the most green vloggers acknowledge their viewers by responding to comments in videos, inviting people to write in, and offering shout-outs that acknowledge other users of the service (Burgess and Green 2009; Lange 2009). Jean Burgess argues, "YouTube is in itself a social network site; one in which videos (rather than "friending") are the primary medium of social connection between participants" (2008, 102).

Furthermore, Burgess suggests that certain videos "act as a hub for further creative activity by a wide range of participants" (2008, 102). These videos are mimicked, copied, mashed up, responded to, emulated, and re-created. They may not be, quantitatively, the "most popular" videos, but they may become more deeply embedded in popular memory through their repetition and variation. These are often the videos identified as "memes"—such as Way's "Crank Dat" or Tay Zonday's hugely popular YouTube music video for the song "Chocolate Rain." Discussing the storm of creativity that the latter video inspired, Burgess notes that "Chocolate Rain"—much like "Crank Dat"—featured various ways for audiences to imitate or remix, from the unique baritone vocals to Zonday's idiosyncratic performance and the video's "liner notes"–style subtitles.

Bruns's notion of produsage suggests that those who produce their own video responses retain their roles as audiences, even while they create and publish content. The same can be said of the people who help to spread these videos and who talk up Soulja Boy. YouTube is one space where we can all watch audiences do the work of being an audience member: the labor of making meaning, of connecting media with their lived realities and their personal and interpersonal identities.

YouTube is driven in part by the clip and the quote—the short grab or edited selection from other media texts. Such videos are evidence of audiences engaging with and appraising content, using it as a resource to express their personal identities and shared interests. Many industry leaders, however, view these mundane practices as significant threats. For instance, Brian Grazer, producer of 8 Mile, said of a mash-up of his film and Napoleon Dynamite, "It bothers me artistically. Here's this thing where you have no control; they are chopping it up and putting your memories in a blender" (quoted in Holson 2007). Meanwhile, Medialink Worldwide CEO and president Laurence Moskowitz said of copyright infringement in 2007 that "the genie has to be put back in the bottle, or the entire economics of the entertainment industry on a global basis are subject to ruinous counterfeiting" (quoted in Whitney 2007). Both statements point toward the media industries' conflation of blatant piracy—the reproduction of a work in full for some degree of commercial gain—and a variety of fan activities that comment on, critique, recommend, or make new creative statements using some portion of an existing work.

These are the kinds of practices John Hartley describes as "redaction"—the production of "new material by a process of editing existing content" (2008, 112). While quoting has become an accepted form of the circulation of printed material online (blogs regularly quote from and then link back to one another, for instance), many companies are not yet equipped to embrace the value generated through audiovisual quotes or other forms of transformative work as a means of incorporating their material into larger, ongoing conversations.

In a world where if it doesn't spread, it's dead, if it can't be quoted, it might not mean anything. The social practices of spreadable media necessitate material that is quotable—providing easy ways for audiences to be able to excerpt from that material and to share those excerpts with others—and grabbable—providing the technological functions which make that content easily portable and sharable. The ability to easily embed videos from the site into other online forums has been key to YouTube's success. Such grabbability is often a key factor in how material spreads. For example, Emma F. Webb (2011) has explored how online videos are often used as a reference point or illustration in soap opera fan discussions and critiques. These appropriations are not simply produced by audiences; they are generating audiences through heightening popular awareness of the programs being quoted and, more importantly, sustaining audiences through fueling ongoing conversations.

The Problem of Unequal Participation

The gains made in making the communication environment more participatory for some people have not been the inevitable consequence of the introduction of new digital technologies and networked communications. They emerge from the choices made, and which continue to be made, about how new tools and platforms are deployed. A 2006 study by the Pew Internet & American Life Project (Lenhart et al. 2007) found that people in households that earned $75,000 or more per year were three times more likely to produce and share Internet content than those whose annual household income was less than $30,000. These inequalities keep expanding: as low-income

U.S. residents have gained access to networked computers through schools and public libraries, their wealthier counterparts have gained access to broadband and enjoy unlimited access from their homes (Livingstone and Bober 2005).

Wikipedians talk about "systemic bias," that is, the ways that the content creation in their grassroots project is limited and unbalanced by the demographics of who participates and who doesn't. The issue of systematic bias has long been discussed amongst Wikipedians, but this bias shapes all "Web 2.0" platforms. It matters when more Asian American contributors have risen to the top ranks on YouTube than African Americans or when user-moderated sites lack mechanisms that promote diversity of perspectives. In each of these cases, the affordances of these platforms may seem neutral in their design but not in their effects because technological "fixes" cannot overcome other factors that shape the relative access of different groups to cultural and communicative power. Limited online participation may reflect a lack of disposable time, especially among those who lack digital access in the workplace, just as it reflects a lack of disposable income (Seiter 2008). Thus, this lack of participation might persist when one has technical access but not the skills and cultural knowledge required to fully take part. Further, those who do not know anyone who uses the Internet to engage in participatory culture practices may lack meaningful role models to inspire their own use of the technologies and platforms.[6]

Changes in these inequalities are unlikely to come from corporations focusing on "underserved markets," an approach which presumes that the primary drivers of the new media landscape are economic and that we should be courted as customers first rather than as community members. Nor will it come from public service projects designed to ensure access to technologies but not training for the skills required to meaningfully participate. Obtaining Internet access for public schools and libraries in the United States was touted as helping to close the "digital divide" during the presidency of Bill Clinton, but governmental policy at all levels has sought to significantly limit access to social network sites and video-sharing platforms or to impose mandatory filters on web content rather than developing skills for negotiating these spaces.

Many of the most powerful efforts to broaden participation have instead come from communities working together to overcome constraints on their communication capacities. Sasha Costanza-Chock (2010), for instance, has described the emergence of new media strategies and tactics among Latin groups in Southern California as "transmedia mobilization," a strategy which taps into any and all available media platforms to spread its message. Historically, these immigrant rights activists have courted coverage through Anglo mass media with limited success: their message was often marginalized or distorted. The rise of ethnic broadcast media in California, especially Spanish-language radio and television, has granted these immigrant rights groups broader but still centralized access to the channels of communication.

While the Locutores—the hosts of Spanish-language talk-radio programs—still play the greatest role in mobilizing immigrant rights supporters to participate in protest marches, Costanza-Chock notes a growing deployment of social media and participatory practices, especially among younger activists but spreading across the movement as activists have come to recognize the ways that such digital practices can lower costs and expand their reach. As he explains, "Transmedia mobilization thus marks a transition in the role of movement communicators from content creation to aggregation, curation, remix and circulation of rich media texts through networked movement formations" (2010).

Transmedia mobilization takes advantage of the community's latent communications capabilities. Costanza-Chock describes how immigrants in Los Angeles had been early adopters of video cameras, collectively recording major community events—such as festivals, weddings, funerals, and concerts—and mailing the tapes back to their hometowns as a way of sustaining family and community ties across geographic distances. More recently, the use of video-sharing sites online has supplemented the physical shipping of tapes. These same practices get deployed when immigrant rights activists record and upload footage of protests or talks by community leaders about their struggles. (Many of these digital skills are then passed informally between friends and co-workers, while young people who have acquired new media literacies through schools end up teaching their parents and grandparents.)

As the value of transmedia mobilization has become clearer, many traditional activist and labor groups in the U.S. have begun providing training in new media skills to their memberships, often in the service of producing media that may spread their messages into other segments of the community. For example, Costanza-Chock documents a project called Radio Tijeras which trained garment workers in audio production practices (2010, 174). Participants created newscasts, recorded poems, generated public service announcements, and captured oral history. They mixed their own productions with popular music in creating *discos volantes* (CD audio magazines) to be distributed inside downtown Los Angeles garment sweatshops. More generally, participation in the production and circulation of movement messages strengthens ties and heightens engagement within the cause, allowing participants a greater sense of ownership over what was produced and a greater sense of involvement in the outcome.

The message may spread through Facebook pages and Twitter postings, talk radio and audio magazines, street art and oratory. Often, the same content gets repurposed or remixed as it travels across platforms. Hybrid systems of communication, especially those between higher- and lower-tech media, bridge literacy gaps in immigrant communities. To cite a historical example, Jewish immigrants working in sweatshops in New York at the turn of the twentieth century would hire someone to read books, newspapers, and magazines aloud to them while they worked (Howe and Libo 1983). Turning to a more recent example, bloggers in Beirut during the 2006 Lebanon War created compelling drawings and graphics which could be printed out and posted by digitally connected supporters in Lebanese immigrant communities around the world, thus conveying their message to people who might lack both digital access and media literacy skills required to follow the blogs themselves (Jenkins 2006a).

There is a strong tradition in policy literature about the developing world of talking about "appropriate technologies"—that is, technologies which accommodate the skills and needs of local populations, are sustainable, respect their environments, and take full advantage of the affordances of often limited technical infrastructures and resources. Many times, these practices straddle media, often bridging between diverse populations while ensuring the communication of core messages. Such practices frequently involve the interplay between low- and high-tech cultures, such as that which John Fiske (1994) describes in his work on the ways pirate radio functioned in the African American and immigrant communities of Los Angeles in the wake of the 1992 L.A. riots. In that instance, participants used grassroots media to contest dominant media framings of the uprisings and to question police authority, in the process often reading aloud and debating printed accounts which might not have been accessible to the entire community. Costanza-Chock's more recent account of immigrant rights activism suggests that a similarly hybrid system of communication continues to function within Los Angeles, challenging and supplementing mass-media representations through more locally constructed and participatory forms of messaging.

Yet it is telling that Costanza-Chock, in his study, describes many of these communication practices as remaining within the Latin immigrant community. Participants in the immigrant rights movement, he argues, believe that they have little chance of reaching Anglo audiences or that they will find little support there, given the demagogic anti-immigrant rhetoric which runs through some English-language television and talk-radio programs. While these groups sometimes use social media to find common cause with other immigrant populations who are engaged in similar struggles, they frequently receive little or no response from mainstream media that could help them reach and persuade Anglo audiences about the justness of their cause. Thus, we find in the immigrant rights movement a rich example of how media texts spread (across generations, across platforms, across national borders) and when and why they do not (across ideological and class divides, across language barriers, and especially across the closed minds of many people outside the movement).

Meanwhile, other researchers have found that online social networks can be as much if not more segregated than social networks in the physical world. As danah boyd (2011) and S. Craig Watkins (2010) have documented, Facebook and other social network sites often operate as the digital equivalent of gated communities, protecting participants from online contact with people outside their social circle as much as enabling easier and quicker communications with their friends and families. Both boyd and Watkins argue that people choose between Facebook and MySpace based on their economic aspirations and educational status, often using language heavily coded in class and racial terms to describe what they dislike about the other platform. Watkins compares this process to the "big sort," which has reintroduced segregation in many U.S. cities through residential patterns.

How seriously we take these inequalities of access and opportunity depends very much on what we see as the value of participation. If, like some skeptics, we see participatory culture as "consumptive behavior by a different name," then we should, as a former Federal Communications Commissioner suggested, see the digital divide as no more consequential than the gap in who owns fancy cars. If we see participatory culture, though, as a vital step toward the realization of a century-long struggle for grassroots communities to gain greater control over the means of cultural production and circulation—if we see participation as the work of publics and not simply of markets and audiences—then opportunities to expand participation are struggles we must actively embrace through our work, whether through efforts to lower economic and technical obstacles or to expand access to media literacies. (These debates become very real when low-income school districts struggle over whether to spend their sparse budgets on teachers, textbooks, or computers.) And, if we see the current moment as one of "collaboration" or co-creation—that is, if we see it as involving more complex relations between companies and audiences—we have all the more reason to expand the struggle over the terms of our participation. Our examples here (ranging from Tecnobrega in Brazil to "snap" videos on YouTube and the immigrant rights struggles in Los Angeles) all suggest ways that our public sphere has been enriched through the diversification of who has the means to create and share culture.

When we describe our culture as becoming more participatory, we are speaking in relative terms—participatory in relation to older systems of mass communication—and not in absolute terms. We do not and may never live in a society where every member is able to fully participate, where the lowest of the low has the same communicative capacity as the most powerful elites. Insofar as participation within networked publics becomes a source of discursive and persuasive power—and insofar as the capacities to meaningfully participate online are linked to educational and economic opportunities—then the struggle over the right to participation is linked to core issues of social justice and equality.

As we've seen here, the nature of participation in the digital age is a complicated matter. For even those groups who have greater access to digital technologies and have mastered the skills to deploy them effectively toward their own end, our capacity to participate can be complicated by issues of who owns the platforms through which communication occurs and how their agendas shape how those tools can be deployed. And, even if we get our messages through, there is often a question of whether anyone is listening. None of this allows us to be complacent about the current conditions of networked communications, even if the expanded opportunities for participation give us reasons for hope and optimism.

What we are calling spreadability starts from an assumption that circulation constitutes one of the key forces shaping the media environment. It comes also from a belief that, if we can better understand the social and institutional factors that shape the nature of circulation, we may become more effective at putting alternative messages into circulation (a goal which brings us back to Enzensberger's talk of "aggressive forms of publicity"). This chapter has looked at the shapes that participation takes in societies increasingly using digital tools to communicate and gather. In chapter 5, we will argue that what spreads in this participatory environment is what John Fiske (1989b) might call the "producerly," texts which constitute resources that participatory communities deploy in their interactions with each other. In doing so, we move between a focus on the properties of the networked audience and the properties of texts which are increasingly being designed to spread through social network sites, whether by brands seeking to reach current or potential customers or by activists seeking to reach supporters.

The May 2010 issue of *Fast Company* profiled the creative agency Mekanism (Borden 2010), the group responsible for such successful online promotions as the double-entendre-laden Axe body wash campaign "Clean Your Balls." Claiming the company can guarantee "viral success," Mekanism proclaims that the language of sharing gifts with its brand communities is too soft for a client-services-driven world (quoted in Borden 2010). In other words, it can make more deals if it claims to be able to infect the world with content. But the agency sometimes falls victim to its own language, admitting that clients say, "You're the viral guys, push a button and make it go viral. Isn't that why we hired you?"

In actuality, rather than having some magic formula, Mekanism deeply understands the U.S. youth market and uses this knowledge to better engage that audience. The agency's staff keep their ears attuned to the needs and wants of those they are courting for the companies that pay them. They seed content aimed at particular audiences and deliver material that provides those audiences something unique to share within their communities. Mekanism deploys various quantitative tools to model how and why their media is spreading, creating metrics for success. The notion that the agency generates "virality" may be a stretch, but Mekanism puts significant effort into understanding audiences and creating texts which resonate with desired audiences. As they say, "post and pray" is not an option.

Through our arguments so far, we hope to have convinced readers that the spread of all forms of media relies as much (or more) on their

DESIGNING FOR SPREADABILITY

circulation by the audience as it does on their commercial distribution, that spreadability is determined by processes of social appraisal rather than technical or creative wizardry and on the active participation of engaged audiences. In this chapter, we explore the creation of material designed to be spread.

Content creators do not work magic, nor are they powerless. Creators don't design viruses, nor do they simply wait for something to happen. Successful creators understand the strategic and technical aspects they need to master in order to create content more likely to spread, and they think about what motivates participants to share information and to build relationships with the communities shaping its circulation. They cannot fully predict whether audiences will embrace what they have designed, but a creator—whether professional or amateur—can place better bets through the listening processes discussed in chapter 4. In addition, creators consider elements of media texts which make them more likely to spread. This chapter explores the strategies, technical aspects, audience motivations, and content characteristics which creators might keep in mind in order to create content with a higher potential for spreadability. Many of our examples here are from marketing initiatives. However, as we will explore later in the chapter, these principles apply to civic groups, nonprofits, and independent media makers, among others.

The Uncertainty Principle

The creative industries have had a long struggle with predicting and measuring their products' success. Economist Richard Caves (2000) argues that uncertainty of demand is an everyday reality within the creative industries. These questions are exponentially harder to answer in today's spreadable media landscape, where many longstanding models for understanding media audiences no longer apply. However, there are a few sets of considerations which can help producers better create content that might resonate with audiences. These include longstanding processes the entertainment industry has used to minimize this uncertainty, technical and strategic considerations that ensure content is made available in forms that audiences will most likely find useful, and approaches for understanding what motivates audiences to circulate content.

First, entertainment companies have long used models of overproduction and formatting to address this uncertainty. As Amanda D. Lotz, a communication studies professor at the University of Michigan, discusses in our enhanced book, these traditional strategies for responding to this unpredictability carry over to a spreadable media environment. Key to understanding the "entertainment-based media industries," she writes, is recognizing the degree to which success is unpredictable. The primary response has been overproduction, writes Lotz:

> Television, film, and recording industry executives all work in a universe in which they know full well that more than 80 percent of what they develop and create will fail commercially. The key problem is that they don't know which 10 to 20 percent might actually succeed. So, while it is painful from a resource-allocation standpoint, the strategy has been to produce far more creative goods than might succeed and then see what works.

Spreadable media might enjoy lower sunk costs of production, Lotz suggests, particularly because audiences don't hold "the same high production-budget expectations that hobble established media" and because spreadable media's "circumvention of paid distribution reduces costs," allowing "creators to release preliminary content and then follow up on successes with sequels or extensions." Despite this, the best response remains relying on formatting; the best way to predict new success is to build on past success.

Second, in an era of digital sharing, there are a variety of technical and strategic considerations that can increase the chances content might be spread. Content is more likely to be shared if it is

- *Available when and where audiences want it*: Producers, whether professional or amateur, need to move beyond an "if you build it, they will come" mentality, taking (or sending) material to where audiences will find it most useful.

- *Portable*: Audience members do not want to be stuck in one place; they want their media texts "on the go." Content has to be quotable (editable by the audience) and grabbable (easily picked up and inserted elsewhere by the audience). Audiences will often abandon material if sharing proves too onerous.
- *Easily reusable in a variety of ways*: Media producers and media audiences circulate content for very different reasons, actually for very many different reasons. Creating media texts that are open to a variety of audience uses is crucial for creating material that spreads.
- *Relevant to multiple audiences*: Content that appeals to more than one target audience, both intended and surplus audiences, has greater meaning as spreadable media.
- *Part of a steady stream of material*: The "viral" mentality leads brands to invest all their energy in a particular media text that is expected to generate exponential hits. Blogging and microblogging platforms emphasize the importance of a regular stream of material, some of which may resonate more than others in ways creators may not always be able to predict.

Third, and most importantly, success in creating material people want to spread requires some attention to the patterns and motivations of media circulation, both of which are driven by the meanings people can draw from content. After all, humans rarely engage in meaningless activities. Sometimes, it may not be readily apparent why people are doing what they are doing, but striving to understand a person's or community's motivation and interest is key for creating texts more likely to spread.

One thing that is clear: people don't circulate material because advertisers or media producers ask them to, though they may do so to support a cause they are invested in. They might give someone a shirt with a designer label or even a T-shirt promoting a favorite film, and they might respond to questions about where someone could buy more shirts—but they are unlikely to stuff a catalog in a gift box.

When it comes to spreadability, not all content is created equal. Audiences constantly appraise media offerings, trying to ascertain their potential value as resources for sharing. Further, not all good content is necessarily good for sharing. In a gift economy, circulated texts say something about participants' perceptions of both the giver and the receiver; we all choose to share materials we value and anticipate others will value. People appraise the content they encounter according to their personal standards and the content they share based on its perceived value for their social circle. In other words, some of what is interesting to individuals may not be material they want to spread through their communities, and some media texts they spread may become more interesting because of their perceived social value.

We may share songs from our favorite band as a way to define ourselves, to communicate something about who we are and what we like to our friends. We may pass along a news article to a former schoolmate to strengthen our social ties with her, to remind her we remember what she is interested in. We may include a video clip in a blog post or Twitter update as a means to provide commentary on it, using that clip as inspiration for our own content and as a means to gain our own notoriety and audience. Or we may share material as a way to grow or activate a community, whether that be passing along a television-show clip for fellow fans to help dissect or spreading a protest video to mobilize or recruit others around a social cause.

Content spreads, then, when it acts as fodder for conversations that audiences are already having. As Douglas Rushkoff has put it, "Content is just a medium for interaction between people. The many forms of content we collect and experience online, I'd argue, are really just forms of ammunition—something to have when the conversation goes quiet at work the next day; an excuse to start a discussion with that attractive person in the next cubicle" (2000). Keep in mind that many of the choices people make in spreading content, as just described, are not grand and sweeping gestures but rather simple, everyday actions such as "liking" a Facebook status update.[1] Yet many active decisions and motivations are involved in even those instantaneous processes.

Producerly Texts and Cultural Resources

The previous section detailed production models, technical and strategic considerations, and questions about audience motivations that can help producers reduce uncertainty when trying to create material with a higher chance of spreading. These are all considerations outside of the text itself—approaches that can apply to any type of text. What we are not trying to imply, however, is that—in a world of spreadable media—content no longer matters. In fact, quite the opposite is true: creators who utilize all the strategies and consider all the questions discussed earlier will still not be successful if they do not create media texts that engage people and that people deem worth sharing with their friends. While there is no simple answer to creating content that resonates with people, the next several sections consider types of material with a higher potential for spreadability.

Communications scholar John Fiske (1989a) draws a distinction between mass culture—which is mass produced and distributed—and popular culture—media texts which have been meaningfully integrated into people's lives. As Fiske points out, only some material from mass culture enters the popular culture: "If the cultural commodities or texts do not contain resources out of which the people can make their own meanings of their social relations and identities, they will be rejected and will fail in the marketplace. They will not be made popular" (2). Under this model, *messages* are encoded into content; *meanings* are decoded from a text. Audience meanings often expand on or deviate from a producer's messages. Fiske recognizes that there are commercial interests working to inspire interest in mass-produced messages, but this commercial material couldn't be "made popular" if it didn't hold meaning-making potential.

Fiske's idea that content can become material for the interactions and interests of diverse communities recognizes and celebrates the generative capacity of participatory culture. Fiske writes that audiences "pluralize the meanings and pleasures [mass culture] offers, evade or resist its disciplinary efforts, fracture its homogeneity or coherence, raid or poach upon its terrain" and that people produce culture when they integrate products and texts into their everyday lives (1989b, 28).

Under the producer's control, it is mass culture. Under the audience's control, it is popular culture. Grassroots circulation can thus transform a commodity into a cultural resource.

Fiske argues that some texts are more apt to produce new meanings than others. The producerly text is one which "offers itself up to popular production. [. . .] It has loose ends that escape its control, its meanings exceed its own power to discipline them, its gaps are wide enough for whole new texts to be produced in them—it is, in a very real sense, beyond its own control" (1989b, 104). Material which fills in every blank limits audience interpretations. Propaganda, for instance, is less producerly because it sets rigid limits on potential meanings (though, as audiences become removed from its immediate context, old propaganda might be reread, such as the recirculation of social-ist realist or Cold War iconography as camp in recent years). Instead, producerly content can be enjoyed and accessed on multiple levels—it can be taken at face value but also can yield hidden levels upon active interpretation and appropriation (such as with the complex television narratives examined in chapter 3).

Fiske's notion of the "producerly" introduces guiding principles for transforming commodities into cultural resources: openness, loose ends, and gaps that allow viewers to read material against their own backgrounds and experiences are key. As we detailed earlier in this chapter, such openness allows people to convey something of them-selves as they pass along content. As Mike Arauz, a strategist at digital consultancy Undercurrent, suggests, "Opportunities for brands to reach individuals in mass audiences are quickly vanishing. In order to reach people now, you have to find a way to cross paths with them on their own terms, where they choose to spend time. And those places are defined by people's passions. People's lives don't revolve around your brand, they revolve around life" (2009).

Traditional branding theory has valued controlling meaning rather than inspiring circulation. Some longtime Madison Avenue types are likely to sputter in rage at the idea that audiences might appropriate and rework their messages (and their corresponding legal depart-ments are even more likely to). They do not want their brands to be "pluralized" (Fiske 1989b) or "multiplied" (to use Grant McCracken's term from his piece in our enhanced book). They worry about losing control when, in fact, they never had it. As this book has detailed, today's spreading behaviors reflect much older patterns in how people have received and discussed media texts. Only now, people's exchanges are much more visible, occurring at a greater scale and frequency as a greater portion of society taps into the online world. As participants circulate branded content for their own purposes, each new viewer encounters the original content afresh and is reminded of the brand and its potential meanings.

Right now, many companies hold onto the idea that a brand may carry a highly restricted range of meanings, defined and articulated by official brand stewards. They avoid creating producerly texts because making material that is open to interpretation leaves the control of meaning out of their hands. But, in doing so, companies limit the spreadability of their messages and constrain the value of the brand as a vehicle for social and personal expression, all of which ultimately damages their reputation and sales. These corporate attempts to rein in grassroots creativity by creating closed works devalue their material by removing it from meaningful circulation. Yet, even so, creative audiences may find "producerly angles" for many of these texts, meaning that such closed strategies still give no guarantee of complete control to a producer. Perhaps the only way to retain complete control over the meaning of a text is never to share it with anyone.

In the next few sections, we highlight a few types of content which are particularly spreadable because they take up the producerly strategies outlined earlier. These include the use of shared fantasies, humor, parody and references, unfinished content, mystery, timely controversy, and rumors.

Shared Fantasies

Lewis Hyde has argued that the commercial culture shaping the sale of commodities and the noncommercial culture shaping the exchange of gifts are formed around fundamentally different fantasies, which in turn shape the meanings ascribed to such transactions: "Because of the bonding power of gifts and the detached nature of commodity exchange, gifts have become associated with community and with being obliged to others, while commodities are associated with alienation and freedom" (1983, 86). Commodity culture emphasizes personal expression, freedom, upward social mobility, escape from constraints, and enabling new possibilities. These themes—often described as "escapist"—have a deep history in advertising theory and practice. Creating individualized fantasies makes sense within an impressions model, in which audience members are understood as atomized individuals.

The fantasies of a commodity culture are those of transformation (McCracken 2008), while the fantasies animating nonmarket exchanges are based on shared experience, whether the reassertion of traditional values and nostalgia, the strengthening of social ties, the acceptance of mutual obligations, or the comfort of operating within familiar social patterns. These are the values closely linked to the reciprocity on which a gift economy depends. When materials move from one sphere to the other, they frequently get reworked to reflect alternative values and fantasies.

Fan-created works often center on themes of romance, friendship, and community (Jenkins 1992). These values shape the decisions fans make at every level—starting, for instance, with choosing a film or television program. A fan music video for *Heroes*, for example, might feature interactions between two characters that rarely share the screen. The music selected further emphasizes the emotional bonds between characters. Fan-made media is shared among a community with common passions. In some cases, fans produce stories or videos to give to one another explicitly as gifts. Most often, though, fans understand their works as a contribution to the community as a whole. Fandom nurtures writers and artists, putting the deepest emphasis on that material which most clearly reflects the community's core values.

Other commonly spread content has an explicitly nostalgic tone. For many baby boomers, for instance, there is enormous pleasure in watching older commercials or programs of their childhood. This generation, as we emphasized in chapter 2, uses eBay to repurchase the old toys, comics, collector cards, and other pieces of content their parents threw away when they went to college. Such material sparks the exchange of memories, especially personal and collective histories of reading, listening, and viewing. A Facebook page, say, focused around the graduates of a particular high school class may routinely post music videos popular during their youth as a springboard for the exchange of shared memories. When producers are part of a community and understand its values and shared fantasies, the content they create is more likely to resonate deeply with fellow community members.

Humor

Anthropologist Mary Douglas (1991) examines the very thin line separating a joke from an insult: a joke expresses something a community is ready to hear; an insult expresses something it doesn't want to consider. Thus, recognizing a joke involves exchanging judgments about the world and defining oneself either with or against others. Content creators can endear themselves to a particular audience by showing they understand its sensibilities and can alienate themselves by miscalculating that audience's sensibilities. Humor is not simply a matter of taste: it is a vehicle by which people articulate and validate their relationships with those with whom they share the joke.

Consider a breakout advertising success from 2010: Old Spice's "Smell Like a Man, Man" campaign. Launched in February by ad agency Wieden+Kennedy, the television commercials feature Isaiah Mustafa as Old Spice Guy, "a handsome but somewhat inscrutable figure who engaged in random acts of manliness": "the man your man could smell like" (Potter 2010). The first spot set the tone. "Hello ladies," Old Spice Guy intones, standing in his bathroom wearing only a towel. Then, he commands the (presumably female) viewer, "Look at your man, now back at me, now back at your man. Sadly, he isn't me, but, if he stopped using lady-scented body wash and switched to Old Spice, he could smell like he's me." After that, the game is afoot. The bathroom is replaced by a boat, a knotted sweater falls onto Old Spice Guy's shoulders, and he reveals he's wearing a pair of tight white trousers. Proving his value as the man ladies would like their man to smell like, he presents an oyster, inside of which are tickets to a favorite event. "Now the tickets are diamonds," he says, and so they are, because "anything is possible when your man smells like Old Spice and not a lady." The receding camera reveals Mustafa sitting on a horse, a situation he underlines with a dry statement of fact: "I'm on a horse."

Promising to transform customers simply through their use of the product, the spots draw on some of advertising's own clichés and cultural touchstones. It parodies not only the pitchman but also the commercially manufactured ideal man—all "chiseled torso and ridiculously self-assured tone" (Edwards 2010). Old Spice has employed such techniques multiple times in the past. For instance, a commercial in 2007 showed how the product could grow chest hair instantly (a feat its competitor in the side-by-side comparison couldn't manage). This manliness made it the ideal choice for "real man situations, like basketball, recon, and frenching." A 2008 spot featured a spokesman sliding around the entirety of a baseball diamond while he promoted Old Spice as the "bare-knuckle, straight-on tackle, heavyweight deodorant that gives the best game, set, and match, high-stepping, sudden-death, double-overtime performance in the pit fight against odor." By 2009, the product was shown as the deodorant of choice for the winners of manly competitions such as arm wrestling, the karate chopping of concrete blocks, and chainsaw carving. In the latter case, the Old Spice deodorized winner carved his own block of wood into a chainsaw, and he then used it to carve his competitor's block of wood into a sculpture, all before the other guy could start his saw. Old Spice has long experimented with parodying the advertising industry's construction of masculinity.

For the impressions minded, by September 2010, the original Old Spice Guy spot had received in excess of 25 million views on YouTube, while the Old Spice channel showcasing all the campaign's videos received about 94 million views. At that time, the brand had acquired more than 90,000 Twitter followers and more than 675,000 Facebook fans. Perhaps in relation, sales of Old Spice grew 30 percent from February through July 2010, the five months after the new advertising campaign had launched (Edwards 2010).

We might see the "Smell Like a Man, Man" campaign as a product of Old Spice's ongoing experiments with finding the right humorous tone to mock notions of masculinity (Caddell 2010). Unlike the previous spots, this campaign engaged both male and female viewers, as the commercials are directly addressed to the "ladies" who are often purchasers of body wash for their significant other. Its self-parodic elements implicitly grant users permission to adopt and adapt the content for their own purposes. Parodies of the Old Spice commercial spread across the Internet as users drew on the spot's form and structure to conduct their own conversations. Men of all body types and sizes shot spoofs featuring "more realistic" men your man could smell like. The children's television show *Sesame Street* produced a version featuring the character Grover that promised to help viewers "smell like a monster." Australian political comedy program *Yes We Canberra!* shot a version critiquing the status of gay marriage down under, and another Australian Broadcasting Corporation spoof featured an animated Tony Abbott, leader of the Australian opposition party, begging to be "the man your PM should be." Brigham Young University's Harold B. Lee Library even produced a version selling the merits of studying in the library.

"Smell Like a Man, Man" serves as a good exemplar of a "producerly" text. The video has a clearly defined message, but the absurdity creates gaps "wide enough for whole new texts to be produced in them" (Fiske 1989b, 104). Wieden+Kennedy enlisted Mustafa to shoot 186 individual videos over 48 hours and posted them on YouTube, responding to comments sent to Old Spice Guy via Twitter, Reddit, and Facebook and to video responses left on YouTube in real time. Old Spice Guy responds multiple times to Alyssa Milano (whom he flirts with), offers a marriage proposal on behalf of a Twitter user, and answers a lot of quite random questions.[2] Many response videos don't feature a single mention of Old Spice products—they respond to people talking about the campaign. Ultimately, the campaign uses its humor in all its extensions to demonstrate how Old Spice "gets" a certain mentality and is a meaningful participant in the dialogue of particular audience members (in the case of the online extension, communities that are cognizant of the traditional logics of advertising, fully conversant in irony, and immersed in social media platforms).

Not every group appreciated the outreach, however. When Old Spice targeted the trolls at 4Chan, they responded with a mixture of bemusement and overt ridicule; one wrote, "This was the first time I've ever seen someone market to /b/ and I am glad it was a thing as epic and funny and as close to our humor as this so fuck off," while another posted an image macro of the Old Spice Guy labeled "marketing campaign troll." In this case, Old Spice's humor may have been directed at the wrong audience, offending some in a community expressly built to be not just noncommercial but often anticommercial.

Parody and References

Fiske specifically cites parody as a popular form closely associated with the "producerly"—one of the ways audiences transform brands into resources for their own social interactions. While all humor builds on whether an audience "gets" the joke or shares a sensibility, parody combines that aspect of humor with a specific shared reference. This is precisely what makes parody valuable—it can express shared experiences and, especially when it plays on nostalgic references, a shared history. Those who are creating humor and parody claim specific common experiences with those who are laughing at the joke.

A particularly potent example of the power of parody to help content spread can be found in a 2007 commercial for Toyota set in the online video game *World of Warcraft*. This spot not only utilizes unique details and aesthetics of *World of Warcraft* but also refers to a very specific event in the history of the online game's culture. The 30-second spot features a group of warriors planning and arming for an attack. In the middle of their discussion about battle strategy, one player suddenly goes rogue. He announces he'll equip himself with "a little Four Wheels of Fury!" and then promptly transforms into a truck and rushes into battle, leaving his teammates to chase behind him. The ad directly references a well-known video based in *World of Warcraft*. Player Leeroy Jenkins was away from his computer while his guildmates meticulously planned a raid. When he returned to the game, he shouted out his own name as a battle cry and tore into the fray with no regard for the plan that had been articulated in his absence, ultimately dooming his guildmates to defeat. This video of Jenkins's "epic fail" spread widely online within, and eventually outside of, the *World of Warcraft* community, and the incident became so well known that it was eventually featured as a question on the television game show *Jeopardy!*

The Toyota parody remained faithful not just to *World of Warcraft* culture but to the Leeroy Jenkins incident in particular. The Toyota ad's warriors use similar matter-of-fact voices to the original players as they plan the raid. The character who turns into a truck issues a crazy, over-the-top battle cry and proclaims, "Let's do this," in much the same way Leeroy Jenkins does. Further, there is an additional layer of self-reflexivity when one of the *World of Warcraft* players responds with an exasperated "No way. There's no trucks in *World of Warcraft!*" The commercial's culturally specific details ultimately establish a playful homage to, and loving spoof of, the original, showing Toyota as a meaningful member of the *World of Warcraft* community rather than as a commercial force mocking or "capitalizing on" a culture of which it is not part.

Culturally specific references such as the Toyota ad provide pleasure to audiences who enjoy mapping links between different texts and recognizing when texts are referencing each other. Designer Jeffrey Zeldman writes in his analysis of the advertising campaign for HBO's 2007 documentary *Alive Day Memories*,

> The poster contains more content than I have listed. Most of that content is externally located. For this poster has been framed and shot, and its subject styled and posed, almost exactly like an American Gap ad. Consciously or unconsciously, an American viewer will almost certainly make an uncomfortable connection between the disfigurement and sacrifice portrayed in this ad, and the upbeat quality of the Gap's long-running, highly successful clothing slash lifestyle campaign. *That connection is content.* (2007)

Zeldman's example highlights how a variety of genres—in this case, a documentary about U.S. Iraq War veterans—might use such references.

When audience members choose to pass along media texts, they demonstrate that they belong to a community, that they are "in" on the reference and share some common experience. Knowing about Leeroy Jenkins helps define someone as a *World of Warcraft* insider while also deflecting outsiders for whom this knowledge carries little to no value. This degree of exclusivity is a key function for the spread of some material, though the inclusion of Jenkins as the basis for a *Jeopardy!* question also suggests how much this information becomes common knowledge beyond the initial community. The Toyota ad both becomes part of the myth of Leeroy Jenkins and drives new audiences to seek out the original *World of Warcraft* material.

Unfinished Content

Chapter 3 argues that a successful media franchise is not only a cultural attractor, drawing like-minded people together to form an audience, but also a cultural activator, giving that community something to do. Content which is unfinished, or not immediately intelligible, drives the individual and collective intelligence of its audiences. Such texts or events often ask people to contribute something or encourage them to look twice because they can't believe what they are seeing; they need to verify its authenticity or figure out how it was done.

One of the most cited advertising examples of this approach, Burger King's Subservient Chicken interactive video site (launched in 2004), literally engaged users in the creation of the video's content. Visitors saw an amateurish video of a man in a chicken suit standing in a room; the view is through a single, low-resolution camera pointed head-on, not unlike a webcam mounted atop a computer. Below, there was a text-input box with the words, "Get chicken just the way you like it. Type command here." Once a recognized command was typed, it triggered a video clip of the man in the chicken suit performing what is demanded of him. There were nearly 300 different clips in all, each set to respond to commands ranging from "jump" to "lay egg" to "moonwalk." Commands that the chicken didn't understand might result in a clip expressing confusion or boredom, while commands deemed inappropriate—such as those that were sexually explicit—resulted in a clip of the chicken wagging his finger in disapproval.

The campaign became so widely referenced as a new way to advertise that it inspired a variety of case studies and many related campaigns. For instance, six years later, European correction-fluid brand Tipp-Ex replicated the model in a YouTube video that featured a hunter too scared to shoot a bear that approaches him in the wilderness. Rather than kill the bear, he uses correction tape to blank out the verb in the title of the video—"Hunter Kills a Bear"—inviting users instead to write in their own verbs. More than fifty recognized verbs triggered clips showing different humorous endings.

Both these campaigns created dynamic interaction, engaging the user as part of the process of creating the final video they see. The "story" required a command to be entered to move forward, so the actual output was controlled and triggered entirely by the user. Both brands declined complete control over the creation of the content; even though the various actions and endings were premade, the text itself—the advertisement—was fundamentally incomplete. Subservient Chicken was the more daring of the two: while Tipp-Ex asked users to engage in a narrative game with two characters (the hunter and the bear) in a heavily and clearly branded space on YouTube, Subservient Chicken was far more obscure, offering fewer clues as to the context for the giant-chicken-suited person staring out from the screen. Not only was there no obvious meaning ascribed to Subservient Chicken, but there was also no action, no finished content, until the user entered a command. Thus, by creating a partial work—an archive of incomplete component parts—the Subservient Chicken campaign offered the user agency that went beyond just access and choice: it offered tangible participation in the work's creation.

Many participants also explored the way Subservient Chicken worked as much as they reinterpreted its meaning. Gamers often seek to test the limits of a game to see how much actual control they can exert. In the case of Subservient Chicken, users wanted to push against the limits of the ad to see what flaws they could locate in its execution. Webpages soon appeared that cataloged the various commands the site recognized and their responses. Similarly, users left comments under the Tipp-Ex videos with the full list of verbs that would trigger responses. The ambiguity and unfinished nature of these campaigns capitalized on the collective intelligence of participatory culture, encouraging the spread of content by setting up a challenge that people could work together to solve. Communities spread the text, trying to expand the ranks of potential puzzle solvers.

Mystery

Subservient Chicken was also interesting because the amateurish qualities of the video production and the site were reminiscent of the proliferation of live fetish online webcams, perhaps driving many viewers to initially question whether the site featured a prerecording or whether the man was actually performing these commands live. Mysteries about the origins of media texts have proliferated in the age of spreadable media, in part because content moves so fluidly from context to context, often stripping away the original motives behind its production. As new audiences encounter such texts, they are often unsure what their rhetorical goals were intended to be or even who produced the material. They may not even be able to initially classify whether the works are commercially or noncommercially motivated.

For instance, in early January 2009, Heidi (an attractive, blonde Australian woman) sent out a somewhat awkward plea via YouTube: she'd recently met a guy in a café in Sydney with whom she had become a little enraptured. After explaining how their orders had gotten mixed up, providing her a chance to speak with him briefly, Heidi showed the camera a black sport coat that the mystery man had left behind. This was her key to finding him again. She hoped someone would recognize the jacket.

Heidi's appeal had many of the hallmarks of a genuine, amateur YouTube video. She addresses the camera directly, sitting in a simple, naturally lit bedroom. She stumbles over her words, her speech filled with repetition and "ums." She appears nervous, and her language is plain. Pink text flashes over the screen at the video's end with a Hotmail account where viewers could contact her and a URL for a website offering more details: hardly a slick and professional production standard.

The video was quickly popular. The 24-year-old appeared on national news and talk programs and was the subject of a profile piece in the lifestyle section of Australian newspaper the *Sydney Morning Herald* (Marcus 2009a). Describing her as a "modern Cinderella," the paper reported that, in just six days, her video had garnered more than 60,000 views and more than 130 comments. Some of these comments, it reported, questioned the story's authenticity. In interviews, Heidi assured the Australian public that she was genuine, but YouTube commenters were less than convinced. Some pointed out that taking a jacket from a café, rather than turning it in to the staff, was odd behavior. News outlets found other inconsistencies in her story, revealing that they couldn't track down Heidi's employer and that staff at the café didn't recall the incident (though they did recall her leaving a note for her mystery man). Others found that the label on the jacket was for a clothing company—Witchery—that didn't have a men's line. When contacted, Witchery denied involvement.

Soon, the video was revealed as a "hoax." Sydney paper the *Daily Telegraph* learned that Witchery was about to launch a men's line (O'Neill 2009). Only two days after the *Sydney Morning Herald's* profile piece, the paper noted that a publicist for Naked Communications, which handles Witchery, confirmed that the company had been behind the video (Marcus 2009b). Some parts of the Australian press reacted with a certain vehemence against the campaign. Guests on *The Gruen Transfer*, a national television panel program that critiques and discusses advertising campaigns and strategies, dismissed the campaign for being disingenuous. Meanwhile, Heidi followed her original video with a second one in which she came clean, acknowledging that she was an actress and that the entire narrative was part of a campaign for Witchery.

The Witchery story is especially interesting because of how closely it resembles the case of Lonelygirl15, the online video experiment that ran from 2006 to 2008 and purported to be the vlog of a homeschooled teenager. In both cases, the public's uncertainty about the status of this content made figuring out the source of these messages the central task. Consider what danah boyd wrote about the now classic example of Lonelygirl15: "They are telling their story, truth or fiction. Of course, this makes many people very uncomfortable. They want blogs and YouTube and MySpace to be Real with a capital R. Or they want it to be complete play. Yet, what's happening is both and neither. People are certainly playing but even those who are creating 'reality' are still engaged in an act of performance" (2006). This fascination with getting to the bottom of "hoaxes" is far from new. Neil Harris recounts how infamous nineteenth-century circus showman P. T. Barnum once shared an anecdote from his ticket seller about Barnum's show: "First he humbugs them, and then they pay to hear him tell how he did it" (1981, 77). Perhaps it's not surprising that someone like pro wrestling impresario Vince McMahon is regularly compared to Barnum today. Almost all wrestling fans know that the performances are not legitimate competitions but often actively watch wrestling matches with an eye toward understanding "how they do it."

The encouragement of such active strategies from the audience is what distinguishes a magic show (where attendees know they are being "tricked") from a scam and stories such as the Witchery Cinderella and Lonelygirl15 from what has become known as "astroturf": commercially produced content which seeks to pass itself off as grassroots media, often in ways that mask the commercial and political motives of those who have produced it. In a culture which increasingly has to work through confusions about the sources and motives of digitally circulating material, there is a strong incentive for bloggers and journalists to unmask the groups which are circulating "fake" or "misleading" messages online, calling them out for their deceptions. The line between a "cool campaign" purporting to be part of "the real world" and marketers exposed as looking to "dupe" the world can be thin and relies on whether creators seem to have wanted the true origins of the text to eventually be discovered and whether creators are seen to be part of the culture with which the content seeks to engage.

Timely Controversy

Controversy and timeliness can also be key to understanding why content spreads. For our purposes, controversy refers to the ways that material may spark intense disagreement among those who encounter it, especially in terms of conflicting values and judgments. Meanwhile, timeliness refers to the ways that a chunk of media may be linked to highly topical discussions within or beyond a given social network site, sometimes fueled by news coverage but also shaped by recurring personal experiences.

Take, for example, the November 2010 online videos depicting computer programmer John Tyner's experience at an airport security checkpoint in San Diego. The U.S. Transportation Security Administration had just introduced "enhanced security procedures," including new scanner technologies that could penetrate travelers' clothing and allow full-body scans, essentially producing an X-ray of travelers. As the new scanners were being phased in, travelers were permitted to "opt out" of passing through them, in which case they would be patted down by TSA agents who would now use the front of their hands and fingers (rather than the back of their hands) to touch passengers in the groin and chest. Tyner declined to walk through the new scanner. When a TSA agent prepared to pat him down, Tyner warned the agent that he would have him arrested if the agent "touched his junk." The agent called over his supervisor, and a verbal altercation ensued between Tyner and his traveling companions and some TSA agents. Eventually, Tyner was escorted back to the airline counter for a ticket refund, and a man believed to be a TSA agent threatened him with a $10,000 fine for leaving the security area.

Before beginning the process just detailed, Tyner had turned on the video-recording function of his cell phone. He posted a three-part series of his experience on YouTube and a full written account on his blog that same day. The videos quickly gained traction because they spoke to an issue prevalent in the public consciousness at the moment of Tyner's experience. Throughout the year, the press and public had been questioning the safety, necessity, and privacy violations of these airport scanners and the invasiveness of more thorough pat-downs. And the release of this content was timely, as news accounts and public discussion alike had come to a head as travelers worried about the potential delays these new security practices could have on their Thanksgiving travel. Perhaps not surprisingly, then, the videos spread rapidly across the Internet, through social network and news sites and through blogs and microblogging sites. Tyner's video was remixed and even Auto-Tuned (electronically processed to distort the audio to make it melodic). People made T-shirts with slogans based on Tyner's challenge: "If you touch my junk, I'll have you arrested." And the story was picked up by mainstream news services that both reported the incident and interviewed Tyner.

Often, a media text spreads particularly far when it depicts a controversy a community cares about at the precise time it is looking for content which might act as its rallying cry. In this case, material becomes spreadable because it articulates the sentiment of the moment, a situation people have experienced but couldn't easily explain, or an insight people hadn't quite been able to put into words. Similarly, content spreads when it states a community's stance on an issue of intense interest at a particular moment better than its members think they can otherwise. Tyner's video arrived at the right time to serve as a proof point for people skeptical of new TSA security measures, especially because Tyner was not a widely known "influencer": rather, he was a citizen "like everyone else" whose sharing of an experience that many people fear and dread became contextually relevant and timely.

Timeliness (and timing) can be particularly tricky because cultural relevance can change quickly. Such timing is hard to predict. This is often the logic behind corporate blogs and Twitter accounts (and online news sites, for that matter), where content is uploaded regularly in hopes of speaking to an issue of importance to the audience at a particular moment but with the mindset that some texts will be widely spread while others will not, depending on how long a community stays engaged on a particular issue and what other content the community might be actively engaging with at a given time.

Controversy can be even trickier for producers to embrace. Many of the examples highlighted in this chapter demonstrate how various groups—creators, marketers, grassroots civic media groups, and loosely organized communities—use controversy to make their content more spreadable. In some cases, however, that controversy can backfire. For instance, video game company Electronic Arts suffered a strong backlash to its decision to host a contest at the San Diego Comic-Con in 2009 which offered a lucky winner "a sinful night with two hot girls" as part of the promotion for its *Dante's Inferno* video game. Intended to depict "lust," one of the seven deadly sins used as a game element in *Dante's Inferno*, the contest created more passionate disgust about the objectification of women than the company was prepared for. As Suzanne Scott (2010) has documented, the promotion became linked to larger debates around the convention's shifting gender balance, a backlash against the mostly female *Twilight* fans, and charges of sexual harassment among event participants. Further, Electronic Arts's campaign gained broader visibility because of the widespread use of social network tools by Comic-Con attendees. Here, timeliness may have helped spread publicity for Electronic Arts but simultaneously intensified the controversy, eventually requiring an apology from the company.

Rumors

Our final quality that makes content spread is also the one with the most potential for causing harm. In Patricia Ann Turner's work with African American populations, she makes the distinction between rumors—informal and temporary constellations of speculation—and contemporary legends—"more solidified rumors" that maintain a reasonable consistency as they are passed (1994, 5). Many of Turner's cases center on commercial products; in particular, the rumors that a number of different companies—from food and consumable-good producers such as Church's Chicken and Marlboro cigarettes to clothing firms such as Troop Sport—were owned by the Ku Klux Klan remained widespread during the period of her research. Such rumors may have inflicted serious damage on these brands: Church's was forced to sell, and Troop went bankrupt as these rumors were spreading (Turner 1994, 96).

Some of the accused organizations were private enterprises and others public, but none had any explicitly racist policies. Though the claims had no basis in fact, the accusations, Turner tells us, were far from random. The accused companies were "white-owned firms [with] advertising directed solely at black consumers, that established nationwide franchises selling popular but nonessential commodities in primarily black neighborhoods" (1994, 97). The rumors became vehicles for shared feelings of frustration among some African American audiences about the shortage of black-owned businesses in their own communities. These rumors reflect the reality of a world where racism most often no longer takes a direct form, such as a KKK rally, but is instead experienced as implicit, tacit, and thus hard to locate or confront. By circulating the story, community members were demonstrating their own active participation in the community, helping to distinguish friend from foe, popularizing an anecdote to express their larger concerns about racism, and establishing the boundaries of their community.[3]

The rumors that Turner discussed were widely shared within the black communities she studied and were little known outside them. Historically, black America generated its own institutions, from the barbershop to the African American press and the black church, counterpublics which enabled the formulation and exchange of the community's own perspectives. Some scholars (for instance, Nunley 2004) have linked these institutions to an older tradition of "hush harbors," spaces where slaves gathered outside the oversight of their masters for vital communication, stressing their capacity to sustain conversations within the race. The rise of networked computers has amplified these messages and expanded their circulation, which, in some cases, allows others to make common cause within and between minority groups.

Yet the porousness of the communication environment also brings new risks for such communities. Consider, for example, the circulation of videos featuring Rev. Jeremiah Wright's sermons to his Trinity United Church of Christ congregation (of which Barack Obama was a member), which played a significant role in the 2008 presidential campaign. Wright's sermons were written for and presented to a predominantly but no longer exclusively black congregation as part of a tradition of fiery black critique of white institutions and practices. But, in the modern media environment, messages are much harder to contain; they travel and spread everywhere. So the Wright videos were posted on YouTube and picked up by bloggers and podcasters, broadcast and reframed on Fox News, covered in the *Washington Post* and the *New York Times*, discussed on talk radio, referenced in political debates, repurposed in political advertising, and so forth. What Wright's comments might have meant in a black-only or black-dominated space is very different from what they meant when spread through these other contexts.

Consider the false claims that President Barack Obama had a Muslim upbringing or that he was not born in the United States, rumors which persist despite repeated attempts to correct them. Some political observers believe these stories were maliciously manufactured; they have certainly been sustained by groups invested in generating anxiety about Obama's election and distrust of his motives. Rumors about the black president functioned among white cultural conservatives as a displaced discourse about race, expressing their sense that Obama is not appropriate to lead the country and shifting the focus from race onto issues of religion, national origins, or patriotism.

For Christian conservatives, rumors about Obama's Muslim roots were especially worrisome when coupled with the departure of George W. Bush—a white, conservative president who openly proclaimed his "Christian values." One particular rumor about President Obama, circulated both online and offline, held that the president had canceled the National Day of Prayer and participated in an Islamic ceremony at the White House. In actuality, Obama had announced the annual proclamation of the day of prayer in 2009 but opted to observe it in private. Some email versions of the rumor misrepresented a picture of the president removing his shoes before entering a mosque during a diplomatic trip in Istanbul as proof of the supposed White House Islamic ceremony. Those who share the values that these rumors expressed knew how to read them. They may or may not have believed them on a literal level, just as the rumors about Church's may or may not have been taken at face value by those in the African American communities who heard and shared them; however, these rumors do culturally and politically significant work in shaping how these communities collectively perceive shifts in U.S. racial composition.

Through investigating these various rumors, we learn something important about how and why content spreads, most notably that the material which gets picked up often is not that which is of the highest quality but rather that which most powerfully speaks to the desires and fears of the participating community. The ease with which the

Obama "birther" controversy could be disproven did not impact its ability to drive debate because—as with the Church's example—it was a parable for deeply held cultural concerns.

We do not mean to indicate that the attributes listed here are the only types of material which might spread. In fact, this book includes a wide range of examples that wouldn't fit into the categories detailed in the preceding few sections. While our list is not exhaustive, our intent has been to detail some types of content that have the highest degree of spreadability. As these sections indicate, texts that are particularly producerly—that leave open processes of analysis, meaning making, or collective activity for the audience to fill in—often drive deep engagement. In short, engaging, producerly texts have a greater tendency to spread.

Avatar Activism and Other Civic Media

While much of the discussion in this chapter has centered on strategies being deployed by marketers to create more spreadable content, the core principles of spreadability can be deployed by any kind of media producer that wants to ensure the circulation of its content across dispersed and diverse populations. Principles of spreadability may, in fact, be most visible when we look at the ways civic media is adopting new styles and strategies in order to encourage free circulation and to attract so-called earned media coverage. Civic media is content intended to increase civic engagement or to motivate participation in the political process. This may include media produced by political candidates, grassroots organizations (including activist groups), and individual citizens. (Some of the examples of rumors described earlier are civic in function, even if they may seem anti-civic in their tone and content.) Without the means to reach wide audiences through broadcast channels and often working with very limited resources, many of these groups hope their calls for action communicated through online media can motivate supporters to help spread the word.

Unlike commercial producers that may be torn between their desire to create buzz and their interest in monetizing and regulating the flow of material, civic media producers typically care more about getting their message out to the world. As such, they have little choice but to embrace the participation of their supporters. In general, spreadability has lowered the costs of political speech. As a result, activist groups find it easier to design and circulate compelling media content, building stronger affiliations with a public that plays a much more active role in spreading their message. These tactics work because they create media (such as YouTube videos) which are easy to circulate, pay attention to the social motives which encourage supporters and more casual viewers to share this content with their friends, and design the content using some of the basic principles we've identified. Yet, as we will see, these civic media producers confront ethical issues, especially concerning what happens when some images of social turmoil and human suffering get decontextualized from the specifics of their historical and political origins, being read in ways which damage rather than strengthen the producers' calls to action.

This spreadable civic media content may be initially jarring in the ways that it abandons the sobriety with which we normally receive political messages, but producers count on the controversy around such unexpected tactics to inspire the further spread and discussion of their media. For instance, in early 2010, a group of five Palestinian, Israeli, and international activists painted themselves blue to resemble the Na'vi from James Cameron's 2009 science fiction blockbuster movie *Avatar* and marched along the fence which runs through the West Bank village of Bil'in. The azure-skinned protesters, whose garb combined traditional keffiyeh and hijab scarfs with tails and pointy ears, were eventually intercepted by the Israeli military, which assaulted them with tear gas and sound bombs. They uploaded a video on YouTube which juxtaposes home video footage of the action with quoted footage from the Hollywood film. As the activists chant about tearing down the fence, the viewer can hear the movie characters proclaim, "We will show the Sky People that they cannot take whatever they want! This . . . this is our land!"

Conservative U.S. critics worried that *Avatar*'s critical depiction of a military-industrial complex might foster anti-Americanism internationally, yet, as the image of the Na'vi has been taken up by protest groups in various parts of the world, the myth has instead been rewritten to focus on local embodiments of the military-industrial complex (Deuze 2010). In Bil'in, the focus was on the Israeli army; in China, it was on the struggles of home owners against land seizures by developers working with the Chinese government; in Brazil, it was the Amazon Indians against dam construction threatening the rain forest; and, in London, it was activists protesting British mining interests on behalf of a tribe in India.[4]

The Bil'in protesters recognized potential parallels between Na'vi struggles to defend their garden planet against the Sky People and their own attempts to regain lands they feel have been unjustly taken from them. Their YouTube video makes clear the contrast between the lush jungles of Pandora and the arid, dusty landscape of the occupied territories, but the film's heroic imagery offered them an empowered view of their own struggles. Viewers worldwide would recognize timely references to the film because of the extraordinary power of the Hollywood publicity machine, and the ways these references are deployed here in relation to struggles over territory in the Middle East was sure to spark controversy. Further, the sight of a blue-skinned protester writhing in the dust and choking on tear gas shocked many people into paying attention to the type of message people often turn off and tune out. While one would hardly call the resulting images humorous, they are defamiliarizing and depend on the audience's access to contextual knowledge in ways similar to the claims made earlier about parody.

Activist and media theorist Stephen Duncombe argues in his book *Dream: Re-imagining Progressive Politics in the Age of Fantasy* (2007) that the American Left has too often adopted a rationalist language which can seem cold and exclusionary, speaking to the head and not the heart. Duncombe argues that the contemporary cultural context—with its focus on appropriation and remixing of elements from popular culture—may offer a new model for activism, one both spectacular and participatory, drawing emotional power from stories that already matter to a mass public and rejecting the wonkish vocabulary through which policy debates are so often conducted. Duncombe cites, for example, a group called Billionaires for Bush, which posed as megatycoons straight out of a Monopoly game to call attention to the corporate interests shaping Republican Party positions. Yet he might have been writing about protesters painting themselves blue, Twitter users turning their icons green in solidarity with the Iranian civil rights movement, or Tea Party activists dressing in garb from the American Revolution to reflect their desire to return to what they see as the original intentions of the U.S. Constitution. In each case, activists have generated powerful images, often by appropriating and transforming elements from a larger shared cultural mythology which people feel an immediate emotional connection with and have an impulse to share.

The Harry Potter Alliance's Andrew Slack calls this process "cultural acupuncture," suggesting that his organization has identified a vital "pressure point" in the popular imagination by building on metaphors from a popular children's franchise (Jenkins 2009, 2012). Young Harry Potter, Slack argues, realized that the government and the media were lying to the public in order to mask evil in their midst. Potter thus organized his classmates to form Dumbledore's Army and went out to change the world. Mirroring that impulse, the Harry Potter Alliance has mobilized more than 100,000 young people worldwide to participate in campaigns against genocide in Africa, supporting workers' rights and gay marriage, raising money for disaster relief in Haiti, and calling attention to media concentration and many other causes.

Slack's efforts draw together passionate fans of J. K. Rowling's fantasy novels to work in concert with more traditional activist groups, asking his followers what Dumbledore's Army would be battling in the real world. Many of the group's supporters said they had never considered themselves "political" before; the ability to move from participatory culture to civic engagement was effective at overcoming their reluctance to become activists (Kligler-Vilenchik et al., 2012). Such efforts tap the realities of a news media apt to pay much more attention to what's happening at Hogwarts (or at least the opening of a new Harry Potter theme park) than what's happening in Darfur.

To be sure, *Avatar* can't solve an age-old struggle over territory, and the YouTube video that the Bil'in protesters produced is no substitute for informed discourse about what's at stake in that conflict. But it wasn't intended to be. Instead, its goal was to circulate beyond the core audience already invested in these issues by speaking to the wants and interests of other communities—fans of *Avatar*, cultural commentators interested in grassroots appropriations of media content, and so on—in a visual language familiar to various international audiences. As Simon Faulkner explained in a discussion which placed the *Avatar* video in a larger context of the Bil'in protesters' ongoing media strategies,

> Viewers of a video of the Bil'in demonstration on YouTube, or photographs of the same demonstration on Flickr might turn to text-based forms of communication as a means of informing themselves about why these images were produced. [. . .] The organisers of the *Avatar* demonstration in Bil'in aimed to produce strong images that would have an impact upon those who saw them and would attract the attention of a much wider audience. [. . .] Whatever loss of conceptual understanding occurs through the immediate impact of the images of '*Avatar* activism' can be made up for in how these images relate to the written word. (2010)

The hope is that such provocative videos will encourage greater information seeking, inspiring those who encounter them to follow links back and to drill deeper into the content-rich sites that these activist groups have constructed around them. In turn, the act of sharing such videos has the potential to pull participants into closer emotional ties with the communities that produced them.

Despite critics who dismiss a politics grounded in the spread of messages through social media as "slactivism," research by Georgetown University's Center for Social Impact Communication and Ogilvy Worldwide in 2010 suggests that the small investments in time and effort required to pass along such messages (or to link to causes via our social network site profiles) may make participants more likely to take more substantive action later (Andresen 2011). In the national survey, people who frequently engaged in promotional social activity were:

- As likely as non-social-media promoters to donate
- Twice as likely to volunteer their time
- Twice as likely to take part in events such as charity walks
- More than twice as likely to buy products or services from companies that supported the cause
- Three times as likely to solicit donations on behalf of their cause

All of this suggests that more spreadable forms of civic media may not only reach unexpected supporters but may be planting seeds which can grow into deeper commitments over time.

Despite the benefits of such strategies, the ease with which such content spreads, and is reshaped, raises significant concerns. Sasha Costanza-Chock writes in his work on the immigrant rights movement in Los Angeles about tensions between younger activists who seek to use social media for spontaneous responses to real-time developments and those who want to maintain the more careful structuring and shaping of the campaign's core media elements:

> Many organizations continue to find transmedia mobilization risky, because it requires opening movement communication practices up to diverse voices rather than relying only on experienced movement leaders to frame the movement's narrative by speaking to broadcast reporters during press conferences. [. . .] Those movement formations that embrace the decentralization of the movement voice can reap great rewards, while those that attempt to maintain top down control of movement communication practices risk losing credibility. (2010, 113–114)

Sam Gregory (2010), a spokesperson for WITNESS (a human rights organization which emerged amid the controversy surrounding the Rodney King videotape in the 1980s), has published a series of reflections about the potential risks and benefits of allowing videos of human rights abuses to circulate freely. When the pop star Peter Gabriel first launched WITNESS, he asked, "What if every human rights worker had a camera in their hands? What would they be able to document? What would they be able to change?" (quoted in Gregory 2010, 192). Expanding access to low-tech tools of media production and distribution has brought the group much closer to fulfilling that vision, with many more human rights abuses documented and made public.

WITNESS's embrace of participatory culture allows activists to produce and share such videos, yet the organization also recognizes that the circulation of human rights videos far beyond their original contexts raises core ethical issues. First, Gregory identifies issues of consent. Those who are victims of abuse may not be able to meaningfully anticipate the range of different uses of their images in the context of a spreadable and remix culture. This concern remains true, whether with images of government torture or videos of school bullying, in developing countries or in the United States. Second, Gregory warns against the potential "re-victimization" which can occur when humiliating footage enters contexts that encourage comic or erotic interpretations:

> The most graphic violations—violent attacks, or even sexual assault—are seen as the material that most easily translates into a loss of dignity, privacy, and agency, and which carries with it the potential for real re-victimization. [. . .] Video distribution in and of itself can also contribute to creating further layers of victimization: individuals in torture videos shot are already being doubly humiliated—in the first instance by what happens to them in custody, and, in the second, by the act of filming. They are then further exposed as the footage achieves widespread circulation. (2010, 201)

Confronting these challenges, Gregory pushed his organization to develop an ethics for the way such material gets circulated. In some cases, WITNESS allowed its content to circulate via YouTube and other video-sharing sites, while other videos were locked down and (in theory) could be seen only via the group's own site, the Hub, where WITNESS could more clearly shape the viewing context. In reality, of course, it is increasingly hard for any group—whether a human rights organization or a company—to control how its material spreads. In 2010, WITNESS shut down its Hub.

The persistence of rumors and the porousness of the communication landscape (as we saw earlier) and the risks associated with the spread of decontextualized videos and images (as WITNESS suggests) represent arguments for us all to take greater responsibility for the media we choose to circulate, to avoid posting information which has not been vetted carefully, to help challenge rumors we know to have been discredited, and to try to help frame materials which may be controversial or disturbing when encountered in inappropriate contexts. In our enhanced book, MIT lecturer and software developer Christopher Weaver and Sam Ford argue for the importance of developing critical skills for appraising content, as well as ethical frameworks for taking ownership of the consequences of what we share with our communities. As Weaver and Ford point out, it is especially important for educational institutions to critically engage with these processes of content evaluation, as digital texts play increasingly prominent roles in how people make informed decisions as citizens. Another important step for increasing the consistency with which we all can vet information online (and for combatting new forms of plagiarism in an era of spreadability) comes from projects like the Curator's Code (http://www.curatorscode.org/), an initiative providing guidelines for standardizing how to credit both the content creator and the circulator from whom a person has found material once he or she chooses to share that material with others.

In short, the collective control over meaning making and content circulation we all now have may provide powerful new ways to participate as citizens and society members. However, it also necessitates new means to vet the quality of the information we share. And responsible use of these new forms of circulation demands that we both make clear where we received the information we share and think twice before passing along material we have not closely evaluated.

This book has embraced the values of circulation, seeing how spreadability gives the public a much more active role in shaping the media environment, but that does raise the ethical stakes in our collective decisions about what media should circulate and how we all ensure the integrity of the information we share with others. We are not arguing here that spreadability necessarily leads to a utopian vision of a more informed, more responsible, more ethical society. Rather, as more people take an active role in shaping the creation and circulation of media texts, the public has access—for better and worse—to a greater range of voices.

Our belief is that content creators of all kinds—from Madison Avenue executives that want to sell us Old Spice to civic groups that want to call attention to social injustices—can design texts that audiences want to spread if they recognize the basic desires and mechanics which inspire these grassroots acts of circulation. As we have seen, material that spreads is producerly, in that it leaves open space for audience participation, provides resources for shared expression, and motivates exchanges through surprising or intriguing content. People want to share media texts which become a meaningful resource in their ongoing conversations or which offer them some new source of pleasure and interest. They want to exchange and discuss media content when the material contains cultural activators, when it offers activities in which they can participate. As we saw with regard to rumors, this content often spreads when it speaks, consciously or not, thoughts that people are compelled by but lack a language to communicate.

This is not to say that such material becomes irresistible, a claim that would take us back to the passivity associated with viral media theory. Rather, participants appraise the content to see whether it is valuable and meaningful for the groups with which they regularly converse.

As we enter more decisively into an era of spreadable media, we are seeing new kinds of brand strategies and new kinds of civic discourses, both imagined to reflect a shift in power away from top-down distribution of content and toward empowering grassroots intermediaries to act on behalf of a larger organization or cause. Advertisements are becoming more playful and participatory, no longer counting on their ability to demand attention by disrupting our chosen entertainment experiences. Instead, advertisers are striving to create texts that people actively seek out and willingly circulate. Meanwhile, the concept of civic media moves away from the discourses of public service institutions, taking on more of the qualities of entertainment media as creators seek to expand the communities through which they circulate. These producers are no longer dependent on traditional kinds of public broadcasting to reach audiences. In chapter 6, we will explore more fully what this push toward spreadability means for independent media producers. Such creators have often been the first to innovate with social media as they seek to route around traditional roadblocks to distributing their content and have tapped into collaborative models as they seek to court and sustain a community of supporters around their works.

Animator Nina Paley and science fiction writer Cory Doctorow are two of a growing number of independent artists rethinking and reinventing the process through which their texts enter circulation. Both offer their art to fans as "gifts," hoping the community will support their efforts. While they differ on the best models (Paley and Doctorow 2010), both artists are strong backers of the concept of a "creative commons," and both want to escape what they see as constricting copyright regimes. Here, for example, is part of Paley's open letter to the fans who visit her website:

> I hereby give *Sita Sings the Blues* to you. [. . .] Please distribute, copy, share, archive, and show *Sita Sings the Blues*. From the shared culture it came, and back into the shared culture it goes. Conventional wisdom urges me to demand payment for every use of the film, but then how would people without money get to see it? How widely would the film be disseminated if it were limited by permission and fees? Control offers a false sense of security. The only real security I have is trusting you, trusting culture, and trusting freedom. (2009)

As we argued in chapter 1, such "gifts" do not represent "free content." This sort of gift-giving frequently implies some form of reciprocity, and that is openly acknowledged in both these cases. But the willingness of these artists to sacrifice some control over the circulation of their works helps the works to spread. Doctorow has been explicit about the publicity and relationship-building potential of embracing

COURTING SUPPORTERS FOR INDEPENDENT MEDIA

grassroots circulation: "Of all the people who failed to buy this book today, the majority did so because they never heard of it, not because someone gave them a free copy" (2008a).

Under a broadcast paradigm, distribution is almost inseparable from promotion: both mechanisms ensure that a commercially produced product grabs the attention of the most broadly defined audience possible. By contrast, the circulation of independent films, games, music, and comics typically demands participatory mechanisms to compensate for the lack of promotional budget. Their communication strategies often court niche and subcultural communities imagined to have a strong affinity with their genre or message, and the creators hope these supporters will promote the work to like-minded others.

Such strategies do not exist in opposition to commercial aims, even if they may not be wholly compatible with them. Doctorow publishes his books (such as his 2003 *Down and Out in the Magic Kingdom* and his 2008 *Little Brother*) through commercial publishers, yet he has gained greater visibility by allowing fans to download his books for free and to remix and recirculate the content in ways that spark discussions. Paley sells DVDs of her 2008 animated feature *Sita Sings the Blues* through her own website, where she also sells themed merchandise, including soundtracks and T-shirts. However, much of the buzz has come from people sharing links to the film online. Some subset of those who watch the film for free ultimately pay to own, and many purchase DVDs to show their respect and support for the artist. When Paley does sell copies of her DVDs, she collects 50 percent of the proceeds because she does not split her revenue with an outside distributor. She donates the other 50 percent to QuestionCopyright. org, making a statement for the value of unlimited access to cultural materials. Paley (2010b) estimates as of November 2010 that she has netted $119,708 through various forms of "gifts" from her fans, while making only $12,551 through theatrical and broadcast distribution. Doctorow's Creative Commons license prohibits commercial and nonprofit appropriation and remixing of his book, while Paley allows her audience members to profit from their own commercial sales of her DVDs but stresses that they must pay a portion of revenue to certain music rights holders.[1]

Paley rejects an either/or argument which sees the choice to "go digital" as opting out of commercial distribution altogether:

> When I decided to give it away free online, what finally made me realize this was viable was when I realized that this didn't mean it wouldn't be seen on the big screen, that the internet is not a replacement for a theater. It's a complement. Many people will see it online and go, "Wow, I wish I could see this on the big screen!" And so they can, and some people like to see it more than once. Another thing is, you see it online, and that increases the demand for the DVDs. So it's the opposite of what the record and movie industries say. Actually, the more shared something is, the more demand there is for it. (Quoted in K. Thompson 2009)

Similarly, Doctorow (2008a) has found that his sales have increased because of the decision to share digital versions of his books online. More people discover his work, and, if they value what he wrote, they often want to add it to their personal libraries. In both cases, fans engage with the content, and a portion later decide to purchase it.

Paley (2009) refers to older forms of distribution as "coercion and extortion" because audience members are forced to pay, whether they value the experience or not. She, on the other hand, trusts that her audiences will pay for what they value. Her distribution practices are often compared with English alternative-rock band Radiohead's decision to let fans pay whatever they wanted for the digital download release of the band's 2007 album *In Rainbows*. While Radiohead still relied on centralized processes of distribution, however, Paley has embraced a much more decentralized approach:

> My personal experience confirms audiences are generous and want to support artists. Surely there's a way for this to happen without centrally controlling every transaction. [. . .] The audience, you and the rest of the world is actually the distributor of the film. So I'm not maintaining a server or host or anything like that. Everyone else is. We put it on archive.org, a fabulous website, and encourage people to BitTorrent it and share it. (2009)

Doctorow similarly revels in the ways that individuals engage with his free content; he showcases grassroots transformations that others create using his material via his blog—everything from amateur films reenacting scenes from his novels or fan-created theatrical adaptations to translations of his texts into foreign languages.

Over the past two decades, the web's powerful impact on the media marketplace has been felt in the construction of alternative systems for the circulation of media texts. This chapter offers a comparative perspective on the ways such shifts hint at new modes of production, alternative genres of content, and new relationships between producers and audiences. Though these examples may take a variety of forms—from sharing content for free in hopes of soliciting other kinds of rewards to seeking free labor and direct financial support from fans—they all rely on a more active role for audiences who often work in concert with alternative media makers. These practices are still emergent and very much in flux, making a definitive approach for supporting alternative media unlikely to emerge anytime soon. This chapter discusses the experiments of independent or alternative filmmakers, video game designers, comic book creators, and recording artists. We describe them here as "alternative" because they frequently position themselves against a commercial mainstream which remains powerful in its ability to ensure widespread distribution of its products yet is slow moving in adapting its infrastructure for this rapidly evolving media landscape.

While we've focused our discussions of developing models around specific media and genres, the reality is that experimentation along similar lines (sometimes with wildly divergent results) is often occurring across media sectors. So, for instance, later in this chapter we consider collaborative production models for independent film but have found experiments in music which are just as innovative and interesting. Because alternative media producers across a wide variety of platforms work outside of fixed institutional and corporate structures, they are driving an immense amount of experimentation. This chapter does not attempt an exhaustive map of everything being tried but instead offers snapshots demonstrating the logics shaping these innovations.

Creating Spreadable Business Models

The University of Southern California's Networked Publics group explains the ramifications of these experimental approaches to media circulation:

> Commercial media, for better and for worse, provide much of the source material for our modern language of communication. The current moment is perhaps less about overthrow of this established modality of common culture, but more a plea for recognition of a new layer of communication and cultural sharing. At best, this is about folk, amateur, niche and non-market communities of cultural production mobilizing, critiquing, remixing commercial media and functioning as a test bed for radically new cultural forms. At worst, this is about the fragmenting of common culture or the decay of shared standards of quality, professionalism, and accountability. (Russell et al. 2008, 72)

The new media landscape, they argue, is characterized by a proliferation of different groups—some grassroots and amateur, some civic (as we saw in chapter 5) or educational, some commercial—producing and circulating content.

Many commercial media producers will hold onto old-school business models as long as they can, attempting to ease the transition to a new state of affairs, but grassroots circulation may be the only way forward for many independent artists lacking mainstream distribution. The Networked Publics group reached a similar conclusion, arguing that participatory culture may be changing the goals of artists or benchmarks for success:

> Music has always been a domain of robust amateur production, making it particularly amenable to more bottom-up forms of production and distribution in the digital ecology, and ripe for the disintermediation of labels and licensors. [. . .] As late as 2001 the prevailing wisdom described local/amateur music being considered by fans, scholars, and musicians alike as "something to get beyond." In other words, the end game for the artist was still "getting signed" and following the

traditional industry model, with the time-honored decision-making chain. However as the lines further blur, remix becomes embedded into the culture (even beyond music), and technological changes continue to occur, it would appear that perhaps "getting beyond" might no longer be the goal. (Russell et al. 2008, 55)

But there is no one model for "getting beyond" amateur status. The greatest advantage may rest with those producers whose work operates within genres with strong fan followings (animation, science fiction, horror) and who speak to well-defined populations (minority and activist groups). (For an account on how Joss Whedon tapped into a network of ardent fans to independently distribute *Dr. Horrible's Sing-Along Blog*, see the essay by Henry Jenkins in our enhanced book.)

Our description of the value network created around Tecnobrega in Brazil in chapter 4 offers one example of the ways strong regional identities can help forge a new model for relations between music producers and their audiences. Microsoft Research New England principal researcher Nancy K. Baym draws on similar logics in her piece in the enhanced book. She has undertaken intensive research on the particularly sophisticated model of independent media circulation found in the Swedish independent music scene. Sweden, Baym notes, is home both to ABBA and a range of other globally successful musical groups and to Pirate Bay, a key torrenting site. In our enhanced book, Baym describes the way that midlevel and emerging groups seek to navigate a space between the two:

> The logic goes like this: We are small and have minimal budgets. There are few mainstream venues that will promote our music, so few people will have the opportunity to hear it through mass media. The more people who hear it, the larger the audience will become. Even if most of that audience does not pay for CDs or mp3s, the slice that does will be bigger than the entire audience would otherwise have been. And the slice that doesn't pay to buy music may well pay for other things. [. . .] The result is not the death of Swedish music but a successful synergy in which the need of small artists and labels to reach an expanded

audience while staying within limited budgets meets the needs of fans to make music listening a collective activity [. . .] and to incorporate music into their own online identities.

For many of these smaller labels, Baym reports anywhere from half to two-thirds of CD and mp3 sales come from beyond Sweden's borders. Swedish groups unlikely to benefit from traditional publicity mechanisms are achieving hits, going on transnational tours, and otherwise reaping the benefits of this system. In embracing spreadability, these artists are sacrificing some ability to shape and control the routes by which their music reaches the public. In return, their songs circulate among audiences they would never have come into contact with before.

In chapter 3, we examined the role that surplus audiences can play for broadcast television. Audiences often ignored by television networks in favor of those thought "most lucrative" have sometimes turned out to be missed opportunities. For independent producers, however, there are no surplus audiences. Creators need every bit of support they can find. They will rarely spend money on audience testing, especially if their work is motivated by noncommercial goals, so they are less likely to too tightly prescribe who their audience should be from a demographics standpoint.

The free and open sharing of content can provide a valuable research tool for these producers, allowing them to see where (culturally and geographically) their texts spread and thus to build business models that might map against those pockets of audience interest. Bands that plan their tour dates around how and where their mp3s are distributed, filmmakers who empower those who advocate for their content, or authors who learn which readers to court more actively based on who is most interested in their work are using the digital circulation of their content as a means to develop new relationships rather than merely selling a single good to an individual. Some of this may look like guesswork when compared to established industry practice, but their guesses are now grounded in much more data on audience behavior and built from anecdotal readings of online flows—means that were not as readily available to alternative media makers in the past. If content creators consider getting noticed one of their primary goals, the best way for them to do so is to listen for how their material spreads.

Spreadability does not offer a panacea for independent media makers, however. Distribution by a major studio still matters for many independently produced films, for instance, and only a small number are picked up each year beyond the film festival circuit. Without the promotional budgets and platforms of big media companies and amid the competition from other independent content producers, independent creators still face an uphill struggle to find audiences for their works. Spreadability can help transform this system, however. Many more films now get circulated through mechanisms that rely heavily on the support of their most enthusiastic fans. As a consequence, spreadability is actively expanding cultural diversity because a broader range of media makers have access to potential audiences and a greater number of people have access to works which might otherwise have been available only in major urban areas.

Reinventing Comics

Scott McCloud's manifesto *Reinventing Comics* (2000) positioned the web as a more open space for newcomers to prove their worth as artists, as well as a technology that might broaden the potential public for comics by allowing writers and artists to explore themes that would never make it into mainstream publications. McCloud also predicted that the web might break the stranglehold centralized distribution exerts on the comics world, so helping to diversify the readership of comics. McCloud's ideas about the possibilities for the comics industry echo many aspects of the visions of the independent filmmakers and musicians described in the previous section. (It's worth noting that, in addition to Paley's experimentation with *Sita Sings the Blues*, she has also used online distribution for her comics series *Mimi and Eunice*.) And, in the case of comics, all of McCloud's forecasts have proven true to some degree.

Today, webcomics thrive across many different communities, and people create comics material for very different reasons. Some are trying to hone their skills, to demonstrate market potential, or to build a reputation before going pro. They might move into print once they've found their niche. Others still choose to remain digital, despite offers from print-based publishers. And a few, such as the game-themed *Penny Arcade* creators Jerry Holkins and Mike Krahulik, have developed communities around their webcomics which can take on a life of their own and, in some cases, become bigger than the comics themselves. For instance, Holkins and Krahulik have created one of the most important trade shows in the games industry, one of the few which facilitates direct interactions between game designers and their audiences.

While the traditional comics model is structured around major publishers, with independent and underground publishers constructed as an alternative, things are much fuzzier online, where amateur and semiprofessional artists appear alongside those who are more commercial and professionally accomplished. And, as alternative comics creators work together to provide mutual support, they often shatter the rigid genre classifications that have long constrained commercial comics publishing. Consider publisher Joey Manley's description of *Modern Tales*, a website showcasing works by a range of independent comics artists: "We've got manga-styled werewolf/cop dramas butting heads (or, um, maybe some other body part) with *Fancy Froglin*, medieval fantasy side-by-side with 'straight' autobiography, space-opera-charged science fiction right next door to Borgesian metafiction. And we like it all (as do our thousands of subscribers)" (quoted in T. Campbell 2006, n.p.).

While comics fans have long passed along battered issues to friends, new media platforms make it much easier for fans to help favorite artists attract new readers. As Microsoft program manager Geoffrey Long writes in our enhanced book,

Unlike traditional print comics, for which most writers and artists labor under "work for hire" contracts for large publishers such as Marvel and DC, webcomics are typically owned and operated by their creators and rely on revenues generated by advertising, fan subscriptions/memberships, or sales of ancillary merchandise. As a result, for creators, getting individuals to purchase a single instance of their work (such as a traditional print floppy) is less important than establishing an ongoing relationship, aggregating a large recurring audience over time.

George Rohac Jr. (2010) surveyed more than 500 webcomics producers and found that almost all of them now give their comics away for free, while seeking revenue through other means (such as the sale of themed merchandise). About 30 percent of those interviewed published their work under a Creative Commons license, and another 15 percent have asserted no copyright claims over their material whatsoever. Almost two-thirds of these artists allowed fans to share their work freely—with attribution. Joel Watson of *HijiNKS Ensue* told Rohac that Watson's fans support his work in different ways: some have the financial resources to pay for the comics they read, while others have the time and energy to help promote what he is doing (2010, 35). Flexible arrangements around copyright have given Watson the ability both to serve and to obtain value from these varied constituencies.

Like the Swedish indie bands examined earlier, webcomics producers often circulate content without immediate monetary compensation in the hopes of capturing the interest of potential customers. Similar to Doctorow's electronic publishing model, the digital circulation of new comics material might drive eventual sales of printed collections or support a range of other business models. In each case, digital distribution lowers the costs of reaching this market, while spreadable strategies allow these independent creators to expand the potential audiences they can reach.

How Long Is the Long Tail?

Chris Anderson's influential *Wired* article (2004) and his 2006 best-selling book, *The Long Tail: Why the Future of Business Is Selling Less of More*, make the case that online retailers operate in a context far more hospitable to diverse material and minority tastes than ever before. *The Long Tail* suggests that niche media content may accrue value at a different pace, on a different scale, through different infrastructure, and on the basis of different appeals than the highest-grossing commercial texts do. The limited shelf space of brick-and-mortar stores often results in very narrow periods of exposure of works to customers (or none whatsoever), generally producing zero tolerance for works that do not quickly generate a profit. And, as McCloud's critique of the role of retailers in the comics world suggests, these operations may sequester media content from those who have casual rather than dedicated interests.

Online retail and rental operations such as Amazon and Netflix, on the other hand, can maintain more extensive backlists of titles, many of which may get little circulation in any given week but which, over time, recoup their costs and may even turn significant profits. Further, for the distributor in such a model, even the titles which never turn a profit are valuable in building the company's reputation as a comprehensive source for material.

Anderson's widely read argument locates the mass, hit-driven market at the front end of the tail, reaching a large and diverse audience. Meanwhile, more niche products sit at the narrow, back end of the tail, appealing to much smaller audiences. This narrow end, he argues, keeps getting longer and longer, and the ability to turn a profit on this so-called Long Tail content rests on being able to maintain a broad and diverse inventory while lowering the costs of distribution (through digital networks) and promotion (by ceding more control of this effort to grassroots intermediaries).

There is strong evidence that the public has access to a much more diverse array of media texts in the digital era than ever before. Anita Elberse (2008) estimates that, at the time of her writing, the average brick-and-mortar record store carried about 15,000 albums, while Amazon, by contrast, offered 250,000 titles. At the time, online sources listed about 80,000 DVD titles, while a neighborhood Blockbuster offered 1,500 titles. The contrast may be even greater for those who live outside large metropolitan areas, for whom such diverse options have never before been available. This new diversity represents expanded opportunities for independent media producers of all kinds. For the moment, let's call this the "soft version" of the Long Tail argument.

Anderson's book, however, pushed his claims much further. Given this context, Anderson asserts that media industries will shift from an emphasis on hits that appeal to a broad customer base toward greater fragmentation and diversification for different niche markets, resulting in an era of "microcultures" (2006, 183–184). This "hard version" of the Long Tail theory, which argues that media industries are evolving from a hit-driven model, has drawn significant criticism. Anita Elberse's *Harvard Business Review* article (2008) challenges some of Anderson's core claims based on her extensive research into two key online distributors: U.S.-based music distributor Rhapsody and the Australian-based DVD rental company Quickflix. Some of Elberse's findings support the idea that the online world sustains a much more diverse array of media options. Looking at Rhapsody, she found that the top 10 percent of songs accounted for 78 percent of rentals in any given month and that the top 1 percent represents 32 percent of all plays. While this evidence supports the claim that popular attention is still focused mostly toward "hits," the category of "hit" has expanded online to include many titles that most likely would have been unavailable in a predigital era. Further, many audiences are tracking down and engaging with more obscure titles that fall even further outside of the so-called mainstream market.

Turning to individuals, Elberse found that those who engage with media most intensely are most likely to seek content from the longer end of the tail, whereas light and casual users are more likely to restrict their interests to more mainstream texts. In other words, those invested deeply in a given genre are more likely to research and sample alternative material in that area. All of this tends to support a softer version of the Long Tail theory—one focused on the ways the web has expanded access to alternatives rather than suggesting that niche markets will totally displace the concentrated attention associated with the broadcast era. (In an essay in our enhanced book, David Edery, CEO of the Spry Fox game studio and principal of the Fuzbi games consulting company, offers the games industry as a particularly rich case study for understanding the strengths and limitations of the Long Tail model.)

Examined side by side, Anderson and Elberse base their analyses on two very different models of taste. In Anderson's account, the public is poorly served by the homogenized content associated with the broadcast model and better served by material which more precisely fits their tastes. Anderson holds that access to more diverse offerings will lead to greater fragmentation of audience interest. Elberse, on the other hand, draws much of her analysis from Robert H. Frank and Philip J. Cook's 1995 book *The Winner-Take-All Society*, which assumes that "hits" are popular because they represent a higher quality and a more desirable alternative to niche content. Arguing that digital dynamics make it even more likely that audiences will "converge in their tastes and buying habits," Elberse writes,

> First and foremost, lesser talent is a poor substitute for greater talent. Why, for example, would people listen to the world's second-best recording of *Carmen* when the best is readily available? Thus even a tiny advantage over competitors can be rewarded by an avalanche of market share. Second, people are inherently social, and therefore find value in listening to the same music and watching the same movies that others do. (2008, 3)

Elberse's *Carmen* example links discriminating taste back to the realm of high art, which has traditionally been organized around hierarchies and canons. The ranking of popular artists is not as clear as this line of thinking would suggest: we defy anyone to identify the "best" or "second-best" pop star in the world, for instance. People typically are interested in more than one example of a given category, seeking not only "quality" (classically defined) but diversity. Anderson's argument is much more consistent with work in the cultural studies tradition which sees taste as highly particular to specific populations—that is, not as a universalized claim about quality but, rather, more localized, context-specific evaluations.

Elberse supports her argument with some compelling evidence that people, on average, are more likely to be satisfied with selections from the broad end of the tail and more likely to be disappointed with choices from the long end of the tail. While all tastes are "acquired" in the sense that they emerge from specific social and cultural experiences that tend to be mutually reinforcing, our limited exposure to alternative culture means we are less likely to have acquired the skills needed to decipher and appreciate its content. But those who do acquire such tastes are likely to have more precise expectations, such as classical music buffs who have a clear (if heatedly disputed) ranking of the best performances of *Carmen*.

But missing from both of these arguments is a simple reality: most people do not engage with only niche material or only mass-media material. People use media texts both to enjoy shared cultural experiences and to differentiate themselves from mass tastes. Mass-media content often becomes spreadable because its relative ubiquity provides common ground for conversation with a wide variety of people. Niche content, on the other hand, spreads because it helps people communicate their more particular interests and sensibilities, to distinguish themselves from most others. Mass-media content often helps us all "be friendly"; niche media content helps us find "best friends." Occasionally, mass-media texts generate the type of passion and deep interest more often reserved for niche interests. Other times, once-niche material attracts mainstream interest. On the whole, however, mainstream and niche media texts will continue to serve different functions.[2]

Curating Independent Games

Success under Anderson's Long Tail model relies on developing mechanisms for educating audiences and tools to help people find the texts they are most apt to value. As Erik Brynjolfsson, Yu Jeffrey Hu, and Michael Smith concluded in another investigation of Anderson's formulations, "Consumers can become overwhelmed when choices are poorly organized, and they may actually reduce their purchases as a result. Thus, the Long Tail makes it critically important that retailers provide tools to facilitate the discovery of products through both active and passive search" (2006, 69). Their research suggests that the public's taste for alternative fare broadens as they are exposed to more options and as they learn how to find the best niche products. Anderson describes technological fixes such as "aggregators" and "filters" which help bring content to the attention of interested publics, yet he also recognizes folksonomic practices such as "tagging" as "amplified word of mouth" for particularly compelling works (2006, 107). In an essay in our enhanced book, Jonathan Gray, a media and cultural studies professor at University of Wisconsin–Madison, sees the figure of the author as a particularly important mechanism for tagging such content. Peter Jackson got people to pay attention to *District 9*, the 2009 film by a little-known South African filmmaker, by officially endorsing the project with his "brand." For independent films and other creative projects, then, known authors can become a tag for new media content that can interest audiences in projects outside the mainstream.

The Long Tail has resulted in new business models in which the aggregation of alternative media texts is combined with the creation of online communities engaged in discussing and evaluating shared works. Such communities represent one form of "curated" content—that is, material which has been appraised and situated via the community's collective action. Yet companies such as Apple have also claimed to provide customers with "curated" material—in this case, material which has been professionally evaluated according to standards of technical polish or commercial potential. This kind of curation represents a reassertion of a traditional gatekeeping function, which some observers read as signaling the end of a more open and participatory web (Anderson and Wolff 2010). Both models are designed to help cut through the clutter of expanding media options, one by calling attention to distinctive work and diverse options, the other by constraining the flow of content based on commercial values.

As an example of the collective curation model, the rise of the independent games movement has been shaped by both the idiosyncratic curatorial practices of individuals and more grassroots and decentralized curatorial practices. Meanwhile, the emergence of the "app" market around the iPhone and the iPad has represented a more centralized and corporate-controlled model of curation. Let's briefly consider an example of each.

Created in September 2005 by game designer Greg Costikyan and trade reporter Johnny Wilson, Manifesto Games sought to change the infrastructure of the gaming industry, making it easier for creative game designers to work outside major studios and publishers. Inspired by the discourse about the Long Tail, Manifesto Games created a platform to showcase video games which never reached physical stores, connecting the best work coming out of the indie games movement to engaged audiences seeking such content. In many ways, Manifesto functioned as a critique of the shift from games as a cottage industry where small bands of innovators worked to experiment with new forms of expression in the early days of home computing toward a mass-scale, studio-based industry where only large companies could meaningfully compete for shelf space at WalMart. Costikyan was relentless in posting his own impressions of the games—positive and negative—via his blog. He encouraged developers to post material that educated audiences about the thinking behind their titles. He provided an open space for his audience members to share their impressions of what worked and what didn't in the titles Manifesto was promoting and hosted regular discussions where designers could talk directly with their players.

As Manifesto was launching, the independent video games movement was itself rapidly growing. IndieCade emerged as a games festival, not unlike a traditional film festival, showcasing both independent games and the audiences who supported them. Meanwhile, the number of university-based game labs expanded, producing an increasing number of talented artists who were working on the fringes of the mainstream games industry. Some of these experiments, such as *Flow* (the inspiration for the commercial game *Flower*) or *Narbacular Drop* (the inspiration for the mainstream *Portal*) won key industry awards. Their innovations were copied and built on, and some of the developers involved were recruited by big studios. Simultaneously, casual games and mobile games became key sectors in the overall games market, suggesting that video games could succeed without massive design and promotional budgets. And many new distribution platforms such as Steam, Xbox Live Arcade, and WiiWare offered independent and entrepreneurial game developers greater access to their potential markets.

In June 2009, Manifesto Games closed shop. Costikyan (2009) cited a number of factors behind Manifesto's collapse, including the downturn of the economy and the drying up of venture-capital resources. The continued success of other independent sites, such as Kongregate, may be in part a result of their targeting a narrower segment of the independent games market—in Kongregate's case, Flash games—and then developing a robust set of tools which support audience efforts to appraise and recommend content to each other.

Ironically, the growth of new mainstream platforms for video game distribution, which provided access for indie developers, sucked some of the urgency out of the cause of constructing a movement around indie games, even if these other new models did not generally provide the autonomy for independent creators that Manifesto's founders had hoped. As Costikyan explained on his blog, following the announcement of Manifesto's shuttering, "Apple, Microsoft, and Nintendo have complete, monopolistic control over distribution through their proprietary channels, and while they may, today, generously grant a high revenue share to developers who sell through them, developers are in the final analysis utterly at their mercy" (2009).

Critics of Apple's App Store for iPhone echo Costikyan's concerns that Apple holds too much power in its relations with independent producers of mobile applications. Apple obviously has a vested interest in distributing a wide variety of apps (or programs) for its proprietary platform, since a diversity of interests helps build its user base. However, the corporation ultimately curates what is made available in the App Store based on what aligns with its own perceived market interests. Jonathan Zittrain (2009) argues such restrictions run counter to the history of innovation on digital platforms. Personal computers, he argues, are relatively open platforms that anyone with the right knowledge can master and leverage for useful tasks. The Internet, he argues, is also a generative platform with an open set of standards and a network of nodes that pass data between them without regard for the material or nature of the data. As a result, both support a "generative revolution where novel and disruptive technologies have come from obscure backwaters—and conquered" (18). The restrictions of Apple's App Store, however, mean only a select group who agree to Apple's terms can access the tools to create content for its platforms; innovation is concentrated and filtered, if not ultimately regulated, by Apple itself.

Zittrain notes that the Software Development Kit (SDK) developers must use to create material for devices such as the iPhone gives Apple the right to approve technology, functionality, content, and design of these applications. Only those approved will be sold through the App Store, the only channel through which apps can officially be sold. Apple reserves the right to recall or stop selling apps as it sees fit, to promote certain apps over others, and to prevent the sale of apps that duplicate the functionality of official programs (such as email) or that provide users with functionality Apple or its network partners (such as the iPhone's U.S. mobile service carriers) dislike. Zittrain suggests that this approach means Apple's App Store and mobile devices are unlikely to become generative platforms.

Manifesto and Apple thus offer two very different models of curation, one remaining relatively open to new content and placing greater control into the hands of audiences to help tag and evaluate material, the other more closed and constrained by commercial criteria. As the logics of spreadable media continue to take hold across the media landscape, the tensions between these two models will likely become more prominent.

Collaborative "Sourcing," "Funding," and "Surfing"

Though Costikyan's experiment in developing an alternative model for independent video game production was ultimately unsuccessful, similar strategies are enjoying success in the world of independent film, where producers are leveraging the energy and excitement of their fan bases to fund, sustain, and promote their projects. Consider filmmakers Susan Buice and Arin Crumley, who tapped every device available to them in an era of participatory culture to get their 2005 feature film *Four Eyed Monsters* in front of an audience. Rather than waiting for the film's DVD release to offer director's extras, Buice and Crumley released videos about the film's production via iTunes, MySpace, and YouTube. As interest in the project grew, the team asked people to provide their email and zip code if they wanted a screening in their local area. Within months, they received more than 8,000 screening requests and were able to self-distribute the film to more than 30 U.S. cities where they had received at least 100 requests, with each of those cities generating ticket sales equivalent to the screening requests they had received (Crumley 2011). As Crumley explained to Indiewire,

Most theaters would normally avoid a project like ours because we don't have a distributor who would be marketing the film and getting people to show up. But because the audience of our video podcast is so enthusiastic about the project and because we have numbers and emails and zip codes for all of these people, we've been able to instill enough confidence in theaters to get the film booked. (Hernandez 2006)

Fans could use Buice and Crumley's website to monitor requests and identify other potential viewers in their neighborhood.

The Sundance Channel used *Four Eyed Monsters* to launch a series of screenings of independent films in virtual world Second Life, where once again it played to packed houses. Based on these experiences, Buice and Crumley have started talking about the "collective curation" of content: a scenario in which independent producers make clips and previews available online, invite fans to express their interest in or support for the work, and identify where the film has a strong enough following to justify the expense of renting theater space and shipping prints. Paramount adopted a very similar "on-demand" strategy for the nationwide U.S. release of low-budget horror film *Paranormal Activity* in 2009, exhibiting the film in the markets where online demand was greatest (B. Johnson 2010).

Buice and Crumley, like Nina Paley, represent a new generation of independent filmmakers experimenting with new media technologies and practices to reach desired and desiring audiences that might otherwise have little or no exposure to their films. While Hollywood often takes fan and brand communities for granted, these independent filmmakers recognize that they must actively identify and partner with existing communities whose interests align with their own (for aesthetic or political reasons).

These tactics fall loosely into the territory of "crowdsourcing," a term coined by Jeff Howe in an influential 2006 *Wired* magazine article that documents the ways media producers solicit insights and contributions from a large base of amateur or pro-amateur creators. Howe discusses iStockPhoto.com, a company crowdsourcing a library of stock photos. Any photographer can upload images to the site, but photographers are only paid when a subscriber licenses an image for commercial purposes. Threadless, where designers post ideas for T-shirts and the public votes on which ones should be produced and sold, is another widely cited example of crowdsourcing businesses (Brabham 2008). Such processes can be understood as a form of microinvesting (of money, time, resources, and attention) which enables dispersed participants to collectively shape the range of media options available to them.

Similar to the tensions explored in chapter 4, some critics argue that crowdsourcing can become another way of exploiting "free" labor toward commercial ends (especially when there is a lack of transparency about a crowdsourced project), while others argue that crowdsourcing models erode rather than bolster the creativity and autonomy of content creators. In some cases, aspects of a story crowdsourced by a brand or media property may be seen as trivial or insubstantial. In others, fans may be frustrated by a creator "outsourcing" a creative decision to the audience when that audience wants to be surprised (Ford 2010d). In short, crowdsourcing is a delicate concept.

Perhaps part of the problem is the term itself. Critics such as Jonathan Gray (2011) have argued that some of the contradictions rest in the use of the concept of the "crowd," historically more associated with "mobs" than with a thinking creative community, to describe the grassroots populations with which these artists are engaging. As Gray explains, "If we see audiences, agents, actors, citizens, individuals as crowds, we're per force rolling them into an undifferentiated bovine mass. [. . .] Once a crowd develops something, we use different words to describe them. Once voices of brilliance rise up from a crowd, we give them a new title and extract them from the crowd."

These "crowd" projects may ascribe more or less power to co-creators or to the artist "curating" the co-creators' contributions. They may ascribe more or less intelligence and creativity to the crowd. Thus, they may be more or less democratic in their logic. In some cases, talk of crowdsourcing is about shifting the power relations between audiences and producers. In others, crowdsourcing represents an effort to court a community of supporters or simply to pass around a cup to garner funds to do what the artist had planned to do with or without public input.

We agree with Gray's point that part of the problem lies with the term "crowd," bringing with it a mentality of an undifferentiated and aggregated audience rather than a community of participants. Just as we call for a purging of terms such as "viral" to describe how content spreads, we hope to see new terms and concepts used to describe collaboration between audiences and producers, in ways that acknowledge rather than minimize the contributions of all involved.

Such collaborative models have started to emerge as a principal strategy for independent filmmakers to connect directly with their audiences. *Lost Zombies*, for example, describes itself as "a social network whose goal is to create the world's first community generated zombie documentary" (Lost Zombies n.d.). The filmmakers behind the project use a website to solicit specific shots or scenes that would fit within the loose framework of their feature-length movie.

Properly sourcing input from co-creators, however, presents a particular challenge. In the early days of the *Lost Zombies* project, the filmmakers fluctuated between requesting too precise contributions from their participants, so stifling their creativity, and offering too open-ended a structure, resulting in contributions that would never have added up to a compelling film. Here's how the producers describe the strategy that has proven most successful for them:

> We came up with beats—it starts out as a flu, it mutates, the government tries to quarantine people, control the outbreak, pharmaceutical companies try to develop a vaccine, it doesn't work, and there are zombies everywhere. That worked very well for the creative filmmakers. For people who were really good artists but who needed more direction, we created something called the grid. You can pick a square on this 128 square grid, and it will say something like "we need a photo of a zombie fight," and once that grid is full, we think we'll have enough footage to compile the documentary, which should be by the end of the year. (Quoted in "25 New Faces" 2009)

Because the zombie genre has such a loyal fan following, the producers were able to sketch broad directions and count on the audience's creativity to elaborate and embellish scenes in highly generative ways.

On the site, members are welcome to submit photos and footage, and, often, multiple versions of the same shots or sequences are publicly evaluated, with networked participants weighing in on which ones best achieve the desired effect.

Thousands of people so far have contributed to the process, though the producers reserve the right to make the final decision about what is included in the completed production. As Skot Leach, one of the filmmakers, explained, "We're doing everything backward. We've built our audience before creating a film and now we are exploring a range of platforms, still with no completed film" (2010). Their innovative process has already led to much greater media attention paid to their work-in-progress than could be expected by most low-budget horror films, and the producers see such publicity as the lifeblood of the independent filmmaking process.

In some cases, such as the *Star Wars Uncut* website, these co-creation processes are intended to produce noncommercial fan films whose pleasure primarily comes from the experimentation with dispersed creative processes. The *Star Wars Uncut* project assigned an individual scene from the original film to each recruited fan filmmaker, who could re-create that scene however he or she wished. The completed work is stylistically eclectic—with, for instance, animated sequences juxtaposed with scenes of Princess Leia as a drag queen—but the film remains coherent because the intended audience knows every shot and line from George Lucas's original.

This model is now being applied to professional or semiprofessional productions. For example, the Finnish production *Iron Sky* (a science fiction film about a Nazi settlement on the dark side of the moon) involves intensive fan participation. Its filmmaking team had enjoyed success with *Star Wreck: In the Pirkinning*, another science fiction film produced through the collaboration and contributions of about 3,300 fans and released online in 2005. As of September 2010, it has been estimated that *Star Wreck: In the Pirkinning* has received more than 10 million downloads (Lavan 2010). With *Iron Sky*, the producers sought to build on this successful model (Vuorensola 2010). The project raised €6 million through traditional film funding channels such as the Finnish Film Foundation, Eurimages, HessenInvestFilm, and Screen Queensland, but they hope to raise another €900,000 from fans and supporters (Iron Sky website n.d.). Not just seeking cash contributions, the producers post creative challenges and requests for assets to their website—requests which might include anything from developing 3-D models and generating special effects to designing and producing costumes, loaning the use of locations, or working on the road crew for a night shoot.

So far, most of the productions embracing these collaborative production models have been genre films, since it is easier to communicate what is desired when working within highly codified kinds of narratives. Genre films also have very well established fan bases that have built explicit and implicit communities, all of which may more easily support the infrastructure to get the word out to potential participants. Nevertheless, these independent efforts may expand the borders of particular genres, introducing new themes or visual styles or otherwise creating stories significantly different from most mainstream productions.

While crowdsourcing has been used to refer to the solicitation of many different kinds of contributions from supporters (from footage to locations), "crowdfunding" typically refers to situations in which audiences make microinvestments in new creative ventures. Sites such as Kickstarter offer a platform that some independent artists (not simply filmmakers but bands, comic book artists, game designers, authors—indeed, anyone who wants to create or build something) are using to solicit and collect funds. These fundraising processes are used to generate everything from seed money to launch a new venture all the way to completion money to handle postproduction. Artists set their own funding goals and challenge the community to help them raise the needed money. They can offer a broad array of incentives to potential contributors and develop their own publicity schemes to spur on support, and contributors only pay if the producers reach their funding goals.

Kickstarter, as of December 2010, had 1,285 successfully funded film projects, representing a total pledge fund of more than $11 million. Some of these were student projects, others documentaries or short subjects, but the list also includes feature films, especially those trying to gather the cash for postproduction and distribution. The average film project on Kickstarter raises $6,400, while the largest film project raised more than $364,000 (Camper 2010).

Some producers are also finding new ways to collaborate with their audiences to circulate content. (In the "crowd" lexicon, this would be "crowdsurfing.") These processes rely on identifying audiences that might help guide the film's circulation and promotion. At the "Seize the Power" symposium at the Los Angeles Film Festival, Caitlin Boyle (2010) of grassroots documentary-distribution company Film Sprout described the process by which her company consults with the producers of politically charged documentaries, helping them sharpen their focus on interest groups that might have reason to promote their projects. Film Sprout then helps the filmmakers identify circulation strategies, such as the kinds of house parties we described in relation to Brave New Films in chapter 4.

Typically, the film becomes part of a larger public education effort. For example, *The End of the Line* (2009), a documentary on overfishing, found its strongest support from owners of local seafood restaurants who wanted their customers to better understand the ways fishing practices impact the environment. In many cases, they accompanied screenings of the film with meals of sustainable seafood. For another film, *Pray the Devil Back to Hell* (2008), Film Sprout worked closely with church groups and shelters for battered women, both of which found resonance in the film's core stories about how a group of Liberian women helped end their country's bloody civil war. In both these cases, rather than building a specific fan community, Film Sprout and film producers listened to conversations already taking place around relevant topics, courted intermediaries and organizations that would help organize and publicize screenings, and offered their documentaries as a resource these partners could use to support their own causes. For this to work, however, Boyle argues that filmmakers need to be transparent in setting the terms of their alliance with these other interests and must give supporters bragging rights within their own communities.

Going one step further, Jamie King and The League of Noble Peers released their documentary series about copyright battles, *Steal This*

Film (2006), in partnership with torrent tracker sites where fans could download it for free (Weiler 2009). The film series was also distributed through mainstream video-streaming sites such as YouTube. *Steal This Film* closed with a simple call for donations, which had, by mid-2009, brought the filmmakers more than $30,000 from some of the more than six million people who had downloaded or streamed their documentary. King has predicted that one can motivate about 5 percent of viewers to donate in support of independent film production and is now testing that model by developing a new service, VODO (Volunteer Donation), that makes it easy to assign and track donations associated with a film's torrent file. As independent filmmaker Lance Weiler explains, "Engaging an audience in a meaningful way does not ensure that your work will not be pirated, but building such relationships may help limit the damage" (2008).

We might think of the examples described throughout this chapter as experiments. In some cases, these films are still under production, and it remains to be seen whether they will be completed and distributed via such practices or how they will be received. Some of these experiments may be successful; others will produce mixed results. For example, in 2010, the Sundance Film Festival partnered with YouTube to make some of its top independent submissions available to audiences online while the buzz was still brewing from their festival screening (Van Buskirk 2010). Filmmakers could set their own rental rates and their own terms of access as a means of experimenting with different alternative value propositions. While this seemed a good idea for broadening access, the results were disappointing, with each title attracting only about 200 to 300 paid downloads during the two weeks it was available online. Industry observers (for instance, Connelly 2010) quickly dismissed the venture as a failed experiment. Yet Mynette Louie (2010), producer of the 2009 film *Children of Invention* (one of the films in the experiment), told the "Seize the Power" symposium audience that her results were more positive than common perceptions might suggest. The experiment increased public awareness of her film, and, over time, she saw a clear surge in the renting and purchasing of her DVDs. She directly linked this increase back to the exposure she received via YouTube.

Taken as a whole, these projects demonstrate how independent filmmakers could, at least in theory, collaborate with their audiences at each step of the production, distribution, and promotion process. Independent filmmakers have historically had to give up some degree of control over their films in working with commercial distributors, and some are embracing these collaborative strategies because they feel more aligned with the values and interests of their supporters than with those of commercial distributors. Under these models for co-creation, supporters may contribute a range of goods or services which help defray the costs of production. Through community funding, audiences are giving filmmakers their support in advance of the completion of the product, in the hope that they may feel a greater sense of satisfaction in seeing a story that matters to them reach the screen. And emerging collaborative circulation models tap into existing communities of potential supporters to shape the distribution and exhibition of the completed work. These systems tend to pull aspects of independent filmmaking closer to gift-economy logic, where the exchange between artists and audience fosters sentimental, symbolic, and, with luck, exchange value through building feelings of reciprocity.

Making a Joyful Noise

While online technologies might have amplified and proliferated the ways material circulates throughout culture, the existence of alternative forms of media production and circulation is hardly new. Niche genre content and independently produced media have circulated through grassroots movements for decades. For instance, perhaps no community in the United States has been more successful in circulating content outside of mainstream platforms than the religious media activities of implicit and explicit evangelical Christian social networks. The alternative models for circulating media content created by Christian communities, and the tensions and challenges these communities have faced, can shed light and give perspective to the range of new approaches we have examined throughout the chapter.

Evangelical Christian media has long spread through the collaboration of producers, Bible bookstores, and churches. Historically and today, events such as "Vacation Bible School" at local churches and

Bible-study classes have generated large volumes of material alongside Christian music and other media designed for home reading, viewing, or listening. And, while many of these Christian media products have not received significant shelf space in mainstream stores or appeared on prominent bestseller lists, they have achieved widespread circulation via alternative platforms.

Take the traditional ways in which gospel music groups gained traction in U.S. regional circuits. On the local music scene, the reputation of acts often spread as members of a congregation would share cassette tapes or even dub copies of the music of their favored bands (a form of grassroots collaborative media circulation). For small churches featuring a monthly gospel music service, deciding which quartet to invite could become a point of contention, with congregation members advocating for one quartet versus another. Many gospel music fans would even begin following their favorite band around the circuit.

Typically, a quartet would travel from church to church, participating in Saturday-night gospel singings, church homecomings, or other special events (Ford 2010c). Such efforts would be collaboratively funded, with the bands often "surprised" with a "love offering" during or at the conclusion of their church singing service. The Sunshine Witnesses may be more like Radiohead than originally imagined! Moreover, these bands would often be allowed to set up a table in the entrance of the church to sell their cassette tapes (and, later, CDs)—or on the church porch for those congregations that took the parable of Jesus overturning the moneychangers' table in the temple particularly seriously. And, in some cases, the music would be collaboratively performed, with a visiting soloist or group singing alongside the local choir or the whole church.

This model of content circulation sustained acts on a local level. Further, Christian communities "scaled up" such processes as well, as similar informal networks were used to circulate content across Bible bookstores, religious associations, religious radio networks, and congregations, nationally and internationally.

While this process provides many potential suggestions for navigating new models designed for a spreadable media landscape, these

Christian communities have also faced a variety of tensions, many of which highlight issues that content creators might have to tackle. To return to the local gospel music scene, as particular musical acts grew their fame, it became unofficially known that some seemed to gravitate toward the churches that had more "love" to give. Other quartets became more open about requiring an up-front fee, to varying reactions among church communities. Today, these questions are also posed in another way: through debates about whether it is possible to "pirate" Christian tunes.

Journalist Geoff Boucher describes these tensions succinctly as "a clash between familiar imperatives: *Spread the Word* and *Thou shalt not steal*" (2006). While the perceived need to curtail the unofficial circulation of media content is a question faced by all media industries, it has become a particularly vexing question in Christian music circles. Some groups have adopted an economic argument to discourage Christian file sharing: the Christian music industry is not as substantially lucrative as other popular music businesses, and, thus, Christian artists and their families are particularly hard hit by unauthorized downloads. Meanwhile, other organizations in the Christian music industry—such as the Christian Music Trade Association—embrace a moral argument, claiming that it is a sin to "steal" any type of music. According to CMTA president John Styll, "You wouldn't walk into a Christian bookstore and steal a Bible off the shelf" (quoted in Boucher 2006).

However, many Christian music fans and artists disagree, arguing that people taking Bibles freely should be the goal, rather than making large profit margins through "God's gift to humanity": "His Word." In short, if the Christian's charge is proselytizing, then content spreading "the Word" should circulate for free as broadly as possible. Said singer/ songwriter Derek Webb on the grassroots spread of Christian music, "Forgive me for saying it this way, but that looks a lot more like Jesus to me than packaging some album and telling people what to do with their art" (quoted in Boucher 2006).

Christian music artists also face another type of tension: the consternation felt by many as their religious media content circulates outside their borders into the larger "secular" culture. Heather Hendershot (2004) has documented the complex set of social negotiations that occur around the production and distribution of Christian music. She finds that this music is perceived as serving two very different goals: reaffirming the shared values within Christian communities and serving as a vehicle for "witnessing" to those who have not yet accepted Christ. As artists seek to ensure their spread beyond the borders of their self-defined Christian community and thus to reach potential new fans in the secular world, they often have to downplay those messages which too heavily signal their membership to Christianity. Thus, the strategies that ensure such groups' circulation in the cultural mainstream might cause them to lose the support of their initial niche market. Hendershot documents how different artists reconcile these contradictory pushes and pulls on their performance, making peace with the decision to remain within or move beyond their initial base of support.

Many of the tactics deployed and challenges faced by independent media makers are amplified versions of what networks such as these grassroots Christian communities have been employing and dealing with for decades. For local gospel quartets, evangelists, literature publishers, and national Christian music acts alike, much like independent media makers of all stripes, success has come through building a reputation and developing relationships, rather than selling a single good to an individual. Instead of seeing "the song" or "the message" as a commodity, these texts have been the means for developing and sustaining community support, for building collaborative models for "spreading the Word." Despite the tensions that often arise in Christian communities between commercial (making a living) and noncommercial (sharing the gospel) impulses for content creation and circulation, media texts—and the reputations of performers—have been built through formal and informal networks outside of mainstream media distribution.

Further, as Christian artists who have seen or sought the spread of their material outside their religious base have witnessed, the circulation of content across cultural borders often creates points of potential conflict among various communities that view and use those texts for sometimes quite different purposes. But such circulation also creates great new promise for audiences to experience works from other cultures and for producers, whether commercial or grassroots, to find surprising new audiences for their texts. Our final chapter examines these issues through looking at how spreadable practices are shaping and being shaped by processes of globalization, opening up the potential for a more diverse media environment (for some more than others) while creating new tensions as well.

A central argument running through this book is that spreadability has expanded people's capacities to both appraise and circulate media texts and thus to shape their media environment. None of this supposes an end to the role of commercial mass media as perhaps the most powerful force in our collective cultural lives. In many cases, producers and brand makers have decided to utilize more participatory means of communication and informal means of circulation, but their ultimate aim is still the propagation of mass-media content. In other cases, circulated mass-media texts have been grabbed and quoted by people who insert these segments into their ongoing social interactions without regard to—or even against the wishes of—commercial creators. Throughout, mass-media content remains that which spreads the furthest, the widest, and the fastest. This book has also focused on situations in which content has circulated socially which audiences could not access through mass-media distribution: archival materials preserved by collectors, material produced by fans and amateur producers, activist and religious media created to spread the word, and independently produced and distributed media. But all of these instances rest on a basic assumption: that a networked culture is easily accessible to those who desire to spread content.

Our final chapter focuses on the transnational spread of both mass and niche media content. Throughout this chapter, we are using the term "transnational" rather than the commonly used "global," in recognition of the uneven nature of these flows. While, as we will demonstrate, media texts are being exchanged between communities

THINKING TRANSNATIONALLY

in many diverse and dispersed countries, there are also many countries (especially in the Global South—much of Africa, parts of Latin America and Asia) not yet able to actively participate in such exchanges. This increased transnational circulation in some cases amplifies the already powerful influence of producers from the developed world and, in others, reflects the efforts of media producers in the developing world to increase their (sometimes already powerful) influence.

Transnational media content sometimes comes through the front door, distributed by commercial interests (large and small) seeking to expand markets. Other times, it comes through the back door, shaped by the efforts of pirates seeking to profit from media produced by others, by immigrants seeking to maintain contact with cultures they have left behind, and by audiences seeking to expand their access to the world's cultural diversity. In every case, participatory cultural practices are transforming transnational media flows, even if access and participation among those audiences remains uneven.

John Fiske has drawn a productive distinction between "multiplicity," which consists of "more of the same," and "diversity," which reflects a range of alternative identities and agendas:

> We live, we might say, in a society of many commodities, many knowledges, and many cultures. Multiplicity is to be applauded only when it brings diversity, and the two are not necessarily the same, though they are closely related. Multiplicity is a prerequisite of diversity, but it does not necessarily entail it—more can all too often be more of the same. Equally, diversity thrives on multiplicity, but does not necessarily produce it. (1994, 239)

While this book has primarily focused on U.S. media and culture, we have throughout called attention to the ways that works produced elsewhere are entering broader circulation—from the British Susan Boyle video and Twitter flows from Tehran in the introduction to the European genre films and music in chapter 6. To be sure, these materials are being filtered according to local cultural norms and interests; only some of the media texts produced around the world are able to find audiences, for example, in the United States. The patterns of this media spread are not simply between center and periphery, as they have been historically understood, but may be multinodal, connecting countries that have had limited communication in the past. This chapter focuses on transnational cultural flows to illustrate the ways that spreadability may enhance cultural diversity. What we say here about the complex interplay of immigrants and fans around shared cultural materials that travel across national borders also applies to other kinds of exchanges between communities—say, for instance, the secular circulation of Christian media. Throughout this chapter, we also call attention to the potential limits, misunderstandings, and frictions that emerge as media content flows across communities with different histories and agendas.

While we currently write from a vantage point in the United States, we do not want to overstate the traditional dominance of U.S. media internationally, considering the many robust media industries that exist across the globe. Nor do we want to exaggerate the impact of transnational media flows on U.S. audiences, given how recently many media producers gained access to the U.S. market and how relatively little media revenue flows back to some producing countries. Of all the trends we discuss in the book, the transnational circulation of media may be the most fragile, given the geopolitical and economic complexities of the situations we are discussing. However, we do believe that the informal spread of media content through networked communications may circumnavigate if not circumvent some of the factors (political, legal, economic, cultural) which have allowed U.S. mass media to maintain its dominance throughout much of the twentieth century.

The Virtue of Impure Culture

In our enhanced book, MIT Center for Civic Media director Ethan Zuckerman shares the story of how Makmende, a "highly remixable Kenyan superhero," emerged from the music video "Ha-He" by the Nairobi-based "experimental boy band" Just A Band and gained more visibility in the West. Makmende, a "karate-kicking badass," reflects the '70s Blaxploitation-themed music video but also suggests something more. Just A Band's video celebrates the capacity of African media makers to appropriate and remix the content that circulates across their national borders—including a series of pastiches featuring Makmende's imagined appearances on *GQ* and *Esquire* covers. In the process, they encouraged their fans to expand the myth of Makmende's prowess. According to Zuckerman, "The Kenyan blogosphere quickly obliged, and remixers contributed a 10,000 Kenyan shilling note (about US$123) featuring Makmende, several movie posters and magazine covers, and the cover of the Kenyan school system's *Primary Mathematics* textbook remixed as 'Primary Makmende'tics'—all featuring Makmende in his iconic pose." Makmende became a popular reference among Kenyan Twitterers as well. Writes Zuckerman,

> Messages such as "They tried to make a Makmende toilet paper, but there was a problem: it wouldn't take shit from anyone" or "Makmende doesn't cheat death—he wins fair and square" may sound familiar to anyone who's followed Internet memes such as "Chuck Norris Facts," a series of testimonials about that American karate champion and movie star's impossible powers. Other Makmende tweets showed a familiarity with U.S. popular culture: "When Makmende wants a massage, he asks Jack Bauer to torture him." And others have a distinctly Kenyan flair: "Makmende bit a mosquito and it died of malaria" and "Makmende hangs his clothes on a Safaricom line to dry"—a line that's funnier if you know that Safaricom, Kenya's leading mobile phone network, doesn't maintain any wired telephone lines.

Historically, critics of cultural imperialism have sought to defend the purity of indigenous cultures against the corrupting influence of outside parties, yet Zuckerman's analysis suggests ways that the intermixing of cultures may be empowering for those who are looking to escape cultural isolation and to enter into a larger transnational conversation. Makmende is neither purely African nor purely American: this grassroots figure is a cultural composite, whose mashed-up and remixed identity is marked by a series of border crossings, moments when two cultures (perhaps more) touch each other across geopolitical distances. Makmende's cultural impurity makes him a particularly powerful example of the way content is developed and circulated in this current phase of globalization. If, as Zuckerman notes, Makmende sounds Kenyan but is actually a mangled version of Clint Eastwood's "Make my day" catchphrase, he might be seen as what the Africans make of the U.S. culture which has been dumped into their marketplace, and his circulation beyond Africa raises the ante in terms of the developed world's willingness to embrace African's participation within Web 2.0 platforms. Spreadable media practices are expanding points of contact between countries. As they do so, they create an unexpected mixing and mingling of cultural materials, allowing multiple points of entry into these composite mythologies.

But the kinds of exchanges emerging through spreadable media may be even more messy because they do not enter through established channels of communication, because they often involve participants who have not been trained in international diplomacy or commerce, and because all participants lay claim to some of the value and meaning that emerges through their transactions. Such exchanges demonstrate many of the properties that cultural historian Mary Louise Pratt has described as "the arts of the contact zone," suggesting that "social spaces where disparate cultures meet, clash, and grapple with each other" may be culturally generative, resulting in a diversity of different narratives and images as parties work through their connections with each other (1991, 34). Writes Pratt, "Autoethnography, transculturation, critique, collaboration, bilingualism, mediation, parody, denunciation, imaginary dialogue, vernacular expression—these are some of the literate arts of the contact zone. Miscomprehension, incomprehension, dead letters, unread masterpieces, absolute heterogeneity of meaning—these are some of the perils of writing in the contact zone" (35).

The product of such transactions is not only "heterogeneous" in its design but also in its interpretation. Pratt says, "It will read very differently to people in different positions within the contact zone" (1991, 35). She argues that such arts do not generate "universal" understandings; rather, they require complex and multiple literacies as we come to understand the process through which we negotiate their meaning and value across a range of different global contexts. Just as we saw in chapter 4 that the complex negotiations between audiences and industry required us to move beyond simple notions of resistance to embrace a more multivocal concept such as collaboration, this chapter suggests that old debates about the homogenizing force of global communication do not deal with the complex interactions between diverse populations which shape the transnational flows of media content.

We see a complex layering of cultures in Ian Condry's study of the hip-hop scene in Japan. Condry rejects either/or claims about the cultural impact of globalization: "I found that neither global homogenization nor localization accurately captured the ways the musical style has changed. Instead, we see a deepening and quickening connection between hip-hop scenes worldwide, at the same time that a wider diversity of styles appears in Japan and globally" (2006, 19).

Something similar occurs with the transnational flows around Kuduro, a contemporary dance movement heavily informed by the martial arts practice Capoeira. While Capoeira is primarily associated today with Brazil, historians believe it was strongly shaped by African practices which came to the New World through the slave trade. The export to Angola of a Jean-Claude Van Damme film using Capoeira may have inspired African youth to adapt some of the martial arts gestures into their dancing, where they mixed Jamaican dancehall music movements, traditional Angolan kilapanga, semba, and kizomba musics, and, finally, Caribbean calypso music, becoming kuduro (de Bourgoing 2009).

Kuduro music and dance reached the urban ghettos of Lisbon by the early 1990s via waves of African immigration. And, more recently, kuduro has been inserted into amateur and professional music videos which get posted on YouTube. The movement gained perhaps its most high-profile international attention through the circulation of "Sound of Kuduro," a video coproduced by the British artist M.I.A. and the Portuguese electronic-dance-music project Buraka Som Sistema (McDonnell 2008). Here, we see an ongoing process of localization and globalization through popular and participatory culture, but also through waves of immigration, economic exploitation, and slavery.

So, first and foremost, the production of the Makmende mythology can be understood as an example of the expanded digital capacity of the African people, their ability to deploy networked systems of cultural production and circulation to serve their own agenda, to give voice to their own creative impulses. Makmende can be seen as a way of claiming space and occupying time in larger transnational systems of exchange. We might read this ability to intervene, however falteringly, as a reaction against the status of the developing world as what Lawrence Liang has described as "the waiting room of history" (2009, 23). Liang argues that "waiting for the latest Hollywood or Bollywood release [. . .] becomes an apt metaphor for those placed differently within the circuit of 'technological time'" (23). Historically, these populations were both geographically and temporally isolated, lacking the "currency" (in all senses of the word) to meaningfully engage with people from faster-moving, more geographically central societies. Piracy, Liang argues, has historically been a way to close those gaps created by the uneven and unequal circulation of culture, allowing entry into contemporary conversations to which marginalized populations might otherwise be excluded.

Engaging with the popular mythology around Makmende is not going to change much in and of itself about how North Americans think about Kenya in the face of much more powerful mass-media representations of the region reasserting familiar stereotypes. However, sharing a joke together may open up new kinds of social and emotional bonds, which can lead people to seek out more information and more contact in their understanding of transnational relations (as seems to have occurred as U.S. Twitter users became more aware of the oppositional forces taking to the streets after the 2009 Iranian presidential elections). It would be hard to measure or prove that the exchange of media increases empathy between cultures, just as it has been hard to prove that the transmission of culture imposes meanings and values on other societies. Such exchanges can provoke conflict as well as understanding, but often the conflict can be a way of clearing the air of preconceptions and forcing participants to look at each other through fresh eyes.

Learning from Nollywood

Material such as the Makmende mashups might also be considered a probe which gives Kenyan and other African producers the opportunity to observe where and how their content gains traction, potentially guiding future efforts at international circulation. As with the appropriation of *Avatar* by Palestinian activists, getting the message out is the first step. If texts attract the interest of transnational audiences, and if producers and grassroots advocates can provide a depth of additional information in and around a work, the potential for a deeper relationship exists.

As this happens, Kenyan filmmakers might learn from the dramatic growth of the Nigerian video industry (popularly known as "Nollywood") beginning in the early 1990s, a movement Brian Larkin (2008) has studied extensively. Nigeria now claims to be the second-largest movie producer in the world (after India), producing at its peak an estimated 2,600 (straight-to-video) films per year and exporting its media content not only across Africa but also through the continent's international diasporic population. Nollywood's influence across the region has grown to the point that many other African countries worry that it is undermining their own local cultural and media practices.

Historically, Africa's governments have generally not supported the expense of producing a sustained national cinema. Many Francophone African countries produced only a few films, typically funded through French arts agencies and shown at international film festivals. Nigeria struggled to create its own national film culture; efforts peaked in the 1980s, constrained by the lack of cinema houses. The rise of video, however, meant lower production budgets, and African filmmakers sold their content directly to audiences via urban marketplaces for home viewing, often through the networks surrounding Pentecostal churches, where the films are frequently used for evangelism. After Ghana launched a popular video culture in the late 1980s (Meyer 2001), Nigeria followed a few years later. Increasingly, Nigerian videos are showing up in African groceries and restaurants in Europe and North America. These more grassroots forms of circulation sidestep the infrastructure required to sustain film production aimed at cinema houses.

Another example of impure culture, Nollywood productions combine aspects of particular U.S. film and television genres (particularly soap opera but also gangster and suspense) with storytelling elements from indigenous folk traditions (such as a strong focus on witchcraft and spirit worship). Larkin (2008) suggests that some Nigerian film-makers have also eagerly engaged with South Asian media in part because of certain similarities in values and traditions—for instance, Indian film influences are strongly felt in Nigerian films with roots in the Hausa people, the mostly Muslim ethnic group in northern Nigeria. Rather than being used as a vehicle for nation building, Nigerian films focus on the entertainment demands of middle-class African audiences, both in the home continent and abroad.

Nollywood films often make lots of money by African standards. The Nigerian film industry sustains a steady stream of video production, with a film taking two weeks to produce and a week to finalize for circulation. And, because Nollywood films are often funded by retailers who market directly to their audiences, they can be highly responsive to shifts in local tastes and interests.

Larkin describes the "highly ambivalent" relationship Nollywood producers and distributors have with piracy—recognizing its inevitability yet anxious that it may destroy their local markets even as it also expands them transnationally. Within Nigeria and across Africa, Nollywood's success has focused in part on displacing pirated copies of international films with locally produced content, so that African audiences might see African performers and African stories. As Larkin explains,

> In many parts of the world, media piracy is not a pathology of the circulation of media forms but its prerequisite. In many places, piracy is the only means by which certain media—usually foreign—are available. And in countries like Nigeria, the technological constraints that fuel pirate media provide the industrial template through which other, nonpirate media are reproduced, disseminated, and consumed. (2008, 240)

Most Nollywood films start out with a 50,000-copy run, which is typically as many as the filmmakers can afford to produce on a first printing (Zuckerman 2010). The creator often has a two-week window to sell that first run, which is the typical time it takes for pirated versions to become available (*Economist* 2010). From there, it is a race between the producer and the pirates, with each selling the titles at more or less the same price (Zuckerman 2010).

Piracy informs the aesthetics of Nollywood and not simply its economics. As Larkin writes, "Cheap tape recorders, old televisions, blurred videos that are the copy of a copy of a copy—these are the material distortions endemic to the reproduction of media goods in situations of poverty and illegality" (2004, 310). One of Hollywood's key advantages in the transnational marketplace has been the high standards of technical polish and perfection which it maintains, standards which historically media makers in the developing world have found impossible to meet. Yet, if the everyday experience of a Hollywood film is a degraded and muddy copy of a copy, then the advantages posed by superior equipment and production processes are devalued. Consequently, audiences in Nigeria and elsewhere have been willing to accept the lower-end look and feel of Nollywood films, shot on video and not celluloid.

Beyond Africa, pirates have performed crucial work in expanding the market for Nigerian films into diasporic communities and beyond, creating deeper awareness of, and interest in, what had at first been an entirely local phenomenon. Now that the Nigerian film industry has become empowered by its increasing international success, though, it has begun seeking the cooperation of authorities, for example, in shutting down dealers that sell Nollywood works without permission and supporting distribution through licensed dealers (Fahim 2010). This is ironic, as unauthorized distribution did so much to help to test and open Nollywood's markets, paving the way for models of official distribution.

Speaking primarily about the "informal" economies through which video circulates throughout India, Ravi Sundaram (1999) has suggested the term "pirate modernity" to refer to an economy which is "disorganized, nonideological, and marked by mobility and innovation" (Larkin 2008, 226) and—perhaps most of all—by its ambivalence toward the promises of capitalism. Pirates' ruthless mercantilism, including a willingness to sell anything to anyone whether or not they have the legal right to do so, makes them as much advocates of capitalism as resisters of its regulatory regimes. As the Nollywood example suggests, pirate culture may ultimately be the foundation on which legal industries and institutions are formed, allowing poorer countries a chance to gain ground without having to bear the full costs of investment in production.

The Brazilian semifictional police movie *Tropa de Elite* provides another compelling example of how piracy lays the groundwork for new business models for circulating media content. Released in 2007, *Tropa de Elite* became one of the most commercially successful Brazilian films in history. While the film was in its final stages of production, a copy was leaked to "pirates," and these forces spread it far and wide. In fact, polling organization IBOPE estimated that 11.5 million people saw the leaked film within two months after its release (Barrionuevo 2007). And, according to Datafolha, 77 percent of São Paulo residents knew about the movie by its launch (Novaes 2007). On opening weekend, approximately 180,000 people saw the film legally in São Paulo and Rio de Janeiro ("Tropa de Elite" 2007), and, by early 2008, more than 2.5 million people had watched the film through official means ("Brazil Cop Drama" 2008).

As the video was further pirated via torrents (as well as legally distributed) in 15 countries across multiple continents, Maurício Mota (2008), chief storytelling officer of the Rio de Janeiro–based transmedia company The Alchemists, estimates that it may have been seen illegally by more than 13 million and legally by more than 5 million people. The Brazilian media industries debated whether the legal box-office returns would have been substantially lower and the costs of equivalent paid promotion much higher if the pirated circulation of the film had not heightened awareness about the title (Cajueiro 2007). The producers themselves sought greater copyright protection for the film's sequel, *Tropa de Elite 2*, which broke the national box-office record with more than 11 million legal viewers and which has been commercially exported to many countries around the world. We will never know for sure how many of the legal viewers of *Tropa de Elite 2* got introduced to the franchise by watching illegal copies of the first film.

Increasingly, piracy allows producers to break into new markets without bearing the full costs of distribution. Nitin Govil describes this process as "the formalization of informality" (2007, 79), describing, for example, how the more corporate structures shaping contemporary Bollywood entertainment took shape from "networks of informal/ occasional labor and craft/trade unions that form intricate itineraries of work linked through custom, patronage, and transitory affiliation" (80). As these informal structures are given greater permanence and acquire legal status, piracy and organized crime give way to corporatization. Yet Govil sees continued traces of this earlier, less formal structure in the ways Bollywood filmmakers freely appropriate and remix Hollywood and Bollywood blockbusters alike, mixing and matching genre elements shamelessly with few expectations of being called out by their audience for a lack of originality or by the state for infringement.

Part of what we can learn from Nollywood (and from "pirate modernism" more generally) is that producing countries do not have to fully control the processes of circulation in order to benefit from the spread of their content across national borders. In practice, pirates can help open markets, experimenting with alternative forms and flows of content in ways that more established players may be reluctant to embrace. Part of what we learn is that the very impurity of these new kinds of cultural production allows them to spread rapidly because these texts can be made to speak to and for multiple audiences and because their illicit quality means that they are not necessarily read in relation to the high technical standards of a high-budget Hollywood release. Though these texts are "impure," they nevertheless remain powerful vehicles of ideologies, traditions, and styles characteristic of a particular nation or region. They may enable greater cultural visibility for their originating cultures and be forces of diversity within their destination countries. They may be part of a process in which countries jockey for influence within their regions and struggle to be heard on the international stage.

Diverting Entertainment

In an environment fostering spreadability, grassroots communities are embracing content from elsewhere, actively facilitating its circulation (often in advance of its commercial availability) and taking responsibility for educating their local public about its traditions and conventions. Such participatory practices coexist with efforts by large media companies to adapt their development and distribution models for transnational markets, which are often leading to the much greater exchange of media formats and texts across national borders. Taken as a whole, then, spreadable media represents a potential force for globalization, understood as "an intensification of global connectedness" achieved through shifting the kinds of culture that people around the world can access (Inda and Rosaldo 2002, 5).

Sociocultural anthropologist Arjun Appadurai (1990) argues that the international cultural economy can be understood by examining the disjunctures and differences that arise between the various "landscapes" through which culture travels. Appadurai is an especially important thinker for our project because he has also written in his book *The Social Life of Things* about the interplay between commodity cultures and traditional gift economies. There, Appadurai discusses "strategies of diversion" which involve the "removal of things from an enclaved zone to one where exchange is less confined and more profitable" (1986, 25). He focuses primarily on examples in which powerful groups or companies extract artifacts from their originating culture, often through acts of "plunder." In the process, these forces strip away local meanings and introduce these goods into an alternative regime of value dominated by commercial interests.

Something similar occurs when media content which has been "enclaved" by media companies is "diverted" as a potential resource within a gift economy. For example, an episode of the U.S. television drama *Prison Break* airs in the United States, and, within less than 24 hours, organized groups of volunteers will have translated it into Cantonese, added subtitles, and enabled its circulation across China and beyond (Jenkins 2008). *Prison Break*, though only a marginal success on U.S. television, has proven to be a cult success with Chinese audiences, perhaps because its themes of strong fraternal ties speak so powerfully to local melodramatic traditions and to the generation that has grown up under the country's one-child policy. These materials are diversions in two senses of the word. In Appadurai's sense, they are diverted, often without authorization, from their country of origin.

But they are also "diverting" insofar as they are engaging, meaningful, and valuable to new Chinese audiences, which engage with them for their own reasons, which may have little or nothing to do with their original reception.

However, current framings of copyright infringement label these supportive international communities as "pirates," even though they generally do not seek to profit from the cultural materials they are helping to spread among their own community. Fans in mainland China, for example, question how they can be accused of diminishing revenues for Western media content when most of what they are circulating is unlikely to be ever legally available to them, given the Chinese government's protectionism and censorship. Such "pirates" might be the most effective agents Hollywood has for generating long-term interest for Western works in markets such as China.

As Chinese fans are translating *Prison Break*, fans in the U.S. and around the world are busy subtitling and circulating the latest Korean television drama or Japanese animated series for a diverse mix of transnational audiences days or even hours after their local broadcasts. In our enhanced book, Xiaochang Li—doctoral student in the Department of Media, Culture, and Communications at New York University—describes the ways that "densely coordinated networks of fansubbers, aggregation sites, curatorial efforts, discussion forums, and blogs" have dramatically expanded access to such programs.

These diversions between commercial and noncommercial systems of value might occur multiple times in the life cycle of a media text. As Appadurai explains, "Diversions that become predictable are on their way to becoming new paths, paths that will in turn inspire new diversions or returns to old paths" (1986, 29). In Li's example, East Asian drama is produced and sold within a local commercial context and then spread freely through fan networks because fans believe it will be meaningful to people outside its originating culture. This movement is inspired by what Appadurai describes as "irregular desires and novel demands" (1986, 29), leading people to depart from preestablished trade routes and thus potentially forging new cultural relations. Producers may not have seen it as worth their investment to court those alternative markets, yet such fan networks may ultimately invite a reappraisal of potential markets as creators hope to distribute commercially what these fans have been circulating as gifts, a move which may or may not be welcomed by the fan communities involved.

Mizuko Ito shows that today's anime fandom is shaped by the "symbiotic and antagonistic" relationship forged between commercial and noncommercial distributors of anime content: "Fansubbing arose to fill an unmet consumer demand not being served by commercial industries. Fans assumed the costs of localization, distribution, and marketing, converting commercial media into a noncommercial peer-to-peer regime out of necessity and passion" (2012, 183). The rapid turnaround of fansubbed videos on a volunteer basis requires a massive amount of financially uncompensated work, including coordination of large networks of participants, as well as the more direct labor of translating, encoding, proofing, and circulating these texts. No commercial interest involved in anime has been able to subtitle material as fast or with the same degree of cultural nuance as high-performing fansubbing groups, which is why many fans still prefer fansubbed versions, even if commercial alternatives become available.

While, historically, fans saw their goal as helping to sustain an anime industry which would serve the growing demand for this content, many younger fans see their primary loyalty as to "a more fluid and hybrid networked public culture in which the industry does not have as privileged a position" (Ito 2012, 193). The community engages in heated debates about when it is appropriate to view fansubbed as opposed to commercially localized versions of particular series, while anime producers are seeking ways to cater to a new generation of overseas viewers through online distribution and simultaneous release in multiple languages. The result, Ito argues, has been hybrid models of localization, advertising, and distribution which include both commercial and noncommercial players.

According to Appadurai, "The flow of commodities in any given situation is a shifting compromise between socially regulated paths and competitively inspired diversions" (1986, 17). Read broadly, what is at stake in such acts of diversion (whether through "plunder" or "piracy") is the unauthorized movement between different "regimes of value," which brings about a fundamental shift in the status of what is being circulated.

To return to a term we introduced in chapter 2, such negotiations over the value and significance of cultural materials represent a transnational form of appraisal. For instance, Jonathan Gray spent time examining which U.S. media texts gain traction in Malawi, an African country with little local media production. In addition to the popularity of the latest U.S. hip-hop and R&B, Gray (2008b) and his wife also encountered children named after U.S. country music star Dolly Parton's 1974 hit "Jolene" and many locals who seemed to know the lyrics to even Dolly's more obscure releases. Gray described the distinctive picture of U.S. media culture that might emerge if U.S. national production were understood through the lens of what made it to Africa:

> Some American texts that are popular in America are popular there. Some that have long since become uncool here are popular there. Some that are seen as "girl" music here have wide masculine appeal there. Some that are seen as lower class here are upper class there. Some that hold court here are completely irrelevant there. The cultural flow between the two countries, then, is remarkably uneven, in terms of genre, temporality, and centrality. [. . .] So, yes, American popular culture was often prevalent, but there were different American popular cultures. Black pride, in particular, was obvious and explicit in numerous respondents' discussion of which movie stars and musicians they enjoyed. Recent film was almost nowhere to be seen, meanwhile, meaning that if any messages regarding what's cool were being taken away from the films, they were messages of what was cool in the eighties and early nineties. (2008a)

As Gray suggests, the uneven distribution of popular media around the globe (in part a product of the various kinds of diversions that Appadurai describes) suggests different practices of appraisal. Parton resonates with a different set of cultural experiences and preferences in Blantyre than she does in Nashville. Such choices reflect the complex imbrication of cultures, often imposed by external forces (for instance, during periods under imperial and colonialist rule), as well as the attempts to sort through and move beyond such influences in the postcolonial period. We cannot understand Malawians as simply recipients of Western media, despite the fact that the country relies heavily on media produced elsewhere. Rather, the process by which these materials are acquired and appraised serves to root them more deeply into local cultural practices and traditions.

Cosmopolitans and Immigrants

Writing about the impact of Japanese transnationalism on popular culture, Koichi Iwabuchi draws a distinction between the circulation of cultural goods that are essentially "odorless," bearing few traces of their cultural origins, and those that are embraced for their culturally distinctive "fragrance" (2002, 27). Writers such as Anne Allison (2006) have built on Iwabuchi's notion of "odorless" cultural imports to explore ways that animated films were stripped of nationally specific references to broaden their appeal to a mass market. However, in the case of the diversions of transnational anime fans, the opposite tendency is felt; often, the fetishization of cultural differences acts as a means of signaling the fans' own "distinctiveness" from the culture around them. These anime fans seek out Japanese "soft cultural goods" because they are Japanese, not despite their Japaneseness. We have a term for this active search for what Iwabuchi calls "fragrance": "pop cosmopolitanism." Pop cosmopolitans embody Appadurai's "irregular desires and novel demands," exerting unanticipated pulls on the system of cultural circulation. The efforts of U.S. fans to access East Asian drama or Japanese anime, discussed earlier, might best be described in terms of this active search for cultural difference (as might be said of Chinese fans of *Prison Break*). These groups are tapping transnational networks in search of something other than what is commercially on offer to them, and they are often willing to work hard or spend a fair chunk of change to access this content.

In practice, the diversions performed by "pop cosmopolitans," seeking to escape the parochialism of their own cultures by embracing materials from elsewhere (Jenkins 2004), are complexly intertwined with the activities of immigrant populations seeking to maintain ties back to their motherlands. Both international networks of diaspora communities and of cosmopolitan fans seek out meaningful material which may not be locally available; both seek content which is heavily marked by its national origins; both have shown a willingness to circulate content illegally when they have difficulty accessing it legally; and both may end up appraising the material differently than it was valued within its originating culture.

Often, as pop cosmopolitans seek media from places they've never been, they solicit expertise and resources from diaspora communities online, even as immigrants increasingly participate in broader online fan networks formed around texts from their countries of origin. For instance, Rebecca Black (2008) explores how Japanese ESL students both contribute to and gain from participation in U.S. fan-fiction communities that have emerged around anime and manga. These students are solicited for their insights into Japanese language and culture and, in return, receive mentorship in mastering the nuances of U.S. culture and the English language. Such collaboration between immigrants and pop cosmopolitans has longstanding precursors. As Lawrence Eng (2012) has documented, even before the popularization of the Internet, the emergence of U.S. fandom around Japanese media properties rested on access to international fan networks which could help members acquire the media content and information they desired. Eng notes, for example, that the informal importation of anime may have started with "somebody's Japanese pen pal who sent tapes in the mail, U.S. servicemen and women stationed in Japan who brought tapes to the United States, Japanese video stores in California, or local television broadcasts intended for the Japanese population of Hawaii" (162). These small, informal networks gained greater traction once Internet communication platforms better facilitated connecting pop cosmopolitan fans to one another and to native and diasporic Japanese anime fans.

College campuses are particularly rich sites for fostering such alliances between pop cosmopolitans and diasporic fans. According to an ethnographic study of media-sharing behaviors in a U.S. college dormitory,

While students often use their media exposure to connect to new ideas and learn about the world, a reverse trend is also prevalent: dorm students use their media consumption to retain ties to their past and their own cultures. For international students, this may include continued consumption of material in their native languages. For American students, media consumption may be a means of retaining common points of discussion with family and friends back home. (Ford et al. 2006, 3)

Among the ten students profiled in the study, Mahamati, a freshman from India, was most pronounced about the importance of staying connected to one's cultural roots through media. Mahamati discussed his love of classical Indian and Bollywood music in great detail, driven by his own lifelong experience with musical performance. Mahamati said Indian classical music left a "residue" with him that outlives his short-term enjoyment of most pop music: "If I were to not go back to India, I believe that I would probably end up even more attached to this music because it's one of the things that reminds me of home" (quoted in Ford et al. 2006, 24).

Mei-Ling, who grew up in Lexington, Massachusetts, said that she continued to watch Malaysian films to stay connected with the culture her family came from: "If I brought it to the hall and had other people watch it, they wouldn't get it. They wouldn't appreciate it, not even as much as I do, and I don't understand it as much as my parents do" (quoted in Ford et al. 2006, 24). Similarly, Anna, who grew up in Chicago, said that her love of 1970s and 1980s Russian rock music comes from the fact that she was born in Russia and that her family are members of the Russian diaspora (24). She said that her enjoyment of Russian music and television increases on her visits back home in Chicago, where this genre is a staple in her parents' lives.

Yet students included in the study also indicated that they gained prestige in their peer groups by being able to introduce their class-mates to fresh and distinctive media texts that the rest of the dorm didn't know about. Because of their often-intimate living quarters, one freshman student's hunger for international material may be fed by a roommate's commitment to maintaining ties back to his or her culture through media content. Pop cosmopolitans are less likely to be exposed to unfamiliar products from other cultures without first- and second-generation immigrants acting as proselytizers. And, in the process, these international students may become fans of both works that reflect their heritage and new content they are introduced to by other students in the dorm.

Dislocating and Relocating Diasporic Media

Of course, the preceding discussion assumes that the relationship between diasporic audiences and content from their countries of origin is simple and immediate. The opposite is often the case, with the flow of media content across national borders serving as a reminder of the differences within immigrant communities, of the gaps between the lived experience of those who remain in the motherland and the perceptions of those who have sought a nostalgic return after extended stays overseas, and of the role of the local in shaping our engagement with transnational content. As we saw through the dorm study, students represent multiple generations of immigrants, some of whom have more immediate ties and deeper knowledge than others, and some of whom only have access to the mother country through their parents' memories.

Hamid Naficy's 1993 case study of the ways Iranian exiles deployed local-access cable television has long been one of the classic examples of media production and exchange within diasporic populations. Yet a growing number of diasporic communities are tapping into the potential to use new media platforms to forge stronger social networks that link the old world and the new on an ongoing basis. While Naficy's Iranian exiles critiqued contemporary developments in Iran as a way of preserving their hopes of restoring the Iranian monarchy, a second generation of Iranian Americans have sought to articulate a new "Persian" identity which is often divorced from any direct knowledge or memories of the country their families left behind. These self-named Persian Americans have created blogs, podcasts, and online videos to express their relationship to Iran and its cultural heritage. Some of these are entirely noncommercial, produced on a volunteer basis, while others are commercial, seeking to capitalize an expanding and "underserved" market. As these groups tap into digital networks, however, they find themselves in dialogue with people still living in Iran, exchanges which may strengthen cultural ties but may also force them to confront what is distinctive about their different cultural locations and histories.

Bebin.tv became the first Iranian American Internet Protocol television station in 2006, focusing on popular music, discussions of traditional culture and history, and spoofs of popular U.S. programs from an Iranian American perspective. (Internet Protocol television is a system in which television-style content is delivered through the Internet, often through specialized high-bandwidth channels, not unlike video on demand. It is a practice increasingly used to bring media content to diasporic populations.) Bebin.tv's original project, Talieh Rohani (2009) notes, was partly one of "cultural repair," reclaiming parts of Iranian oral culture in danger of being lost while also responding to the "nostalgia without memory" experienced by a generation which knew Iran primarily through their parents' stories. Bebin.tv's programming was also attracting a strong following back in Iran, especially given its focus on traditions which had been profoundly disrupted by the Islamic Revolution but preserved by those who left the country for Europe and North America.

Responding to this demand, Bebin.tv launched two new satellite television channels in 2009 for both younger- and older-generation viewers in Iran. It also encouraged its viewers to upload videos of their everyday lives. Bebin.tv sponsored competitions among Persian-language musicians from around the world. Viewers compared notes to reconstruct the texts of pre-Islamic Persian literature that had been lost to some of them and responded to each other's questions about nightclubs in Tehran which had been closed for decades. The online exchanges became one factor among many that strengthened the interest of young Iranian Americans in the controversial 2009 Iranian presidential election and its aftermath. As Rohani writes, "The increasing sensation of nostalgia without memory in the aftermath of Iran's presidential election among the second generation Iranian-Americans urged them to participate even more in Iranian events and to join the first generation Iranians in diaspora in live protests" (2009, 105).

Yet the expanded capacity for communication could not entirely overcome several decades of isolation and misinformation. As the Iranian diaspora's conception of Iran came into increased contact with Iranian citizens' views on Bebin.tv, heated debates also arose in the site's discussion forums about different perceptions of the nation's culture and politics among various "Iranian" audiences. Those in Iran grumbled about the poor language skills displayed by the Iranian Americans, for instance, and various groups questioned each other's takes of the current state of the country.

While we often use the concept of localization to describe the ways that media from one part of the world must be remade or at least reframed for audiences elsewhere, tracing the paths of diasporic media suggests that localization has to occur even within the same ethnic population, since the processes of travel and immigration result in considerable cultural dislocation. Sangita Shresthova (2011) has explored the transnational circulation of Bollywood dance sequences—sometimes excerpted and shared via YouTube and other online video sites, sometimes contained within tapes and DVDs spread through local merchants. These digital practices of circulation mirror older forms of export and exchange of South Asian media, such as those which Aswin Punathambekar, professor of communication studies at the University of Michigan, discusses in an essay on "Desi media" in our enhanced book:

> We can draw an arc from the late 1970s to the current moment—from VHS tapes that circulated via Indian grocery stores to remix music events (DJ Rekha's Basement Bhangra in New York City, for example), one-hour shows featuring Bollywood song sequences broadcast on public-access stations, performances on college campuses, and, now, vast pirate networks that make Desi media content available to audiences across the globe—to show that the notion of spreadability has always been a defining feature of Desi media culture.

The musical numbers from Bollywood films, in their original Indian contexts, are often distributed via audio and video in advance of the film's release so that the songs are familiar to audiences by the time they enter the movie theater. These practices now extend transnationally through, for example, the efforts of Eros Entertainment, a primary distributor of Bollywood films in the West. Eros shares hundreds of Bollywood clips online, attempting both to head off pirating and to broaden the market for particular titles. Of what Shresthova estimates as the more than 325,000 Bollywood clips circulating internationally on YouTube (2011, 9), many are recordings of amateur performers seeking to duplicate favorite dance sequences from films. These practices have contributed to the rise of Bollywood dance classes in major metropolitan areas worldwide, including some in cities which do not have a substantial South Asian diasporic population.

Despite this transnational distribution and circulation, the meaning making around these Bollywood dance practices is often highly localized. For example, Shresthova discusses the ways Bollywood dance classes in Los Angeles operate within a U.S. culture that prides itself on multiculturalism (2011, 105–142). Gradually, Bollywood dance classes here are displacing classical Indian dance classes (often originally established as one way of preserving distinctive traditional and national cultural practices among the Indian immigrant communities) for first- and second-generation Desi youths. These youths find greater affinity with the hybridity of Bollywood style, which often combines South Asian and Western influences for expressing their emergent identities. Meanwhile, the inclusion of elements of hip-hop and other Western dance styles in Bollywood films expands the movies' appeal to contemporary audiences (even as traditionalist Bollywood fans bemoan the incorporation of elements not deemed sufficiently "Indian"). Here, again, despite debates about "odorlessness" or "fragrance," what travels most readily across national borders may well be that which is the least culturally pure, that which is already shaped by multiple points of contact between dispersed cultural influences. These "impure" products create openings for pop cosmopolitans to find something familiar even amid their search for diversity, and they give expression to the unsettled feelings of diasporic audiences that may not feel fully at home in either culture.

Transnational Telenovelas

The soap opera and the telenovela have traditionally been particularly vibrant sites of the international spread of content, both officially through distribution deals and unofficially through fan circulation (as in Li's examples of the circulation of East Asian dramas in the West). Following the U.S. launch of radio soap operas in the 1930s, the format was tweaked for what eventually came to be known as the radionovela and later telenovela, inspired by serialized novels. According to Jaime Nasser, particularly post–World War II, "The U.S. took an interest in Latin American radio and television in order to discourage government-owned and operated broadcasting networks because the U.S. government feared the rise of socialist forms of national mass media industries after the fall of Nazi Germany and the rise of communism. Therefore, the U.S. government sought to promote a commercial model of broadcasting in Latin America" (2011, 51). A pivotal part of this approach was the telenovela, sponsored by transnational soap companies in much the same way U.S. soaps were created. However, whereas U.S.-based soaps focus on "worlds without end," telenovelas are stories told through daily texts but with finite endings, thus making them more easily exportable and replayed over time.

As local broadcasting companies developed in many other countries, they began in part with the importation of soap opera or telenovela programs, which are cheaper to import than higher-budget U.S. prime-time fare. Over time, these shows have inspired and later been joined or even replaced by indigenous productions. And, increasingly, as local versions of soap opera/telenovela formats have evolved, these new formats are being recirculated and are gaining greater popularity outside local audiences. Take, for instance, the history of the *MariMar* telenovela, which demonstrates not only the crossover between official distribution and unofficial circulation but likewise the ways media flows across borders. A popular Mexican telenovela in the 1990s, *MariMar* was exported to the Philippines, where it enjoyed particular success—so much success, in fact, that a Filipino version launched in 2007 on the GMA Network, starring Dingdong Dantes and Marian Rivera, who plays the title role of MariMar. The combined series have led to more than 5,000 related videos uploaded to YouTube at the time of this writing, with content that, during the show's initial 2007–2008 broadcast airing, often was among the video-sharing site's most popular (Ford 2008b).

While the telenovela genre was inspired by the U.S. soap opera, the format's innovations are now having a reciprocal impact back on U.S. programming. U.S. Spanish-language television networks Telemundo and Univision have become prominent through serving many members of the country's Latin population who want to remain connected to their cultural roots, and other Latin American–based television networks are expanding their access via the web and on-demand video. Latin immigrants in the United States might follow telenovelas to fuel their regular conversations within their local community or as material for their discussions with family "back home."

This influence is spreading to include a range of U.S. media producers and distributors not explicitly targeting U.S. Latin viewers. For example, consider MyNetworkTV's short-lived experiment in 2006–2007 to move its prime-time programming production to a telenovela-inspired model or the development of Colombian telenovela *Yo soy Betty, la fea* (1999–2001) into the critically acclaimed U.S. series *Ugly Betty* (2006–2010) on the ABC television network (Nasser 2011). Something of the complexities of these transnational exchanges of the telenovela is also suggested by the trajectory of the 2009 *Caminho das Índias* (internationally titled *India—A Love Story*), a telenovela produced by Brazil's Globo in response to growing local interest in South Asia in the wake of the 2008 British Oscar-winning film *Slumdog Millionaire*. The series was later sold to TeleFutura, a Spanish-language station owned by Univision, which hoped to create a crossover success in the United States (Villarreal 2010).

These examples demonstrate how the telenovela format has developed and evolved as an impure genre over decades. A U.S. format imported to Latin America takes its own localized and unique shapes which eventually become exportable programming circulated around the world. Those local cultures eventually begin adapting the programs and format to their own local productions. Meanwhile, the Latin American diaspora in the U.S. seeks official and unofficial ways to bring that content into the country, and the telenovela's influence eventually starts to be felt on the U.S. prime-time drama. These processes of adaptation and localization and this flow which sees reciprocal paths of influence as formats and content cross cultural borders demonstrate how impure culture is inevitable as content is continuously relocated and localized.

However, such transnational flows can unearth cultural tensions as well. Jaime Nasser (2011) documents a tendency in U.S. television critics to express surprise that *Ugly Betty* was a high-quality television series, often dismissing what they describe as the inferior quality and low budget of telenovelas. Such reviews, Nasser argues, treat the telenovela as utterly foreign, ignoring its ties to the U.S. soap opera or the potential that many U.S. viewers were already familiar with this format. Nasser shows how *Ugly Betty*'s makers sought to distance themselves from the show's roots, ultimately creating a narrative about the series's production that mirrored that of its protagonist: from the ugly, inferior Colombian telenovela "duckling" arises the beautiful U.S. prime-time "swan."

The World Is Not Flat

Contrary to what you may have read, the world is not flat. Thomas Friedman's (2005) bestseller sparked intense debate about the consequences of globalization on the twenty-first-century media landscape. Friedman sees the development of the Internet browser as akin to the end of the Cold War or the outsourcing of labor from developed countries to the developing world: a flattening force which enables goods and content to move more fluidly across national borders, ultimately increasing the influence of transnational capitalism in the everyday lives of people around the world. As Friedman explains,

> The falling of the walls, the opening of the Windows, and the rise of the PC all combined to empower more individuals than ever to become authors of their own content in digital form. Then the spread of the Internet and the coming to life of the Web, thanks to the browser and fiber optics, enabled more people than ever to be connected and to share their digital content with more other people for less money than any time before. [. . .] There was suddenly available a platform

for collaboration that all kinds of people from around the globe could now plug and play, compete and connect on—in order to share work, exchange knowledge, start companies, and invent and sell goods and services. (92)

And we've seen throughout this chapter many different examples of the accelerated flow of cultural materials across national and cultural borders through various kinds of diversions—both plunder and piracy, both commercial and grassroots, both pulled by pop cosmopolitans and pushed by local producers. As we have documented, these processes can often become the site of cultural clashes between diasporic audiences and the cultures they left behind.

While Friedman is often read as arguing that technology has evened the playing field between national economies, he is also attentive to segments of the population left out of the general economic surge emerging from these platforms for collaboration and circulation. Friedman's argument has become a focal point for heated discussions about the impact of globalization and mass media. These range from concerns about the marginalization or elimination of local culture as content from powerful international media industries attains greater reach, on the one hand, to concerns even among dominant media-producing countries that their industries might eventually be damaged from increased transnational competition. Yet others (for instance, Ghemawat 2007) complicate these perspectives, arguing that—despite changes in transnational distribution and access to media and technology—most communication still happens on geographically local levels (which, of course, includes mediated communication through calling, texting, emailing, etc.), and many people still lack the technical, social, and economic resources to meaningfully communicate beyond the community of people they know face-to-face. Ethan Zuckerman's Global Voices project focuses on these issues, facilitating the exchange of citizen media and blogs around the world and, in the process, bringing attention to sites often neglected by mainstream media coverage. His network of more than 400 volunteers collectively translate and summarize the words of local bloggers, podcasters, and video creators into a range of languages.

Thus far, our discussion of the potentially complementary, potentially conflicting spread of material among multiple communities has nevertheless focused only on certain types of communities: those likely to have the technical and cultural capacity to spread that material. A variety of economic, social, and geographic divides preclude some communities from having a prominent role in a spreadable media culture. There are divides within countries as well as between countries which ensure that not everyone gets to participate on the empowered terms we have described. Inside Google's corporate headquarters in Mountain View, California, there is a dynamic visualization mapping in real time the searches the company receives from countries around the world, representing each language in a different color. As a result, the countries of the Global North—especially those in Europe and North America—are fireworks displays, with constant activity depicted in a range of different colors. Meanwhile, over much of Africa, one or two queries drift up at a time, reflecting the degree to which these countries have been cut off from the larger communication flows this book has been describing. Despite the Makmende story which opened this chapter and its suggestion of expanded (if still contested) African participation in global Internet culture, the reality is that U.S. residents are far more likely to be aware of Nigerian-based digital scam artists than they are of the generation of new kinds of media content from Kenya or of the explosion of Nollywood movies.

Even within the same country, there can be more or less impermeable barriers to meaningful communications between different populations. Writing about the rise of digital cultures in India in our enhanced book, Parmesh Shahani—general manager of the Culture Lab at Godrej Industries Limited and editor at large for *Verve* magazine—contrasts India's embrace of new media platforms with "Bharat" (the Hindi name for the country), which has struggled to keep pace with these changes. Bharat, as Shahani characterizes it, is poor, rural, traditional, and young, by comparison with "India." The English-speaking "India" is ignorant of what happens in Bharat, whose successes remain highly localized as compared to the country's thriving commercial media and whose social reform messages are often drowned out by the more affluent population's search for celebrity gossip and lifestyle news. Shahani asks poignantly, "In this context, is spreadability a curse? [. . .] Is 'spreadable media' an intoxicant that is keeping India's middle classes happy and ignorant, while Bharat whirls by, as though on a different planet?"

Shahani's account of two very different lived realities illustrates rising concerns about the uneven access to technologies and skills between and within different national cultures. Most of Shahani's examples of modern "India" originate in the corporate sector, often in partnership with nonprofit organizations, suggesting a form of social entrepreneurship that represents a specific aspect of the new hybrid systems of communication we have been discussing throughout this book. In some ways, it may easier for the digital elites in, say, India, Japan, Nigeria, Brazil, Iran, and the United States to communicate with each other than it is for them to communicate with lower-income, rural, or less-educated residents of their own countries—in part because access to networked computers carries with it so many other implications about economic level, educational background, cultural cosmopolitanism, travel, and trade which separate "the digerati" from their fellow countryfolk.

Despite the despair over the disparities between the two Indias reflected in Shahani's comments quoted earlier, he also writes about local efforts to expand who has access to networked computers and which voices get heard through participatory culture. He reports, for instance, on Rikin Gandhi's Digital Green project, which seeks to "help small and marginal farmers to share agricultural information with other villagers using low-cost video production, screening devices, and a participatory philosophy." In its first year, the project produced and distributed more than 700 videos, involving the work of 26,000 farmers scattered across more than 400 villages (Gandhi 2010). Shahani stresses the group's ingenuity in deploying low-cost digital technologies to connect geographically dispersed and isolated rural communities. But he notes, "The real reason for its success is the spreadability of its content. It achieves this by tapping into the power of people and village-level social dynamics and by spreading content through DVDs." Such examples illustrate the urgency with which people from remote areas are seeking to plug into larger communication flows, to make their perspectives heard in the conversations which impact their lives and within which they are too often neglected, and to express their cultural traditions in forms which may keep them alive for future generations. Spreadable practices offer them perhaps the most effective means to achieve this expanded communication practice. In a world where everyday citizens may help select and circulate media content, playing active roles in building links between dispersed communities, there are new ways of working around the entrenched interests of traditional gatekeepers and in allegiance with others who may spread their content.

In chapter 6, we found that independent media makers have expanded opportunities to connect with a desired public in an era of networked communication, but they still struggle harder (and with greater risk) than those working within the commercial mainstream. They remain on the far end of the Long Tail in a world nowhere close to giving up on the hits-driven production model of the older broadcast-industry paradigm. Something similar has emerged here, where media products are being circulated across national borders with much more fluidity than ever before—sometimes expanding their cultural influence and prestige, sometimes expanding their opportunity to profit from their works. Yet their creators do so under terms which are still far from ideal, trying to overcome uneven access to the conditions of production and distribution while confronting existing stereotypes which may encourage others to belittle and dismiss what they've made and while often being caught between contradictory sets of expectations from their local and transnational supporters.

Spreadability has increased diversity and not simply multiplicity, yet the fragmentation of content may make it difficult for people to locate the diversity which does exist and may make it hard for minority groups to communicate outside their own communities. International and independent media producers must confront the glut of material on the international market today, depending on their most passionate supporters to help them cut through the clutter. Neither can afford the budget for large-scale advertising, so they are increasingly dependent on spreadable media practices. Such practices do ensure that their material gains circulation yet do not always compensate for the lack of focused attention that broadcast media still offers.

Spreadable practices are allowing more content to circulate across national borders according to criteria very different from the criteria of those who once managed the distribution of culture: commercial interests, film festival programmers, and government agencies, for instance. Yet, as always, these exchanges between cultures are far from friction-free. Part of the problem has to do with the uneven flow of information across transnational communication networks. Bollywood dance videos travel much faster and further than any nuanced or deep explanation for what they might mean in their original cultural context. Access to transnational media content can foster curiosity about other cultures and may motivate further investigation, as occurred as many non-Indian fans have sought to learn more about Bollywood dance after being exposed to it through Western media such as the musical *Bombay Dreams*, the movie *Slumdog Millionaire*, or the television show *So You Think You Can Dance*.

However, that curiosity must be met with deeper kinds of cultural exchanges, ones designed to foster richer understandings that address both common experiences and diverse perspectives. In theory, networked communication allows diverse groups to speak with each other; too often, they speak past each other. U.S. fans may love *Ugly Betty* but be disdainful of telenovelas, for example. Yet this is not always the case, as might be suggested by the complex interactions described earlier between pop cosmopolitans and diasporic audiences. The college dorm residents were inhabiting a contact zone where they lived in close quarters with people from very different cultural backgrounds, developing a deeper appreciation of other traditions. Similarly, the online communities which grow up around fansubbing and the exchange of media content between different parts of the world have the potential to be context-rich sites, which can foster deeper understandings across cultural differences.

While commercial distribution can strip media content of all markers of its originating culture, these more grassroots practices often require a deeper knowledge of where the content originates, motivating some people to master local languages, say, in order to contribute to fan-based translation projects or to develop an understanding of local media industries or to monitor online discussions among local audiences in order to anticipate desirable content. Such contact zones may generate forms of culture which seem "impure" when read through a lens which values preservation of distinctive local cultures, but they may be highly generative insofar as they facilitate new kinds of understandings among people who are being increasingly shoved toward each other through other globalizing forces. For the moment, this deep cultural empathy may be largely the stuff of the utopian imagination, yet the kinds of cultural practices we describe in this chapter represent perhaps our greatest hope for making such understandings a lived reality.

Writing for *Locus*, a trade publication for science fiction writers, Cory Doctorow challenges established assumptions surrounding the need for maintaining tight control over intellectual property. He suggests such norms are "hard-wired" into us as mammals:

> Mammals invest a lot of energy in keeping track of the disposition of each we spawn. It's only natural, of course: we invest so much energy and so many resources in our offspring that it would be a shocking waste if they were to wander away and fall off the balcony or flush themselves down the garbage disposal. [. . .] It follows naturally that we invest a lot of importance in the individual disposition of every copy of our artistic works as well, wringing our hands over "not for resale" advance review copies that show up on Amazon and tugging our beards at the thought of Google making a scan of our books in order to index them for searchers. (2008c)

Such attitudes may emerge "naturally" from our mammalian predispositions, but Doctorow notes that they are not the only ways we can understand our creative output. We might reimagine our current intellectual property regimes as they might operate in a world dominated by dandelions. The dandelion is playing a law of averages, with each plant producing more than 2,000 seeds per year and sending them blowing off into the wind. The results are hard to deny when we see the number of dandelions sprinkling the U.S. landscape each spring.

Doctorow draws parallels between this dispersal of seeds and the ways that artists increasingly tap into participatory systems of circulation in order to reach desired audiences:

CONCLUSION

If you blow your works into the net like a dandelion clock on the breeze, the net itself will take care of the copying costs. Your fans will paste-bomb your works into their mailing list, making 60,000 copies so fast and so cheaply that figuring out how much it cost in aggregate to make all those copies would be orders of magnitude more expensive than the copies themselves. What's more, the winds of the Internet will toss your works to every corner of the globe, seeking out every fertile home that they may have—given enough time and the right work, your stuff could someday find its way over the transom of every reader who would find it good and pleasing. (2008c)

Doctorow's own example as an author, discussed in chapter 6, demonstrates how a dandelion-style strategy may help an obscure writer gain greater visibility and build a readership over time.

Doctorow's account of circulation fits nicely with the themes of this book: value and meaning get created as grassroots communities tap into creative products as resources for their own conversations and spread them to others who share their interests. As institutions constructed by and for mammals, media companies, educational institutions, newspapers, and political campaigns display fear of this potential loss of control and concern for the fates of their intellectual offspring. The result has been, on the one hand, the development of "enclaves" and "monopolies" which tighten the distribution of their content and, on the other, a tendency to see grassroots acts of circulation as random, unpredictable, even irrational.

But nothing seems to be stopping the dandelion seeds from flowing beyond their walled gardens. As people pursue their own agendas in sharing and discussing media content, they are helping to spread the seeds—transforming commodities into gifts, turning texts into resources, and asserting their own expanding communication capacities.

The contemporary focus on the "viral" nature of circulation expresses media companies' and brands' utter terror of the unknown cultural processes now influencing all aspects of the media and entertainment industries. To manage that terror, they have often professed a mastery over a mysterious science that allows them to produce "viral content," rather than acknowledge (and benefit from) the loss of control inherent in our networked culture. Indeed, we have argued that these producers are increasingly dependent on networked communities to circulate, curate, and appraise their output. Web 2.0 companies have sought to capture and capitalize on these generative activities; brands have sought to corral their own brand communities; and trolls have sought to manufacture and spread "memes" for their own malicious joy and to disrupt the operations of groups which take the web too seriously. Perhaps we might understand content creators as mammals occasionally pretending to be dandelions but then reverting often back to their true natures, like the fable of the scorpion who cannot resist stinging the frog carrying him halfway through their journey across the river. If it doesn't spread, it's dead; true enough. But sometimes producers would rather die than give up control.

However, often, audiences are as ambivalent about being the wind scattering the seeds as the production companies and brands are about letting their spawn fly away. And audiences have reason to be nervous: many Web 2.0 practices are far from benign, seeking to tap into their "free labor" in ways which profit the companies but may not respect the traditions and norms of participatory culture.

Those who are most prepared to embrace spreadability have often been the people with the least to lose from changing the current system—the civic activists described in chapter 5, the independent and Christian media producers in chapter 6, and people from the developing world discussed in chapter 7. In each case, these groups accept a loss of control, seeking to forge partnerships with audiences that helped them expand and accelerate the circulation of their output.

Of course, we need to be cautious about displacing one biological metaphor with another: we began this book critiquing the use of "viral" metaphors that depict culture as "self-replicating," and we now appear to be on the verge of ending it by comparing culture to the dandelion seeds simply blowing on the wind. However useful Doctorow's analogy may be, it is a metaphor, not a system by which we propose to make sense of spreadable media. The choices over how we deal with intellectual property are ultimately cultural, political, and economic—not biologically hardwired. We should be concerned if the economic interests of companies are the only forces determining the terms of our cultural participation, which is why this book has stressed some of the "noncommercial" aspects of our cultural experiences.

Audience members are using the media texts at their disposal to forge connections with each other, to mediate social relations and make meaning of the world around them. Both individually and collectively, they exert agency in the spreadability model. They are not merely impregnated with media messages, nor are they at the service of the brand; rather, they select material that matters to them from the much broader array of media content on offer (which now includes audience creations alongside industrially produced works). They do not simply pass along static texts; they transform the material through active production processes or through their own critiques and commentary, so that it better serves their own social and expressive needs. Content—in whole or through quotes—does not remain in fixed borders but rather circulates in unpredicted and often unpredictable directions, not the product of top-down design but rather the result of a multitude of local decisions made by autonomous agents negotiating their way through diverse cultural spaces.

Similarly, so-called consumers do not simply consume; they recommend what they like to their friends, who recommend it to their friends, who recommend it on down the line. They do not simply "buy" cultural goods; they "buy into" a cultural economy which rewards their participation. And, in such an environment, any party can block or slow the spread of texts: if creators construct legal or technical blocks, if third-party platform owners choose to restrict the ways in which material can circulate, or if audiences refuse to circulate content which fails to serve their own interests.

Spreadable media expands the power of people to help shape their everyday media environment, but it does not guarantee any particular outcomes. Nevertheless, we believe these processes may hold the potential for social and cultural change. We hope we have illustrated the many ways that expanding access to the tools of media production and circulation is transforming the media landscape, allowing for greater responsiveness to audience interest, for greater support for independent media producers, for the wider circulation of civic and religious media, and for expanded access to transnational media content.

This book is describing a moment of transition, one in which an old system is shattering without us yet knowing what is going to replace it, one which is ripe in contradictions as audiences and producers make competing bids for the new moral economy that will displace the broadcast paradigm which has dominated cultural production and distribution throughout the twentieth century. Our various case studies represent snapshots of this new culture-in-development, glimpses into possible futures if some of these tensions can be resolved. The arguments in this book represent appeals to construct a system which pays more attention to the public interest—defined not through elite institutions but by the public itself, through its acts of appraisal, curation, and circulation.

Toward that end, let us revisit the claims about spreadability which opened the book. Some of those statements about what constitutes a "spreadable media" environment may have—at that time— seemed arbitrary, overstated, or even overwhelming to some of you. But our hope is that, in light of our various investigations and examples throughout this book, our claims will now be clear. Our intention is that the journey we've taken throughout this book gives you a road map for a better understanding of how value and meaning are being made and appraised in an age of spreadability, a better understanding of some of the models for understanding and transforming business practice in this environment, and some language that might help us more accurately describe and discuss the evolution of media circulation. So to revisit our opening salvo of claims, spreadability focuses on the following:

The flow of ideas. This book has sought to explain the rapid and widespread circulation of media content not through a metaphor of "virality" but through analyzing the social motives of those who are actually doing the spreading. These practices often occur at the intersection between an old media ecology based on corporate control and a new media ecology based on noncommercial sharing. These peer-to-peer exchanges may take many forms—from the kinds of reciprocity characteristic of traditional and modern forms of a gift economy to contexts of competition and contestation among rival groups. The exchange of media helps to anchor ongoing relationships and thus occurs most often when the content being exchanged says something significant about the parties involved. We have questioned the industry's assumption that it can create "brand communities" and "fan communities" around its products, suggesting instead that most of these exchanges occur within existing communities and ongoing conversations. As marketers and other content creators enter these spaces, they must think about questions of transparency and authenticity and the differences in their own commercial motivations and the social motivations of community members. They must think about the types of content these communities most want and need, which best provides fodder for the conversations and activities in which such groups are already invested. And they must think about what happens as content travels across cultural boundaries, sometimes stripped of its original context, creating "impure" texts which are not simply distributed from culture to culture but—in the process—often bear the mark of audiences that remake, reinterpret, and transform content.

Dispersed material. While part of this book's argument has centered on ways the public can shape localized and participatory acts of curation and circulation to their own ends, it is clear that content creators of all types have deep stakes in how their content spreads. Brands, for example, have seen spreadable media as a means of expanding the resonance of company messages and developing more meaningful relationships with current or potential customers. Broadcast networks and producers have seen transmedia strategies as a means of intensifying audiences' engagement and deepening fans' investment in their success. Activist groups have deployed "cultural acupuncture" to accelerate the spread and to amplify the reach of their messages, even as they have also struggled with the consequences of having their ideas and images sometimes used against them. Thus, creators have to think about creating multiple access points to content and texts that are both "grabbable" and "quotable"—which are technically and aesthetically easy for audiences to share.

Diversified experiences. Under the spreadability paradigm, mass-produced and mass-distributed content is often customized and localized for niche audiences, not by commercial producers but rather by other community members. Fans evangelize for entertainment they want others to enjoy. In the process, they function as translators between a text's contexts of production and reception. Audiences act as "multipliers" who attach new meaning to existing properties, as "appraisers" who evaluate the worth of different bids on our attention, as "lead users" who anticipate new markets for newly released content, as "retro curators" who discover forgotten content which may still hold cultural and economic value, and as "pop cosmopolitans" who seek cultural difference and help to educate others about content they've discovered from other parts of the world. And producers must think about these various motivations as they design content and respond to audience feedback.

Open-ended participation. These acts of appraisal and circulation reflect the practices of participatory culture. Participatory culture is not new—it has, in fact, multiple histories (through fandom, through struggles for greater popular control over media, through histories of craft or activism) which go back at least to the nineteenth century. What we are calling participatory culture has much in common with these and much older forms of folk cultural production and exchange. In thinking about these various histories, it is crucial to realize that participatory activities differ substantially, depending on the community and the media property in question. We must be careful not to define participation too narrowly in ways that prioritize "drillable texts" over "accretion texts," video creation over fan debate, or "affirmational" fan activity over "transformational" fan activity.

Cultural participation takes different forms within different legal, economic, and technological contexts. Some people have confused participatory culture with Web 2.0, but Web 2.0 is a business model through which commercial platforms seek to court and capture the participatory energies of desired markets and to harness them toward their own ends. While these Web 2.0 platforms may offer new technical affordances that further the goals of participatory culture, friction almost always exists between the desires of producers and audiences, a gap which has resulted in ongoing struggles around the terms of participation.

Contemporary culture is becoming more participatory, especially compared with earlier media ecologies primarily reliant on traditional mass media. However, not everyone is allowed to participate, not everyone is able to participate, not everyone wants to participate, and not everyone who participates does so on equal terms. The word "participation" has a history in both political and cultural discourse, and the overlap between the two begs closer consideration. In some cases, networked publics are tapping this expanded communication capacity to create a more diverse culture—challenging entrenched institutions, expanding economic opportunities, and even, in the case of religious media, perhaps saving our souls. Others are simply using it to get on with the business of their everyday lives.

Motivating and facilitating sharing. The current media environment has become increasingly conducive to the spread of media content. Partially, spreadability is the result of shifts in the nature of technologies which make it easier to produce, upload, download, appropriate, remix, recirculate, and embed content. Digitization has made it simpler to change formats and cheaper to circulate content. Partially, spreadability is the result of legal struggles, as many groups are questioning the logic of tight control over intellectual property and as mundane practices of unauthorized use are making legal claims that seek to regulate circulation moot. Whether media producers desire it or not, they can no longer control what their audiences do with their content once it leaves their hands. Seeking to compensate for this loss of control, media producers and networks are developing new business models seeking to benefit from at least some forms of grassroots circulation. The result is a more permissive climate, one where cease-and-desist letters are giving way to appeals to help spread the word. And even more radical experimentation is taking place around independent and alternative media, which must collaborate with supporters to survive. As producers consider how audiences will create "divergences" from official systems of distribution, listening to such practices might provide insight for new models for content creation and circulation, proof of an unanticipated surplus audience eager to engage with material, or indications of emerging popularity for texts that had been removed from commercial circulation.

Temporary and localized communication. There is little that is static or predictable in the current media environment, which is why traditional controlled models of top-down distribution have needed to give way to a hybrid model of circulation which is shaped partially top-down and partially bottom-up. Channels of communication are highly fluid and often improvised, in the spirit of "making shit up as it happens." Thus, content creators are often making their communication more frequent, more timely, and more responsive to particular audiences, with the acknowledgment that producers and communicators often don't know which video segment, blog post, or Twitter thought will get picked up and which will be greeted with silence. Creators are listening closely to their audiences, meeting them when and where the audience is having a conversation to address questions related to the audience's agenda rather than just what the company wants to say. Those who seek to lock down their content or communication cut themselves off from this larger ebb and flow of the culture.

Grassroots intermediaries who advocate and evangelize. Marketing literature, discussed in chapter 1, suggests that brand messages gain greater credibility if shared by someone the listener already knows and trusts. For that reason, companies have sought to identify and bolster their strongest supporters, giving them what they need to help spread the word through the various networks to which they belong. Sometimes, this process backfires, with companies crossing the line in ways which damage public trust in these advocates or which offend the very audiences they hoped to reach. At the same time, "grassroots intermediaries" can become the sharpest critics of brands and media properties when those products fail to live up to their promises. Because these grassroots intermediaries are trusted by other community members, because their voices are widely heard, and because they also have access to empowered decision-makers, they become the locus for campaigns to encourage greater accountability and responsiveness.

It is crucial for those content creators to realize that, if an audience is going to take it upon themselves to spread media content or discussion about that content, it is because it serves some communicative purpose for them and because it fits into the conversations they were already having. Producers must also be careful about too narrowly restricting which voices matter, about ignoring the voices of disgruntled customers, surplus audiences, and major swaths of audience outside a prechosen "target demographic" or who have not been deemed "influencers." Such mistakes lead to missed opportunities or, worse, communication crises. And, finally, brands and other organizations have to think about the ways they organize themselves and communicate internally, to ensure they are efficiently and effectively responding to audiences and—as they can—realigning their focus based on what they are finding from these listening efforts. If successful, organizations have the potential to create two-way channels of communication that are more appropriate to the emergent peer-to-peer culture.

Collaboration among roles. Early in the book, we talked about the blurring relations between producers, marketers, and audiences, suggesting that few of us today are simply passive audience members in the classic sense of the term, and, increasingly, we all are becoming publicists for the things we care about. In fact, any given participant may be reconciling different motives in him- or herself, whether it is a corporate insider who wants to balance his profit motive with other personal and social concerns, a marketer who also sees herself as a member of the community she is marketing toward and thus has to balance her professional motivation with her personal identity, or a fan who is troubled by the racial and cultural politics represented in a favorite text.

How far should spreadability go? Veteran production designer David Brisbin (2009–2010) captures the industry's discomfort about the public's expanded communication capacities in an essay, widely read and discussed by other Hollywood insiders, about his experiences working on *Twilight: New Moon*. From beginning to end, this production—based on the bestselling novels about a vampire/human love story—was under close observation by very active fans, including some who staked out the locations as they were being scouted, altered, and filmed. In the process, many people offered collective judgment in real time on every decision the designers made. Brisbin writes,

Late in the production, I was building a fountain and dressing a public piazza in Tuscany for our last week of shooting. The fan machine was so hungry and efficient that they shot and posted every step of our construction, paint and dressing progress in that piazza so that when the art department in Vancouver came to work each day, they could scrutinize stills and video on public blogs showing precisely what had been accomplished by wrap time in Italy a few hours earlier. (56)

The fans were not simply spoilers, seeking to reconstruct what happened on the set or to anticipate what would be in the movie. Nor were they simply helping to create buzz and public awareness. They were also sharp critics who read those leaked details in relation to firm expectations forged through their close and intimate engagement with the novel. As Brisbin describes,

How many times do we as designers work out visual detail with our directors and choose when to embrace and when to alter source material? Suddenly, entering into this discussion, in very real time, is a vocal fan base equipped with sound and picture. [. . .] On *New Moon*, when the fans discovered a new location—they launched (online) into traditional Art Department–type debates, informed by intense knowledge of the source text, about which colors, buildings, and set dressing worked—or didn't. (57–58)

Brisbin acknowledges that fans were often highly supportive of choices they felt preserved what they valued; yet the production team found the process of having their real-time design decisions monitored and appraised unnerving. In some cases, the fan photographers and scouts were faster than the production team itself. And, in some cases, the unauthorized images became the basis of profit making by online participants who charged admission for a virtual tour of the production sites.

Brisbin's essay ends on a note of ambivalence about what all this means for his profession: "It is perhaps also worth a moment of speculation on what this forecasts for Production Design. It is surely unavoidable that instant fan-made media will, depending on the story, be insinuating itself into our future work. It seems likely that heightened levels of production security will settle over us as we romp around in public spaces pulling together sets" (59). At risk here are a number of things once taken for granted by commercial media producers: control over the flow of intellectual property, to be sure—though, more than this, control over creative decisions and control over the public's access to information, which may in turn shape how people respond to the work when they encounter it in the theater. The public's appraisal of a film's merits may increasingly rest not on the finished product on the screen but the process by which it got there.

Brisbin seems prepared to accept the inevitability of such information flow. He predicts that Hollywood will tighten security and demand that its personnel remain mum about details, but it will not be able to contain what the Internet has unleashed. Yet the relations between fans and producers about the *Twilight* franchise became even more conflicted as it reached its closing chapters. When stolen images and raw footage from *Twilight: Breaking Dawn* were found circulating online, Summit Entertainment hired a detective to track down their unauthorized source (Belloni 2011). Meanwhile, in a statement, producers appealed to dedicated fans not to reward this breach of studio security: "Please, for those who are posting, stop. And please, though the temptation is high, don't view or pass on these images. Wait for the film in its beautiful, finished entirety to thrill you" (quoted in Belloni 2011).

Many of those fans cooperated, working with the producers to curtail the unauthorized spread of the video. Ultimately, when the detectives completed their investigation, the producers identified by name a specific Argentinian fan and announced their plans to take legal action. Said Summit executive vice president and general counsel David Friedman, "While we very much appreciate the legions of committed fans of the franchise and encourage them to create community online, we cannot ignore that property was stolen. It is not fair to the majority of fans that want to see the final chapter of the *Twilight Saga* film franchise fully realized by the filmmaker and dedicated cast and crew to have these images out and available on the Internet" (quoted in Belloni 2011).

Readers may disagree about when and where producers should draw the line in terms of public circulation of such material. Some will side with producers who feel that their rights to creative control over the film's production and their efforts to protect the security of their processes should supersede the desires of fans. Others may feel that movie audiences have the right *not* to have the first-time experience of watching the film "spoiled" (in the positive and negative sense of the word) by leaked images and information. Even those who support the sharing of amateur photographs taken at public locations may draw the line when it comes to gaining illegal access to actual production materials or making money off their access to these images.

Others may be much more suspicious of the industry's attempts to restrict the public's right to scrutinize and criticize their production decisions. They may be outraged by the producers' decision to publicly identify the responsible fan, feeling that it is an inappropriate response to someone who was almost certainly motivated by a desire to support rather than damage the film franchise.

Twilight is an interesting test case, because it takes us beyond issues of intellectual property or viral marketing. It speaks to inevitable conflicts in expectations and values, to almost unavoidable friction within a spreadable media ecology. What's striking, then, is that so many fans did respond to the producers' calls to slow the circulation of these unauthorized images, that there was so much public discussion within the fandom about how the community should respond to this request. At the same time, the fact that many fans chose not to comply suggests that these participatory cultures are asserting their own philosophy about what should be circulated to whom and under what circumstances.

The circulation of these images reflects a desire to know what's happening so the community can exert a collective influence on the production decisions while it is still possible—in theory—to change them. And that type of audience intervention from engaged fans who have been at least somewhat empowered with greater potential to organize and have their voices heard is the type of activity we've documented throughout this book.

If, for many of us, the long-term goal is to create a more democratic culture, which allows the public a greater role in decision-making at all levels, then a key requirement is going to be timely access to information and transparency in decision-making. We are still far more accustomed to applying such standards to governmental policy than to commercial decision-making. Yet, insofar as new models of spreadability rest on acknowledging customers, fans, and other audiences as stakeholders in the success of brands and franchises, these expectations about responsiveness bring with them corresponding expectations about access to meaningful information.

Perhaps the most impactful aspect of a spreadable media environment, though, is the way in which we all now play a vital role in the sharing of media texts. The everyday, often mundane decisions each of us makes about what to pass along, who to share it with, and the context under which we share that material is fundamentally altering the processes of how media is circulated. In some cases, participants are remixing this content as it spreads; in others, they are recontextualizing. But in every case, these participants are expanding the potential meaning the content had and, in some cases, enhancing its value. This means material, and perspectives, that previously would never have had a chance to be heard are being circulated through grassroots movement and that the potential exists for a more connected, collective, and active society in what has often been labeled an "information age." Yet, as Uncle Ben said to Peter Parker in *Spider-Man*, "With great power comes great responsibility." Just as companies and governments will and should face increasing pressure to be transparent in an era when information is more likely than ever to come to light, each of us has to think about our complicity in the materials we pass along, about the responsibility we hold as citizens to vet what we share, and about our reputations as curators for the information we choose to circulate.

The spreading of media texts helps us articulate who we are, bolster our personal and professional relationships, strengthen our relationships with one another, and build community and awareness around the subjects we care about. And the sharing of media across cultural boundaries increases the opportunity to listen to other perspectives and to develop empathy for perspectives outside our own. We believe that building a more informed and more engaged society will require an environment in which governments, companies, educational institutions, journalists, artists, and activists all work to support rather than restrict this environment of spreadability and the ability of everyone to have access—not just technically but also culturally—to participate in it.

For the foreseeable future, these issues will be under debate between and among all participating parties. The shape of our culture, thank goodness, is still under transition, and—as a consequence—it is still possible for us to collectively struggle to shape the terms of a spreadable media environment and to forge a media environment that is more inclusive, more dynamic, and more participatory than before.

Notes to How to Read This Book

1. We feel it is important to note that, despite this overall trend, there are a range of media studies scholars and projects that are taking a more collaborative approach to find productive ways to converse with industry voices. We hope *Spreadable Media* contributes to that trend.

2. For the purposes of this book, we distinguish between social network sites such as Facebook and the larger concept of social networks, which refer to the interconnections between social agents; social network sites may serve as tools for sustaining and expanding social networks, but few people participate in social networks consisting only of people they can meet on Facebook.

Notes to the Introduction

1. Some groups had commercial motives that in some way contributed to the video's creation and circulation—FremantleMedia (the production company), ITV (the television network), YouTube (an important distribution channel)—but their motives had very little to do with why any individual user chose to circulate it.

2. Something like viral media was described by science fiction writers years before the idea appeared in business literature. Cordwainer Smith, as early as 1964, writes, "A bad idea can spread like a mutated germ. If it is at all interesting, it can leap from one mind to another halfway across the universe before it has a stop put to it. Look at the ruinous fads and foolish fashions which have nuisanced mankind even in the ages of the highest orderliness" ([1964] 1975, 193). This passage demonstrates some of the defining traits of viral media theory: ideas are transmitted, often without critical assessment, across a broad array of minds, and this uncoordinated flow of information is associated with "bad ideas" or "ruinous fads and foolish fashions."

Notes to Chapter 1

1. It is worth noting how commonplace these comments seem. Legal action by recording labels, movie studios, or their lobbying groups are regularly met with claims that large copyright holders are "out of touch" with audience behavior and the norms of the culture at large.

2. Henry Jenkins (1992) brought the concept of "moral economy" to fan studies, exploring how fan fiction writers legitimate their appropriation of media texts and set "limits" on acceptable uses for borrowed materials. Through discussion, fan communities often develop a firm consensus about the moral economy, which provides a strong motivation for them to speak out against media producers that they feel are damaging a media property or "exploiting" fans. The popularity of illegal downloads among music audiences, for instance, reflects an oft-spoken belief that record labels "rip off"

NOTES

audiences and artists alike through inflated prices and poor contractual terms. Similarly, recent controversies about fan or user relations and user rights have emerged around key Web 2.0 sites—from LiveJournal to Twitter. These controversies spread rapidly, thanks to the often well-articulated ideas possessed by many communities about what constitutes appropriate use.

3. This intersection of value and meaning has a deep history in consumer culture theory. In the essay "Meaning Manufacture and Movement in the World of Goods," in *Culture and Consumption* (1998), Grant McCracken brings together anthropological and marketing literature to offer an account of the way "meaning transfer" shapes the exchange of objects. McCracken starts from the premise that the circulation of goods is accompanied by the circulation of meaning: "Meaning is constantly flowing to and from its several locations in the social world, aided by the collective and individual efforts of designers, producers, advertisers, and consumers" (71). Both designers and advertisers draw on meanings already in the culture around them as they seek to construct offerings that will be valued by their potential customers. In a later revision of this argument that evokes the work of Russell Belk (1984), McCracken writes, "Consumers turn to their goods not only as bundles of utility with which to serve functions and satisfy needs but also as bundles of meaning with which to fashion who they are and the world in which they live" (2005, 112).

Notes to Chapter 3

1. However, cross-platform viewers might particularly matter to an advertiser that has bought a product placement in the media text itself. For instance, Hyundai's deal to have its Tucson car driven by characters in *The Walking Dead* means that the results of that advertising deal will remain embedded in the show throughout all its forms of distribution. Thus, Hyundai has reason to be interested in the show's viewership across any platform. Product-placement deals remain complicated, however, as there has been little standardization as to how such cross-platform deals are made.

2. Such practices have led to great consternation among human resources professionals and IT experts, who are trying to decide whether such activities during the workday constitutes a sign of lost productivity or heightened camaraderie. For example, a 2010 survey of British workers by employment site MyJobGroup reported on the amount of time people were using social media at work, concluding that the equivalent of up to approximately US$22 billion was lost per year to the British economy (Ingram 2010). Others have refuted such claims. A 2009 survey of 300 Australian workers led by marketing professor Brent Coker found that 70 percent of respondents engaged in "leisure browsing" online while at work but that such activities make workers about 9 percent more productive—as long as those workers spend no more than a fifth of their time online recreationally during work hours (University of Melbourne 2009).

3. It's also crucial for producers to listen to these most deeply engaged audiences if they seek to reach them, to ensure that the content they create for them actually match what those audiences want. See Levine 2011 for an example in which soap opera producers designed a transmedia text (a character's blog) that interfered with a key fan activity (speculating on what characters are thinking and what is motivating them, based on their actions on the show). In this case, the blog offered straightforward access to a character's thoughts rather than providing a resource which could sustain the fan community's own efforts to examine, debate, and interpret what they saw on the show and subsequently drew scorn from some dedicated fans.

4. The impact of these strategies might be suggested by the rising celebrity of Harry Shum Jr., the Asian American dancer who was a regular extra on *Glee*'s first season (jokingly referred to on the show as "unnamed Asian guy") and who emerged as a more prominent character by season two. Shum, already well known in the Los Angeles dance community, was also associated with *Legion of Extraordinary Dancers* (*LXD*), a web-based video series featuring spectacular street dance within a narrative framework that borrowed heavily from superhero comics and professional wrestling. *LXD* was the opening act for the *Glee* cast in the summer of 2010, increasing Shum's visibility with the fans who turned out to see the concert tour. And *LXD*'s cross-promotion on *So You Think You Can Dance* and performances at both the 2010 Oscars and TED2010 helped to further raise Shum's profile. Shum's elastic-limbed solo performance in an early episode of *LXD* probably prefigured the "Make 'Em Dance" number on *Glee*'s season two. Such strategies allowed the program's most hardcore fans a sense of having helped discover Shum, a reward for tracing his performances across a range of media platforms and venues.

5. This way of thinking is making its way into the advertising industry itself. Faris Yakob (2006), among others, argues that the marketing world should focus on "transmedia planning." As with transmedia storytelling, transmedia planning would emphasize how narratives flow and audiences engage with content across multiple media platforms. Yakob writes, "In this model, there would be an evolving non-linear brand narrative. Different channels could be used to communicate different, self-contained elements of the brand narrative that build to create [a] larger brand world. Consumers then pull different parts of the story together themselves."

Note to Chapter 4

1. By pointing this out, we don't mean to further the myth of a division between "digital natives" and "digital immigrants" (Jenkins 2007a). Rather, we want to emphasize the relationships these youths who have grown up immersed in online participation have with those who are just starting to embrace these communication platforms. By doing so, we can see transgenerational networks of people who are increasingly active in communication online. For instance, a 2009 Nielsen report found that 50 percent of people surveyed who were 65 and older had posted or viewed photos online in the past month and that 8.2 percent of those who visit social network sites and blogs are senior citizens (which, as a demographic group, was virtually equal to the number of teenagers engaging on such platforms) (Nielsen 2009). As boomer audiences age into older demographics and as transgenerational ties (and promises of grandchildren's photos) bring older audiences into social network sites and onto media-sharing platforms, these numbers continue to grow. Many of these older users may not be producers in the narrowest sense of the term, but to paint them as passive "consumers" of digital media content doesn't capture the active social dynamics that have driven them to increasingly participate in social spaces online.

2. Games scholar James Paul Gee (2004) characterizes many forms of participatory culture in terms of "affinity spaces"—affinity, that is, for a common endeavor. He argues that romantic notions of community do not apply to many of these groups; engaging with one another is a secondary objective in many cases, if it exists at all. Participants in an affinity space may or may not feel a strong sense of affiliation with each other: some simply pass through, engaging with content, gathering information, and returning to their own play. Others may become more closely connected. They

may participate via different modes—some active, some passive; some leading, some following other participants. Gee is interested in the informal learning taking place in relation to gaming, which often depends heavily on gamers sharing knowledge to sustain their competitions and collaborations. Such affinity spaces can motivate the production and circulation of information, which may intensify affiliation and inspire other kinds of contributions. People form nonexclusive relationships to these kinds of affinity spaces: they may have multiple interests and thus engage with several different affinity spaces. And, as they travel, information spreads.

3. We might also consider the widespread local use of radio technology through police scanners. Communication across local networks of emergency responders, police departments, school bus drivers, and other groups is conducted on public channels, giving people in the community the opportunity to listen and actively start up word-of-mouth networks to circulate community happenings (a school bus running late, a fire in town, an altercation the police has been called to). However, while the community can listen, they have no way to get actively involved in producing such content.

4. Of course, calling podcasts "radio" emphasizes the formats and relationships of radio much more than the technology; radiolike technologies continue to operate in largely invisible ways today through devices such as cell phones and garage-door openers. But these shifts in the structures of media circulation are at the heart of what we are calling the spreadable media paradigm.

5. We realize that, within cultural studies, the language of "alignment" most typically describes situations in which people in power force, cajole, or mislead people to their side, using their considerable resources. What happens when companies use those resources instead to better understand their audiences' priorities and to force alignment on themselves, pushing their company to better address what their audiences seek?

6. Writing at the dawn of the digital age, John Fiske argues, "The multiplication of communications and information technologies extends the terrains of struggle, modifies the forms struggle may take, and makes it even more imperative that people grasp the opportunities for struggle the multiplying of technologies offers" (1994, 240). Fiske does not romanticize new media as a ready solution for all inequalities and injustices: he discusses, for example, the continued inequalities between those who had access to high-tech and low-tech modes of communication, differences which reflected their economic resources, cultural capital, and social status as much as it reflected the particular tools at their disposal.

Notes to Chapter 5

1. On Reddit, for instance, users contribute links to news stories and/or comment and vote on others' links. People use the site to discover new material and simultaneously contribute their interests back to the site, collectively vetting and curating what users believe is the most "valuable" information. Reddit is useful inasmuch as its users agree that the material it surfaces matches their sense of quality and importance. Reddit employs a points-based system through which users can achieve greater notoriety within a community on the site and simultaneously reward others they agree with or of whom they approve. Consequently, many active site users are motivated by the desire to improve their own standing to share the types of stories that will interest and engage others. And less engaged users are still making active (if instant) decisions to communicate something about themselves when they publicly record their preferences.

2. The mix of Twitter users whom Old Spice Guy responded to included both celebrities and people who did not have large Twitter followings and who would certainly not be considered "influencers," creating a variety and unpredictability of exactly whom he would respond to next that fueled the popularity of the Twitter video initiative.

3. In some cases, such negative publicity can enhance corporate interests, as we examined in the introduction regarding the widespread circulation of criticisms about cable operator Comcast's customer service, which forced the company to improve its own performance and to become more effective at engaging its customers (at least through its online efforts), or in chapter 4 regarding Domino's build up of its marketing through correcting longstanding customer frustrations with the pizza-delivery company. It is hard to imagine that Church's felt there was a potential upside, though, to false claims about its ties to the Ku Klux Klan. If Turner is right that the rumors were really displaced criticisms of white-owned-and-run companies aggressively targeting minority populations, perhaps the solution rests in going after the implicit causes of the critique rather than trying to suppress the urban myth that expresses it.

4. In some senses, the Bil'in activists and their counterparts elsewhere were tapping into a very old language of popular protest. Cultural historian Natalie Zemon Davis (1975) reminds readers in her now-classic essay "Women on Top" that protesters in early modern Europe often masked their identity through various forms of role play, dressing as peoples both real (Moors) and imagined (Amazons) who were a perceived threat to the civilized order. The Sons of Liberty in colonial Boston continued this tradition when they dressed as Native Americans to dump tea in the harbor, and African Americans in New Orleans have formed their own Mardi Gras Indian tribes (Lipsitz 2001), taking imagery from Buffalo Bill's Wild West Show to signify their community's struggles for respect and dignity in a segregated South. These protesters—historical and modern day—adopt fictive identities in order to tap the mythic powers associated with "warrior peoples."

Notes to Chapter 6

1. Paley has opted not to exert strong control over her content, but she has not escaped the constraints of current copyright law. She has been involved in an ongoing struggle over her use of vocals by the 1920s jazz singer Annette Hanshaw. Paley had discovered Hanshaw's songs through a collector and felt they provided the right soundtrack for her film. Paley (2010a) attended a workshop on fair use and worked closely with student lawyers at American University to determine the rights for this music. While the songs might have fallen into public domain if copyright terms had not been dramatically extended in 1998, the rights holders have demanded steep rents on their circulation, even though they have no intention themselves of doing anything with the music.

2. Mass-media content gives people shared material to sustain a variety of relationships. The value of *Dancing with the Stars*, the performance of an area's favorite sports teams, or last night's weather report will continue to serve vital functions for fueling conversations in the supermarket line. Mass-media content also provides familiarity and a level of trust. Think of the vital role chain restaurants play for travelers. Local (niche) restaurants might provide a more satisfying meal for travelers, but they carry with them a much greater risk for disappointment. The implicit contract that the traveler has with a chain brand, meanwhile, sets

expectations. And mass-media content still carries momentary value in the "broadcast" sense. Morning news programs, Weather Channel segments, syndicated game shows, and the like stand little chance of being appraised as having long-term value as "spreadable media," but they may still be useful as one-time viewing or background noise against which advertising can be sold. Rather, the material most endangered in such an environment is that which neither draws a large up-front audience nor generates passion from supporters.

Aday, Sean, Henry Farrell, Marc Lynch, John Sides, John Kelly, and Ethan Zuckerman. 2010. *Blogs and Bullets: New Media in Contentious Politics.* Washington,
DC: United States Institute of Peace/Peaceworks.

Allison, Anne. 2006. *Millennial Monsters: Japanese Toys and the Global Imagination.*
Berkeley: University of California Press.

Anderson, Chris. 2004. "The Long Tail." *Wired* 12 (10) (October). http://www.wired.
com/wired/archive/12.10/tail.html.

———. 2006. *The Long Tail: Why the Future of Business Is Selling Less of More.*
New York: Hyperion.

———. 2009. The Economics of Giving It Away." *Wall Street Journal*, Jan. 31. http://
online.wsj.com/article/SB123335678420235003.html.

Anderson, Chris, and Michael Wolff. 2010. "The Web Is Dead, Long Live the Internet!" *Wired*, Aug. 17. http://www.wired.com/magazine/2010/08/ff_webrip/.

Anderson, Nate. 2009. "Vimeo Sued: Have Staffers Uploaded Infringing Content?"
Ars Technica, Dec. 19. http://arstechnica.com/tech-policy/news/2009/12/vimeo-sued-
have-staffers-uploaded-infringing-content.ars.

Andrejevic, Mark. 2007. "Surveillance in the Digital Enclosure." *Communication
Review* 10 (4): 295–317.

———. 2008. "Watching Television without Pity: The Productivity of Online Fans."
Television and New Media 9 (24): 24–46.

———. 2009. "Exploiting YouTube: Contradictions of User-Generated Labor." In Pelle
Snickars and Patrick Vonderau (eds.), *The YouTube Reader*, 406–421. Stockholm:
National Library of Sweden.

Andresen, Katya. 2011. "Why Slactivism Is Underrated," *Mashable*, Oct. 24. http://
mashable.com/2011/10/24/slactivism-cause-engagement/.

Ang, Ien. 1991. *Desperately Seeking the Audience.* London: Routledge.

Appadurai, Arjun. 1986. "Introduction: Commodities and the Politics of Value." In
The Social Life of Things: Commodities in Cultural Perspective, 3–63. Cambridge:
Cambridge University Press.

———. 1990. "Disjuncture and Difference in the Global Cultural Economy." *Public
Culture* 2 (2) (Spring): 1–24.

———. 2010. "How Histories Make Geographies: Circulation and Context in a Global
Perspective." *Transcultural Studies* 1:4–13.

Arauz, Mike. 2008. "Pass-along Is Made of People! Peeeeeeeoplllle!" *Mike Arauz*
(blog), Dec. 1. http://www.mikearauz.com/2008/12/pass-along-is-made-of-people.
html.

REFERENCES

————. 2009. "Is Your Brand Passionate about Something More Important than Your Product?" *Mike Arauz* (blog), Feb. 26. http://www.mikearauz.com/2009/02/is-your-brand-passionate-about.html.

Arrington, Michael. 2009. "YouTube Full of Creepy, Soundless Music Videos." *TechCrunch*, Jan. 14. http://www.techcrunch.com/2009/01/14/youtube-full-of-creepy-soundless-music-videos/.

Askwith, Ivan. 2009. "'Do You Even Know Where This Is Going?': *Lost*'s Viewers and Narrative Premeditation." In Roberta Pearson (ed.), *Reading* Lost, 159–180. London: I. B. Tauris.

————. 2010. "Stop Spreading Viruses and Start Giving Gifts." In *Society of Digital Agencies Two Thousand and Ten Digital Marketing Outlook*, 47–48. http://www.scribd.com/doc/25441346/Two-Thousand-and-Ten-Digital-Marketing-Outlook.

Asur, Sitaram, and Bernardo Huberman. 2010. "Predicting the Future with Social Media." *arXiv.org*, Cornell University Library, March 29. http://arxiv.org/pdf/1003.5699v1.

Aufderheide, Pat, and Peter Jaszi. 2008. "Recut, Reframe, Recycle: Quoting Copyrighted Material in User-Generated Video." *American University Center for Social Media*, January. http://www.centerforsocialmedia.org/fair-use/related-materials/documents/recut-reframe-recycle.

Bacon-Smith, Camille. 1992. *Enterprising Women: Television Fandom and the Creation of Popular Myth*. Philadelphia: University of Pennsylvania Press.

Baldwin, Mike. n.d. "mban768." *CartoonStock*, http://www.cartoonstock.com/newscartoons/cartoonists/mba/lowres/mban768l.jpg.

Banet-Weiser, Sarah. 2012. *Authentic™: The Politics of Ambivalence in a Brand Culture*. New York: NYU Press.

Banks, John, and Sal Humphreys. 2008. "The Labour of User Co-Creators." *Convergence: The International Journal of Research into New Media Technologies* 14 (4): 401–418.

Barbrook, Richard. 1998. "The Hi-Tech Gift Economy." *First Monday* 3 (12) (December). http://www.firstmonday.org/issues/issue3_12/barbrook/.

Barrionuevo, Alexei. 2007. "A Violent Police Unit, on Film and in Rio's Streets." *New York Times*, Oct. 14. http://www.nytimes.com/2007/10/14/world/americas/14tropa.html.

Bartle, Richard. 2003. *Designing Virtual Worlds*. San Francisco: New Riders.

Bebergal, Peter. 2007. "The Age of Steampunk." *Boston Globe*, Aug. 26. http://www.boston.com/news/globe/ideas/articles/2007/08/26/the_age_of_steampunk/.

Belk, Russell. 1984. "Cultural and Historical Differences in Concepts of the Self and Their Effects on Attitudes towards Having and Giving." In Thomas C. Kinnear (ed.), *Advances in Consumer Research* 11:753–760. Provo, UT: Association for Consumer Research.

Belloni, Matthew. 2011. "'Twilight: Breaking Dawn' Alleged Pirate Identified by Summit." *Hollywood, Esq.* (blog), *Hollywood Reporter*, Aug. 1. http://www.hollywoodreporter.com/thr-esq/twilight-breaking-dawn-alleged-pirate-217664.

Benkler, Yochai. 2006. *The Wealth of Networks*. New Haven: Yale University Press.

Bishop, Ronald. 2001. "Dreams in the Line: A Day at the Antiques Roadshow." *Journal of Popular Culture* 35 (1): 195–209.

Black, Rebecca. 2008. *Adolescents and Online Fan Fiction*. New York: Peter Lang.

Blom, Philipp. 2002. *To Have and to Hold: An Intimate History of Collectors and Collecting*. Woodstock, NY: Overlook.

Booth, Paul. 2010. *Digital Fandom: New Media Studies*. New York: Peter Lang.

Borden, Mark. 2010. "The Mekanism Guarantee: They Engineer Virality." *Fast Company* 145 (May). http://www.fastcompany.com/magazine/145/repeat-offenders.html.

Boucher, Geoff. 2006. "Pirating Songs of Praise." *Los Angeles Times*, Oct. 10. http://articles. latimes.com/2006/oct/10/entertainment/et-christian10.

boyd, danah. 2006. "Lonelygirl15." *apophenia: making connections where none previously existed* (blog), Sept. 7. http://www.zephoria.org/thoughts/archives/2006/09/07/lonely-girl15.html.

———. 2011. "White Flight in Networked Publics? How Race and Class Shaped American Teen Engagement with MySpace and Facebook." In Lisa Nakamura and Peter Chow-White (eds.), *Race after the Internet*, 203–222. New York: Routledge.

Boyle, Caitlin. 2010. "Making Change: An Introduction to Advocacy-Driven Distribution." Talk at "Seize the Power: A Marketing and (DIY)stribution Symposium" at the Los Angeles Film Festival in Los Angeles, June 20.

Brabham, Daren C. 2008. "Crowdsourcing as a Model for Problem Solving: An Introduction and Cases." *Convergence* 14 (1): 75–90.

"Brazil Cop Drama Wins Berlinale." 2008. *The Local*, Feb. 17. http://www.thelocal.de/lifestyle/20080217-10325.html.

Brecht, Bertolt. (1932) 1986. "The Radio as an Apparatus of Communication." In John Hanhardt (ed.), *Video Culture: A Critical Investigation*, 53–55. Rochester: Visual Studies Workshop.

Brisbin, David. 2009–2010. "Instant Fan-Made Media." *Perspective* 27 (December–January): 54–59.

Brown, Mary Ellen. 1990. "Motley Moments: Soap Operas, Carnival, Gossip and the Power of the Utterance." In Mary Ellen Brown (ed.), *Television and Women's Culture: The Politics of the Popular*, 183–198. London: Sage.

Bruns, Axel. 2008. *Blogs, Wikipedia, Second Life, and Beyond: From Production to Produsage*. New York: Peter Lang.

Brunsdon, Charlotte. 1984. "Writing about Soap Opera." In Len Masterman (ed.), *Television Mythologies: Stars, Shows & Signs*, 82–87. London: Comedia.

Bryant, Susan L., Andrea Forte, and Amy Bruckman. 2005. "Becoming Wikipedian: Transformation of Participation in a Collaborative Online Encyclopedia." *GROUP '05 Proceedings of the 2005 International ACM SIGGROUP Conference on Supporting Group Work*. http://www.cc.gatech.edu/~asb/papers/conference/bryant-forte-bruckman-group05.pdf.

Brynjolfsson, Erik, Yu Jeffrey Hu, and Michael D. Smith. 2006. "From Niches to Riches: The Anatomy of the Long Tail." *Sloan Management Review* 47 (4): 67–71.

Burgess, Jean. 2008. "'All Your Chocolate Rain Are Belong to Us'? Viral Video, YouTube and the Dynamics of Participatory Culture." In Geert Lovnik and Sabine Niederer (eds.), *The Video Vortex Reader*, 101–110. Amsterdam: Institute of Network Cultures.

Burgess, Jean, and Joshua Green. 2009. *YouTube: Online Video and Participatory Culture*. Cambridge: Polity.

Caddell, Bud. 2008. "Becoming a Mad Man." *We Are Sterling Cooper*. http://wearester-lingcooper.org/becoming-a-mad-man.pdf.

———. 2009a. "Mad Men on Twitter at SXSW." *What Consumes Me* (blog), March 2. http://whatconsumesme.com/2009/what-im-writing/mad-men-on-twitter-at-sxsw/.

———. 2009b. "Stop Saying Viral Video." *What Consumes Me* (blog), Dec. 10. http://whatconsumesme.com/2009/posts-ive-written/will-i-share-your-branded-content/.

———. 2010. "The Art of Repetition and Recombinance." *What Consumes Me* (blog), Aug. 6. http://whatconsumesme.com/2010/posts-ive-written/the-art-of-repetition-recombinance/.

Cajueiro, Marcello. 2007. "'Elite' Stirs Controversy, Box Office." *Variety*, Oct. 19. http://www.variety.com/article/VR1117974360.

Campbell, John Edward. 2009. "From Barbershop to BlackPlanet: The Construction of Hush Harbors in Cyberspace." Paper presented at the Media in Transition 6 conference, MIT, Cambridge, Massachusetts, April 25. http://web.mit.edu/comm-forum/mit6/papers/Campbell.pdf.

Campbell, Mel. 2009. "YouCan'tTube." *The Enthusiast*, Jan. 24. http://www.theenthusiast.com.au/archives/2009/youcanttube/.

Campbell, T. 2006. *The History of Webcomics*. San Antonio, TX: Antarctic.

Camper, Brett (vice president of product development at Kickstarter). 2010. Email correspondence with Henry Jenkins, Dec. 18.

Carafano, James Jay. 2009. "All a Twitter: How Social Networking Shaped Iran's Election Profile." *Backgrounder* (Heritage Foundation), July 20.

Carroll, Sam. 2007. "Are You Hep to This Jive? The Fan Culture Surrounding Swing Music." *Confessions of an Aca-Fan*. http://henryjenkins.org/2007/01/are_you_hep_the_fan_culture_su.html.

Caves, Richard. 2000. *Creative Industries: Contracts between Art and Commerce*. Cambridge: Harvard University Press.

Chapman, C. C. 2010. "The Going Viral Myth." *C. C. Chapman* (blog), Nov. 19. http://www.cc-chapman.com/2010/11/19/the-going-viral-myth/.

Clark, Jessica. 2009. *Public Media 2.0: Dynamic, Engaged Publics*. Washington DC: Center for Social Media at American University. http://www.centerforsocialmedia.org/resources/publications/public_media_2_0_dynamic_engaged_publics/.

Clouse, Abby. 2008. "Narratives of Value and the Antiques Roadshow: A Game of Recognitions." *Journal of Popular Culture* 41 (1): 3–20.

Cohen, Lizabeth. 2003. *A Consumers' Republic: The Politics of Mass Consumption in Postwar America*. New York: Vintage.

Collins, Dan. 2007. "'Jericho' Fans Go Nuts." *CBS News*, May 25. http://www.cbsnews.com/stories/2007/05/25/entertainment/main2851525.shtml.

Condry, Ian. 2004. "Cultures of Music Piracy: An Ethnographic Comparison of the US and Japan." *International Journal of Cultural Studies* 7 (3): 343–363.

———. 2006. *Hip-Hop Japan: Rap and the Paths of Cultural Globalization*. Durham: Duke University Press.

Connelly, Brendon. 2010. "Analyst Declares Sundance's YouTube Streaming Initiative a Flop." */film*, Jan. 26. http://www.slashfilm.com/analyst-declares-sundances-youtube-streaming-inititative-a-flop/.

Coppa, Francesca. 2008. "Women, *Star Trek* and the Early Development of Fannish Vidding." *Transformative Works and Cultures* 1. http://journal.transformativeworks.org/index.php/twc/article/view/44/64.

Costanza-Chock, Sasha. 2010. "Se Ve, Se Siente: Transmedia Mobilization in the Los Angeles Immigrant Rights Movement." Ph.D. dissertation, University of Southern California.

Costikyan, Greg. 2009. "Shuttering Manifesto." *Play This Thing* (blog), June 23. http://playthisthing.com/shuttering-manifesto.

Crumley, Arin. 2011. Online correspondence with Henry Jenkins, Feb. 22.

Davis, Natalie Zemon. 1975. "Women on Top." In *Society and Culture in Early Modern France*, 124–151. Stanford: Stanford University Press.

Dawkins, Richard. 1976. *The Selfish Gene*. Oxford: Oxford University Press.

———. 1989. *The Selfish Gene*. 2nd ed. Oxford: Oxford University Press.

———. 2006. *The Selfish Gene*. 3rd ed. Oxford: Oxford University Press.

Dayan, Daniel. 2005. "Mothers, Midwives and Abortionists: Genealogy, Obstetrics, Audiences and Publics." In Sonia Livingstone (ed.), *Audiences and Publics: When Cultural Engagement Matters for the Public Sphere*, 43–76. Bristol, UK: Intellect.

Dean, Jodi. 2002. *Publicity's Secret: How Technoculture Capitalizes on Democracy*. Ithaca: Cornell University Press.

———. 2005. "Communicative Capitalism: Circulation and the Foreclosure of Politics." *Cultural Politics* 1 (1): 51–74.

de Bourgoing, Marguerite. 2009. Untitled student paper, University of Southern California.

de Certeau, Michel. 1984. *The Practice of Everyday Life*. Berkeley: University of California Press.

De Kosnik, Abigail. 2010. *Piracy Is the Future of Television*. Report prepared for the members of the MIT Convergence Culture Consortium, Cambridge, Massachusetts. http://convergenceculture.org/research/c3-piracy_future_television-full.pdf.

Delwiche, Aaron. 2012. "The New Left and the Computer Underground: Recovering Political Antecedents of Participatory Culture." In Aaron Delwiche and Jennifer Jacobs Henderson (eds.), *The Participatory Cultures Handbook*, 10–20. New York: Routledge.

Desjardins, Mary. 2006. "Ephemeral Culture/eBay Culture: Film Collectibles and Fan Investments." In Ken Hillis and Michael Petit with Nathan Scott Epley (eds.), *Everyday eBay: Culture, Collecting, and Desire*, 31–44. New York: Routledge.

Deuze, Mark. 2010. "Survival of the Mediated." *Journal of Cultural Science* 3 (2): 1–11.

Deuze, Mark, and John Banks. 2009. "Co-Creative Labor." *International Journal of Cultural Studies* 12 (5) (September): 419–431.

Doctorow, Cory. 2003. *Down and Out in the Magic Kingdom*. New York: Tor.

———. 2008a. "About This Book." In *Little Brother*. http://craphound.com/littlebrother/about/.

———. 2008b. *Little Brother*. New York: Tor.

———. 2008c. "Think like a Dandelion." *Locus*, May. http://www.locusmag.com/Features/2008/05/cory-doctorow-think-like-dandelion.html.

Dodds, Peter Sheridan, Roby Muhamad, and Duncan J. Watts. 2003. "An Experimental Study of Search in Global Social Networks." *Science* 301 (5634) (Aug. 8): 827–829.

Douglas, Mary. 1991. "Jokes." In Chandra Mukerji and Michael Schudson (eds.), *Rethinking Popular Culture*, 291–311. Berkeley: University of California Press.

Douglas, Susan J. 1989. *Inventing American Broadcasting, 1899–1922*. Baltimore: Johns Hopkins University Press.

Driscoll, Michael. 2007. "Will YouTube Sail into the DMCA's Safe Harbor or Sink for Internet Piracy?" *John Marshall Review of Intellectual Property Law* 6 (May): 550–569.

Duncombe, Stephen. 2007. *Dream: Re-imagining Progressive Politics in an Age of Fantasy*. New York: New Press.

Economist. 2010. "Nollywood: Lights, Camera, Africa." Dec. 16. http://www.economist.com/node/17723124.

Edwards, Jim. 2010. "Smells like Clean Spirit." *Brandweek* 51 (32) (Sept. 13): 18–20.

Elberse, Anita. 2008. "Should You Invest in the Long Tail?" *Harvard Business Review*, July–August, 1–9.

Eng, Lawrence. 2012. "Anime and Manga Fandom in a Networked Culture." In Mizuko Ito, Daisuke Okabe, and Izumi Tsuji (eds.), *Fandom Unbound: Otaku Culture in a Connected World*, 158–178. New Haven: Yale University Press.

Engler, Craig. 2010. "Why Watching TV Online (Mostly) Doesn't Help Ratings (for Now)." *Boing Boing*, May 5. http://boingboing.net/2010/05/05/why-watching-tv-onli.html.

Enzensberger, Hans Magnus. (1970) 2000. "Constituents of a Theory of the Media." In Paul Marris and Sue Thornham (eds.), *Media Studies: A Reader*, 68–91. New York: NYU Press.

Epley, Nathan Scott. 2006. "Of PEZ and Perfect Price: Sniping, Collecting Cultures, and Democracy on eBay." In Ken Hillis and Michael Petit with Nathan Scott Epley (eds.), *Everyday eBay: Culture, Collecting, and Desire*, 151–166. New York: Routledge.

Fahim, Kareem. 2010. "Pirated Films from Nigeria Are Seized in Brooklyn." *New York Times*, Nov. 4. http://www.nytimes.com/2010/11/05/nyregion/05nollywood.html.

Faulkner, Simon. 2010. "Not Just Avatar Activism." *Simon's Teaching Blog*, Sept. 18. http://simonsteachingblog.wordpress.com/2010/09/18/not-just-avatar-activism/.

Fiske, John. 1987. *Television Culture*. London: Methuen.

———. 1989a. *Reading the Popular*. London: Routledge.

———. 1989b. *Understanding Popular Culture*. London: Routledge.

———. 1994. *Media Matters: Race and Gender in U.S. Politics*. Minneapolis: University of Minnesota Press.

Ford, Sam. 2008a. "Soap Operas and the History of Fan Discussion." *Transformative Works and Cultures* 1. http://journal.transformativeworks.org/index.php/twc/article/view/42/50.

———. 2008b. "YouTube and Non-English Media Content." *Futures of Entertainment Weblog*, Feb. 4. http://www.convergenceculture.org/weblog/2008/02/youtube_and_nonenglish_media_c.php.

———. 2010a. "For Best Brand-Building Results, Listen Up!" *PR News*, Aug. 2.

———. 2010b. "Get Advertising and PR to Work Together for a Spreadable Approach." *Chief Marketer*, June 9. http://chiefmarketer.com/disciplines/branding/0609-spreadable-approach/.

———. 2010c. "Sharing vs. Selling: A Lesson from Gospel Music." *Fast Company*, Oct. 19. http://www.fastcompany.com/1696259/sharing-vs-selling-a-lesson-from-gospel-music.

———. 2010d. "Understanding Motivations." In Rick Liebling (ed.), *Everyone Is Illuminated*. eBook. http://www.slideshare.net/eyecube/everyone-is-illuminated-3129260.

———. 2010e. "What's the Rush? Creating Meaningful Dialogue with Social Media Messages." *Public Relations Strategist*, Aug. 23. http://www.prsa.org/Intelligence/TheStrategist/Articles/view/8756/1019/What_s_the_Rush_Creating_Meaningful_Dialogue_with.

Ford, Sam, Abigail De Kosnik, and C. Lee Harrington. 2011. "Introduction: The Crisis of Daytime Drama and What It Means for the Future of Television." In Sam Ford, Abigail De Kosnik, and C. Lee Harrington (eds.), *The Survival of Soap Opera: Transformations for a New Media Era*, 3–21. Jackson: University Press of Mississippi.

Ford, Sam, with Rachel Shearer, Parmesh Shahani, Joshua Green, and Henry Jenkins. 2006. *No Room for Pack Rats: Media Consumption and the College Dorm*. Report prepared for the members of the MIT Convergence Culture Consortium, Cambridge, Massachusetts. http://convergenceculture.org/research/c3_no_room_for_pack_rats.pdf.

Frank, Robert H., and Philip J. Cook. 1995. *The Winner-Take-All Society: Why The Few at the Top Get So Much More than the Rest of Us*. New York: Penguin.

Fraser, Nancy. 1990. "Rethinking the Public Sphere: A Contribution to the Critique of Actually Existing Democracy." *Social Text* 25/26:56–80.

The Freeconomy Community. n.d. "Philosofree." http://www.justfortheloveofit.org/philosofree.

Friedman, Thomas. 2005. *The World Is Flat: A Brief History of the 21st Century*. New York: Farrar, Straus, and Giroux.

Gandhi, Rikin. 2010. "Annual Report: Introduction." Digital Green website. http://www.digitalgreen.org/annualletter/.

Garfield, Bob. 2007. "Comcast Must Die." *Advertising Age*, Sept. 9. http://adage.com/garfieldtheblog/post?article_id=120338.

———. 2009. Letter on *ComcastMustDie.com*. http://comcastmustdie.com/.

Garvey, Ellen Gruber. 2013. *Writing with Scissors: American Scrapbooks from the Civil War to the Harlem Renaissance*. New York: Oxford University Press.

Gee, James Paul. 2004. *Situated Language and Learning: A Critique of Traditional Schooling*. New York: Routledge.

Gehl, Robert. 2009. "YouTube as Archive: Who Will Curate This Digital Wunderkammer?" *International Journal of Cultural Studies* 12 (1): 43–60.

Ghemawat, Pankaj. 2007. "Why the World Isn't Flat." *Foreign Policy* 159 (March–April): 54–60.

Gillespie, Tarleton. 2006. "Designed to 'Effectively Frustrate': Copyright, Technology, and the Agency of Users." *New Media & Society* 8 (4): 651–669.

Gladwell, Malcolm. 2000. *The Tipping Point: How Little Things Can Make a Big Difference*. Boston: Little, Brown.

Gogoi, Pallavi. 2006a. "Wal-Mart's Jim and Laura: The Real Story." *BusinessWeek*, Oct. 9. http://www.businessweek.com/bwdaily/dnflash/content/oct2006/db20061009_579137.htm.

———. 2006b. "Wal-Mart vs. the Blogosphere." *BusinessWeek*, Oct. 17. http://www.businessweek.com/bwdaily/dnflash/content/oct2006/db20061018_445917.htm.

Golijan, Rosa. 2010. "Comcast to Customer: Pay Us $0.00 or We'll Cancel Your Service." *Gizmodo*, July 28. http://gizmodo.com/5599103/comcast-to-customer-pay-us-000-or-well-cancel-your-service.

Gorman, Steve. 2003. "Anti-Bush Iraq Documentary Makes the Party Circuit." Reuters. *Common Dreams*, Dec. 20. http://www.commondreams.org/headlines03/1220-04.htm.

Gould, Scott. 2010. "Gather What You Scatter." *Scott Gould* (blog), July 13. http://scottgould.me/gather-what-you-scatter/.

Govil, Nitin. 2007. "Bollywood and the Friction of Global Mobility." In Daya Kishan Thussu (ed.), *Media on the Move: Global Flow and Counter-Flow*, 76–88. London: Routledge.

Grad, Shelby. 2009. "Sorting Out the Facts in Obama-Joker 'Socialist' Posters around L.A." *L.A. Now* (blog), *Los Angeles Times*, Aug. 3. http://latimesblogs.latimes.com/lanow/2009/08/sorting-out-the-facts-in-obamajoker-socialist-posters-around-la.html.

Gray, Jonathan. 2008a. "Cultural Imperialism and 'Newness': More on Malawian Media Consumption." *The Extratextuals* (blog), Sept. 14. http://www.extratextual.tv/2008/09/cultural-imperialism-and-"newness"-more-on-malawian-media-consumption/.

———. 2008b. "Malawian Media Consumption, Part III: The Music." *The Extratextuals* (blog), July 19. http://www.extratextual.tv/2008/07/malawian-media-consumption-part-iii-music/.

———. 2011. "Crowds, Words, and the Futures of Entertainment Conference." *Antenna* (blog), Nov. 15. http://blog.commarts.wisc.edu/2011/11/15/crowds-words-and-the-futures-of-entertainment-conference/.

Gray, Mary L. 2009. *Out in the Country: Youth, Media, and Queer Visibility in Rural America*. New York: NYU Press.

Green, Joshua. 2008. "'Why in the World Won't They Take My Money?': Hulu, iTunes and the Value of Attention." *Flow*, April 15. http://flowtv.org/2008/04/"why-in-the-world-won't-they-take-my-money"-hulu-itunes-and-the-value-of-attention/.

Greenwall, Robert. 2010. Director's commentary, *Brave New Films 5th Anniversary Activist Collection*. DVD box set.

Gregory, Sam. 2010. "Cameras Everywhere: Ubiquitous Video Documentation of Human Rights, New Forms of Video Advocacy, and Considerations of Safety, Security, Dignity and Consent." *Journal of Human Rights Practice* 2 (2): 191–207.

Guizzo, Erico. 2008. "The Steampunk Contraptors." *IEEE Spectrum*, October. http://spectrum.ieee.org/consumer-electronics/gadgets/the-steampunk-contraptors.

Habermas, Jürgen. (1962) 2000. "The Public Sphere." Trans. Thomas Burger and Frederick Lawrence. In Paul Morris and Sue Thornton (eds.), *Media Studies: A Reader*, 2nd ed., 92–97. New York: NYU Press.

Harrington, C. Lee, and Denise D. Bielby. 1995. *Soap Fans: Pursuing Pleasure and Making Meaning in Everyday Life*. Philadelphia: Temple University Press.

Harris, Neil. 1981. *Humbug: The Art of P. T. Barnum*, Chicago: University of Chicago Press.

Hartley, John. 2008. *Television Truths: Forms of Knowledge in Popular Culture*. Malden, MA: Blackwell.

Hasson, Eva. 2010. "Stop Saying Viral—A Case for Spreadable Media." *SlideShare*, March 23. http://www.slideshare.net/evahasson/stop-saying-viral-a-case-for-spreadable-media-3517863.

Hayes, Gary. 2007. "Web 2.0 and the Myth of Non-participation." *Personalized Media* (blog), Nov. 26. http://www.personalizemedia.com/the-myth-of-non-participation-in-web-20-social-networks/.

Hayward, Jennifer. 1997. *Consuming Passions: Active Audiences and Serial Fictions from Dickens to Soap Opera*. Lexington: University of Kentucky Press.

Heffernan, Virginia. 2008. "Art in the Age of Franchising." *New York Times Magazine*, Jan. 20. http://www.nytimes.com/2008/01/20/magazine/20wwln-medium-t.html.

Helft, Miguel, and Geraldine Fabrikant. 2007. "WhoseTube? Viacom Sues Google over Video Clips." *New York Times*, March 14. http://www.nytimes.com/2007/03/14/technology/14viacom.html.

Hendershot, Heather. 2004. *Shaking the World for Jesus: Media and Conservative Evangelical Culture*. Chicago: University of Chicago Press.

Herman, Andrew, Rosemary J. Coombe, and Lewis Kaye. 2006. "Your Second Life? Goodwill and the Performativity of Intellectual Property in Online Digital Gaming." *Cultural Studies* 20 (2–3) (March–May): 184–210.

Hernandez, Eugene. 2006. "DIY Distribution: Coming Soon via the Filmmakers of *Four-Eyed Monsters* and *Head Trauma*." *Indiewire*, Aug. 17. http://www.indiewire.com/article/diy_distribution_coming_soon_via_the_filmmakers...four_eyed_monsters_and_he/.

Herrman, Gretchen M. 1997. "Gift or Commodity: What Changes Hands in the U.S. Garage Sale?" *American Ethnologist* 24 (4): 910–930.

Herrman, John. 2009. "Hulu's Free Glory Days Are Officially Numbered." *Gizmodo*, Oct. 22. http://gizmodo.com/5387909/hulus-free-glory-days-are-officially-numbered.

Hilderbrand, Lucas. 2007. "YouTube: Where Cultural Memory and Copyright Converge." *Film Quarterly* 6 (1): 48–57.

Hillis, Ken, Michael Petit, and Nathan Scott Epley. 2006. "Introducing *Everyday eBay.*" In Ken Hillis and Michael Petit with Nathan Scott Epley (eds.), *Everyday eBay: Culture, Collecting, and Desire*, 1–18. New York: Routledge.

Hills, Matt. 2002. *Fan Cultures*. London: Routledge.

Holson, Laura M. 2007. "Hollywood Asks YouTube: Friend or Foe?" *New York Times*, Jan. 15. http://www.nytimes.com/2007/01/15/technology/15youtube.html.

Horowitz, Bradley. 2006. "Creators, Synthesizers, and Consumers." *Elatable* (blog), Feb. 15. http://blog.elatable.com/2006/02/creators-synthesizers-and-consumers.html.

Howe, Irving, and Kenneth Libo. 1983. *How We Lived: A Documentary History of Immigrant Jews in America, 1880–1930*. New York: Putnam.

Howe, Jeff. 2006. "The Rise of Crowdsourcing." *Wired* 14 (6) (June). http://www.wired.com/wired/archive/14.06/crowds.html.

Huddleston, Kathie. 2010. "*Heroes* Is a Hit—as the Most Pirated TV Show, That Is." *SyFy Blastr*, Jan. 5. http://blastr.com/2010/01/heroes-is-a-hit-as-the-mo.php.

Hyde, Lewis. 1983. *The Gift: Imagination and the Erotic Life of Property*. New York: Vintage.

Inda, Jonathan Xavier, and Renato Rosaldo. 2002. "Introduction: A World in Motion." In Jonathan Xavier Inda and Renato Rosaldo (eds.), *The Anthropology of Globalization: A Reader*, 1–34. Malden, MA: Blackwell.

Ingram, Mathew. 2010. "News Flash: Your Employees Are Wasting Time on the Internet." *GigaOM*, Aug. 6. http://gigaom.com/2010/08/06/news-flash-your-employees-are-wasting-time-on-the-internet/.

Innis, Harold. 1951. *The Bias of Communication*. Toronto: University of Toronto Press.

Iron Sky. n.d. "Crowdfunding—The New Way to Finance Movies." http://www.ironsky.net/site/support/finance/.

Ito, Mizuko. 2012. "Contributors vs. Leechers: Fansubbing Ethics and a Hybrid Public Culture." In Mizuko Ito, Daisuke Okabe, and Izumi Tsuji (eds.), *Fandom Unbound: Otaku Culture in a Connected World*, 179–204. New Haven: Yale University Press.

Ito, Mizuko, Sonia Baumer, Matteo Bittani, danah boyd, Rachel Cody, Becky Herr-Stephenson, Heather A. Horst, Patricia G. Lange, Dilan Mahendran, Katynka Z. Martinez, C. J. Pascoe, Dan Perkel, Laura Robinson, Christo Sims, and Lisa Tripp. 2009. *Hanging Out, Messing Around, and Geeking Out: Kids Living and Learning with New Media*. Cambridge: MIT Press.

Iwabuchi, Koichi. 2002. *Recentering Globalization: Popular Culture and Japanese Transnationalism*. Durham: Duke University Press.

Jenkins, Henry. 1992. *Textual Poachers: Television Fans and Participatory Culture*. New York: Routledge.

———. 2004. "Pop Cosmopolitanism: Mapping Cultural Flows in an Age of Media Convergence." In Marcelo Suarez-Orozco and Desiree B. Qin-Hilliard (eds.), *Globalization: Culture and Education in the New Millennium*, 114–140. Berkeley: University of California Press.

———. 2006a. "City Blogging in Beirut." *Confessions of an Aca-Fan* (blog), Aug. 17. http://www.henryjenkins.org/2006/08/city_blogging_in_beirut.html.

———. 2006b. *Convergence Culture: Where Old and New Media Collide*. New York: NYU Press.

———. 2007a. "Reconsidering Digital Natives." *Confessions of an Aca-Fan* (blog), Dec. 5. http://www.henryjenkins.org/2007/12/reconsidering_digital_immigran.html.

———. 2007b. "Transforming Fan Culture into User-Generated Content: The Case of Fan-Lib." *Confessions of an Aca-Fan* (blog), May 22. http://www.henryjenkins.org/2007/05/transforming_fan_culture_into.html.

———. 2008. "Field Notes from Shanghai: Fansubbing in China." *Confessions of an Aca-Fan* (blog), Jan. 23. http://henryjenkins.org/2008/01/field_notes_from_shanghai_fans.html.

———. 2009. "How 'Dumbledore's Army' Is Transforming Our World: An Interview with Andrew Slack." *Confessions of an Aca-Fan* (blog), July 23. http://henryjenkins.org/2009/07/how_dumbledores_army_is_transf.html.

———. 2010a. "ARGS, Fandom and the Digi-Gratis Economy: Interview with Paul Booth (Part Three)." *Confessions of an Aca-Fan* (blog), Aug. 18. http://henryjenkins.org/2010/08/args_fandom_and_the_digi-grati.html.

———. 2010b. "The Hollywood Geek Elite Debates the Future of Television." *Confessions of an Aca-Fan* (blog), June 2. http://henryjenkins.org/2010/06/the_hollywood_geek_elite_debat.html.

———. 2012. "'Cultural Acupuncture': Fan Activism and the Harry Potter Alliance." *Transformative Works and Cultures*, 10. http://journal.transformativeworks.org/index.php/twc/article/view/305.

Johnson, Brian David. 2010. *Screen Future: The Future of Entertainment, Computing and the Devices We Love*. Portland, OR: Intel.

Johnson, Derek. 2010. "New Battlegrounds: Modding Cultural Studies." Presentation at Fiske Matters: A Conference on John Fiske's Continuing Legacy for Cultural Studies at University of Wisconsin–Madison, Madison, Wisconsin, June 12.

Johnson, Steven. 2005. *Everything Bad Is Good for You: How Today's Popular Culture Is Actually Making Us Smarter*. New York: Riverhead.

Jung, Helin. 2009. "Mad Men Creator Matthew Weiner Goes Off on the Internet." *New York Magazine Vulture*, Oct. 18. http://nymag.com/daily/entertainment/2009/10/mad_men_creator_matthew_weiner_goes.html.

JupiterResearch. 2007. "JupiterResearch Finds Viral Marketing Missteps Reach Epidemic Proportions." *Business Wire*, Sept. 4. http://www.businesswire.com/news/google/20070904005784/en.

Jurvetson, Steve, and Tim Draper. 1997. "Viral Marketing: Viral Marketing Phenomenon Explained." *Netscape M-Files* newsletter, Jan. 1.

Keen, Andrew. 2007. *The Cult of the Amateur: How the Democratization of the Digital World Is Assaulting Our Economy, Our Culture, and Our Values*. New York: Doubleday.

Kincaid, Jason. 2009. "YouTube Extends Revenue Sharing Program to Anyone with a Viral Video." *TechCrunch*, Aug. 25. http://www.techcrunch.com/2009/08/25/youtube-extends-revenue-sharing-program-to-anyone-with-a-viral-video/.

King, Lindy. 2009. "The Dual Universe of the Twitter Mad Men—they're alive!" *Examiner.com*, July 19. http://www.examiner.com/mad-men-in-national/the-dual-universe-of-the-twitter-mad-men-they-re-alive.

Kligler-Vilenchik, Neta, Joshua McVeigh-Schultz, Christine Weitbrecht, and Chris Tokuhama. 2012. "Experiencing Fan Activism: Understanding the Power of Fan Activist Organizations through Member's Narratives." *Transformative Works and Cultures*, 10. http://journal.transformativeworks.org/index.php/twc/article/view/322.

Klink, Flourish. 2011. "The Fan Manifesto." The Alchemists, unpublished document. In authors' possession.

Knowledge@Wharton. 2006. "Coming Attraction: YouTube's Business Model." Oct. 4. http://www.knowledgeatwharton.com.cn/index.cfm?fa=viewArticle&articleID=1490.

Kompare, Derek. 2006. "Publishing Flow: DVD Box Sets and the Reconception of Television." *Television New Media* 7 (4): 335–360.

Kopytoff, Igor. 1986. "The Cultural Biography of Things: Commoditization as Process." In Arjun Appadurai (ed.), *The Social Life of Things: Commodities in Culture*, 64–91. Cambridge: Cambridge University Press.

Koster, Raph. 2006. "User Created Content." *Raph Koster's Website*, June 20. http://www.raphkoster.com/2006/06/20/user-created-content/.

Kozinets, Robert V. 1999. "E-Tribalized Marketing? The Strategic Implications of Virtual Communities of Consumption." *European Management Journal* 17 (3): 252–264.

Kreps, Daniel. 2009. "EMI Sues Vimeo for Hosting 'Lip Dub' Music Videos." *Rolling Stone*, Dec. 17. http://www.rollingstone.com/rockdaily/index.php/2009/12/17/emi-sues-vimeo-for-hosting-lip-synched-music-videos/.

Lake Superior State University. 2010. "LSSU's 36th Annual List of Banished Words Goes Viral." Dec. 31. http://www.lssu.edu/whats_new/articles.php?articleid=2135.

Lange, Patricia G. 2009. "Videos of Affinity on YouTube." In Patrick Vonderau and Pelle Snickars (eds.), *The YouTube Reader*. Stockholm: National Library of Sweden.

Lanier, Jaron. 2010. *You Are Not a Gadget: A Manifesto*. New York: Knopf.

Lankshear, Colin, and Michele Knobel. 2010. *DIY Media: Creating, Sharing and Learning with New Media*. New York: Peter Lang.

Lapowsky, Issie. 2009. "Susan Boyle's Upcoming Debut Album Bigger than the Beatles and Whitney, Hits No. 1 on Amazon List." *New York Daily News*, Sept. 4. http://www.nydailynews.com/entertainment/music/2009/09/04/2009-09-04_susan_boyles_upcoming_debut_album_bigger_than_the_beatles_and_whitney_hits_no_1_.html.

Larkin, Brian. 2004. "Degraded Images, Distorted Sounds: Nigerian Video and the Infrastructure of Piracy." *Public Culture* 16 (2) (Spring): 289–314.

———. 2008. *Signal and Noise: Media, Infrastructure, and Urban Culture in Nigeria*. Durham: Duke University Press.

Lavan, Rosie. 2010. "Crowd Fuels Sci-Fi Parody." *The Pixel Report*, Sept. 5. http://thepixel-report.org/2010/09/05/star-wreck/.

Lave, Jean, and Etienne Wenger. 1991. *Situated Learning: Legitimate Peripheral Participation*. Cambridge: Cambridge University Press.

Lawler, Ryan. 2009. "Vimeo Sued over Lip Dubs." *GigaOM*, Dec. 15. http://gigaom.com/video/vimeo-sued-over-lip-dubs/.

Leach, Skot (co-creator of *Lost Zombies*). 2010. Email correspondence with Henry Jenkins, Dec. 21.

Learmonth, Michael. 2008. "Twitter, AMC, Wise Up, Restore 'Mad Men' Accounts." *Silicon Alley Insider, Business Insider*, Aug. 26. http://www.businessinsider.com/2008/8/twitter-amc-wise-up-restore-mad-men-.

LeechesofKarma. 2009. "EMI Sues Vimeo for Encouraging Users to Lip Dub." *Digg*, Dec. 18. http://digg.com/music/EMI_Sues_Vimeo_For_Encouraging_Users_To_Lip_Dub.

Lenhart, Amanda, Mary Madden, Aaron Smith, and Alexandra Macgill. 2007. "Teens and Social Media." *Pew Internet & American Life Project*, Dec. 19. http://www.pewinternet.org/Reports/2007/Teens-and-Social-Media.aspx.

Leonard, Sean. 2005. "Progress against the Law: Anime and Fandom, with the Key to the Globalization of Culture." *International Journal of Cultural Studies* 8 (September): 281–305.

Lessig, Lawrence. 2007. "Lucasfilm's Phantom Menace." *Washington Post*, July 12. http://www.washingtonpost.com/wp-dyn/content/article/2007/07/11/AR2007071101996.html.

———. 2008. *Remix: Making Art and Commerce Thrive in a Hybrid Economy*. New York: Penguin.

Levine, Elana. 2011. "'What the Hell Does TIIC Mean?' Online Content and the Struggle to Save the Soaps." In Sam Ford, Abigail De Kosnik, and C. Lee Harrington (eds.), *The Survival of Soap Opera: Transformations for a New Media Era*, 201–218. Jackson: University Press of Mississippi.

Levy, Steven, and Brad Stone. 2006. "The New Wisdom of the Web." *Newsweek*, April 3. http://www.newsweek.com/id/45976.

Li, Xiaochang. 2007. "Fanfic, Inc.: Another Look at FanLib.Com." *MIT Convergence Culture Consortium C3 Weekly Update*, Dec. 7.

———. 2009. *More than Money Can Buy: Locating Value in Spreadable Media*. Report prepared for the members of the MIT Convergence Culture Consortium, Cambridge, Massachusetts. http://convergenceculture.org/research/C3LocatingValueWhitePaper.pdf.

Liang, Lawrence. 2009. "Piracy, Creativity and Infrastructure: Rethinking Access to Culture." Alternative Law Forum. July 20. Available at SSRN: http://ssrn.com/abstract=1436229.

Lipsitz, George. 2001. *Time Passages: Collective Memory and American Popular Culture*. Minneapolis: University of Minnesota Press.

Livingstone, Sonia. 2005. "On the Relation between Audiences and Publics." In Sonia Livingstone (ed.), *Audiences and Publics: When Cultural Engagement Matters for the Public Sphere*, 17–42. Bristol, UK: Intellect.

Livingstone, Sonia, and Magdalena Bober. 2005. *UK Children Go Online*, April. London: Economic and Social Research Council, http://www.lse.ac.uk/collections/children-go-online/UKCGOfinalReport.pdf.

Lopez, Lori Kido. 2011. "Fan-Activists and the Politics of Race in *The Last Airbender*." *International Journal of Cultural Studies*, 15(5): 431-445.

Lost Zombies. n.d. "What Is This?" http://www.lostzombies.com/.

Louie, Mynette. 2010. "How Did They Do It? Distribution Case Studies." Talk at "Seize the Power: A Marketing and (DIY)stribution Symposium" at the Los Angeles Film Festival in Los Angeles, California, June 20.

Manjoo, Farhad. 2009. "Tweeting Avengers: Does Venting Consumer Outrage on Twitter Actually Work?" *Slate*, Sept. 1. http://www.slate.com/id/2226927/pagenum/all/.

Marcus, Caroline. 2009a. "A Lost Jacket and a Stolen Heart." *Sydney Morning Herald*, Jan. 18. http://www.smh.com.au/news/lifeandstyle/lifematters/a-lost-jacket-and-a-stolen-heart/2009/01/17/1231609053191.html.

———. 2009b. "You've Been Had: Sydney Cinderella's 'Jacket Man' Exposed as Viral Ad." *Sydney Morning Herald*, Jan. 20. http://www.smh.com.au/news/technology/cinderellas-jacket-man-exposed-as-viralad/2009/01/20/1232213599896.html.

Masnick, Michael. 2009. "Vimeo Sued for Lip Dub Videos." *TechDirt*, Dec. 15. http://www.techdirt.com/articles/20091214/1409257345.shtml.

Mauss, Marcel. (1922) 1990. *The Gift: Forms and Functions of Exchange in Archaic Societies*. London: Routledge.

McCloud, Scott. 2000. *Reinventing Comics: How Imagination and Technology Are Revolutionizing an Art Form*. New York: Harper.

McCracken, Grant. 1988. "Meaning Manufacture and Movement in the World of Goods." In *Culture and Consumption*, 71–91. Bloomington: Indiana University Press.

———. 2005. *Culture and Consumption II: Markets, Meaning, and Brand Management.* Bloomington: Indiana University Press.

———. 2008. *Transformations: Identity Construction in Contemporary Culture.* Bloomington: Indiana University Press.

———. 2009. *Chief Culture Officer: How to Create a Living, Breathing Corporation.* New York: Basic Books.

McDonnell, John. 2008. "Scene and Heard: Kuduro." *Guardian Music Blog*, Oct. 6. http://www.guardian.co.uk/music/musicblog/2008/oct/06/urban.mia.sceneandheard.kuduro.

Meehan, Eileen R. 2005. *Why TV Is Not Our Fault: Television Programming, Viewers, and Who's Really in Control.* Lanham, MD: Rowman & Littlefield.

Meyer, Birgit. 2001. "Ghanaian Popular Cinema and the Magic in and of Film." In Birgit Meyer and Peter Pels (eds.), *Magic and Modernity: Interfaces of Revelation and Concealment*, 200–222. Stanford: Stanford University Press.

Milgram, Stanley. 1967. "The Small World Problem." *Psychology Today* 2:60–67.

Miller, Nancy. 2007. "Minifesto for a New Age." *Wired* 15 (3) (March). http://www.wired.com/wired/archive/15.03/snackminifesto.html.

Mittell, Jason. 2005. "Exchanges of Value." *Flow TV*, Oct. 21. http://flowtv.org/2005/10/exchanges-of-value/.

———. 2006. "Narrative Complexity in Contemporary American Television." *Velvet Light Trap* 58:29–40.

———. 2009. "Sites of Participation: Wiki Fandom and the Case of Lostpedia." *Transformative Works and Cultures* 3. http://journal.transformativeworks.org/index.php/twc/article/view/118/117.

Monello, Michael (partner and executive creative director at Campfire). 2010. Email correspondence with Henry Jenkins, June 25.

Moonves, Leslie. 2007. Q&A with Ken Auletta at Syracuse University, June 12. Available at http://www.c-spanvideo.org/program/198594-1.

Moses, Kim. 2009. Personal interview with Henry Jenkins, Los Angeles, California, Oct. 28.

Moses, Kim, and Ian Sander. 2008. *Ghost Whisperer: Spirit Guide.* London: Titan Books.

Mota, Maurício. 2008. Remarks as part of the "Global Flows, Global Deals" panel at MIT Futures of Entertainment 3 in Cambridge, Massachusetts, Nov. 22. http://techtv.mit.edu/videos/1668-futures-of-entertainment-3---session-7-global-flows-global-deals.

Musser, John, with Tim O'Reilly and the O'Reilly Radar Team. 2006. *Web 2.0 Principles and Best Practices.* Sebastopol, CA: O'Reilly Radar.

Naficy, Hamid. 1993. *The Making of Exile Cultures: Iranian Television in Los Angeles.* Minneapolis: University of Minnesota Press.

Nasser, Jaime. 2011. "Giving Soaps a Good Scrub: ABC's *Ugly Betty* and the Ethnicity of Television Formats." In Sam Ford, Abigail De Kosnik, and C. Lee Harrington (eds.), *The Survival of Soap Opera: Transformations for a New Media Era*, 49–57. Jackson: University of Mississippi Press.

Newcomb, Roger. 2011. "*As the World Turns*' Luke and Noah and Fan Activism." In Sam Ford, Abigail De Kosnik, and C. Lee Harrington (eds.), *The Survival of Soap Opera: Transformations for a New Media Era*, 293–299. Jackson: University Press of Mississippi.

Nielsen. 2009. "Six Million More Seniors Using the Web than Five Years Ago." *Nielsen Wire* (blog), Dec. 10. http://blog.nielsen.com/nielsenwire/online_mobile/six-million-more-seniors-using-the-web-than-five-years-ago/.

———. 2010. "Facebook, Google and Yahoo! Are Top Sites When Watching Big TV Events." *Nielsen Wire* (blog), March 16. http://blog.nielsen.com/nielsenwire/online_mobile/facebook-google-and-yahoo-are-top-sites-while-watching-big-tv-events.

Nine Inch Nails. 2008. "nin.com [download]—the slip." http://dl.nin.com/theslip/signup.

Novaes, Tereza. 2007. "'Tropa de Elite' Já Foi Visto por 19% Dos Paulistanos." *Folha Online Ilustrada*, Oct. 6. http://www1.folha.uol.com.br/folha/ilustrada/ult90u334403.shtml.

Nunley, Vorris L. 2004. "From the Harbor to Da Academic Hood: Hush Harbors and an African American Rhetorical Tradition." In Ronald Jackson and Elaine Richardson (eds.), *African American Rhetorics: Interdisciplinary Perspectives*. Carbondale: Southern Illinois University Press.

obsession_inc. 2009. "Affirmational Fandom vs. Transformative Fandom." *obsession_inc* (blog), June 1. http://obsession-inc.dreamwidth.org/82589.html.

O'Neill, Marnie. 2009. "Heidi's YouTube Love Hunt." *Sunday Telegraph*, Jan. 18. http://www.dailytelegraph.com.au/news/sunday-telegraph/heidis-youtube-love-hunt/story-e6frewt0-1111118590773.

Onion, Rebecca. 2008. "Reclaiming the Machine: An Introductory Look at Steampunk." *Neo-Victorian Studies* 1 (1) (Autumn): 138–163. http://www.neovictorianstudies.com/past_issues/Autumn2008/NVS%201-1%20R-Onion.pdf.

O'Reilly, Tim. 2005. "What Is Web 2.0? Design Patterns and Business Models for the Next Generation of Software." *O'Reilly Media*, Sept. 30. http://oreilly.com/web2/archive/what-is-web-20.html.

O'Reilly, Tim, and John Battelle. 2009. "Web Squared: Web 2.0 Five Years On." *Web 2.0 Summit*. http://www.web2summit.com/web2009/public/schedule/detail/10194.

Paley, Nina. 2009. "Dear Audience." *Sita Sings the Blues*, Feb. 28. http://www.sitasingsthe-blues.com/.

———. 2010a. Email correspondence with Henry Jenkins, Dec. 22.

———. 2010b. "Frequently Asked Questions." *Nina Paley's Blog*, Nov. 15. http://blog.nina-paley.com/2010/11/15/frequently-asked-questions/.

Paley, Nina, and Cory Doctorow. 2010. "Paley & Doctorow Argue over Non-commercial Licenses." *Nina Paley's Blog*, Sept. 1. http://blog.ninapaley.com/2010/09/01/paley-vs-doctorow/.

Paul, Keith. 2010. "Comcast (Still) Doesn't Care." *Keith Paul* (blog), Dec. 2. http://keithpaul.net/2010/12/comcast-doesnt-care/.

Petrik, Paula. 1992. "The Youngest Fourth Estate: The Novelty Toy Printing Press and Adolescence, 1870–1886." In Elliot West and Paula Petrik (eds.), *Small Worlds: Children and Adolescents in America, 1850–1950*. Kansas City: University Press of Kansas.

Phillips, Whitney. 2009. "'Why So Socialist?': Unmasking the Joker." *Confessions of an Aca-Fan* (blog), Aug. 14. http://www.henryjenkins.org/2009/08/unmasking_the_joker.html.

Postigo, Hector. 2008. "Video Game Appropriation through Modifications: Attitudes Concerning Intellectual Property among Fans and Modders." *Convergence: The International Journal of Research into New Media Technologies* 14 (1): 59–74.

Potter, Andrew. 2010. "The Ode: The Old Spice Guy (Feb.–July 2010)." *Canadian Business*, Sept. 13. http://www.canadianbusiness.com/article/11125--the-ode-the-old-spice-guy-feb-july-2010.

Powell, Jenni. 2010. "Producers Guild Officially Sanctioned 'Transmedia Producer' Credit." *Tubefilter*, April 6. http://news.tubefilter.tv/2010/04/06/producers-guild-officially-sanctions-transmedia-producer-credit/.

Pratt, Mary Louise. 1991. "The Arts of the Contact Zone." In Phyllis Franklin (ed.), *Profession 91*, 33–40. New York: Modern Language Association of America.

Purcell, Kristen, Lee Rainie, Amy Mitchell, Tom Rosenstiel, and Kenny Olmstead. 2010. *Understanding the Participatory News Consumer*. Pew Center for Internet and American Life. March 1. http://pewinternet.org/Reports/2010/Online-News/Summary-of-Findings.aspx.

Quote Database. n.d. "Quote #779320." http://www.bash.org/?779320.

Rand, Erica. 1995. *Barbie's Queer Accessories*. Durham: Duke University Press.

Reisner, Rebecca. 2009. "Comcast's Twitter Man." *BusinessWeek*, Jan. 13. http://www.businessweek.com/managing/content/jan2009/ca20090113_373506.htm.

Reynolds, Simon. 2011. *Retromania: Pop Culture's Addiction to Its Own Past*. New York: Faber and Faber.

Rheingold, Howard. 1993. *The Virtual Community: Homesteading on the Electronic Frontier*. Reading, MA: Addison-Wesley.

Rohac, George, Jr. 2010. "Copyright and the Economy of Webcomics." Master's thesis, New York University.

Rohani, Talieh. 2009. "Nostalgia without Memory: Iranian-Americans, Cultural Programming, and Internet Television." Master's thesis, MIT. Available at http://cms.mit.edu/research/theses/TaliehRohani2009.pdf.

Rose, Frank. 2011. *The Art of Immersion: How the Digital Generation Is Remaking Hollywood*. New York: Simon and Schuster.

Rosen, Jay. 2006. "The People Formerly Known as the Audience." *PressThink* (blog), June 27. http://journalism.nyu.edu/pubzone/weblogs/pressthink/2006/06/27/ppl_frmr.html.

Ross, Andrew. 1991. *Strange Weather: Culture, Science and Technology in the Age of Limits*. London: Verso.

Rushkoff, Douglas. 1994. *Media Virus: Hidden Agendas in Popular Culture*. New York: Ballantine.

———. 2000. "Second Sight: The Internet Is Not Killing Off Conversation but Actively Encouraging It." *Guardian*, June 28. http://www.guardian.co.uk/technology/2000/jun/29/onlinesupplement13.

Russell, Adrienne, Mizuko Ito, Todd Richmond, and Marc Tuters. 2008. "Culture: Media Convergence and Networked Participation." In Kazys Varnelis (ed.), *Networked Publics*. Cambridge: MIT Press.

Russo, Julie Levin. 2009. "User-Penetrated Content: Fan Video in the Age of Convergence." *Cinema Journal* 48 (4) (Summer): 125–130.

Sandler, Kevin. Forthcoming. *Scooby-Doo*. Durham: Duke University Press.

Sass, Erik. 2006. "Engagement Panel: No Currency, No Clarity." *MediaPost MediaDailyNews*, April 28. http://www.mediapost.com/publications/?fa=Articles.showArticle&art_aid=42771.

Scott, Suzanne. 2009. "Repackaging Fan Culture: The Regifting Economy of Ancillary Content Models." *Transformative Works and Cultures* 3. http://journal.transformativeworks.org/index.php/twc/article/view/150/122.

———. 2010. "Revenge of the Fanboy: Convergence Culture and the Politics of Incorporation." Ph.D. dissertation, University of Southern California.

Seiter, Ellen. 2008. "Practicing at Home: Computers, Pianos, and Cultural Capital." In Tara McPherson (ed.), *Digital Youth, Innovation, and the Unexpected*, 27–52. Cambridge: MIT Press.

Sennett, Richard. 2008. *The Craftsman*. New Haven: Yale University Press.

Serpe, Gina. 2007. "Nut Job Saves *Jericho.*" *E! Online*, June 6. http://www.eonline.com/uberblog/b55326_Nut_Job_Saves_Jericho.html.

Shahani, Parmesh. 2008. "Great Khali and Multiple Narrative Universes." *P Spot* (blog), April 22. http://parmesh.net/2008/04/great-khali-and-multiple-narrative.html.

"'Shared News Matters More,' Say Results from CNN's First International Study into Social Media Recommendation." 2010. *CNN International*, Oct. 7. http://cnninternational.presslift.com/socialmediaresearch.

Shirky, Clay. 2005. "Institutions vs. Collaboration." Talk at TEDGlobal 2005 in Oxford, England, July 14. http://www.ted.com/talks/clay_shirky_on_institutions_versus_collaboration.html.

———. 2009. "Q&A with Clay Shirky on Twitter and Iran." *TED Blog*, June 16. http://blog.ted.com/2009/qa_with_clay_sh.php.

Short, Iain. 2010. "Viral Marketing vs. Spreadable Media." *EngageSciences*, Aug. 24. http://www.engagesciences.com/readytoland/2010/08/viral-marketing-vs-spreadable-media.

Shresthova, Sangita. 2011. *Is It All about the Hips? Around the World with Bollywood Dance*. London: Sage.

Siegler, MG. 2008. "DMCA Takedown Notice Forces Twitter to Blacklist Mad Men Characters." *Venture Beat DigitalBeat*, Aug. 25. http://venturebeat.com/2008/08/25/twitter-blacklists-mad-men-characters-some-of-them/.

Sisario, Ben. 2009. "Susan Boyle, Top Seller, Shakes Up CD Trends." *New York Times*, Dec. 1. http://www.nytimes.com/2009/12/03/arts/music/03sales.html.

Smillie, Dirk. 2009. "Fightin' Words: Murdoch Wants a Google Rebellion." *Forbes*, April 3. http://www.forbes.com/2009/04/03/rupert-murdoch-google-business-media-murdoch.html.

Smith, Cordwainer. (1964) 1975. "The Dead Lady of Clown Town." In J. J. Pierce (ed.), *The Best of Cordwainer Smith*, 124–209. New York: Ballantine.

Smythe, Dallas W. 1981. "On the Audience Commodity and Its Work." In *Dependency Road: Communications, Capitalism, Consciousness, and Canada*, 22–51. Norwood, NJ: Ablex.

Snelson, Chareen, and Ross A. Perkins. 2009. "From Silent Film to YouTube: Tracing the Historical Roots of Motion Picture Technologies in Education." *Journal of Visual Literacy* 28 (1): 1–27.

Snow, Blake. 2006. "Sony Marketers Are Horrible Liars, Pretend to Run Fansite." *Joystiq*, Dec. 11. http://www.joystiq.com/2006/12/11/sony-marketers-are-horrible-liars-pretend-to-run-fansite/.

Standage, Tom. 2006. *A History of the World in Six Glasses*. New York: Walker.

Steinberg, Brian. 2007. "TV Measurement Comes Up Short." *Advertising Age*, July 23. http://adage.com/mediaworks/article?article_id=119440.

Stelter, Brian. 2010. "Hulu Unveils Subscription Service for $9.99 a Month." *Media Decoder* (blog), *New York Times*, June 29. http://mediadecoder.blogs.nytimes.com/2010/06/29/hulu-unveils-subscription-service-for-9-99-a-month/.

Stephenson, Neal. 1992. *Snow Crash*. New York: Bantam.

Straw, Will. 2007. "Embedded Memories." In Charles R. Acland (ed.), *Residual Media*, 3–15. Minneapolis: University of Minnesota Press.

Sundaram, Ravi. 1999. "Recycling Modernity: Pirate Electronic Cultures in India." *Third Text* 47 (Summer): 59–65.

Tarnoff, Andy. 2007. "Waukesha's Beyer Talks about New Life for CBS' 'Jericho.'" *OnMilwaukee.com*, June 9. http://onmilwaukee.com/ent/articles/jerichoreturns.html.

Terranova, Tiziana. 2003. "Free Labor: Producing Culture for the Digital Economy." *Electronic Book Review*, June 20. http://www.electronicbookreview.com/thread/technocapitalism/voluntary.

Thompson, Clive. 2008. "Is the Tipping Point Toast?" *Fast Company* 122 (Feb. 1). http://www.fastcompany.com/magazine/122/is-the-tipping-point-toast.html.

Thompson, E. P. 1971. "The Moral Economy of the English Crowd in the Eighteenth Century." *Past and Present* 50:76–136.

Thompson, Kristin. 2009. "Take My Film, Please." *Observations on Film Art* (blog), May 7. http://www.davidbordwell.net/blog/?p=4529.

Tinkcom, Matthew, Joy Van Fuqua, and Amy Villarejo. 2002. "On Thrifting." In Henry Jenkins, Tara McPherson and Jane Shattuc (eds.), *Hop on Pop: The Politics and Pleasure of Popular Culture*, 459–471. Durham: Duke University Press.

Travers, Jeffrey, and Stanley Milgram. 1969. "An Experimental Study of the Small World Problem." *Sociometry* 32 (4) (December): 425–443.

Trodd, Zoe. 2006. "Reading eBay: Hidden Stores, Subjective Stories, and the People's History of the Archive." In Ken Hillis and Michael Petit with Nathan Scott Epley (eds.), *Everyday eBay: Culture, Collecting, and Desire*, 77–90. New York: Routledge.

"'Tropa de Elite' Provoca Tensão e Conquista Público em Sala Paulistana." 2007. *Último Segundo*, Oct. 9. http://ultimosegundo.ig.com.br/cultura/2007/10/09/tropa_de_elite_provoca_tensao_e_conquista_publico_em_sala_paulistana_1037915.html.

Trust, Gary. 2011. "'Glee' Cast Tops Elvis Presley for Most Hot 100 Hits." *Billboard.com*, Feb. 16. http://www.billboard.com/news/glee-cast-tops-elvis-presley-for-most-hot-1005036732.story.

Turner, Fred. 2008. *From Counterculture to Cyberculture: Stewart Brand, the Whole Earth Network, and the Rise of Digital Utopianism*. Chicago: University of Chicago Press.

Turner, Patricia Ann. 1994. *I Heard It through the Grapevine: Rumor in African-American Culture*. Berkeley: University of California Press.

"25 New Faces of Independent Film: *Lost Zombies*." 2009. *Filmmaker*, Summer. http://www.filmmakermagazine.com/issues/summer2009/25faces.php.

Tyron, Chuck. 2009. *Reinventing Cinema: Movies in the Age of Media Convergence*. New Brunswick: Rutgers University Press.

University of Melbourne. 2009. "Freedom to Surf: Workers More Productive If Allowed to Use the Internet for Leisure." April 2. http://uninews.unimelb.edu.au/news/5750/.

Van Buskirk, Eliot. 2010. "YouTube Movie Rentals: Today Sundance, Tomorrow the World." *Wired*, Jan. 21. http://www.wired.com/epicenter/2010/01/youtube-movie-rentals-today-sundance-tomorrow-the-world/.

van der Graaf, Shenja. 2005. "Viral Experiences: Do You Trust Your Friends?" In Sandeep Krishnamurthy (ed.), *Contemporary Research in E-Marketing*, vol. 1, 166–185. Hershey, PA: Idea.

Van Dijck, José, and David Nieborg. 2009. "Wikinomics and Its Discontents: A Critical Analysis of Web 2.0 Business Manifestoes." *New Media & Society* 11 (4): 855–887.

Vedrashko, Ilya. 2010a. "Five Things 'Jersey Shore' Taught My Agency about Social Media." *Advertising Age*, July 21. http://adage.com/article/digitalnext/mtv-s-jersey-shore-taught-social-media/145024/.

———. 2010b. "The Spreadable War on Viral Media." *Marketshare* (blog), *Forbes*, June 17. http://blogs.forbes.com/marketshare/2010/06/17/the-spreadable-war-on-viral-media/.

Villarreal, Yvonne. 2010. "'India' an Exotic Hit for TeleFutura." *Los Angeles Times*, Dec. 27. http://articles.latimes.com/print/2010/dec/27/entertainment/la-et-telefutura-india-20101227.

Visakowitz, Susan. 2008. "Nine Inch Nails Offers Freebie of New Album." *Billboard*, May 5. http://www.billboard.com/bbcom/news/article_display.jsp?vnu_content_id=1003798490.

Von Hippel, Eric. 2005. *Democratizing Innovation*. Cambridge: MIT Press.

Vranica, Suzanne, and Chad Terhune. 2006. "Mixing Diet Coke and Mentos Makes a Gusher of Publicity." *Wall Street Journal*, June 12, B1.

Vuorensola, Timo (producer of *Iron Sky*). 2010. Email correspondence with Henry Jenkins, Dec. 23.

Waldman, Allison J. 2006. "*World* Turns 50: 'Digital Comfort Food.'" *Television Week*, Dec. 19.

Wasik, Bill. 2009. *And Then There's This: How Stories Live and Die in a Viral Culture.* New York: Viking.

Watkins, S. Craig. 2010. *The Young and the Digital: What the Migration to Social Network Sites, Games, and Anytime, Anywhere Media Means for Our Future.* New York: Beacon.

Webb, Emma F. 2011. "The Evolution of the Fan Video and the Influence of YouTube on the Creative Decision-Making Process for Fans." In Sam Ford, Abigail De Kosnik, and C. Lee Harrington (eds.), *The Survival of Soap Opera: Transformations for a New Media Era*, 219–230. Jackson: University of Mississippi Press.

Web Ecology Project. 2009. *The Iranian Election on Twitter: The First Eighteen Days.* June 26. http://www.webecologyproject.org/2009/06/iran-election-on-twitter/.

Weiler, Lance. 2008. "When the Audience Takes Control." *Filmmaker*, Summer. http://www.filmmakermagazine.com/issues/summer2008/audience.php.

———. 2009. "Culture Hacker." *Filmmaker*, Spring. http://www.filmmakermagazine.com/issues/spring2009/culture-hacker.php.

Whitney, Daisy. 2007. "Protecting Assets Is Talk of the Town: Copyright, Filtering Solutions Prove Key to Keeping Video Web Sites." *Television Week*, Feb. 26. http://www.tvweek.com/news/2007/02/protecting_assets_is_talk_of_t.php.

Williams, Raymond. 1974. *Television: Technology and Cultural Form*. London: Fontana.

———. 1977. *Marxism and Literature*. New York: Oxford University Press.

Witchel, Alex. 2008. "Mad Men Has Its Moment." *New York Times Magazine*, June 22. http://www.nytimes.com/2008/06/22/magazine/22madmen-t.html.

Wyatt, Edward. 2007. "CBS Revives 'Jericho,' with a Plea to Fans." *New York Times*, June 9. http://www.nytimes.com/2007/06/09/arts/television/09jeri.html.

Yakob, Faris. 2006. "Transmedia Planning." *Talent Imitates, Genius Steals* (blog), Oct. 3. http://farisyakob.typepad.com/blog/2006/10/transmedia_plan.html.

———. 2008. "Spreadable Media." *Talent Imitates, Genius Steals* (blog), Nov. 25. http://farisyakob.typepad.com/blog/2008/11/spreadable-media.html.

Yellin, Emily. 2009. *Your Call Is (Not That) Important to Us: Customer Service and What It Reveals about Our World and Our Lives.* New York: Free Press.

YouTube. n.d. "Frequently Asked Questions." http://www.youtube.com/t/faq.

Zeldman, Jeffrey. 2007. "What Is Art Direction (No. 9)." *Jeffrey Zeldman Presents the Daily Report*, Aug. 17. http://www.zeldman.com/2007/08/17/what-is-art-direction-no-9/.

Zimmerman, Patricia R. 1995. *Reel Families: A Social History of Amateur Film*. Bloomington: Indiana University Press.

Zittrain, Jonathan. 2009. "Law and Technology: The End of the Generative Internet." *Communications of the ACM* 54 (1) (January): 18–20.

Zuckerman, Ethan. 2010. "Nollywood: Is Better Distribution the Remedy for Piracy?" *My Heart's in Accra* (blog), Oct. 6. http://www.ethanzuckerman.com/blog/2010/10/06/nollywood-is-better-distribution-the-remedy-for-piracy/.

4Chan, 27–29, 207
8 Mile, 187
20 Years Too Soon: Superstar Billy Graham, 110
24, 146

ABBA, 234
Abbott, Tony, 206
ABC (Australia), 206
ABC (U.S.), 132, 283
accretion texts, 137, 142, 297
activism, xi, 9, 23, 28–29, 40–43, 45, 53–54, 159, 162, 165, 167–169, 171, 190–192, 194, 199, 215, 219–228, 234, 259, 266, 293, 296–297, 305, 311c5n4
adaptation, 86, 186, 206, 232, 264, 271, 283–284
Aday, Sean, 41
advertising, ix, 1, 4–5, 8–9, 13, 17, 20, 24–25, 30–36, 40, 48, 50–51, 74–75, 77, 80, 86, 91, 100, 106, 114–116, 118–120, 122–123, 125–127, 129–130, 144, 152, 154, 163, 176–177, 179–182, 195, 198, 203–213, 215–217, 227, 237, 273, 288, 308c1n3, 308c3n1, 309c3n5, 312c6n2
Advertising Age, 25, 121
affinity portals/spaces, 174, 309–310c4n2
Africa, 222, 260–268, 274, 286
African American, 159, 170, 189, 192, 216–218, 311c5n4
agency (audience/user), xv, 19, 21–22, 39, 44, 55, 71, 80, 157, 178, 210, 225, 294
aggregation, 45, 68, 93, 95, 166, 175–176, 178, 190, 238, 242–243, 249, 272, 292
The Alchemists, ix, 60, 269
Alive Day Memories, 208
Alkhateeb, Firas, 28

Allison, Anne, 275
"All I Want for Xmas Is a PSP," 77
All My Children, 132
alternate-reality experiences, 134
Amateur Press Association, 29, 159
Amazon, 66, 122, 221, 239, 291
AMC (U.S.), 30–33, 35
American Idol, 9, 14, 142, 147
American University, 311c6n1
American Wrestling Association (AWA), 110
Anderson, Chris, 72, 238–243
Anderson, Nate, 48
Andrejevic, Mark, 126–128, 164–165, 174–176
Andresen, Katya, 223
Ang, Ien, 118–119, 178
Angola, 264
animation, 171, 206, 229–230, 234, 250; anime/Japanese animation, 62, 68–69, 101, 272–273, 275–276
anthropology, 40, 65–66, 123, 155, 204, 271, 308c1n3
Antiques Roadshow, 87–89, 96
Appadurai, Arjun, 40–42, 271–274
Apple, 14, 120, 138, 147, 164, 243, 245–246; Software Development Kit, 245–246
appraisal of media content, 45, 59, 63, 66–67, 72, 84–89, 94–96, 98, 104, 108, 110–112, 117, 124, 128, 133, 154, 176, 184, 187, 196, 198–199, 226–227, 241, 243, 245–246, 250, 259, 273–276, 293, 295, 297, 301–302, 312c6n2
appropriation, 16, 28, 56, 58, 69, 75, 86, 105, 150, 186, 188, 201, 221–223, 230, 262, 266, 270, 298, 307c1n2
Arab Spring, 41
Arauz, Mike, 21, 201

INDEX

Argentina, 302
Arrington, Michael, 51
Ars Technica, 47
Asian American, 171–172, 189, 309c3n4
Askwith, Ivan, 21, 134
The Assassination of Jesse James by the Coward Robert Ford, 105
As the World Turns, 131, 167–168
astroturfing, 77–78, 176, 213
Asur, Sitaram, 142
Atom Films, 151
Auferheide, Pat, 50
Austin, Alec, 53
Australia, 206, 211–212, 240, 308c3n2
authenticity, 71, 76–78, 83, 89, 98, 141, 209, 212, 296
Avatar, 219–223, 266
Avatar: The Last Airbender, 171
Axe, 195

Bacon-Smith, Camille, 29
Baldwin, Mike, 54
Banet-Weiser, Sarah, 59
Banks, John, 49, 56–57
Barbie's Queer Accessories, 180
Barbrook, Richard, 65
Barnett, Steve, 14
barn raising, 63–64, 71
Barnum, P.T., 213
Barrionuevo, Alexei, 269
Bartle, Richard, 157
Basement Bhangra, 280
Batman (character) 28
Battelle, John, 175–176
Battlestar Galactica Video Maker Toolkit, 151
Bauer, Jack (character, *24*), 262
Baym, Nancy K., 234–235
BBC (U.K.), 96
The Beatles, 147
Bebergal, Peter, 101
Bebin.tv, 279–280
Bed, Bath, & Beyond, 70
Beirut, 191
Belk, Russell, 308c1n3
Belloni, Matthew, 302
Benkler, Yochai, 92, 154–155, 159
Beyer, Brad, 121
Bharat, 286–287

The Bias of Communication, 37
The Bible, 254–256
Bielby, Denise D., 130
The Big Bang Theory, 69–71, 73
Big Deal PR, 34
Bil'in, 220–223, 311c5n4
Billboard, 147
Billionaires for Bush, 221–222
The Birth of a Nation, 159
Bishop, Ronald, 88
bitly, 11
BitTorrent, 98, 231
BlackPlanet, 174
Black, Rebecca, 276
The Blair Witch Project, 138, 144
Blastr, 113–114
Blaxploitation, 261
Blockbuster, 239
Blogs and Bullets, 41
Blom, Philipp, 98–99
Bloodbath: The Most Incredible Steel Cage Matches, 110
Bluefin Labs, 122
Bober, Magdalena, 189
The Bold and the Beautiful, 129
Bollywood, 265–266, 270, 277, 280–281, 289
Bombay Dreams, 289
Boo Boo (character, *Yogi Bear*), 105
Booth, Paul, 91, 96
Borden, Mark, 195
Borges, Jorge Luis, 237
Boston Globe, 169
Boucher, Geoff, 256
boyd, danah, 192, 212–213
Boyle, Caitlin, 252
Boyle, Susan, 9–11, 13–16, 39, 44, 95, 135, 260
Brabham, Daren C., 248
brand communities, 102–103, 163–164, 172–173, 195, 205, 247, 293, 296
brands. *See* marketing
Brave New Films, 169–170, 252
Brazil, 9, 182–184, 221, 234, 264, 269, 283, 287
Brecht, Bertolt, 160–162
Brigham Young University, 206
Brisbin, David, 300
Britain. *See* United Kingdom
Britain's Got Talent, 9, 14, 16

broadcast mentality, xiv, 1, 4, 7, 15–17, 24, 30, 44–46, 53, 58, 79, 95, 116–117, 119, 125–126, 148, 176, 180–181, 230, 240, 288, 295
broadcast television. *See* television
Brown, James, 147
Brown, Mary Ellen, 167
Bruckman, Amy, 158
Bruns, Axel, 183–187
Brunsdon, Charlotte, 130
Bryant, Susan L., 158
Brynjolfsson, Erik, 242
Buffalo Bill's Wild West Show, 311c5n4
Bugbee, Carri, 33–35
Buice, Susan, 246–247
Burger King, 209–210
Burgess, Jean, 50, 93, 186–187
Bush, George W., 218
BusinessWeek, 25

cable television. *See* television
Caddell, Bud, 21, 33–35, 206
Cajueiro, Marcello, 269
calypso, 264
Cameron, James, 220
Caminho das Índias, 283
Campbell, John Edward, 174
Campbell, Mel, 51
Campbell, Pete (character, *Mad Men*), 31
Campbell, T., 237
Camper, Brett, 252
Campfire, 144, 148*f*
capitalism, xii, 15, 35, 40, 43, 56, 63, 65, 69, 71, 124, 156, 268, 284
Capitol Records, 47–48
Capoeira, 264
Carafano, James Jay, 41
Caribbean, 264
Carmen, 241–242
Carroll, Sam, 100
Cartoon Network (U.S.), 105
Cash Camp, 186
Caves, Richard, 196
CBS (U.S.), 1, 69, 121–122, 129, 131, 138
CDs, 191, 234–235, 255
censorship, 41–42, 272
Center for Civic Media, 261
Center for Social Impact Communication, 223

Chapman, C. C., 21
Chicken McNuggets, 86
Chief Culture Officer, 178
Children of Invention, 253
China, 10, 221, 271–272, 275
"Chocolate Rain," 187
Christianity. *See* religion
Christian Music Trade Association, 256
Chuck, 122–123, 125, 128
"Chuck Norris Facts," 262
churches. *See* religion
Church's Chicken, 216, 218–219, 311c5n3
cinema, 28, 46, 50, 56–57, 97, 100–101, 105, 138, 142–145, 151, 159, 169–172, 187, 197–198, 203, 219–223, 229–232, 235–236, 241, 243–244, 246–247, 249–254, 260, 262, 264–270, 274–275, 277, 280–281, 283, 286, 289, 300–303, 307c1n1, 311c6n1
circulation of media, xii, xiv–xv, 60, 80, 82–84, 86, 102, 111–112, 117–118, 127, 136, 145, 183, 186, 188, 196–199, 202, 213, 223, 287–289, 302, 308c1n3, 310c4n2, 310c4n3, 310c4n4, 311c5n3, 311c6n1; appraisal and, 89, 94–95; collectors and, 98–100, 107–110; control and, 32, 53–56; core definition of, 1–4, 291–299, 303–304; cultural resources and, 201; ethics of, 224–227; gift economy and, 67–72; Harold Innis on, 37–40; independent media and, 170–171, 229–236, 252; Iran Revolution and, 40–44; Long Tail and, 238–239; as political mobilization, 190–191; as participatory practice, 27–29, 33–36, 155–156, 160–162, 169–172, 193–194; public relations and, 27; religious music and, 254–257; recirculation, 12, 16, 27–28, 96, 104, 154, 201, 230, 298; rumors and, 217–220; stickiness vs., 4–9; Susan Boyle, 10–16, 307"Introduction"n1; transnational, 46, 62, 259–276, 280–283, 285; viral media vs., 16–23
Citi, 25
City of Lost Children, 101
civic media/citizenship, xi, xiii, 13, 39–42, 45, 156, 161, 163, 167–168, 174, 196, 215, 219–228, 233, 248, 261, 280, 285, 288, 293–295, 304
Clark, Jessica, 170

Clinton, Bill, 189
Clinton, Hillary, 28
Clouse, Abby, 88
CNN (U.S.), 12; CNN iReport, 41
co-creation. *See* collaboration
Cohen, Lizabeth, 159
Coker, Brent, 308c3n2
collaboration, xi, 7, 32, 47, 49, 58, 172, 74,
    77–79, 83, 94, 140, 155, 172–175, 179–188,
    193, 228, 232, 246–255, 257, 263–264, 276,
    285, 298, 300, 307"How to Read This
    Book"n1, 309–310c4n2
collective intelligence, 48, 137, 176, 209, 211,
    248
collectors, 12, 29, 54, 85, 87, 89–90, 96–103,
    106–111, 157, 203, 259, 311c6n1
Collins, Dan, 121
Colombia, 283–284
Columbia College Chicago, 165
Columbia Records, 14
Comcast, 23–26, 44, 311c5n3
ComcastMustDie.com, 25
Comedy. *See* humor
comic books, 28, 46, 99, 101, 132, 134,
    136–137, 148, 172, 203–204, 230, 232,
    236–239, 251, 309c3n4
Comic-Con (San Diego), 143–145, 215–216
commercial logic, xii, xiv–xv; 1, 3, 15–16, 18,
    35, 43, 45, 48–50, 52–54, 56–79, 82–112,
    115–132, 151–152, 154, 157, 161, 163, 165,
    172–173, 175, 183, 187, 193, 202–203, 294,
    298, 308c1n3
commodity economy. *See* commercial
    logic
communication studies, 135, 197, 280
Condry, Ian, 62, 264
Connelly, Brendon, 253
consumer/consumption, 2, 22, 24, 27, 33,
    35, 49, 56, 71, 76, 90, 93, 118–119, 123–124,
    126, 143, 147, 150, 153–156, 159, 174, 184,
    193, 216, 242, 267, 273, 277, 294, 308c1n3,
    309c3n5, 309c4n1; communities of
    consumption, 128–129
contact zone, 263, 289–290
control, xii–xiii, 1, 6, 17, 23–24, 28, 32, 35,
    37–42, 53, 56–57, 74, 127, 129, 150, 162, 165,
    170, 174, 178, 180, 187, 193, 201–202, 210,
    224–226, 229, 231, 235, 239, 243–246, 254,

270, 291–293, 295, 297–299, 300–303,
    311c6n1
controversy, 33–34, 93, 106, 202, 213–216,
    218–221, 224
Convergence Culture, 136, 151, 153
Convergence Culture Consortium, ix–xi
Cook, Philip J., 241
Coombe, Rosemary J., 58
Cooper, Mary Ann, 131
Cooper, Sheldon (character, *The Big Bang
    Theory*), 69–70
Coppa, Francesca, 29
copyright. *See* legal issues
corporate communications. *See* public
    relations
Costanza–Chock, Sasha, 190–192, 224
Costa Rica, 182
Costikyan, Greg, 243–246
CourtTV (U.S.), 117
Cowell, Simon, 10
Crank Dat, 185–187
craftsmen, 58–61, 71, 101–102, 128, 297
Creative Commons, 72, 229–230, 238
crowdsourcing (see also crowdfunding/
    crowdsurfing), 247–254
Crumley, Arin, 246–247
Crunchyroll.com, 68
CSI, 122
Cunétame, 169
cult media, 113–114, 141–148, 151–152, 271
cultural acupuncture, 222, 296
cultural activator, 136, 209, 227
cultural attractor, 209
cultural studies, x, xii–xiii, 68, 123, 133, 155,
    163, 241–243, 310c4n5, 311c5n4
curation, 12, 61, 85, 94, 100, 108, 157–158,
    160, 170–171, 184, 186, 190, 226, 242–243,
    246–248, 272, 293, 295–297, 304, 310c5n1
Curator's Code, 226
customer service, 2, 23–26, 44, 73, 75, 164,
    179–181, 300, 311c5n3
CW Network (U.S.), 141

Dailymotion, 10
Daily Telegraph, 212
The Dark Knight, 28
Datafolha, 269
Davis, Natalie Zemon, 311c5n4

dance, 16, 59, 100–101, 145, 183, 185–186, 264, 280–281, 289, 309c3n4, 311c6n2

Dancing with the Stars, 311c6n2

dandelion, 291–293

Dantes, Dingdong, 282

Dante's Inferno, 215–216

Darfur, 222

Dawkins, Richard, 18–19

Dawson's Creek, 138

Dayan, Daniel, 166

daytime serial drama. *See* soap opera

DC Comics, 237

Dean, Jodi, 43–44, 165

de Bourgoing, Marguerite, 264

de Certeau, Michel, 174

Deep Focus, 33–35, 78

De Kosnik, Abigail, 57, 114, 132

deliberation, 45, 161, 175–176

Delwiche, Aaron, 161

demographics of audiences, 7, 114, 118–119, 129–132, 135, 138, 148–149, 152, 154, 189, 235, 300, 309c4n1

Department of Defense, 169

Desi, 280–281

Desjardins, Mary, 90

Deuze, Mark, 57, 221

Dexter, 113

The Diamond Age, 101

diaspora, 42, 46, 266, 268, 276–281, 283, 285, 289

Dickens, Charles, 134

Diet Coke, 86

The Difference Engine, 101

Digg, 47

digi-gratis, 91

digital divide, 189, 193

digital fingerprinting, 50–51

Digital Green, 287

digital immigrants/natives, 309c4n1

digital Maoism, 55

Digital Millennium Copyright Act, 32, 51

digital rights management, 38–39

digital video recorder (DVR), 116, 121–122

DirecTV, 141

Disney, 146, 172

distribution of media, xiii, 1–2, 8, 10, 14–18, 20, 22, 48–50, 53, 57, 62–63, 82, 93–94, 106–111, 113–116, 119–120, 124, 127–128,

132, 144, 149, 160, 162, 169–170, 184, 191, 195–197, 200, 225, 228–236, 239–240, 243–247, 252–254, 257, 259–260, 266–274, 280–283, 285, 287–289, 292, 295–299, 307"Introduction"n1, 308c3n1

District 9, 143, 243, 246–247, 252–254

diversity, xii–xiv, 6, 46, 50, 89, 92, 118–119, 161–162, 168, 171–172, 191–193, 200, 219, 224, 236, 238–241, 243, 245, 258, 260–261, 263–264, 270, 272, 281, 288,–289 294, 296–298

Diversity (dance troupe), 16

diverted media, 270–275, 285

DIY ("Do-It-Yourself") media, 53, 60, 93, 154, 166, 184

DJ Rekha, 280

Dobratz, Ronald, 107

Doctorow, Cory, 229–232, 238, 291–292

Doctor Who, 96

documentary, 169–170, 208, 251–253

Dodds, Peter Sheridan, 80–81

Domb, Ana, 182–184

Domino's Pizza, 182

Douglas, Mary, 204

Douglas, Susan J., 159–160

Down and Out in the Magic Kingdom, 230

Draper, Don (character, *Mad Men*), 31–32

Draper, Tim, 19–20

Dream: Re-imagining Progressive Politics in the Age of Fantasy, 221

Dreamwith, 30

Dr. Horrible's Sing-Along Blog, 234

drillable texts, 135–137, 223, 297

Driscoll, Kevin, 185–186

Driscoll, Michael, 50–51

Dumbledore's Army (fictional organization, Harry Potter), 222

Duncombe, Stephen, 221–222

durability of media, 37–39, 44

DVD, 90, 110–111, 113–116, 118, 120, 133–134, 230–231, 239–240, 246, 253, 280, 287

early adopters, 30, 96, 103, 138, 144, 159, 169, 190

East Asia, 272, 275, 282

East West Players, 171

Eastwood, Clint, 263

eBay, 86–87, 89–90, 96, 101, 203

Economist, 267
Edelman, 77–78
Edery, David, 240
education, x–xi, 16, 92–94, 100, 155, 158, 160, 169, 189–190, 193–194, 226, 233, 292, 305, 310c4n3
Edwards, Jim, 205
Elberse, Anita, 239–241
Electronic Arts, 180, 215–216
Eliason, Frank, 25
EMI, 47
Emmy Awards, 30
enclaved media, 271, 292
Ender, Chris, 121
The End of the Line, 252
Eng, Lawrence, 276
engagement of audiences, 4, 7, 13, 22, 31–35, 45, 49, 55, 57–61, 75–76, 80, 83, 93, 99, 112–155, 157–159, 165–166, 171–173, 176–177, 179, 183, 185, 187, 189, 191, 195–196, 200, 206, 209–210, 213, 215, 219, 222–224, 240, 243–244, 265, 272, 278, 296, 298, 301, 303–305, 308c3n3, 309c3n5, 310c5n1, 311c5n3; "total engagement experience," 137–141
Engler, Craig, 119–120, 122
entrepreneurship, 67, 93, 244, 287
Enzensberger, Hans Magnus, 160–161, 194
Epley, Nathan Scott, 89
equipes, 183–184
Eros Entertainment, 281
Esquire, 262
Eurimages, 250
Evaluation. *See* appraisal of media content
The Event, 146

Fabrikant, Geraldine, 50
Facebook, 11, 13, 21–22, 41, 57, 125, 169, 177, 191–193, 199, 204–206, 307"How to Read This Book"n2; Open Graph, 22
Fahim, Kareem, 268
fair use. *See* legal issues
Fancast, 119
fan communities/fandom, 2, 9, 11, 28–29, 73, 77–79, 83, 86, 105, 113–114, 117–118, 124–128, 176–177, 180–181, 199, 213, 236, 246–247, 251–253, 259, 261–262, 275, 278, 281, 289–290, 292, 296–297, 304,
307–308c1n2, 308c3n3, 309c3n4; aca-fan, x; affirmational fandom, 150–151, 297, 300–303; as brand communities, 103, 164–166, 205; as collectors, 97–102, 106–111; comics fans, 237–238; fan activism, 171–172, 220–223; fan campaigns, 121–123; fan filmmakers, 248–250; fan labor, 53–64; female fans, 29–30, 149–151, 216; forensic fandom, 135–136, 140, 146; and gift economy, 62–72, 91, 229–232; Gleeks, 147–148; horror fans, 249–250; marginalization of, 148–152; music fans, 183, 186–188, 233–235, 255–257; performance, 184–185, 281–282; poaching, 174–175; as publics, 166–169; soap opera fans, 129–133, 167–168; ; and social media, 10, 31–37; spoiling, 300–303; transformational fandom, 150–151, 297; transmedia and, 137–151; wrestling fans, 106–111. *See also* fan fiction; fansubbing; fanvids
Fancy Froglin, 237
fan fiction, 33, 69, 91, 140, 147, 149–151, 276, 307c1n2
FanLib, 69
fansubbing, 62–63, 68, 271–273, 289; leechers, 63
fanvids, 29, 149, 151
Farmville, 21–22
Fast Company, 195
Faulkner, Simon, 223
Federal Communications Commission, 193
Federal Trade Commission, 79
Fidelity Investments, ix
film. *See* cinema
Film Sprout, 252
Finkelstein, Brian, 24
Finland, 250
Finnish Film Foundation, 250
Fiske, John, 45, 149, 192, 194, 200–201, 206–207, 260, 310c4n6
The Five Fists of Science, 101
Flash, 245
Flash Forward, 146
Fleishman, Glenn, 26
Flickr, 49, 223
Flow, 244
Flower, 244

Ford, Sam, x, 132, 177–178, 180, 226, 255, 277, 283
Forrester, 154
Forte, Andrea, 158
forums (for online discussion), 25, 79, 109, 131, 156–157, 167–168, 188, 272, 280
Four Eyed Monsters, 246–247
Fox News (U.S.), 169, 217
fragmentation of audiences, 17, 53–54, 116, 233, 239–241, 288
fragrance of cultural goods, 275, 281, 289–290
franchises, 7, 35, 45, 104–105, 119, 133, 141, 143, 146, 151, 166, 171, 209, 216, 222, 269, 302–304
Frank, Robert H., 241
Fraser, Nancy, 173
"free" content, 54–55, 67, 72–75, 94, 114, 127, 129, 163, 219, 229–232, 235, 238, 253, 256, 272; free and open source software, 59, 183
The Freeconomy Community, 72
FremantleMedia, 14, 307"Introduction"n1
Friday Night Lights, 141–142, 146, 149
Friedman, David, 302
Friedman, Thomas, 284–285
Futures of Entertainment, ix–xi
Fuzbi, 240

Gabriel, Peter, 224
GAP, 208
Games. *See* video games
Gandhi, Rikin, 287
garage sales. *See* rummage sales
Garfield, Bob, 25
Garvey, Ellen Gruber, 12
Gawker, 146
Gee, James Paul, 309–310c4n2
Gehl, Robert, 93
gender and sexuality, 29–30, 31, 35, 54, 114, 118, 149, 167–168, 173, 206, 215–216, 222
Georgetown University, 223
Georgia State University, 135
Ghana, 266
Ghemawat, Pankaj, 285
Ghost Whisperer, 138–140, 142, 146, 149
Ghost Whisperer: Spirit Guide, 139
The Gift (Mauss), 65
The Gift (Hyde), 48, 67–69, 73, 76

gift economy, 48, 62–63, 65–73, 76–78, 84–87, 90–92, 107–108, 138, 150, 195, 198–199, 202–203, 229–230, 254, 256, 271, 273, 292, 295–296
Gillespie, Tarleton, 38–39
Gizmodo, 25–26
Gladwell, Malcolm, 4, 9, 80
Glee, 146–149, 309c3n4
globalization, 40, 258, 263–264, 271, 284–285, 290
global media flows. *See* transnational media flows
Global Voices, 285
Globo (Brazil), 283
GMA Network (U.S.), 282
Godrej Industries Limited, 286
Gogoi, Pallavi, 78
Golijan, Rosa, 25–26
Good Morning America, 10
Google, 50, 66, 127, 286, 291; Google News, 72
Gordon, Melinda, 139
Gorman, Steve, 169
gossip. *See* rumors
Gould, Scott, 81–82
Govan, LaChania, 24
governments, 23, 38, 41–43, 79, 92, 173, 189, 221–222, 225, 249, 266, 277, 282, 289, 304–305
Govil, Nitin, 269–270
GQ, 262
grabbability. *See* mobility of media
Grad, Shelby, 28
grassroots intermediaries, 7, 11, 15, 21, 74, 83, 115, 125, 142–143, 146, 149, 152, 227, 232, 239, 252, 299
Gray, Jonathan, 242–243, 248–249, 274
Gray, Mary L., 173
Grazer, Brian, 187
Green, Joshua, x, 50, 93, 128–129, 186
Greenwall, Robert, 169–170
Gregory, Sam, 224–225
Grillo-Marxuach, Javier, 114–115
Grover (character, *Sesame Street*), 206
The Gruen Transfer, 212
GSD&M, ix
Guitar Hero, 147
Guizzo, Erico, 101

Habermas, Jürgen, 173–174
"Ha-He," 261
Haiti, 222
Hanna-Barbera, 105
Hanshaw, Annette, 311c6n1
Harley-Davidson, 164
Harold B. Lee Library, 206
Harrington, C. Lee, 130, 132, 167
Harris, Neil, 213
Harry Potter (franchise), 141, 222
Harry Potter Alliance, 222
Hartley, John, 188
Harvard Business Review, 240
Harvard University, 41
Hasson, Eva, 21
Hausa, 267
Hayes, Gary, 157
Hayward, Jennifer, 134
HBO (U.S.), 144, 208
hearing. *See* monitoring of audiences
Heffernan, Virginia, 141
Heidi (character, Witchery campaign),
    211–213
Helft, Miguel, 50
Hendershot, Heather, 256–257
Herman, Andrew, 58
Hernandez, Eugene, 247
Heroes, 113–115, 141, 143, 146
Herrman, Gretchen M., 91
Herrman, John, 72
HessenInvestFilm, 250
Hewitt, Jennifer Love, 138
High School Musical, 146
HijiNKS Ensue, 238
Hilderbrand, Lucas, 15
Hill Holliday, 8, 177
Hillis, Ken, 89
The Hills, 141
Hills, Matt, 143, 155
hip-hop, 185, 264, 274, 281
Hogwarts (fictional school, Harry Potter),
    222
Holkins, Jerry, 237
Holloway, Joan (character, *Mad Men*), 31
Holson, Laura M., 187
Horowitz, Bradley, 156–157
Hotmail, 19–20
Hovet, Ted, 94

Howe, Irving, 191
Howe, Jeff, 247
Howl's Moving Castle, 101
HP Labs, 142
Hu, Yu Jeffrey, 242
The Hub (WITNESS), 225
Huberman, Bernardo, 142
Huddleston, Kathie, 113
Hulu, 72, 119, 128–129; Hulu Plus, 72
humor, 17, 122, 202, 204–207, 265, 210, 221,
    309c3n4
Humphreys, Sal, 49
"Hunter Kills a Bear," 210
hush harbors, 217
Hyde, Lewis, 48, 67–69, 73, 76, 202–203
Hyundai Tucson, 308c3n1

io9, 146
IBOPE, 269
"I Dreamed a Dream," 9
Illustrated Wrestling Digest, 107
immersive story worlds, 132, 136–137
impressions. *See* measurement of media
    audiences
impure culture, 261–266, 270, 281, 283–284,
    290, 296
Inda, Jonathan Xavier, 271
independent artists, xii, 29, 35, 46, 92, 110,
    145, 185, 196, 228–259, 288, 293–295 298,
    305
India, 221, 265–268, 270, 277, 280–281, 283,
    286–287, 289
India—A Love Story. See *Caminho das*
    Índias
IndieCade, 244
Indiewire, 246
Infernal Devices, 101
influencers, 26, 79–83, 145, 215, 300, 311c5n2
Ingram, Mathew, 308c3n2
Innis, Harold, 37–41, 44
innovation, 11–12, 29, 37, 39, 47, 99, 103, 148,
    228, 232, 244–245, 250, 268, 283
In Rainbows, 231
intellectual property. *See* legal issues
Internet Group do Brasil, ix
ION (U.S.), 140
Iran, 41–44, 260, 265, 278–280, 287
Iranian Americans, 278–280

Iraq, 208
Iraq for Sale, 169
Iron Sky, 250–251
Isakson, Paul, 33
Islam. *See* religion
Israel, 220–221
Istanbul, 218
Ito, Mizuko, 13, 63, 273
iPad, iPhone, iTunes. *See* Apple
iStockPhoto.com, 247
ITV, 307"Introduction"n1
Iwabuchi, Koichi, 275

Jack of All Trades (character, *Profiler*), 139
Jackson, Peter, 243
Jamaica, 264
Japan, 9, 101, 264, 272–273, 275–276, 287
Jaszi, Peter, 50
Jenkins, Henry, x, 2, 29, 41, 69, 91, 114, 136,
    151, 153, 174, 180, 191, 203, 222, 234, 271,
    275, 307c1n2, 309c4n1
Jenkins, Leeroy, 207–209
Jeopardy!, 208–209
Jericho, 121–122, 125
Jersey Shore, 8
Jerzify Yourself, 8–9
Jesus Christ, 255–256
John Deere, 164
Johnson, Brian David, 247
Johnson, Derek, 133, 172
Johnson, Steven, 134
The Joker (character, *Dark Knight Returns*),
    28
jokes. *See* humor
"Jolene," 274
journalism, x, 9, 12–13, 24–26, 41–42, 44, 47,
    55–56, 72–73, 75, 77, 79–80, 109, 162–163,
    173, 185, 199, 201, 211–215, 224, 256, 285, 292,
    305, 312c6n2; newspaper advertising, 144
Jung, Helin, 32
JupiterResearch, 22
Jurvetson, Steve, 19–20
Just A Band, 261

Kaye, Lewis, 58
Keen, Andrew, 55–56
Kenya, 261–263, 265–266, 286
Kick-Ass, 143

Kickstarter, 251–252
kilapanga, 264
Kincaid, Jason, 51
King, Jamie, 252–253
King, Lindy, 31
King, Rodney, 224
Kingler-Vilenchik, Neta, 222
kizomba, 264
Klink, Flourish, 60–61, 68
Knobel, Michele, 53
Knowledge@Wharton, 50
Kompare, Derek, 118
Kongregate, 244–245
Kopytoff, Igor, 66
Koster, Raph, 157
Kozinets, Robert V., 102–103, 128–129
Krahulik, Mike, 237
Kreps, Daniel, 47
Kring, Tim, 114–115
Kuduro, 264
Ku Klux Klan, 216–217, 311c5n3

labor, xiii, 45, 48, 54–66, 68–69, 71, 73–76,
    104, 116, 126–129, 134, 151–152, 154, 165,
    174–175, 187, 191, 232, 237, 248, 270, 273,
    284, 293
Lake Superior State University, 21
Lange, Patricia G., 186
Lanier, Jaron, 55–56, 67
Lankshear, Colin, 53
Lapowsky, Issie,
Larkin, Brian, 266–268
Latin audiences/media, 9, 169, 182–184,
    190–192, 221, 234, 260, 264, 269, 282–284,
    287, 289
Latin American, 282–283
The Laughing Man (character, *Ghost
    Whisperer*), 139
Lavan, Rosie, 250
Lave, Jean, 158
Lawler, Ryan, 47
Leach, Skot, 250
lead users, 96, 103, 178, 297
The League of Extraordinary Gentlemen, 101
Learmonth, Michael, 33
Leavitt, Alex, 147
Lebanon, 191
LeechesofKarma, 48

legal issues, xi, xiv; 3, 151–152, 159, 294, 307c1n1; cease and desist, 32; censorship, 38–40; contracts, 104; copyright/intellectual property, 31–33, 35, 74, 83, 110–112, 126, 186–187, 252–253, 261, 291–293, 297–298, 300–303, 307c1n1, 311c6n1; Creative Commons, 229–230, 238; fair use, 50, 54, 57; digital rights management, 39; Federal Trade Commission, 79; legal battles over video sharing, 47–48, 50–51, 68–69, 92, 94; moral economy and, 54–58, 62; open source, 183; piracy, 15–16, 46, 48, 53, 113–115, 117, 187–188, 256, 265, 267–270, 272, 281, 285; privacy, 57, 214, 225

legends. *See* rumors

Legion of Extraordinary Dancers (*LXD*), 309c3n4

Lenhart, Amanda, 155, 188

Leno, Jay, 123–124

The League of Noble Peers, 252

Leonard, Sean, 63

Lessig, Lawrence, 56–57, 66–67, 91

Levinator25, 181

Levine, Elana, 308c3n3

Levy, Steven, 49

Li, Xiaochang, 68–69, 272, 282

Liang, Lawrence, 265

Liberia, 252

Libo, Kenneth, 191

licensing, 47, 50–51, 72, 74–75, 133, 230, 233, 238, 247–248, 268

Life Unexpected, 141

Lindy Hop, 100

Lipsitz, George, 311c5n4

lip dubs, 47–48

listening, xi–xii, 2, 6, 16, 24–27, 45, 82, 106, 111, 143, 146, 152, 155, 175–182, 196, 236, 252, 298–300, 308c3n3

Little Brother, 230

LiveJournal, 30, 308c1n2

Livingstone, Sonia, 166, 189

localization, 7, 241, 264, 273, 280–281, 283–284–286, 294, 296–297, 299

Locus, 291

Locutores, 190

Lonelygirl15, 212–213

Long, Geoffrey, 237–238

Longlostperfume.com, 97

Long Tail, 238–243, 288

Lopez, Lori Kido, 171

Los Angeles Film Festival, 252

Los Angeles Times, 28

Lost, 113, 134, 136–137, 142–143, 146, 149

Lostpedia, 134 ,136–137, 149

Lost Zombies, 249–250

Lotz, Amanda, 197

Louie, Mynette, 253

Lucas, George, 250

Lucasfilm, 56

lurking, 155–159

Mad Men, 30–36, 39, 44, 78

Makmende (character, "Ha-He"), 261–265, 286

Malawi, 274–275

Malaysia, 277

manga, 237, 276

Manifesto Games, 243–245

Manjoo, Farhad, 26

Manley, Joey, 237

Marcus, Caroline, 212

Mardi Gras Indians, 311c5n4

MariMar, 282

Marlboro, 216

marketing, ix–xi, xiii–xv, 1–2, 6–9, 15, 17, 19–24, 27, 29–36, 44–45, 49, 60–61, 68, 73–83, 86, 93–94, 103–104, 106, 109, 111, 118–119, 127–128, 133, 135, 144–146, 148, 152, 155, 163, 165, 173–177, 179–183, 194, 198, 201–202, 205, 207, 210, 213, 215–216, 219, 227, 243, 248, 259, 292–294, 296, 299–300, 304, 308c1n3, 308c3n2, 309c3n5, 311c6n2; buzz marketing, 20; direct mail marketing, 23; guerrilla marketing, 20; telemarketing, 23. *See also* retro audiences: retrobranding; viral media: viral marketing

Marvel Comics, 172, 237

Marxism, 17

mash-ups, 20, 186–187

Masnick, Michael, 47

Massachusetts Institute of Technology (MIT), ix, 37, 92, 226 261

mass culture, 71, 200–201

The Matrix, 138

Mauss, Marcel, 65

McCain, John, 28
McCloud, Scott, 236, 239
McCracken, Grant, 95–96, 123–125, 127, 178, 201–203, 308c1n3
McDonald's, 86
McDonnell, John, 264
McMahon, Vince, 109, 213
measurement of media audiences/customers, 1, 4–7, 14, 23, 34, 45, 48, 57, 59–60, 67–68, 74, 106, 113–153, 166, 176–179, 195–196, 203, 205. *See also* television: television ratings
Media Action Network, 171
media concentration, xiii, 137, 162, 169
Medialink Worldwide, 187
media studies, ix–xiii, 9, 37, 57, 92, 94, 99, 135, 179, 242–243, 307"How to Read This Book"n1
Media Virus, 17–18
Meehan, Eileen R., 119
Mekanism, 195
Melman, Bud (character, *Mad Man* fan culture), 31
Meltzer, Dave, 108–109
memes, 18–19, 27–28, 44, 187, 262, 293
Mentos, 86
Mexico, 282
Meyer, Birgit, 266
M.I.A., 264
Miami University, 167
Michael Gill's Media Domain, 168
Mickey Mouse Club, 140
Microsoft, 237, 245; Microsoft Research New England, 234; Microsoft Windows 284
Middlebury College, 135
The Middleman, 114–115
Milano, Alyssa, 206
Milgram, Stanley, 80
Miller, Nancy, 135
Mimi and Eunice, 236
Mittell, Jason, 115, 134–137, 146
mix tapes, 54
mobility of media, 37–39, 44, 151, 188, 198, 259, 268, 296
modders, 58
Modern Tales, 237
Monello, Michael, 144–145
monitoring of audiences, xiii, 5, 41, 45, 47,

103, 127, 139–140, 142, 155, 166, 175–182, 290
Monopoly, 221
Moonves, Leslie, 121–122
Moors, 311c5n4
moral economy, 48, 52–53, 55–56, 58, 60–62, 65–67, 71, 75–77, 82, 118, 295, 303, 307c1n2; social/moral contract, 52–53, 55, 75, 111, 311c6n2
Moses, Kim, 138–140, 148
Moskowitz, Laurence, 187
Mota, Maurício, 269
Movies. *See* cinema
mp3, 30, 160, 234–235
MTV (U.S.), 8
MTV Networks (U.S.), ix
Muhamad, Roby, 80–81
multiplicity, 260, 288, 310c4n6
multiplier, 124, 126–127, 183, 201, 297
Murdoch, Rupert, 72
music, 14, 18, 46–48, 50–52, 54–55, 62, 72–73, 98, 100–101, 146–149, 182–187, 191, 193, 197, 199, 203–204, 230, 232–236, 238, 240–242, 251, 255–257, 260–261, 264, 274, 277, 279–281, 289, 307c1n1, 307c1n2, 309c3n4, 311c6n1
Muslim. *See* religion
Musser, John, 49
Mustafa, Isaiah, 204–206
MyJobGroup, 308c3n2
MyNetworkTV, 283
MySpace, 185, 193, 212, 246
mystery, 202, 211–213

NAACP, 170
Naficy, Hamid, 278–279
Nagravision, ix
Naked Communications, 212
Narbacular Drop, 244
Napoleon Dynamite, 187
Nasser, Jaime, 282–284
National Day of Prayer, 218
Native Americans, 311c5n4
Na'vi (fictional race, *Avatar*), 220–221
Nazi, 250, 282
NBC (U.S.), 122–123, 139, 141
Netflix, 66, 169, 239
The Netherlands, 9

net neutrality, 162
networked culture/communication. *See* social networks
Networked Publics Group, 233–234
Newcomb, Roger, 168
New York Times, 1, 121, 217
New York University, 272
news. *See* journalism
News Corporation, 72
newspapers. *See* journalism
niche communities, 22, 27–29, 32, 34, 36, 38, 90, 93–95, 100, 113, 118, 138, 142–146, 148, 170, 230, 233, 237–242, 254, 257, 259, 296–297, 311–312c6n2
Nickelodeon, 171
Nieborg, David, 49, 153–156
Nielsen, 113, 115–117, 119, 122–123, 142, 148, 309c4n1; C3s, 116–117
Nieman Marcus, 2
Nigeria, 265–268, 270, 286–287
Nimoy, Leonard, 70
Nine Inch Nails, 72–73
Nintendo, 245
Nolan, Christopher, 28
Nollywood, 265–268, 270, 286
noncommercial logic, xv, 16, 36, 45, 48–50, 55, 61–79, 82–87, 94–112, 123–124, 149–151, 154, 157, 173, 183, 188, 199, 202–203, 207, 211, 235, 250, 272–273, 278, 294–295, 308c1n3
nonprofit organizations, xi, 5, 92, 196, 230, 287
North Carolina State University, 76
Novaes, Tereza, 269
Nunley, Vorris L., 217

Obama, Barack, 28, 217–219
obsession_inc., 150–151
Occupy Wall Street, 41
odorless culture, 275, 281, 289
Ogilvy Worldwide, 223
Old Spice, 204–207, 227, 311c5n2
Olson, Peggy (character, *Mad Men*), 33–34
Omidyar, Pierre, 89
O'Neill, Marnie, 212
One Life to Live, 132
Onion, Rebecca, 102
O'Reilly Media Group, 48

O'Reilly, Tim, 48, 175–176
Organization for Transformative Works, 69
Oscars, 142, 283, 309c3n4
"The Other Side," 139
Outfoxed, 169
ownership, fans' sense of, 35, 60, 68, 164, 191, 307c1n2

Palestine, 220, 266
Paley, Nina, 229–230, 236, 247, 311c6n1
Palin, Sarah, 28
Paramount, 171, 247
Paranormal Activity, 143, 247
Parker, Peter (character, Spider-Man), 304
parody, 151, 202, 205, 207–209, 221, 263
participatory culture, xi, xiii–xv, 27–37, 45, 48, 53–54, 63–64, 87, 153–194, 291–294, 296–298, 305 309c4n1, 309c4n2; anti-social implications, 216–219, 226–228 architecture of participation, 55, 175; "brand communities" and, 163–166; circulation and, 1–3, 35; as collaboration, 172–175, 180; and corporate interests, 35–37, 48, 53–54, 63–65, 83, 163–166, 172–182, 210–211; and critique of viral media, 17, 19–20; crowdsourcing and, 246–254; as a globalizing force, 274–278; grassroots participation, xi, xiv–xv, 1–2, 7, 10, 29, 37–43, 46, 58, 63, 77, 82, 86, 99, 111, 147, 150, 156, 159, 163, 172, 192–193, 201, 202, 213, 215, 219, 223, 227, 232–233, 252, 254–257, 262, 266, 270, 285, 289, 298, 304; history of, 29–30, 159–166; 298; inequality in participation, xiii, 37, 39–42, 45–46, 49, 148–152, 153–155, 188–194, 285–290, 292, 297–298, 300–305, 310c4n6; kinds of participation, 54; memes and, 27–29; labor and, 57–61, 127–128; lurking and, 156–159; open-ended participation, 6, 297; participatory platforms, 11, 49; performance, 147; peripheral participation, 158–159; piracy, 271–275; political participation, 3, 41–43, 160–162, 166–172, 190–193, 217–226; produsage and, 182–188; pyramids of participation, 156–157; and resistance, 162–163; as sharing, 65–72; and spoiling,

300–303; and transmedia, 141–143;
terms of participation, 36–37, 63–65;
user-generated content and, 15; and
Web 2.0, 48–49
Parton, Dolly, 274
Paul, Keith, 26
PBS (U.S.), 88
peer-to-peer networks, 55, 61, 69, 74–75, 86,
91, 111, 273, 295, 300
Penny (character, *The Big Bang Theory*),
69–70
Penny Arcade, 237
Perkins, Ross A., 93
Petit, Michael, 89
Petrik, Paula, 29, 159
Petrobras, ix
Pew Research Center/Pew Center for the
Internet & American Life, 12, 155, 188
Philippines, 282
Phillips, Whitney, 27–28
piracy. *See* legal issues
Pirate Bay, 234
PlanetOut, 174
PlayStation Portable, 77
plunder, 271, 273, 285
podcasts, 30, 162, 167, 217, 247, 278, 285,
310c4n4
political issues, xiv, 2–3, 9, 18, 35, 38, 92,
128, 136, 143, 247, 252, 261, 280, 292–293,
300; audiences vs. publics, 165–174; civic
media, 220–225; cultural and political
participation, 155–156, 159–163, 298;
fan activism, 171–172, 220–223; gender
politics, 29–31, 35, 149–152, 206, 215–216,
222; memes as political speech, 28–29,
31, 213–215; political rumors, 216–219;
sexual politics, 167–168, 173; transmedia mobilization, 190–193; Twitter and
revolutions, 38–44
pop cosmopolitans, 46, 275–278, 281, 285,
289, 297
popular culture, 18, 143, 168, 200–201, 221,
262, 264, 274–275
portability. *See* mobility of media
Portal, 244
Portugal, 264
Postigo, Hector, 58
Potter, Andrew, 204

Potter, Harry (character, Harry Potter), 222
Powell, Jenni, 134
Pratt, Mary Louise, 263
Pray the Devil Back to Hell, 252
Presley, Elvis, 147
"Primary Makmende'tics," 262
Primary Mathematics, 262
Princess Leia (character, Star Wars), 250
Prison Break, 271–272, 275
The Prisoner, 146
privacy issues. *See* legal issues
producerly texts, 45–46, 194, 200–204,
206–207, 219, 227
Producers Guild of America, 134
production of media, xiv–xv, 1–2, 7, 9, 15,
29, 32, 36, 46, 118, 130, 133, 139–140, 154–
155, 158–162, 171, 183, 191, 193, 200, 232,
248–251, 254, 264–265, 284, 288, 294–295,
297, 300–303, 307"Introduction"n1
produsage, 182–185, 187
professional wrestling, 106–111, 133, 136–137,
142–143, 213, 309c3n4
Profiler, 139
prohibitionists. *See* control
Project Runway, 141
Prospect Park Productions, 132
public relations, x, xiii–xv, 2, 19, 24–27,
30, 34, 36, 48, 73, 75–81, 83, 86, 145–146,
176–177, 179–181
publics, 152, 155–156, 161, 163, 165–172,
176–180, 193–194, 217, 242, 298; boundary publics, 173
publishing, 29, 37, 46, 55, 106–108, 230–231,
235, 236–238, 251, 254–256, 291–292
Punathambekar, Aswin, 280
Purcell, Kristen, 12

Q Scores, 119
quantitative data about audiences. *See*
measurement of media audiences/
customers
Quickflix, 240
Quote Database, 55
quote/quotability, 54, 187–188, 198, 220, 259,
294, 296
Queensland University of Technology, 56
QuestionCopyright, 230
Racebending, 171–172

Rand, Erica, 180
Random House, 1
radio, 24, 159–162, 170, 190–192, 217, 255, 282, 310c4n3
radionovela. *See* telenovela
Radiohead, 231, 255
Radio Tijeras, 191
Ray, Burt, 107
reality television. *See* television
recirculation. *See* circulation of media
recommendations, 8, 75–77, 83, 294, 299
redaction, 188
Reddit, 206, 310c5n1
references, 31, 202, 207–209, 217, 221, 262, 275
Rehak, Bob, 99
Reichig, Deborah, 117
Reinventing Comics, 236
Reisner, Rebecca, 25
religion, xi, 9, 13, 17, 29, 40–41, 46, 54, 73, 128, 160, 167, 261, 293–295, 298; Christian music, 254–257; churches as exhibition outlets, 169, 266–267; cult, 143; fundamentalism, 40–41; rumors about Obama's religious beliefs, 217–218
Remix, 66
remixing, 2, 27–29, 50, 56, 167, 169–172, 185, 187, 190–191, 214–215, 221, 225, 230, 233–234, 261–262, 270, 280, 296, 298, 304. *See also* fanvids
Republican Party, 222
residual material, 29, 45, 71, 85, 95–101, 103–106
resistance, 18, 37, 53, 155, 162–166, 171–173, 263–264
Rethink Afghanistan, 169
retro audiences/material, 29, 98–102–106, 100, 178, 297; retrobranding, 102–103, 105; retrogames, 99
Retromania, 98
Reynolds, Simon, 98–99
Reznor, Trent, 73
Rhapsody, 240
Rheingold, Howard, 65–66
Rivera, Marian, 282
Rock Band, 147
Rohac, George, Jr., 238

Rohani, Talieh, 279
Rolling Stone, 47
Rolls Royce, 104
Romano, Salvatore (character, *Mad Men*), 31
Rosaldo, Renato, 271
Rose, Frank, 136
Rosen, Jay, 153–154, 162
Ross, Andrew, 29
Ross, Sharon Marie, 165
rummage sales, 91, 96
rumors, 17, 22, 42, 102, 167, 202, 216–219, 226–227, 286–287, 311c5n3
Runaways, 172
Rushkoff, Douglas, 17–18, 199
Russell, Adrienne, 233–234
Russia, 277
Russo, Julie Levin, 151

Safaricom, 262
Sander, Ian, 138–139
Sandler, Kevin, 105–106
Sass, Erik, 117
Schools. *See* education
science fiction, 17, 29, 70, 101–102, 151, 220, 229, 234, 237, 250, 291, 307"Introduction"n2
Scooby-Doo (character, many cartoon series), 105–106
Scotland, 9
Scott Pilgrim vs. the World, 143, 145
Scott, Suzanne, 150–151, 216
Screen Queensland, 251
Second Life, 177, 247
Seiter, Ellen, 189
"Seize the Power," 252–253
self-branding, 59–60, 65, 186
The Selfish Gene, 18–19
Seles, Sheila, 122–123
semba, 264
Sennett, Richard, 58–61, 128
serialized storytelling, 113, 129–134, 139, 149, 282
Serpe, Gina, 121
Sesame Street, 206
sexuality. *See* gender and sexuality
Shahani, Parmesh, 286
Shamalyan, M. Night, 171

sharing, 7, 11, 124–125, 226–227, 229, 295, 298; file sharing, 53, 61–63, 73–74, 90–91, 98, 115, 207, 256, 276–277, 307c1n2, 309c4n1; commercial vs. sharing economies, 66–67; motives for sharing, 20, 195–199, 304, 311–312c6n2; shared fantasies, 202–204; shared identity, 166; shared mythology, 222; stealing vs., 61–63; video sharing, 2, 6, 10, 13–15, 30, 47, 50–52, 94, 101, 110, 127, 142, 147, 169, 185, 188–190, 223, 225, 276, 280–281, 283. *See also* circulation of media; gift economy

Shaw, Mona, 24

Shell, Hanna Rose, 92

Shirky, Clay, 42, 153, 162

Short, Iain, 21

Shorty Awards, 34

Shresthova, Sangita, 280–281

Shum, Harry Jr., 309c3n4

Siegler, MG, 33

Sisario, Ben, 14

Sita Sings the Blues, 229–230, 236

"six degrees of separation," 80–81

Slack, Andrew, 222

slactivism, 223

Slashdot, 183

Slate, 26

The Slip, 72–73

Slumdog Millionaire, 283, 289

"Small World Problem," 80

Smillie, Dirk, 72

Smith, Cordwainer, 307"Introduction"n2

Smith, Michael D., 242

Smythe, Dallas W., 126–128

snacks (media), 135–136

Snelson, Chareen, 93

Snow, Blake, 77

Snow Crash, 17

Snyder, Luke (character, *As the World Turns*), 167

soap opera, 129–133, 136–137, 146–147, 149, 164, 167–168, 188, 266, 282–284, 308c3n3

social change. *See* activism

The Social Life of Things, 271

social media, 6, 12, 25, 33, 122, 148, 177–178, 190, 192, 207, 223–224, 228, 308c3n2

social networks, xiii–xiv, 4, 7, 9, 11–13, 17, 20, 30, 32, 39, 60, 67, 94–95, 123, 128, 130–131, 145, 149, 159, 167, 171, 184, 192, 249, 254–256, 278, 307"How to Read This Book"n2, 309c4n1; networked culture, xiv, 2, 12–13, 16, 20, 29, 36, 45, 60, 65, 89, 102, 128, 133–134, 152, 155–156, 163, 166, 169, 175, 180, 182–183, 188–190, 194, 217, 250, 259, 261, 264–265, 273, 287–289, 293, 298; social connections, 5–6, 11, 13, 60, 93, 186; social network sites, 11–13, 17, 20–22, 30, 37, 41–42, 57, 68, 125, 142–143, 169, 177, 183–186, 189, 191–194, 199, 204–206, 212–214, 223, 246, 307"How to Read This Book"n2, 309c4n1

software as a service, 48

Sons of Liberty, 311c5n4

Sony, 77

Soulja Boy, 185–187

Soundclick, 185

"Sound of Kuduro," 264

South Africa, 243

South by Southwest Interactive, 30, 35

South Korea, 272

So You Think You Can Dance, 289, 309c3n4

space150, 33

The Spectacular Legacy of the AWA, 110

Spider-Man (franchise), 304

Mr. Spock (character, *Star Trek*), 70

sports, 1, 108,–109, 132, 136, 142, 170, 180–181, 311c6n2

Spry Fox, 240

Standage, Tom, 173

Star Trek (franchise), 70

Star Wars (franchise), 56, 103, 151, 250

Star Wars Uncut, 250

Star Wreck: In the Pirkinning, 250

Steal This Film, 252–253

Steam, 244

Steamboy, 101

steampunk, 101–102

Steinberg, Brian, 121

Stelter, Brian, 72

Stephenson, Neal, 17

Sterling Cooper (fictional firm, *Mad Men*), 30–31, 33

Sterling, Roger (character, *Mad Men*), 31

stickiness, 3–9, 16–17, 33–34, 43–44, 56, 114, 176

Stone, Brad, 49

Straw, Will, 97–98
Stribling, Eleanor Baird, 124–125
Styll, John, 256
Summit Entertainment, 302
Sundance Channel, (U.S.) 247
Sundance Film Festival, 253
Sundaram, Ravi, 268
The Sunshine Witnesses, 255
surplus audiences, 14, 106, 112, 129–132, 152, 167–168, 178–179, 198, 235, 298, 300
surveillance of audiences. *See* monitoring of audiences
subcultures. *See* niche communities
Subservient Chicken (character, Burger King), 209–211
Subway, 122–123
Super Bowl, 142
Survivor, 142
Sweden, 234–235, 238
Sydney Morning Herald, 212
SyFy Channel, 113, 119–120, 140
syndication, 109, 120, 138, 140, 312c6n2
Syracuse University, 121

Tarnoff, Andy, 121
Tassler, Nina, 121
Tea Party, 28, 169–170, 222
TechDirt, 47
Tecnobrega, 182–184, 193, 234, 284–285, 294, 296–298
TED, 309c3n4
TeleFutura, 283
Telemundo (U.S.), 283
telenovela, 282–284, 289
television, ix, 24, 29–30, 45, 59, 72, 75–76, 86–89, 96, 113–152, 162, 174, 176, 190, 192, 197, 199, 201, 206, 208, 212, 235, 266, 276, 279, 282–284; appointment-based, 116–117; 123–124, 129, 133, 152; broadcast television, 9–10, 14–15, 39, 43, 105, 113–115, 119–125, 128–133, 134, 136–143, 146–147, 149, 164, 167–168, 170, 224, 271; cable/satellite television 14–15, 30–36, 106, 109, 113–114, 117, 119–120, 132–133, 136–137, 140–141, 143–149, 151; engagement-based, 116, 123–124, 127, 133, 136, 140, 152; game shows, 131, 208, 312c6n2; reality television, 8–11, 13–16, 59, 142;

talk shows, 123, 131; television ratings, 10, 32, 96, 113–123, 126, 141, 148
Television Without Pity, 174
Tequila, Tila, 59
Terhune, Chad, 86
Terranova, Tiziana, 56–57, 60
Thompson, Clive, 81
Thompson, E. P., 48, 52
Thompson, Kristin, 231
Threadless, 248
thrift shop, 92, 96
Tiger Woods PGA Tour, 180–181
timeliness, 16, 39, 95, 128, 202, 213–216, 221, 299, 304
Tinkcom, Matthew, 92
Tipp-Ex, 210
The Tipping Point, 4, 80
TiVo, 115
To Have and to Hold, 98
Tonight Show, 10
torrents, 98, 113, 115, 129, 231, 234, 253, 269
TorrentFreak.com, 113
Toyota, 207–209
transformative works, 16, 69, 152, 188
transgenerational audiences, 130–131, 147, 192, 309c4n1
Transmedia Hollywood, x–xi
transmedia storytelling/performance, ix, 45, 49, 60, 118, 132–152, 269, 296, 308c3n3; transmedia mobilization, 190–191, 224, 233; transmedia planning, 309c3n5
transnational media flows, xii, 14–16, 35, 37–38, 40–43, 46, 113–114, 192, 235, 257–290, 293, 295–296
transparency, 65, 75–80, 83, 248, 252, 296, 304
Transportation Security Administration, 214–215
Travers, Jeffrey, 80
Trinity United Church of Christ, 217
Trodd, Zoe, 90
trolls, 27–28, 207, 293
Troop Sport, 216
Tropa de Elite, 269
True Blood, 144–145, 147–149
Trust, Gary, 147
TubeMogul, 125

Tudou, 10
Tumblr, 31
Turner Broadcasting (U.S.), ix
Turner, Fred, 161
Turner, Patricia Ann, 216–217, 311c5n3
Tussey, Ethan, 135
Twilight (franchise), 216, 300–303
Twitter, 2, 11, 21, 25–26, 30–34, 41–43, 59, 79,
    125, 142, 191, 205–206, 215, 260, 262, 265,
    299, 308c1n2, 311c5n2
Tyner, John, 214–215
Tyron, Chuck, 170

Ugly Betty, 283–284, 289
Uncle Ben (character, Spider-Man), 304
Undercurrent, 201
unfinished content, 202, 209–211
United Kingdom, 9–10, 13–14, 18, 95, 221,
    231, 260, 264, 283, 308c3n2
Universidad Veritas, 182
University of California—Berkeley, 57
University of Melbourne, 308c3n2
University of Michigan, 197, 280
University of Oregon, 27
University of Southern California, 185,
    233–234
University of Wisconsin—Madison, 133, 243
Univision (U.S.), 283
urban legends. See rumors
Uricchio, William, 37
USA Network (U.S.), 109
U.S. Constitution, 222
user-generatedcontent,xi,12,15,48,50,52,59,
    64,72,83,86,140–141,147–152,154,175,179

V, 146
Vacation Bible School, 254
value. See commercial logic
Van Buskirk, Eliot, 253
Van Damme, Jean-Claude, 264
van der Graaf, Shenja, 20–21
Van Dijck, José, 49, 153–156
Van Fuqua, Joy, 92
VCR. See videotape
Vedrashko, Ilya, 8, 21–22, 177
Veronica Mars, 115
Verve, 286
VHS. See videotape

Viacom, 50, 92–94
video games, 46, 53, 58, 77, 79, 99, 105,
    133–134, 147–148, 157, 180–181, 207–208,
    210, 215–216, 230, 232, 237, 240, 242–246,
    251, 309–310c4n2
video on demand (VOD), 110, 113, 118, 120,
    143–144
videotape, 106–109, 116, 190, 224, 276, 280
Villarreal, Yvonne, 283
Villarejo, Amy, 92
Vimeo, 47
viral media, xiv, 16–23, 34, 44, 51, 82,
    135, 139–140, 196, 198, 227, 249,
    292–293, 295; viral marketing,
    19–22, 34, 77, 79, 81, 95, 195–196, 303,
    307"Introduction"n2
The Virtual Community, 65
Visakowitz, Susan, 73
vlogging, 93, 186, 212
VODO (Volunteer Donation), 253
Volkswagen Beetle, 103
Von Hippel, Eric, 96
Vranica, Suzanne, 86
Vuorensola, Timo,250

Waldman, Allison J., 131, 275
The Walking Dead, 308c3n1
Wall Street Journal, 1
Walmart, 77–78, 169, 173
"Wal-Marting Across America," 78
Wal-Mart: The High Cost of Low Price, 169
Warner Brothers, 1
Warner Music Group (WMG), 50–51
Washington Post, 57, 217
Wasik, Bill, 93
Watkins, S. Craig, 192
Watson, Joel, 238
Watts, Duncan J., 80–81
Way, DeAndre, 185, 187
WE (U.S.), 140
The Wealth of Networks, 92
WeAreSterlingCooper.org, 33
Weather Channel (U.S.), 312c6n2
Weaver, Chris, 226
Web 2.0, xiii–xiv, 15, 36, 43, 45, 48–49,
    52–53, 55–58, 63–64, 67–68, 71–72, 74,
    76, 78–80, 82–83, 92, 127, 153, 156, 165,
    174–176, 189, 263, 293, 297, 308c1n2

Webb, Derek, 256
Webb, Emma F., 188
Web Ecology Project, 41
Weiler, Lance, 253
Weiner, Matthew, 32
Wenger, Etienne, 158
Western Kentucky University, 94
Whedon, Joss, 234
White House, 218
Whitney, Daisy, 187
Wieden+Kennedy, 181, 204, 206
WiiWare, 244
Wikipedia, 3, 10, 66, 134, 158, 183, 189
The Wild Wild West, 101
Williams, Raymond, 95–97, 100, 104, 118
Wilson, Johnny, 243
The Winner-Take-All Society, 241
Wired, 72, 238, 247
Witchel, Alex, 32
Witchery, 212
WITNESS, 224–226
Wolff, Michael, 243
Wood, Stacy, 76
Woods, Tiger, 180–181
World Cup, 170
World Championship Wrestling (WCW), 109
World Wrestling Entertainment (WWE), 106, 109–111, 133, 137, 143; WWE Classics on Demand, 110; WWE Greatest Matches, 110; WWE Hall of Fame, 110; WWE Home Video, 109
World Wrestling Federation. *See* World Wrestling Entertainment

word of mouth, 2, 7–8, 20, 75–77, 79, 141, 143, 242, 310c4n3
Working Families for Walmart, 78
World of Warcraft, 207–209
worth. *See* noncommercial logic
wrestling. *See* professional wrestling
Wrestling Information Bulletin, 107
Wrestling Observer Newsletter, 108–109
Wright, Jeremiah, 217
Wurzelbacher, Joe, 31
Wyatt, Edward, 121

Xbox Live Arcade, 244
Xerox, 31

Yahoo!, ix, 155–156
Yakob, Faris, 20, 309c3n5
Yellin, Emily, 23–25
Yes, We Canberra!, 206
Yogi Bear (character, Yogi Bear), 105
York University, 102
Yo soy Betty, la fea, 283
YouTube, 6, 9–11, 13, 15, 20, 30, 39, 41, 47, 49–52, 59, 74, 86, 90, 92–96, 98, 100–101, 110, 144, 147, 181, 184–187, 189, 193, 205–206, 210–212, 214, 217, 220, 222–223, 225, 246, 253, 264, 280–282, 307"Introduction"n1; Partner Program, 52

Zeldman, Jeffrey, 208
Zimmerman, Patricia R., 159
Zipatoni, 77
Zittrain, Jonathan, 245–246
Zonday, Tay, 187
Zuckerman, Ethan, 261–263, 267–268, 285

Henry Jenkins is Provost's Professor of Communication, Journalism, Cinematic Arts, and Education at USC. He is author of *Convergence Culture* (2006), *Fans, Bloggers, and Gamers* (2006), *The Wow Climax* (2006), *Textual Poachers* (1992), and *What Made Pistachio Nuts?* (1992); coauthor of *Confronting the Challenges of Participatory Culture* (2009); editor of *The Children's Culture Reader* (1998); and coeditor of *Rethinking Media Change* (2004), *Democracy and New Media* (2003), *Hop on Pop* (2003), *From Barbie to Mortal Kombat* (2000), and *Classical Hollywood Comedy* (1994). From 1993 to 2009, he was the MIT Peter de Florez Professor of Humanities and codirected MIT's Comparative Media Studies graduate degree program. Since coming to USC, Jenkins has formed the Participatory Culture and Learning Lab, which includes Project New Media Literacies and Media Activism and Participatory Politics. He holds a Ph.D. in communication arts from the University of Wisconsin, Madison, and a master's degree in communication studies from the University of Iowa.

Sam Ford is Director of Digital Strategy at Peppercomm Strategic Communications, an affiliate with the MIT Program in Comparative Media Studies and the Western Kentucky University Popular Culture Studies Program, and a regular contributor to *Fast Company*. He also serves on the Membership Ethics Advisory Panel for the Word of Mouth Marketing Association. Ford is coeditor of *The Survival of Soap Opera* (2011) and has written for *BusinessWeek*, the *Huffington Post*, the *Christian Science Monitor*, *Portfolio*, and *Chief Marketer*. He and his work have appeared in *Investor's Business Daily*, *New York Times Magazine*, *Financial Times*, CNN, NPR, BBC, Australian Broadcasting

ABOUT THE AUTHORS

Corporation, *Mental Floss, Boing Boing, Slashdot, Mashable, ESPN: The Magazine, Soap Opera Weekly,* and *Reader's Digest,* among other outlets. In 2011, *Bulldog Reporter* named him Social Media Innovator of the Year. He holds a master's degree from MIT and a bachelor's degree from WKU. He is also a Kentucky Press Association award-winning journalist.

Joshua Green is a strategist at Undercurrent, a digital strategy firm in New York City. He is coauthor (with Jean Burgess) of the 2009 book *YouTube: Online Video and Participatory Culture,* the first large-scale analysis of YouTube's content, structure, and uses. Green cofounded the Futures of Entertainment conference (with Henry Jenkins) in 2006. Before joining Undercurrent, he served as Project Manager of the Media Industries Project at the University of California–Santa Barbara's Carsey-Wolf Center. Previous to that, he was a Postdoctoral Researcher in the Program in Comparative Media Studies Program at MIT, where he was also Research Manager of the Convergence Culture Consortium project. Green has published work about television, new media, and participatory culture. He holds a Ph.D. in media studies from the Queensland University of Technology in Brisbane, Australia.

POSTMILLENNIAL POP

GENERAL EDITORS: KAREN TONGSON AND HENRY JENKINS

Puro Arte: Filipinos on the Stages of Empire
Lucy Mae San Pablo Burns

Spreadable Media: Creating Value and Meaning in a Networked Culture
Henry Jenkins, Sam Ford, and Joshua Green